PRICE GUIDE TO
Pocket Knives

BY JACOB N. JARRETT

1993

Published by:
L-W Book Sales
P.O. Box 69
Gas City, IN 46933

ISBN # 0-89538-024-2

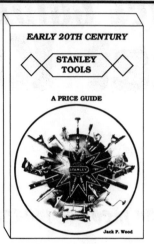

Table of Contents

Introduction

This book is a reprint of various catalogs before 1970. As you will notice all measurements and descriptions have been left to better help you identify your knives. We do not claim to be experts in the knife collecting field, however after many years in the publishing business we do feel we know what is helpful to collectors. There is a separate price guide included which is only the opinion of the author. We hope you enjoy "Price Guide to Pocket Knives".

Pricing Information

All prices in the price guide are for knives in good condition. Knives in <u>mint</u>, <u>unsharpened</u> condition are worth considerably more and are much more desirable. Remember, the prices are retail and a dealer will pay much less. L-W Book Sales cannot be held responsible for losses or gains in using this book.

Dates of Catalog Pages

Case – 1969
George Wostenholm & Sons' – 1913
Hibbard, Spencer, Bartlett & Co.'s – 1899
Imported Knives – 1903
John Primble – 1937
Joseph Allen & Son's – 1899
Keene Cutlery – 1903
Keen Kutter – 1910

Marble's – 1939
Miscellaneous – 1899, 1935, 1962
New York Knife Co. – 1899
Remington – 1933
Schrade Walden – 1937
Tree Brand – 1913
Van Camp – 1933
Watauga – 1913
Winchester – 1934

WHERE *KEEN KUTTER* POCKET KNIVES ARE MADE—NEW YORK STATE.
THE LARGEST FACTORY OF ITS KIND IN THE UNITED STATES.

Water Power
from these Falls
used to run our
KEEN KUTTER
Tool Factory.

Location of one
of our
KEEN KUTTER
Tool Factories
in
New Hampshire.

WHERE *KEEN KUTTER* TOOLS ARE MADE.

KEEN KUTTER POCKET KNIVES.

HOW THEY ARE MADE.

The above is a photograph of Mr. Holden, one of the workmen of the Walden Knife Company, who for over thirty years has been **Forging by Hand** the Blades for our *KEEN KUTTER* Pocket Knives.

Mr Holden is now 72 years of age, and has spent his entire life in the manufacture of Pocket Knives, having learned the trade directly from his father, and after learning the trade, has spent a number of years in the factories of Joseph Rodgers & Sons, and Geo. Wostenholm & Son, Sheffield, England.

He is a man of artistic temperament in many ways, thoroughly honorable in every respect, and absolutely loyal to his faith in the superiority of *KEEN KUTTER* Hand Forged Pocket Knives over all other brands. He fairly represents the type of English workmen by whom nearly every number of our entire line of *KEEN KUTTER* Pocket Knives is made.

Information Regarding *KEEN KUTTER** Pocket Knives (Continued).

Coverings—As illustrated in their Natural Colors

German Silver—Producing an appearance quite similar to Sterling Silver.

Pearl—Obtained through the London markets from the Dutch East Indies and Australian Fisheries, where the Highest Quality of Pearl is found.

Genuine Ivory—Obtained from the elephants of the West Coast of Africa, where the Ivory is found to be much Superior in Quality—especially in hardness—to that of the Eastern Coast, and of Asia.

Cut Stag—Made by Artificially Cutting the Second Layer of Genuine Stag, or sometimes Bone, and carefully coloring until it so closely resembles Genuine Stag, both in its irregular surface, and color, as to be difficult to distinguish from the real article.

White Bone—The shin bone of beef cattle, which, when carefully selected and cured, gives a covering capable of High Finish and Good Wearing Qualities.

Aluminum—Which is especially adapted for Engraving Fancy Decorations.

Genuine Stag—Outside cut of the horn, obtained from Hungary, Bohemia, Ceylon and China, which countries produce the Highest Quality of Stag.

Tortoise Shell—Obtained chiefly from the Hawk's Bill Tortoise, found in various parts of the world, especially in Asia and Australia.

Buffalo Horn—From the Buffaloes of Siam and India.

Cocobolo—A hard, red wood of very fine grain, which grows chiefly on the Isthmus of Panama.

Genuine Ebony—A hard, black wood of very fine grain, obtained chiefly from the East Coast of Africa and Madagascar.

Celluloid—A manufactured composition; produced either Transparent or in a great Variety of Colors. It may be made in Imitation of almost any of the other coverings which are used on the Knives, except German Silver.

Linings—The Linings are of German Silver, Brass or Steel, whichever is best adapted to the particular Knife on which it is used. The outside edges are Milled (or Knurled), in several of the more expensive patterns.

Bolsters—The Bolsters are, in the great majority of cases, of German Silver, or in a few cases, on the heavier Knives, of Steel.

Rivets—The Rivets are of German Silver and Steel.

Shields are made of German Silver, in various shapes and sizes, as best adapted to each individual pattern.

Back Springs are made of Forged Steel, Uniformly Tempered, Carefully Fitted and Full Polished, as specified in the descriptions; some of the patterns have Fancy Hand Engraved Backs.

Care of a Knife—Much trouble is caused, and many Knives prove unsatisfactory from the lack of proper care.
A well made Pocket Knife is a piece of very fine mechanism, and should be kept cleaned and oiled at the joints as carefully as any other piece of fine mechanism. If this is done we are confident that every Pocket Knife bearing the *KEEN KUTTER* Brand will give the user complete and lasting satisfaction. If it does not, he is amply protected by the liberal guarantee which accompanies *KEEN KUTTER* Pocket Knives, and all other *KEEN KUTTER* goods.
WE ABSOLUTELY GUARANTEE ALL *KEEN KUTTER* POCKET KNIVES AGAINST DEFECTS OF TEMPER OR FLAWS.

INFORMATION
REGARDING *KEEN KUTTER** POCKET KNIVES.

It is our aim to furnish, under the *KEEN KUTTER* Brand, the Highest Quality of Pocket Cutlery which can be produced. That we have accomplished this is shown by the Awards for the Highest Quality, granted to this line at the Louisiana Purchase Exposition, held in St. Louis, Mo., in 1904, and the Lewis & Clark Exposition, held in Portland, Ore., in 1905, illustrations of which are shown on pages 2634 and 2635. We believe this result cannot fail to follow from the method which we use in the manufacture of the goods.

It is our constant aim to see that everything about the line is of absolutely the Highest Quality, from the selection of the Raw Material to the Wrapping and Packing of the finished product.

Workmanship—Nearly 90 per cent of the men who manufacture this line were schooled in the art of making Fine Cutlery in the best English factories, where they learned their trade, and where their fathers and grandfathers spent their lives in the manufacture of Pocket Knives. The men are liberally paid for their work, and are constantly reminded that the item of quality is of much more importance than quantity.

Blades are made from the Highest Grade of English Crucible Steel imported especially for the purpose. They are Forged by hand from the Bar, and not stamped out from sheet steel (the method employed by many makers of Knives). They have an absolutely Uniform Temper, and are Whetted by Hand on an Oil Stone to a Sharp Cutting Edge, Ready for Use.

As specified in the description, the Blades are either Full Crocus Polished (i. e., each Blade Polished on Both Sides) or Half Polished (i. e., Large Blade Polished on One Side and other Blades Glazed Finish).

Patterns of Blades—The line contains every possible shape of Blades which is at all practical, as is shown by the following illustrations:

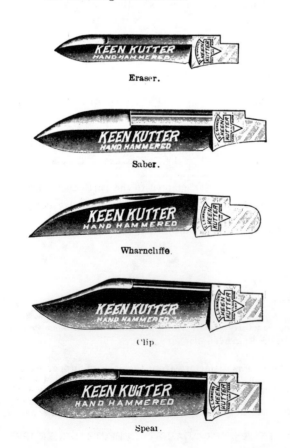

Eraser.

Saber.

Wharncliffe.

Clip

Spear.

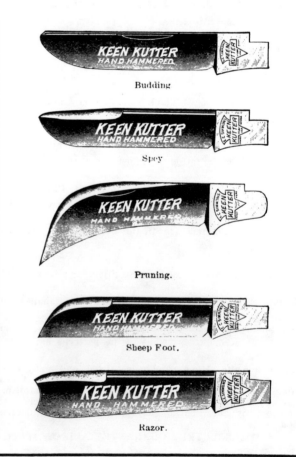

Budding

Spey

Pruning.

Sheep Foot.

Razor.

KEEN KUTTER POCKET KNIVES

HOW THEY ARE MADE.

Pocket Blades.

No. 1—Pocket Blade, for No. K2420, Partially Forged; Showing Steel Bar from which it is being Fashioned.

No. 2—Pocket Blade Forged, Ready for Hardening and Tempering or Grinding.

No. 3—Pocket Blade Ground, Ready for Drilling and Filing, or Drilling and Squaring.

No. 4—Pocket Blade Ready for Assembling, Filed and Dressed, or Drilled, Squared and Dressed.

Pen Blades.

No. 1—Pen Blade for No. K2420, Partially Forged; Showing Steel Bar from which it is being Fashioned.

No. 2—Pen Blade Forged, Ready for Hardening and Tempering or Grinding.

No. 3—Pen Blade Ground, Ready for Drilling and Filing, or Drilling and Squaring.

No. 4—Pen Blade Ready for Assembling, Drilled, Filed and Dressed, or Drilled, Squared and Dressed.

KEEN KUTTER POCKET KNIVES.

HOW THEY ARE MADE.

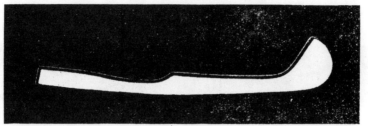

No. 5—Spring Steel, from which Spring is Produced.

No. 6—Spring, Dressed and Drilled, Ready for Adjusting.

No. 7—Spring Adjusted, Filed, Hardened, Tempered and Dressed.

No. 8—Sheet Brass, from which Linings are Pressed.

No. 9—German Silver, from which Bolsters are made.

No. 10—Blank for Bolster, Pressed Ready for Stamping.

No. 11—Bolster Stamped up, Ready to Fasten to Lining.

No. 12—Brass Strip, Pierced, Ready to Receive Bolster.

No. 13—Bolsters "Chopped on" Lining, Ready for Passing through Pattern Dies.

No. 14—Scale Pressed, Ready for Drilling.

KEEN KUTTER POCKET KNIVES.

HOW THEY ARE MADE.

No. 15—Handle Covering Ready for Fitting.

No. 16—Covering Fitted, Ready for Name Plate.

No. 17—Name Plates, or Shields, and German Silver from which they are made.

No. 18—Scales, with Covering Fitted, Showing Name Plate and Reverse Side, Ready for Assembling into Handle

No. 19—Division Scale, or Center Lining.

No. 20—Knife Ready for Final Adjusting—Note Loose Rivets and General Rough Appearance of Knife.

No. 21—The Finished Article.

Information regarding *KEEN KUTTER** Pocket Knives (Continued).

Patterns of Handles—A great variety of shapes and designs of Handles are used in this line, the principal ones of which, with the names by which they are most commonly known are given below:

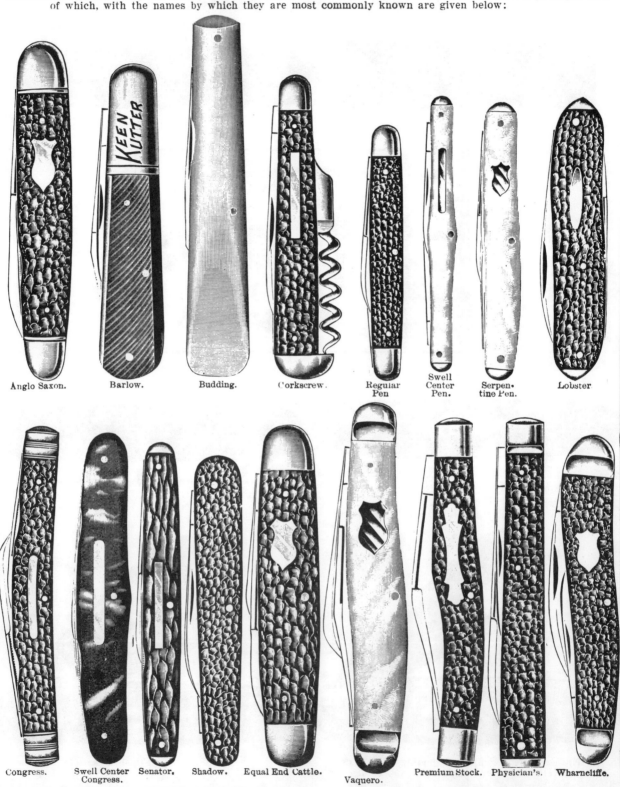

Anglo Saxon.   Barlow.   Budding.   Corkscrew.   Regular Pen   Swell Center Pen.   Serpentine Pen.   Lobster

Congress.   Swell Center Congress.   Senator.   Shadow.   Equal End Cattle.   Vaquero.   Premium Stock.   Physician's.   Wharncliffe.

Information regarding *KEEN KUTTER** Pocket Knives (Continued).

Patterns of Handles—A great variety of shapes and designs of Handles are used in this line, the principal ones of which, with the names by which they are most commonly known are given below:

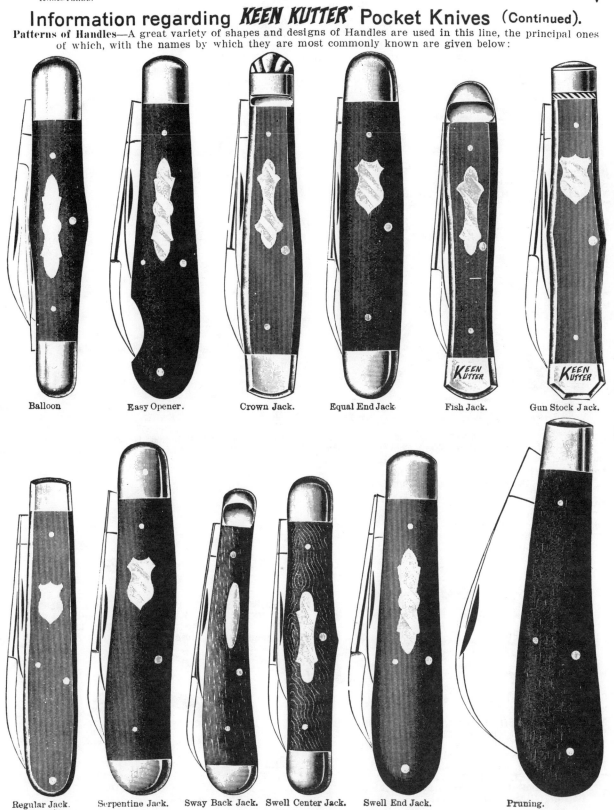

| Balloon | Easy Opener. | Crown Jack. | Equal End Jack | Fish Jack. | Gun Stock Jack. |

| Regular Jack. | Serpentine Jack. | Sway Back Jack. | Swell Center Jack. | Swell End Jack. | Pruning. |

POCKET KNIVES
KEEN KUTTER.*

Highest Grade English Crucible Steel Blades, Uniformly Tempered, Hand Hammered, SHARPENED AND WHETTED ON AN OIL STONE, BY HAND, READY FOR USE.

No. K343.

Full Polished Blades; German Silver Tips and Shield; Brass Lining; Milled Back.

No. K343—3¼ INCH PEARL HANDLE; THREE BLADES, 1 Large Spear Point, 1 Pen and 1 File ....

No. K32566—3⅛ INCH GENUINE STAG HANDLE; THREE BLADES, 1 Large Spear Point, 1 Pen and 1 File...............

No. K42566—3⅛ INCH GENUINE STAG HANDLE; FOUR BLADES, 1 Large Spear Point, 2 Pen and 1 File.....................

No. K429.

FOUR BLADES, 1 Large Sheep Foot Point, 2 Pen and 1 File, Full Polished.

No. K429—3⁵/₁₆ INCH PEARL HANDLE; German Silver Bolsters and Shield; Brass Lining; Milled Back ....

No. K4979—3½ INCH PEARL HANDLE; Steel Bolsters and Lining ....

No. K4679—3¼ INCH PEARL HANDLE; Brass Lining; WITHOUT BOLSTERS; MILLED BACK ....

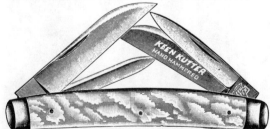

No. K4299.

FOUR BLADES, 2 Large Sheep Foot Point, 1 Pen and 1 File, Half Polished.

No. K4299—3 INCH PEARL HANDLE; Steel Bolsters; Brass Lining ....

No. K4297—3 INCH STAG HANDLE; Steel Bolsters; Brass Lining ....

No. K3769—3⁵/₁₆ INCH PEARL HANDLE; THREE BLADES, 1 Large Spear Point, 1 Pen and 1 File, Full Polished; Steel Bolsters; Brass Lining ....

No. K3113.

Full Polished Blades; German Silver Tips; Brass Lining; Milled Back.

No. K3113—3 INCH PEARL HANDLE; THREE BLADES, 1 Large Spear Point, 1 Pen and 1 File ....

No. K4408—3 INCH PEARL HANDLE; FOUR BLADES, 1 Large Spear Point, 2 Pen and 1 File ....

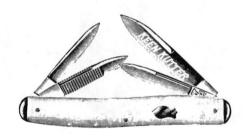

No. K4849—3 INCH PEARL HANDLE; FOUR BLADES, 1 Large Spear Point, 2 Pen and 1 File, Full Polished; German Silver Tips and Shield; Brass Lining ....

No. K3483—3⅛ INCH PEARL HANDLE; THREE BLADES, 1 Large Spear Point and 2 Pen, Half Polished; German Silver Tips and Shield; Brass Lining; Milled Back........

No. K3808—2⅞ INCH PEARL HANDLE; THREE BLADES, 1 Large Spear Point, 1 Pen and 1 File; Full Polished; German Silver Shield and Lining ....

One-half Dozen in a Cardboard Box; Weight per Dozen about 1½ lbs.

POCKET KNIVES.

KEEN KUTTER.*

Highest Grade English Crucible Steel Blades, Uniformly Tempered, Hand Hammered, SHARPENED AND WHETTED ON AN OIL STONE, BY HAND, READY FOR USE.

No. K488.

Full Polished Blades; German Silver Tips; Brass Lining; Milled Back.

No. K488—2⅞ INCH PEARL HANDLE; FOUR BLADES, 1 Large Spear Point, 2 Pen and 1 File ....

No. K0488—2⅞ INCH PEARL HANDLE; TWO BLADES, 1 Large Spear Point and 1 Pen ....

No. K3908—2⅞ INCH PEARL HANDLE; THREE BLADES, 1 Large Spear Point, 1 Pen and 1 File; GERMAN SILVER SHIELD.....

No. K3489.

THREE BLADES, 1 Large Spear Point, 1 Pen and 1 File, Full Polished.

No. K3489—3½ INCH PEARL HANDLE; Hand Engraved Aluminum Bolster; German Silver Lining; Milled Back ....

No. K3486—3½ INCH STAG HANDLE; German Silver Bolsters and Shield; Brass Lining ....

No. K3488—3½ INCH PEARL HANDLE; German Silver Bolsters and Shield; Brass Lining ....

No. K4328—3⅝ INCH STAG HANDLE; FOUR BLADES, 1 Large Sheep Foot Point, 2 Pen and 1 File, Full Polished; Polished Steel Bolsters; GERMAN SILVER SHIELD ON EACH SIDE; Brass Lining ....

No. K02339.

Half Polished Blades; German Silver Tips, Shield and Lining.

No. K02339—3⅜ INCH PEARL HANDLE; TWO BLADES, 1 Large Spear Point and 1 Pen ....

No. K02337—3⅜ INCH STAG HANDLE; TWO BLADES, 1 Large Spear Point and 1 Pen ....

No. K32339—3⅜ INCH PEARL HANDLE; THREE BLADES, 1 Large Spear Point, 1 Pen and 1 File ....

No. K32337—3⅜ INCH STAG HANDLE; THREE BLADES, 1 Large Spear Point, 1 Pen and 1 File ....

No. K0382.

Full Polished Blades; German Silver Tips and Shield; Brass Lining.

No. K0382—3½ INCH PEARL HANDLE; TWO BLADES, 1 Large Spear Point and 1 Pen ....

No. K03833—3½ INCH GENUINE STAG HANDLE; TWO BLADES, 1 Large Spear Point and 1 Pen ....

No. K38333—3½ INCH GENUINE STAG HANDLE; THREE BLADES, 1 Large Spear Point, 1 Pen and 1 File.....................

No. K48333—3½ INCH GENUINE STAG HANDLE; FOUR BLADES, 1 Large Spear Point, 2 Pen and 1 File.....................

No. K3389—2⅞ INCH PEARL HANDLE; THREE BLADES, 1 Large Spear Point and 2 Pen, Full Polished; Hand Engraved Aluminum Bolsters; German Silver Lining ....

One-half Dozen in a Cardboard Box; Weight per Dozen about 1½ lbs.

POCKET KNIVES.

KEEN KUTTER *.

Highest Grade English Crucible Steel Blades, Uniformly Tempered, Hand Hammered, SHARPENED AND WHETTED ON AN OIL STONE, BY HAND, READY FOR USE.

No. K4429.

FOUR BLADES, 1 Large Clip, 1 Large Sheep Foot, 1 Large Spey Point and 1 Pen, Full Polished; German Silver Shield and Lining.

No. K4429 —4 INCH PEARL HANDLE; German Silver Bolsters ....

No. K4429E—4 INCH PEARL HANDLE; Engraved Back; German Silver Bolsters.

No. K44288—4 INCH GENUINE STAG HANDLE; German Silver Bolsters.............

No. K4428 —4 INCH STAG HANDLE; German Silver Bolsters ....

No. K4426 —4 INCH BUFFALO HORN HANDLE; German Silver Bolsters ....

No. K4829 —4 INCH PEARL HANDLE; Hand Engraved Aluminum Bolsters........

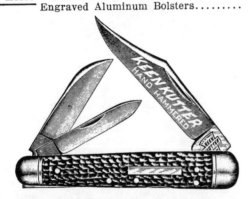

No. K3008—3⅞ INCH STAG HANDLE; THREE BLADES, 1 Large Clip, 1 Large Sheep Foot Point and 1 Pen, Half Polished; German Silver Bolsters and Shield; Brass Lining; Lock Back ....

No. K44833—3¾ INCH GENUINE STAG HANDLE; FOUR BLADES, 1 Large Clip, 1 Large Sheep Foot, 1 Large Spey Point, and 1 Pen, Full Polished; German Silver Bolsters and Shield; Brass Lining; Milled Back ....

No. K3219.

THREE BLADES, 1 Large Spear, 1 Large Sheep Foot Point, and 1 Pen, Half Polished; German Silver Bolsters and Shield; Brass Lining.

No. K3219 —3⅜ INCH PEARL HANDLE........

No. K3216 —3⅜ INCH EBONY HANDLE........

No. K32188—3⅜ INCH GENUINE STAG HANDLE

No. K3215A—3⅜ INCH HAND ENGRAVED ALUMINUM HANDLE; THREE BLADES, 1 Large Spear, 1 Large Sheep Foot Point and 1 Pen, Half Polished........................

No. K37288—3½ INCH GENUINE STAG HANDLE; THREE BLADES, 1 Large Sheep Foot, 1 Large Clip Point, and 1 Pen, Half Polished; German Silver Bolsters and Shield; Brass Lining ....

One-half Dozen in a Cardboard Box; Weight per Dozen about 2½ lbs.

POCKET KNIVES.

KEEN KUTTER *

Highest Grade English Crucible Steel
Blades, Uniformly Tempered, Hand
Hammered, SHARPENED AND
WHETTED ON AN OIL
STONE, BY HAND,
READY FOR
USE.

No. K3433.

THREE LARGE BLADES, 1 Clip, 1 Sheep Foot and
1 Spey Point, Half Polished; German Silver Shield.
German Silver Bolsters and Lining.

No. K3433 —4 INCH STAG HANDLE...........

No. K34333—4 INCH GENUINE STAG HANDLE.

No. K3434 —4 INCH PEARL HANDLE.........
Polished Steel Bolsters; Brass Lining.

No. K32322—4 INCH GENUINE STAG HANDLE
German Silver Bolsters; Brass Lining.

No. K3828 —4 INCH STAG HANDLE..........

No. K3825 —4 INCH BUFFALO HORN HANDLE

No. K3829 —4 INCH PEARL HANDLE........

No. K3903¾—4⅛ INCH STAG HANDLE........

No. K8433—4 INCH STAG HANDLE; THREE
LARGE BLADES, 1 Clip, 1 Wharn-
cliffe, 1 Spey Point, Half Polished; German
Silver Bolsters, Shield and Lining..........

No. K3278.

THREE LARGE BLADES, 1 Spear, 1 Clip and 1
Spey Point, Half Polished; German Silver Shield.

German Silver Bolsters; Brass Lining.

No. K3278 —3⅝ INCH STAG HANDLE .....

No. K3278S—3⅝ INCH GENUINE STAG HANDLE

No. K3276 —3⅝ INCH BUFFALO HORN HAN-
DLE ....

No. K3277 —3⅝ INCH WHITE BONE HANDLE.

Polished Steel Bolsters; Steel Lining.

No. K3375—3⅝ INCH GRANADILLA HANDLE..

No. K3378—3⅝ INCH STAG HANDLE ....

No. K72085.

TWO BLADES, 1 Spear Point; 1 PATENT LEATHER PUNCH, Half Polished; German Silver Bolster and
Shield, Brass Lining.

No. K72085—3½ inch ROSEWOOD HANDLE ....

No. K72086—3½ inch EBONY HANDLE ....

No. K72088—3½ inch STAG HANDLE ....

Showing Possi-
bilities of Leather
Punch Blade.

Per Dozen

No. K738¾—3¾ INCH STAG HANDLE; THREE
BLADES, 1 Large Clip, 1 Large Spey
Point and 1 PATENT LEATHER PUNCH,
Half Polished; German Silver Bolster and
Shield, Brass Lining.......................

No. K73878—3⅝ INCH STAG HANDLE; THREE
BLADES, 1 Large Spear, 1 Large Sheep
Foot Point and 1 PATENT LEATHER PUNCH,
Half Polished; German Silver Bolster and
Shield, Brass Lining ....

One-half Dozen in a Cardboard Box; Weight per Dozen about 2½ lbs.

POCKET KNIVES.

KEEN KUTTER.*

Highest Grade English Crucible Steel Blades, Uniformly Tempered, Hand Hammered, SHARPENED AND WHETTED ON AN OIL STONE, BY HAND, READY FOR USE.

No. K1201.

TWO BLADES, 1 Large Spear Point and 1 Pen; German Silver Bolster, Cap and Shield; Brass Lining.

No. K1201—3½ INCH STAG HANDLE; Half Polished Blades ....

No. K1200—3½ INCH EBONY HANDLE; Half Polished Blades ....

No. K22033—3½ INCH GENUINE STAG HANDLE; Half Polished Blades ....

No. K1203—3½ INCH PEARL HANDLE; Full Polished Blades ....

No. K2621.

TWO BLADES, 1 Large Spear Point and 1 Pen, Half Polished; Steel Bolster and Cap; German Silver Shield; Brass Lining.

No. K2621 —3¾ INCH EBONY HANDLE ....

No. K2623 —3¾ INCH STAG HANDLE.........

No. K26233—3¾ INCH GENUINE STAG HANDLE

TWO BLADES, 1 Large Clip Point and 1 Pen, Half Polished; Steel Bolster and Cap; German Silver Shield; Brass Lining.

No. K2623¾—3¾ INCH STAG HANDLE ....

TWO BLADES, 1 Large Spear Point and 1 Pen, Half Polished; German Silver Shield.

No. K25233—3¾ INCH GENUINE STAG HANDLE; Steel Bolster, Cap and Lining..

No. K21988—4 INCH GENUINE STAG HANDLE; Polished Steel Bolster and Cap; Steel Lining ....

No. K2613.

TWO BLADES, 1 Large Spear Point and 1 Pen, Half Polished; German Silver Bolster, Cap and Shield; Brass Lining.

No. K2613—3¾ INCH STAG HANDLE ....

No. K2611—3¾ INCH EBONY HANDLE .....

No. K2048¾.

No. K2048¾—3⅞ INCH STAG HANDLE; TWO BLADES, 1 Large Clip Point and 1 Pen, Half Polished; German Silver Bolster, Cap and Shield; Brass Lining ....

No. K2273¾—3⅞ INCH STAG HANDLE, WITHOUT CAP; Otherwise same as No. K2048¾ ....

No. K2063.

TWO BLADES, 1 Large Spear Point and 1 Pen, Half Polished; German Silver Bolster and Shield; Brass Lining.

No. K2063 —3¾ INCH STAG HANDLE ....

No. K20633—3¾ INCH GENUINE STAG HANDLE

One-half Dozen in a Cardboard Box; Weight per Dozen about 2 lbs.

POCKET KNIVES.

KEEN KUTTER.*

Highest Grade English Crucible Steel Blades, Uniformly Tempered, Hand Hammered, SHARPENED AND WHETTED ON AN OIL STONE, BY HAND, READY FOR USE.

No. K2850.

Half Polished Blades; German Silver Bolster and Shield; Brass Lining.

Two Blades, 1 Large Spear Point and 1 Pen.

No. K2850 —3¾ INCH GRANADILLA HANDLE.

No. K2851 —3¾ INCH EBONY HANDLE.......

No. K2853 —3¾ INCH STAG HANDLE ....

No. K28533—3¾ INCH GENUINE STAG HANDLE

Two Blades, 1 Large Clip Point and 1 Pen.

No. K2851¾—3¾ INCH EBONY HANDLE ......

No. K2853¾—3¾ INCH STAG HANDLE ....

No. K2695—3⅞ INCH ROSEWOOD HANDLE; TWO BLADES, 1 Large Spear Point and 1 Pen; Steel Bolster; Otherwise same as No. K2850 ....

No. K98.

EASY OPENER.

TWO BLADES, 1 Large Spear Point and 1 Pen, Half Polished; German Silver Bolster, Cap and Shield; Brass Lining.

No. K98 —3⅜ INCH STAG HANDLE ......

No. K95 —3⅜ INCH COCOBOLO HANDLE ....

No. K93 —3⅜ INCH STAG HANDLE, Without Cap ....

No. K90 —3⅜ INCH COCOBOLO HANDLE; Without Cap ....

No. K2719—3⅜ INCH GERMAN SILVER HANDLE; Without Cap ....

No. K50.

TWO BLADES, 1 Large Spear Point and 1 Pen, Glazed Finish; German Silver Shield; Polished Steel Bolster and Cap; Brass Lining.

No. K50—3⅜ INCH ROSEWOOD HANDLE .....

No. K51—3⅜ INCH EBONY HANDLE ....

TWO BLADES, 1 Large and 1 Pen, Half Polished; German Silver Shield; Polished Steel Bolster, Cap and Lining.

No. K2778 —3⅜ INCH STAG HANDLE; Spear Point Large Blade ....

No. K2778¾—3⅜ INCH STAG HANDLE; Clip Point Large Blade ....

TWO BLADES, 1 Large and 1 Pen, Half Polished; German Silver Shield, Bolster and Cap; Brass Lining.

Spear Point Large Blade.

No. K2780 —3⅜ INCH GRANADILLA HANDLE.

No. K2781 —3⅜ INCH EBONY HANDLE ....

No. K2783 —3⅜ INCH STAG HANDLE ....

No. K20333—3⅜ INCH GENUINE STAG HANDLE

No. K2030/SC—3⅜ INCH SILVER CELLULOID HANDLE ....

Clip Point Large Blade.

No. K2780¾—3⅜ INCH GRANADILLA HANDLE

No. K2781¾—3⅜ INCH EBONY HANDLE ......

No. K2783¾—3⅜ INCH STAG HANDLE ....

No. K26755.

TWO BLADES, 1 Large Spear Point and 1 Pen, Half Polished; German Silver Bolster, Shield and Lining.

No. K26755—3⅝ INCH COCOBOLO HANDLE ...

No. K26756—3⅝ INCH EBONY HANDLE ....

No. K23758—3⅝ INCH STAG HANDLE, Polished Steel Bolster and Steel Lining; Otherwise same as No. K26755....................

One-half Dozen in a Cardboard Box; Weight per Dozen about 1½ lbs.

POCKET KNIVES.

*KEEN KUTTER**

Highest Grade English Crucible Steel Blades, Uniformly Tempered, Hand Hammered, SHARPENED AND WHETTED ON AN OIL STONE, BY HAND, READY FOR USE.

No. K510.

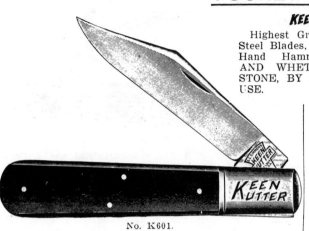

No. K601.

BARLOW PATTERN.

ONE LARGE BLADE, Glazed Finished; Polished Steel Bolster; Steel Lining.

No. K601—5 INCH BROWN BONE HANDLE; Clip Point Blade ....

No. K600—5 INCH BROWN BONE HANDLE; Spear Point Blade.....................

No. K2305.

TWO BLADES, 1 Large and 1 Pen, Glazed Finish; Polished Steel Bolster; German Silver Shield; Steel Lining.

No. K2305 —3⅜ INCH COCOBOLO HANDLE; Spear Point Large Blade............

No. K2305¾—3⅜ INCH COCOBOLO HANDLE; Clip Point Large Blade.............

No. K2306 —3⅜ INCH EBONY HANDLE; Spear Point Large Blade................

No. K2306¾—3⅜ INCH EBONY HANDLE; Clip Point Large Blade.................

TWO BLADES, 1 Large and 1 Pen, Glazed Finish; Polished Steel Bolster; Steel Lining.

No. K2105 —3⅜ INCH COCOBOLO HANDLE; Spear Point Large Blade.............

No. K2105¾—3⅜ INCH COCOBOLO HANDLE; Clip Point Large Blade.............

No. K2106 —3⅜ INCH EBONY HANDLE; Spear Point Large Blade.................

No. K2160R—3⅜ INCH COCOBOLO HANDLE; with Long Bolster; Spear Point Large Blade ....

BARLOW PATTERN.

TWO BLADES, 1 Large and 1 Pen, Glazed Finish; Polished Steel Bolster; Steel Lining.

No. K510—3⅜ INCH BROWN BONE HANDLE; Spear Point Large Blade..............

No. K511—3⅜ INCH BROWN BONE HANDLE; Clip Point Large Blade..............

No. K512—3⅜ INCH BROWN BONE HANDLE; Spey Point Large Blade...............

No. K513—3⅜ INCH BROWN BONE HANDLE; Razor Point Large Blade..............

No. K514—3⅜ INCH WHITE BONE HANDLE; Spear Point Large Blade..............

ONE LARGE BLADE, Glazed Finish; Polished Steel Bolster; Steel Lining.

No. K500 —3⅜ INCH BROWN BONE HANDLE; Spear Point Blade....................

No. K1883—3⅜ INCH BROWN BONE HANDLE; Razor Point Blade...................

No. K2583.

TWO BLADES, 1 Large and 1 Pen, Glazed Finish; Polished Steel Bolster; German Silver Shield; Steel Lining.

No. K2583 —3¼ INCH STAG HANDLE; Spear Point Large Blade.................

No. K2583½—3¼ INCH STAG HANDLE; Sheep Foot Point Large Blade............

No. K2580 —3¼ INCH COCOBOLO HANDLE; Spear Point Large Blade...........

No. K2580½—3¼ INCH COCOBOLO HANDLE; Sheep Foot Point Large Blade.......

One-half Dozen in a Cardboard Box; Weight per Dozen about 2 lbs.

PRESS BUTTON <u>POCKET</u> KNIVES.

First Quality English Crucible Steel Blades, Hand Hammered, Highly Tempered, SHARPENED READY FOR USE.

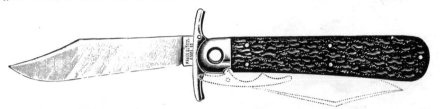

No. 1005WG—5 INCH STAG HANDLE; One Large Clip Point Blade, Full Polished; German Silver Bolster and Folding Guard; Steel Lining...

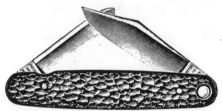

No. 115PB.

No. 115PB—3⅝ INCH STAG HANDLE; Two Large Blades, 1 Clip Point and 1 Spey Point, Half Polished; Brass Lining.........

No. 116PB—3⅝ INCH STAG HANDLE; Two Blades, 1 Large Spear Point and 1 Pen, Half Polished; Brass Lining...............

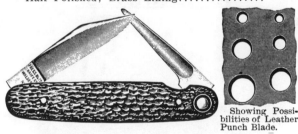

Showing Possibilities of Leather Punch Blade.

No. 117PB—3⅝ INCH STAG HANDLE; Two Blades, 1 Large Clip Point and 1 PATENT LEATHER PUNCH BLADE, Half Polished; Brass Lining.....................

No. 1000PB.

ONE LARGE BLADE, Full Polished; German Silver Bolster; Steel Lining.

No. 1000PB—5 INCH STAG HANDLE; Clip Point Blade ....

No. 1100PB—5 INCH STAG HANDLE; Spear Point Blade ....

No. 1007PB—5 INCH EBONY HANDLE; Clip Point Blade ....

No. 1200PB—5 INCH STAG HANDLE; Clip Point Saber Pattern Blade...............

No. 500PB.

ONE LARGE BLADE, Full Polished; German Silver Bolster; Steel Lining.

No. 500PB—4 INCH STAG HANDLE; Spear Point Blade ....

No. 501PB—4 INCH STAG HANDLE; Clip Point Blade ....

No. 507PB—4 INCH EBONY HANDLE; Spear Point Blade ....

No. 517PB—4 INCH EBONY HANDLE ; Clip Point Blade ....

No. 105PB.

TWO BLADES, 1 Large Spear Point and 1 Pen, Full Polished; Brass Lining.

No. 105PB—3⅝ INCH PEARL HANDLE......

No. 100PB—3⅝ INCH STAG HANDLE..........

No. 102PB—3⅝ INCH IMITATION SHELL HANDLE ....

No. 103PB—3⅝ INCH WHITE CELLULOID HANDLE ....

No. 107PB—3⅝ INCH BLACK CELLULOID HANDLE ....

One-half Dozen in a Cardboard Box; Weight per Dozen about 2 lbs.

POCKET KNIVES.

KEEN KUTTER.*

Combination Knife: Highest Grade English Crucible Steel Blades, Uniformly Tempered, Hand Hammered, Full Polished, SHARPENED READY FOR USE; TWO BLADES, 1 Large Spear Point and 1 Pen; One Each, Polished Steel Combination Hoof Cleaner and Nut Cracker, Cork Screw, Screw Driver, Tweezers, Pipe Cleaner, Gouge and Tempered Steel Fleam.

No. K830—*KEEN KUTTER**; 4 INCH GENUINE STAG HANDLE; Polished Steel Bolster; German Silver Shield; Steel Lining ....

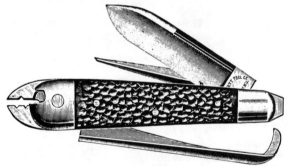

Combination Knife; First Quality English Crucible Steel Blade, Highly Tempered, Half Polished; 1 Large Spear Point Blade, and 1 Each Polished Steel Gouge, Hoof Cleaner, Screw Driver and Combination Pliers and Wire Cutter.

No. 3H—STAG HANDLE; Length Over All 4½ inches; German Silver Bolsters; Brass Lining ....

VETERINARY FLEAMS.

No. 829.

First Quality English Crucible Steel Blades, Highly Tempered, Glazed Finish.

No. 829—3 INCH BRASS HANDLE, with THREE BLADES ....

No. 828—3 INCH BRASS HANDLE, with TWO BLADES.................................

RASE KNIVES.

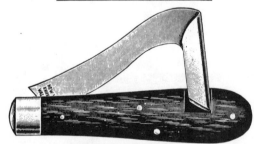

LUMBERMAN'S.

No. 135R—3⅝ INCH COCOBOLO HANDLE; First Quality Crucible Steel Blade, Highly Tempered, Glazed Finish; Polished Steel Bolster; Steel Lining ....

One-half Dozen in a Cardboard Box; Weight per Dozen about 1½ lbs.

BUDDING KNIVES.

No. 3—3⅝ INCH COCOBOLO HANDLE, 2½ inch Extra Grade Crucible Steel Blade, Glazed Finish, with Tang extending half way into the Handle, secured by Two Brass Pins ....

One Dozen in a Cardboard Box; Weight per Dozen about 1½ lbs.

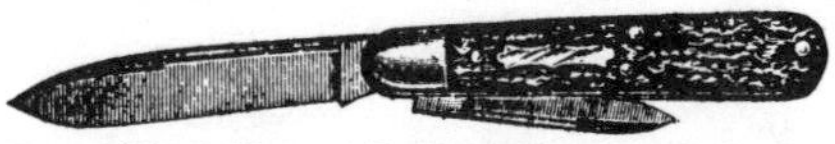

No. 28V916 Keene Cutlery Co.'s Goliath Jack Knife. It has stag handle, German silver long heavy bolsters, and shield, brass lined, finished inside and out. Length of handle, 4½ inches; length with large blade open, 8 inches. Price.........................
If by mail, postage extra, 6 cents.

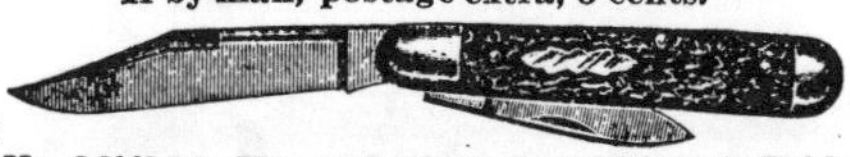

No. 28V920 Keene Cutlery Co.'s Hunter's Pride Knife. It has stag handle, long heavy German silver bolsters, cap and shield, brass lining, highly finished inside and out. The blades open and close freely without wearing. The knife blade is always true in the center, and it is these little points to which we pay so much attention that cause our knives to give better satisfaction than those you can procure from any other dealer. Length of handle, 4½ inches; length with large blade open, 8 inches. Price.........................
If by mail, postage extra, 6 cents.

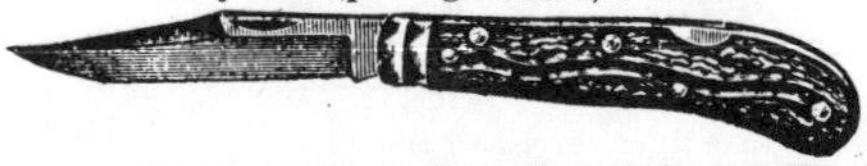

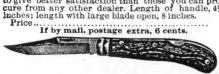

No. 28V945 Keene Cutlery Co.'s Arkansas Hunter. A knife in which nearly every cent of the cost is spent in quality, and not looks. It has clip point saber blade, flush lock back so blade cannot shut on the finger, curved stag handle which just fits the hand nicely, fancy iron bolsters, steel lining. Length of handle, 4⅝ inches; length with blade open, 8½ inches. Price.........................
If by mail, postage extra, 7 cents.

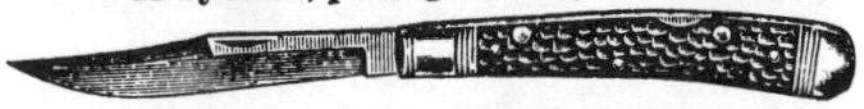

No. 28V946 Keene Cutlery Co.'s Hudson Bay Hunting Knife. A very nicely finished hunting knife. Clip point saber blade, flush lock back, curved stag handle, fancy German silver bolster, caps and lining. Length of handle, 5¼ inches; length with blade open, 9¾ inches. Price...........
If by mail, postage extra, 8 cents.

KEENE CUTLERY CO.'S KNIVES ARE THE BEST ON EARTH. There is no better method of manufacturing; there is no better method of tempering, and we have not yet seen any line of pocket knives in which so much care was used in grinding, finishing and fitting, and the chief point, the one above all others is, that our knives will cut; they will carry an edge; they will give better satisfaction in every way than any knife you have ever purchased, no matter where it was made.

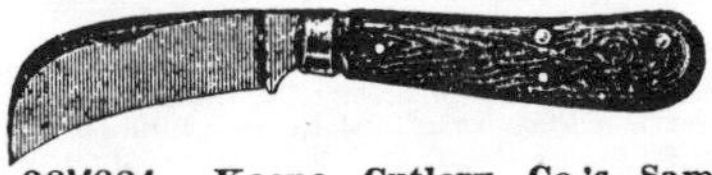

No. 28V884 Keene Cutlery Co.'s Sampson Pruning Knife. Blade made of 10-gauge steel. The shape of blade, method of grinding, etc., being according to the ideas of one of the best fruit growers in the country, who had the original made just exactly the way he wanted it regardless of expense. Length of handle, 4 inches; length with blade open, 7 inches. Price,.........................
If by mail, postage extra, 6 cents.

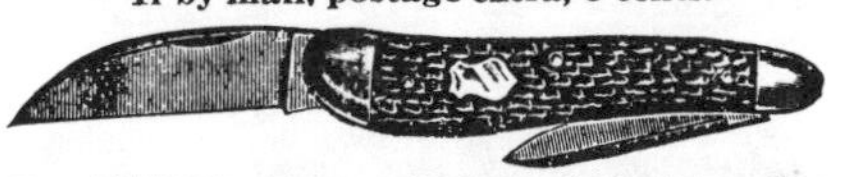

No. 28V925 Keene Cutlery Co.'s New England Workman's Knife. A great favorite with carpenters, cabinet makers and other wood workers. It has stag handle, German silver bolster and shield, brass lining, finely finished, and polished inside and out. Length of handle, 3¾ inches; length with large blade open, 6 inches. Price.........................
If by mail, postage extra, 4 cents.

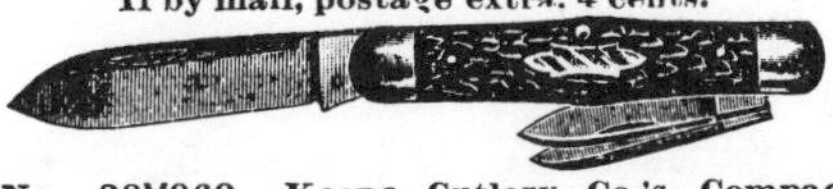

No. 28V969 Keene Cutlery Co.'s Compact Three-Blade Pocket Knife. The large blade is wide and strong; has two pen blades, stag handle, German silver bolsters and shield, brass lining, finely finished inside and out. Length of handle, 3⅜ inches; length with large blade open, 5⅞ inches. Price.........................
If by mail, postage extra, 5 cents.

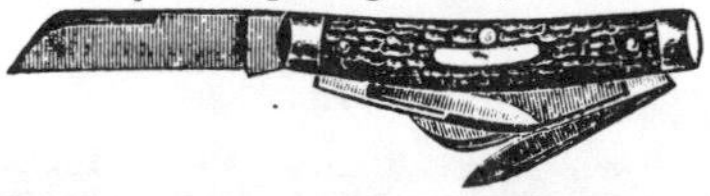

No. 28V980 Keene Cutlery Co.'s Large Congress Knife has two large blades and two pen blades, stag handle, German silver bolsters and shield, brass lined, nicely finished throughout. Length of handle, 3¾ inches; length with large blade open, 6 inches. Price.........................
If by mail, postage extra, 5 cents.

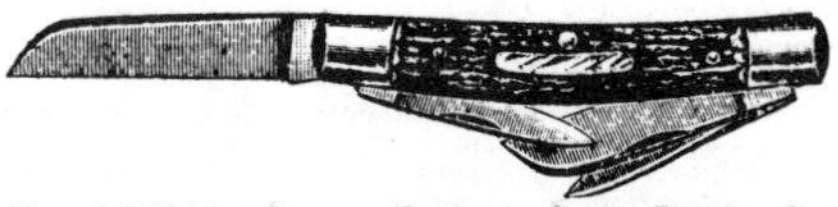

No. 28V982 Keene Cutlery Co.'s Jumbo Congress Knife, with two large blades and two pen blades. Stag handle, iron bolsters, German silver shield, brass lined. Finely finished. Those who prefer a congress pattern knife and want something strong and heavy will find this a most desirable pattern. Length of handle, 4⅛ inches; length with large blade open, 6¾ inches. Price.........................
If by mail, postage extra, 6 cents.

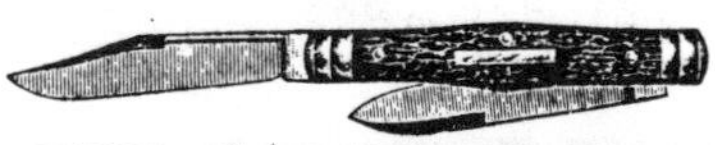

No. 28V890 Keene Cutlery Co.'s Favorite Double Ender, with spear and clip point blades. Stag handle. German silver fancy bolsters and shield, brass lined and finished inside and out. Length of handle, 3¾ inches; length with clip point blade open, 6⅝ inches. Price.........................
If by mail, postage extra, 5 cents.

IF A RAZOR EDGE is put on any of the Keene Cutlery Co.'s blades we will guarantee any of them to shave, but a razor edge should never be put on a pocket knife. To get a proper edge on a pocket knife blade, the blade should be held at an angle of about 20 or 25 degrees, and drawn from shoulder to point on each side until a true edge is obtained. This makes a stiff, keen cutting edge, and enables us to furnish a much higher tempered knife blade than we would were the blade to be laid flat and brought down to a razor edge.

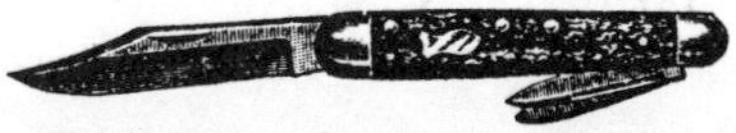

No. 28V892 Keene Cutlery Co.'s Western Chief. Has clip point saber blade, very heavy, made of full 10-gauge steel; has stag handle, German silver bolsters and shield, brass lining, finished inside and out. The large blade has a flush lock back, which prevents the blade from closing on the hand. Length of handle, 4 inches; length with large blade open, 6¾ inches. Price.........................
If by mail, postage extra, 6 cents.

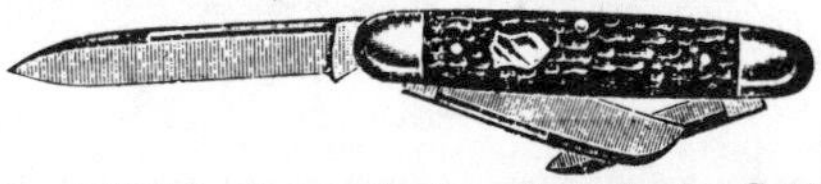

No. 28V911 Keene Cutlery Co.'s Junior Cattle Knife. Has spear, pen and sheep foot blades, It has stag handle, German silver bolster and shield, brass lining, finished inside and out. Length of handle, 3¼ inches; length with large blade open, 5¾ inches. Price.........................
If by mail, postage extra, 5 cents.

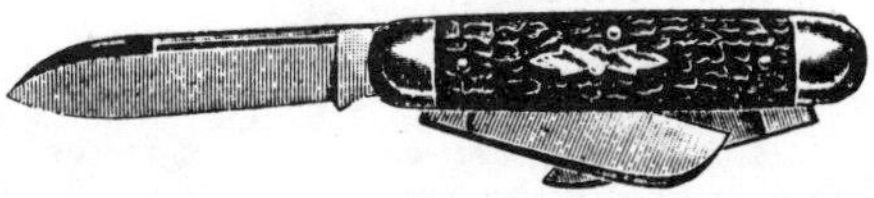

No. 28V912 Keene Cutlery Co.'s Wild West Cowboys' Knife. Has spear, sheep foot and pen blades, stag handle, iron bolsters, German silver shield, brass lined; finished inside and out. This is a strong, heavy knife, and is a great favorite with stockmen, hunters, trappers and others who wish a strong, heavy knife in as compact form as possible. Length of handle, 3⅝ inches; length with large blade open, 6¼ inches. Price.........................
If by mail, postage extra, 6 cents.

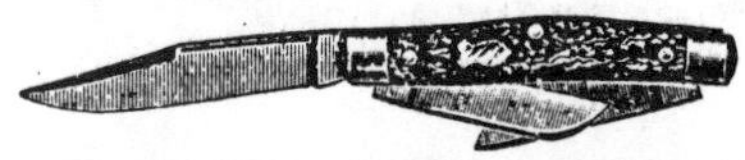

No. 28V881 Keene Cutlery Co.'s Texas Stock Knife. A pattern of knife which is popular with stock raisers all over the world, has clip, sheep foot and spaying blades, stag handle, German silver bolsters and shield, brass lined, highly finished inside and out. This is our most popular cattle knife, and is made just as good as we know how to make them. Length of handle, 4 inches; length with clip point blade open, 6⅞ inches. Price.........................
If by mail, postage extra, 5 cents.

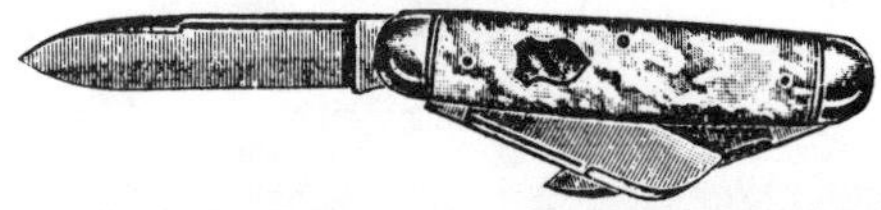

No. 28V899 Keene Cutlery Co.'s Ranchero Cattle Knife. Has pearl handle, German silver bolsters and shield, German silver lining, satin finish. The blades are full crocus polished. It cannot fail to give satisfaction to those who want a knife of superior cutting qualities, workmanship and beauty. Length of handle, 3⅝ inches; length with large blade open, 6⅝ inches. Price.........................
If by mail, postage extra, 5 cents.

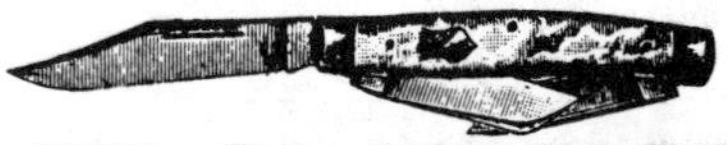

No. 28V901 Keene Cutlery Co.'s Montana Beauty Stockman's Knife. Has clip sheep foot and spaying blades, pearl handle, German silver lining, satin finish; the blades are beautifully crocus polished. In our ordinary grades of knives, knives which must sell at popular prices, we pay very much more attention to quality and workmanship than we do to beauty and finish, but in this particular knife we excel all others in finish as well as in quality. Length of handle, 3⅝ inches; length with large blade open, 6¾ inches. Price,.........................
If by mail, postage extra, 5 cents.

EVERY ONE OF KEENE CUTLERY CO.'S KNIFE BLADES IS TEMPERED by the copper plate process, by a man who has been doing this work for thirty years in the best cutlery factories in the world.

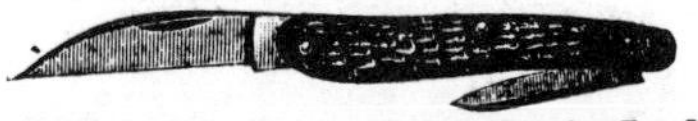

No. 28V949 Keene Cutlery Co.'s Ladies' Penknife. Large blade, just the proper shape for ripping seams, etc.; slender small pen blade, stag handle, brass lining, finished inside. Length of handle, 2¾ inches; length with large blade open, 4¾ inches. Price.........................
If by mail, postage extra, 3 cents.

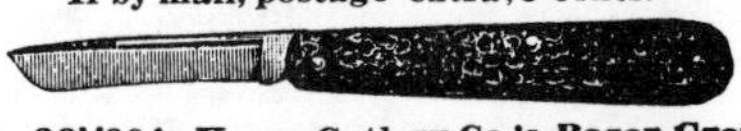

No. 28V904 Keene Cutlery Co.'s Razor Ground Corn Knife. Is razor ground, razor tempered, and must not be put to any use excepting that for which it is designed. It has stag handle, brass lined, finished in a first class manner inside and out. Length of handle. 3¼ inches; length with blade open, 5¼ inches. Price.........................
If by mail, postage extra, 3 cents.

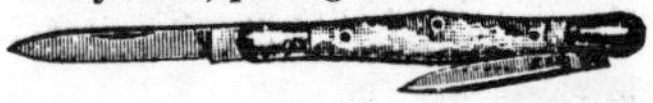

No. 28V954 Keene Cutlery Co.'s Popular School or Ladies' Knife. Pearl handle, German silver bolsters, German silver lining, finished inside. Length of handle, 2⅞ inches; length with large blade open, 4⅝ inches. Price.........................
If by mail, postage extra, 3 cents.

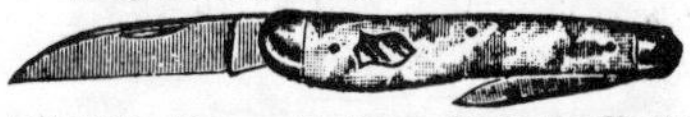

No. 28V928 Keene Cutlery Co.'s Ladies' Pearl Handle Pocket Knife. It has a selected pearl handle, German silver bolsters, German silver lining, satin finish, full crocus polished blades. It is a very desirable pattern. Length of handle, 3 inches; length with large blade open, 4¾ inches. Price.........................
If by mail, postage extra, 3 cents.

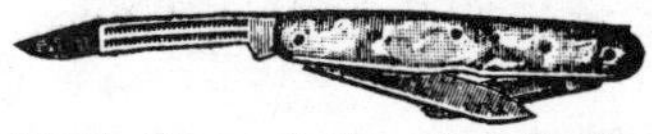

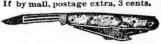

No. 28V931 Keene Cutlery Co.'s Ladies' Fine Three-Blade Shadow Pattern Penknife. Has large blade, pen blade and latest improved nail blade. Has very superior pearl handle, German silver lining, satin finish. The blades are full crocus polished, giving it a beautiful appearance. Length of handle, 2⅝ inches; length with nail blade open, 4⅛ inches. Price.........................
If by mail, postage extra, 3 cents.

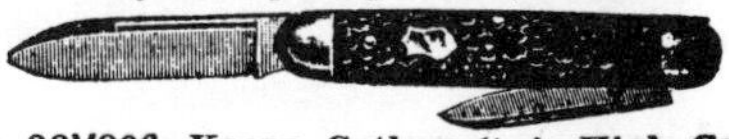

No. 28V906 Keene Cutlery Co.'s High Grade Two-Blade Penknife, has stag handle, German silver bolsters and shield, brass lined, finely polished throughout. The blades are extra heavy, and are stronger than ordinarily found in a knife of this size. Length of handle, 3¼ inches; length with large blade open, 5⅝ inches. Price.........................
If by mail, postage extra, 4 cents.

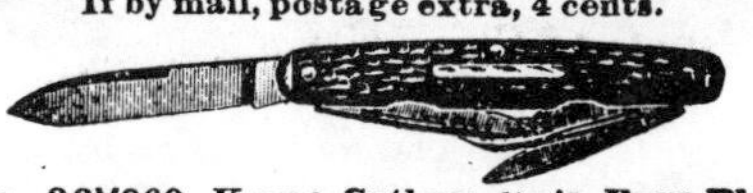

No. 28V960 Keene Cutlery Co.'s Four-Blade Stag Handle Senator Pattern Penknife, with large blade, two pen blades and nail blade, stag handle, German silver tips and shield, brass lining, finely finished inside and out, all blades full crocus polished. Length of handle, 3¼ inches; length with large blade open, 5¼ inches. Price.........................
If by mail, postage extra, 4 cents.

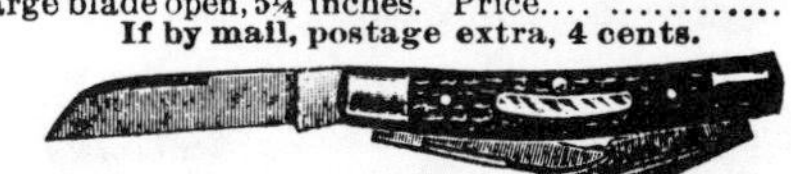

No. 28V963 Keene Cutlery Co.'s Small Congress Knife, has one large blade, two pen blades and one nail blade, stag handle, German silver bolsters and shield, brass lined, finely finished throughout. Length of handle, 3⅛ inches; length with large blade open, 5⅜ inches. Price.........................
If by mail, postage extra, 4 cents.

NEW POCKET KNIVES DIRECT FROM OUR OWN FACTORY.

WE CALL YOUR ATTENTION especially to this handsome new line of highest grade American made pocket and penknives, our Keene Cutlery Co. brand.

THE BLADES ARE FORGED from S. C. Wardlow's best English special blade steel, the finest and the best that can be procured for knife blades. We also use Wardlow's steel for the springs, which costs nearly double the price at which ordinary spring steel can be bought, but which greatly improves the wearing qualities of the knife, and adds greatly to its durability. **Every blade, from the cheapest to the best which bears our brand, is hammered out by hand.** Instead of using iron for the lining of our cheaper knives, we pay more for steel because it makes a much stronger and better knife. All work is done by skilled mechanics, particular attention being paid to making a keen cutting knife that will carry a lasting edge.

OUR POCKET KNIVES are fully guaranteed in every way. This means we guarantee the blades to be free from flaws, and guarantee them to be neither too hard nor too soft. This does not mean that we guarantee the knives not to break. If we were to do this, we would be obliged to temper them so soft they would be of no practical use for cutting. They are not intended to be used as mortising chisels, tack pullers, can openers, screwdrivers, crowbars, or any of the purposes by which pocket knives are frequently misused.

ALL POCKET KNIVES should occasionally be oiled at the joint so the blade will not wear into the spring. Vaseline makes a very good lubricant for this purpose.

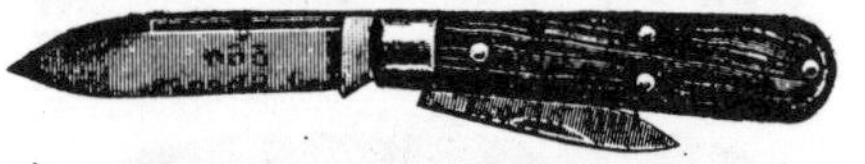

No. 28V830 Keene Cutlery Co.'s Pocket Knife. Has rosewood handle, steel lining, iron bolster. **Length of handle, 3⅜ inches. Length with large blade open, 6 inches.** Price......................

If by mail, postage extra, 4 cents.

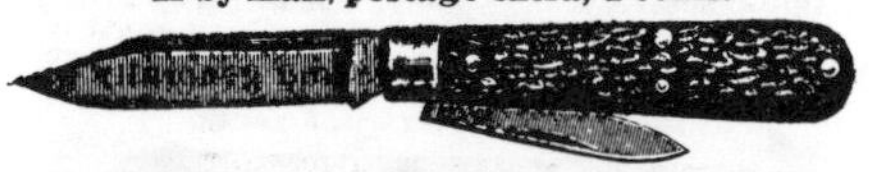

No. 28V833 Keene Cutlery Co.'s Pocket Knife, clip point, stag handle, two blades, steel lining, iron bolster. This is a standard size full weight knife; is durable, and will give splendid satisfaction. **Length of handle, 3⅜ inches. Length, with large blade open, 6⅛ inches.** Price....................

If by mail, postage extra, 5 cents.

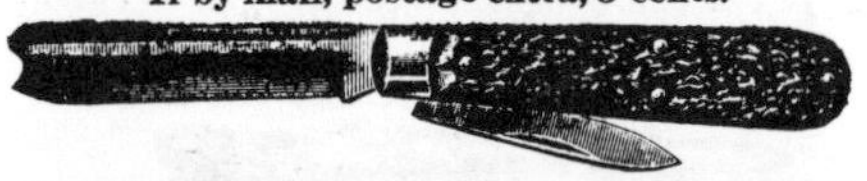

No. 28V836 Keene Cutlery Co.'s Razor Blade Jack Knife, stag handle, steel lining, iron bolster; a pattern which is very popular in certain localities. **Length of handle, 3⅜ inches. Length with large blade open, 6 inches.** Price......................

If by mail, postage extra, 5 cents.

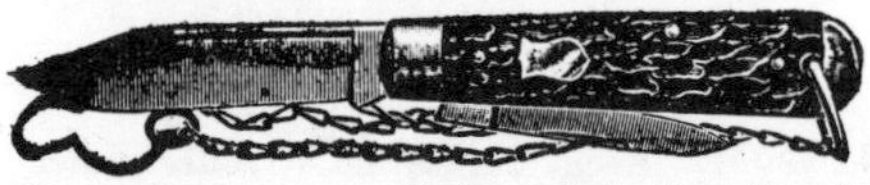

No. 28V838 Keene Cutlery Co.'s Stag Handle Chain Knife, clip point, two blades, steel lining, iron bolster and caps, German silver shield, with chain of suitable length to fasten over button. Length of handle, 3⅜ inches. Length with large blade open, 6⅛ inches. Price......................

If by mail, postage extra, 6 cents.

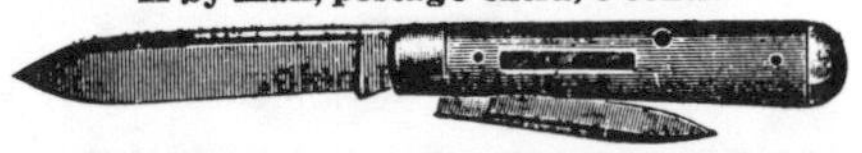

No. 28V840 A medium weight, finely finished Keene Cutlery Co.'s knife, with white bone handle, brass lining, finished inside and out, German silver bolster and caps and shield. Length of handle, 3⅜ inches. Length with large blade open, 6⅛ inches. Price......................

If by mail, postage extra, 5 cents.

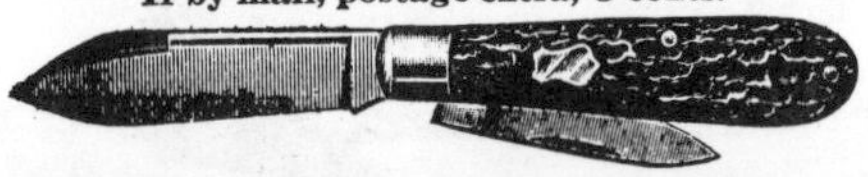

No. 28V842 Keene Cutlery Co.'s Jack Knife, stag handle, swell butt, steel lining, iron bolsters, German silver shield. Length of handle, 3⅜ inches. Length with large blade open, 6⅛ inches.

If by mail, postage extra, 5 cents.

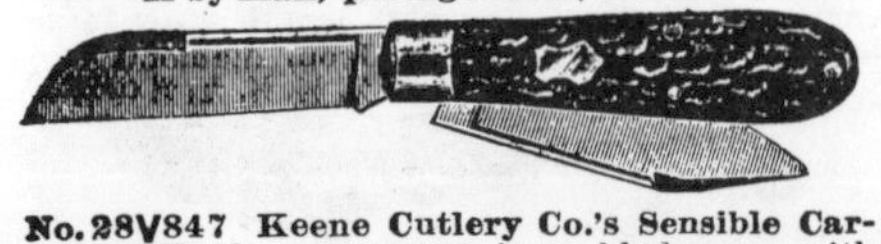

No. 28V847 Keene Cutlery Co.'s Sensible Carpenters' Knife, having two large blades, one with clip point and one sheep foot or carpenter marking blade. The blades of this knife are made of 11-gauge steel; has stag handle, steel lining, iron bolsters, German silver shields, finished inside and out. Length of handle, 3½ inches. Length with large blade open, 6½ inches. Price......................

If by mail, postage extra, 6 cents.

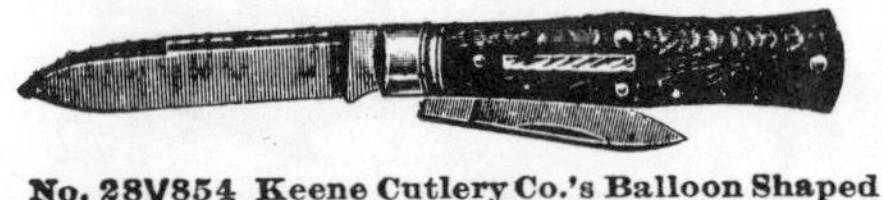

No. 28V854 Keene Cutlery Co.'s Balloon Shaped Two-Blade Cocoa Handle Pocket Knife, German silver fancy bolster and shield, brass lining, finely **finished** inside and out. Length of handle, 3⅜ inches. Length with large blade open, 6⅛ inches.

If by mail, postage extra, 5 cents.

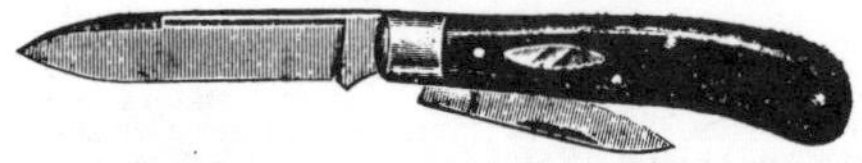

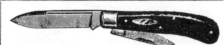

No. 28V849 Keene Cutlery Co.'s Hand Fitting Easy Opener Pocket Knife, with ebony handle, brass lining, German silver bolster and shield. Finished inside and out. Length of handle, 3¼ inches. Length with large blade open, 6⅛ inches.

If by mail, postage extra, 6 cents.

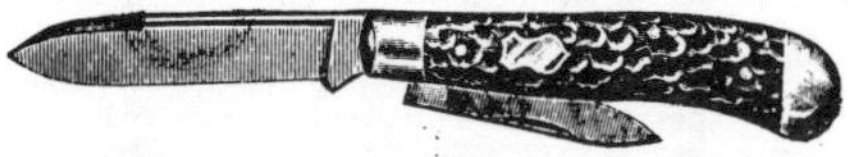

No. 28V850 Another Keene Cutlery Co.'s Easy Opener Pocket Knife, with stag handle, German silver bolster caps and shield, brass lining. Finished inside and out. Length of handle, 3½ inches. Length with large blade open, 6⅛ inches. Price.........

If by mail, postage extra, 6 cents.

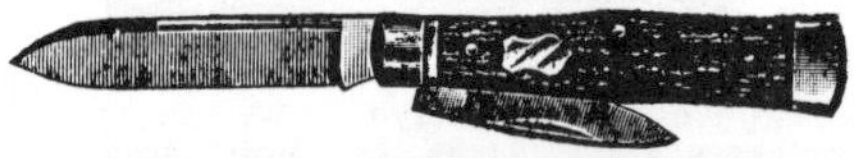

No. 28V875 Keene Cutlery Co.'s balloon shaped knife, stag handle, fancy German silver bolster and caps, German silver shield, brass lining, finished inside and out. Length of handle, 3⅜ inches. Length with large blade open, 6⅛ inches. Price.........

If by mail, postage extra, 6 cents.

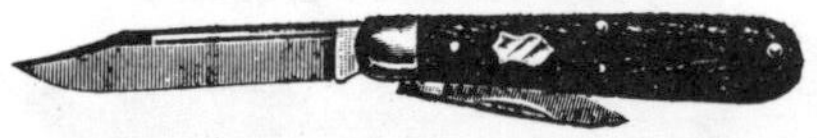

No. 28V860 Keene Cutlery Co.'s Gentlemen's Jack Knife has a cocoa handle, German silver bolster and shield, brass lined, finely finished inside and out. Length of handle, 3¼ inches. Length with large blade open, 5⅜ inches. Price...............

If by mail, postage extra, 5 cents.

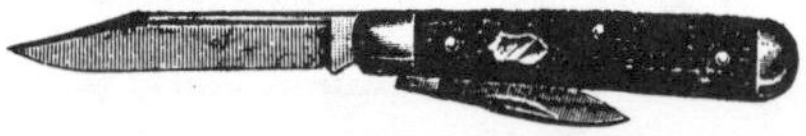

No. 28V861 Keene Cutlery Co.'s Gentlemen's Jack Knife, stag handle, German silver bolster, caps and shield, brass lining, thoroughly finished in every particular inside and out. Length of handle, 3¼ inches. Length with large blade open, 5¾ inches. Price......................

If by mail, postage extra, 5 cents.

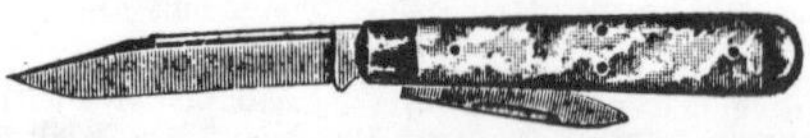

No. 28V878 Keene Cutlery Co.'s Pearl Handle Gentlemen's Jack Knife with clip point blade. Has German silver bolster and caps, brass lining, finished inside and out. The blades are full crocus polished, and the finish of the knife throughout is equal to the very finest penknife. Length of handle, 3¼ inches. Length with large blade open, 5⅜ inches. Price......................

If by mail, postage extra, 5 cents.

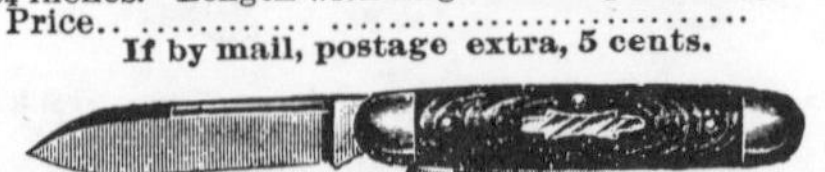

No. 28V864 Keene Cutlery Co.'s Equal End Pocket Knife, has cocoa handle, German silver bolster, cap and shield, brass lined, finished inside and out. Length of handle, 3¼ inches. Length with large blade open, 5⅜ inches. Price...............

If by mail, postage extra, 5 cents.

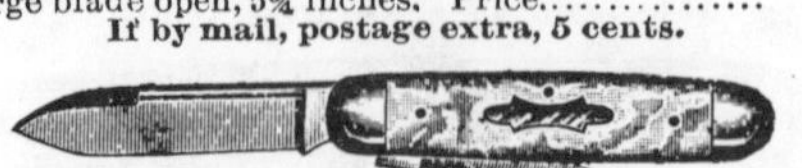

No. 28V869 Keene Cutlery Co.'s Gentlemen's Pearl Handle Jack Knife. Has pearl handle, German silver bolster, caps and shield, German silver lining, satin finish. The blades are full crocus polished. The knife is in every way finished as finely as the best penknife you ever saw. Length of handle, 3¼ inches; length with large blade open, 5¾ inches. Price......................

If by mail, postage extra, 5 cents.

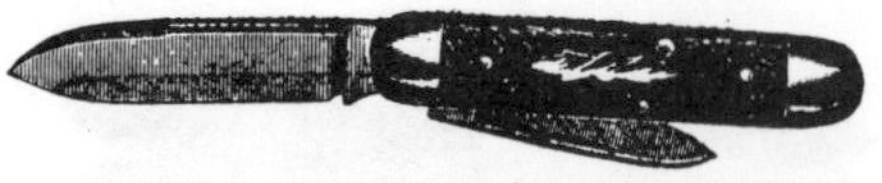

No. 28V856 Keene Cutlery Co.'s Equal End Jack Knife. Has cocoa handle, brass lining, finished inside and out, German silver bolster, caps and shield. Length of handle, 3½ inches; length with large blade open, 6⅛ inches. Price..............

If by mail, postage extra, 6 cents.

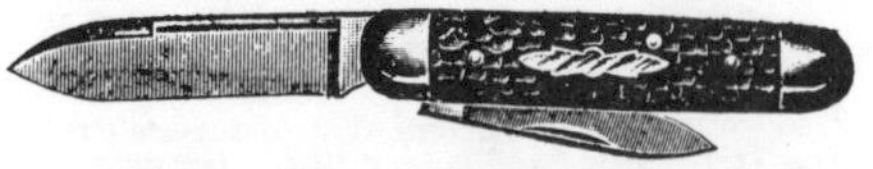

No. 28V857 Keene Cutlery Co.'s equal end knife, has stag handle, brass lining, German silver bolster cap and shield. Length of handle, 3½ inches; length with large blade open, 6⅛ inches. Price..

If by mail, postage extra, 6 cents.

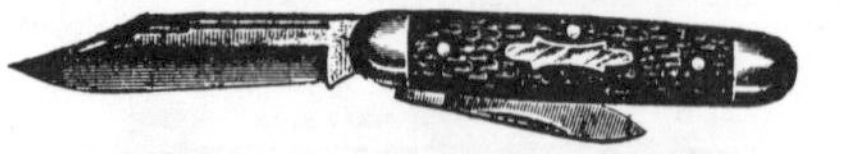

No. 28V866 Keene Cutlery Co.'s Little Giant Equal End Pocket Knife, with saber clip blade, stag handle, German silver bolster, caps and shield, brass lined, finished inside and out. The amount of work which this knife will do is something never before attained in a knife of its size. Length of handle, 3¼ inches; length with large blade open, 5⅝ inches. Price......................

If by mail, postage extra, 5 cents.

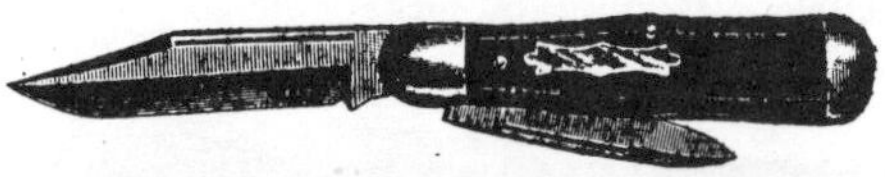

No. 28V908 Keene Cutlery Co.'s Missouri Favorite, has clip point, saber blade made of full 12-gauge steel. Has ebony handle, long German silver bolsters, caps and shield, brass lined, finished inside and out. Length of handle, 3¼ inches; length with large blade open, 6 inches. Price..................

If by mail, postage extra, 6 cents.

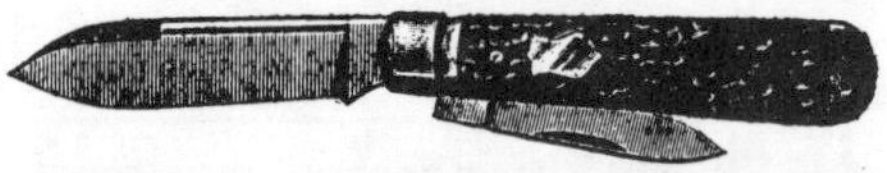

No. 28V845 Keene Cutlery Co.'s Solid Worth Jack Knife. Stag handle, brass lining, finished inside and out, iron bolsters and caps, German silver shield. Length of handle, 3½ inches; length with large blade open, 6¼ inches. Price...............

If by mail, postage extra, 6 cents.

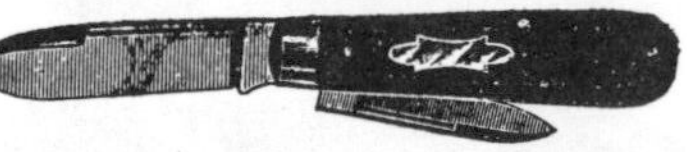

No. 28V886 Keene Cutlery Co.'s Jumbo Pocket Knife, with ebony handle 4 inches long; German silver bolster and shield, brass lined, finished inside and out. **The blades are made of full size 10-gauge steel.** This is a big, strong, heavy, durable knife. Length of handle, 3⅞ inches; length with large blade open, 6⅞ inches. Price......................

If by mail, postage extra, 6 cents.

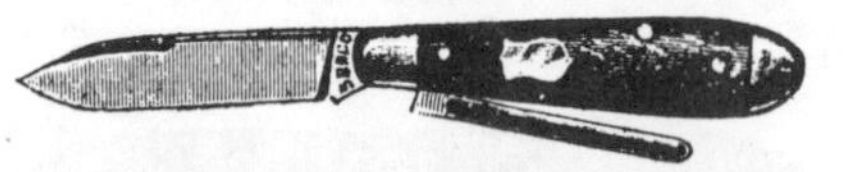

No. 28V1328 Keene Cutlery Co.'s Teamsters' Knife. Has cocoa handle, German silver bolster, tips and shields, brass lined. Length of handle, 3½ inches; length with the large blade open, 6¼ inches. Instead of having an ordinary small blade, this knife is furnished with a gouge shaped blade, which will bore a $\frac{3}{16}$-inch hole through the traces or any part of the harness, and will bore equally well in wood. Price......................

If by mail, postage extra, 6 cents.

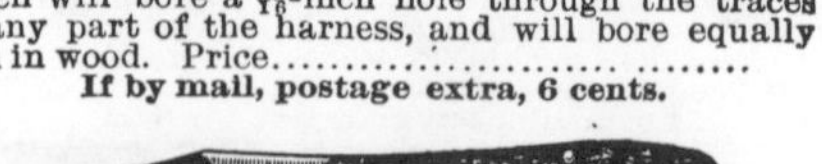

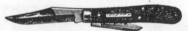

No. 28V895 Keene Cutlery Co's Texas Tooth Pick, has stag handle, German silver bolsters and shield, brass lining, finely finished inside and out. Clip point saber blade. While the blade is long and slim, the peculiar shape makes it very strong and durable as well as an excellent whittler. Length of handle, 3⅜ inches; length with large blade open, 6⅜ inches. Price......................

If by mail, postage extra, 6 cents.

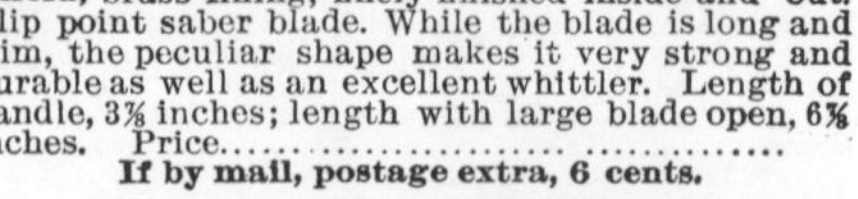

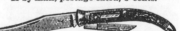

No. 28V896 Keene Cutlery Co.'s Austrian Hunter. It has a clip point blade, stag handle, fancy iron bolster and caps, German silver shield, steel lining, finely finished inside and out. Length of handle, 3¾ inches; length with large blade open, 7 inches. Price......................

If by mail, postage extra, 5 cents.

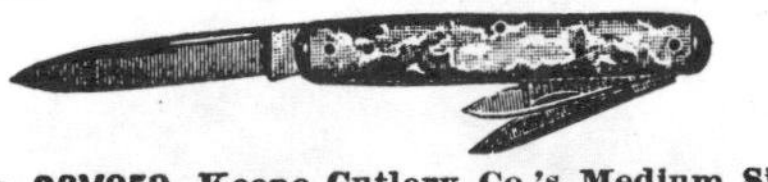

No. 28V959 Keene Cutlery Co.'s Medium Size Three-Blade Pearl Handle, Senator Pattern Penknife, German silver tips and lining, blades full crocus polished, well finished throughout. Length of handle, 3 inches; length with large blade open, 4¾ inches. Price..
If by mail, postage extra, 4 cents.

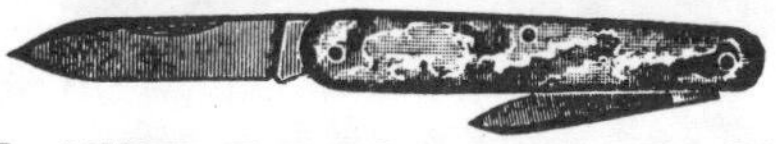

No. 28V932 Keene Cutlery Co.'s Two-Blade Shadow Pattern Penknife, pearl handle, German silver lined, satin finish, large blade and pen blade. **Blades are full** crocus polished; the knife is everything that could be desired in quality and appearance. Length of handle, 3¼ inches; length with large blade open, 5⅝ inches. Price..............
If by mail, postage extra, 4 cents.

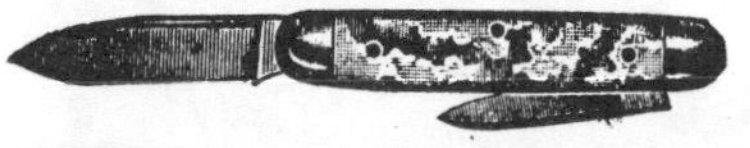

No. 28V935 Keene Cutlery Co.'s Two-Blade Favorite Penknife, has a fine grade of pearl handle, German silver bolster, brass lining, finished inside and out. The big blade is short, wide and heavy. The pen blade is correctly proportioned. Length of handle, 3¼ inches; length with large blade open, 5⅝ inches. Price..
If by mail, postage extra, 4 cents.

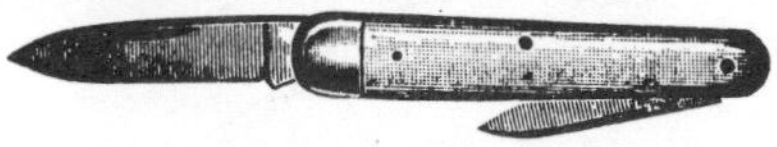

No. 28V953 Keene Cutlery Co.'s Two-Blade Penknife, German Silver Bolster and Lining, imitation ivory handle which will not crack and does not discolor with use. Length of handle, 3⅜ inches; length with large blade open, 5⅝ inches. Price..
If by mail, postage extra, 4 cents.

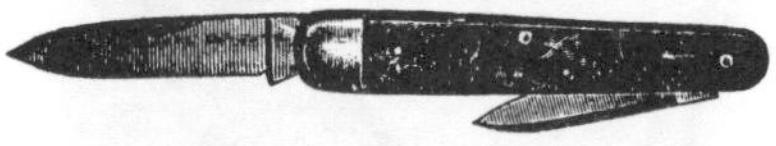

No. 28V955 Keene Cutlery Co.'s Two-Blade Penknife, imitation shell handle, German silver bolster and lining. Length of handle, 3⅜ inches; length with large blade open, 5⅝ inches. The handle is really better than the genuine shell as it is more durable, and every piece is as handsome as the very best selection of shell. Price....................
If by mail, postage extra, 4 cents.

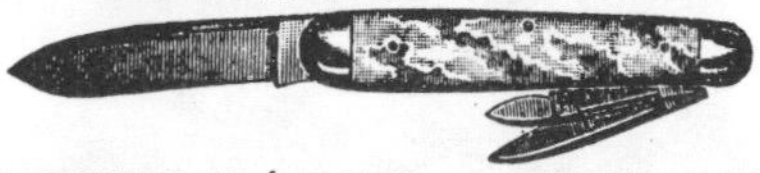

No. 28V956 Keene Cutlery Co.'s Three-Blade Pearl Handle Penknife, German silver bolsters and lining, blades full crocus polished, finely finished. Length of handle, 3¼ inches; length with large blade open, 5½ inches. Price..............................
If by mail, postage extra, 4 cents.

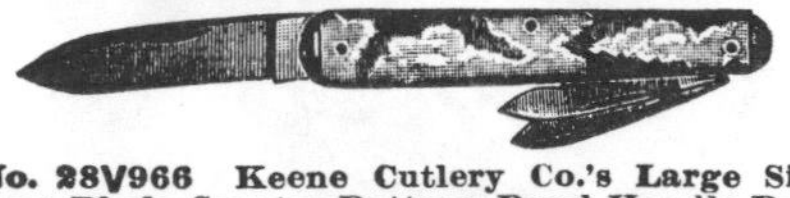

No. 28V966 Keene Cutlery Co.'s Large Size Three-Blade, Senator Pattern, Pearl Handle Penknife, German silver tips and lining, blades full crocus polished, finely finished. Length of handle, 3¼ inches; length with large blade open, 5½ inches. Price..
If by mail, postage extra, 5 cents.

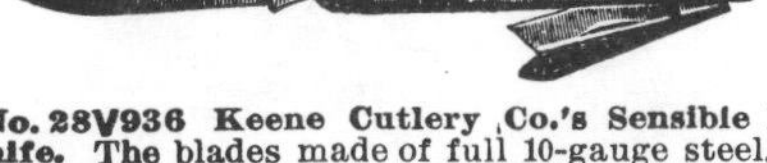

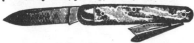

No. 28V936 Keene Cutlery Co.'s Sensible Pen Knife. The blades made of full 10-gauge steel. It has spear point large and one bevel point and one spear point pen blade. It has a very fine quality pearl handle with German silver bolster, brass lined, finished inside and out. The blades are full crocus polished, making an attractive as well as a sensible pocket knife. Length of handle, 3¼ inches; length with large blade open, 5½ inches. Price.......
If by mail, postage extra, 4 cents.

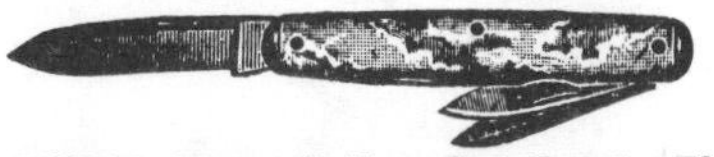

No. 28V940 Keene Cutlery Co.'s Senator Three-Blade Pearl Handle Penknife. It has a good, heavy, strong, big blade, a pen blade and a nail blade. Fine quality pearl handle, German silver tip, German silver lining, satin finish. The blades are full crocus polished, burnished finish back. In quality, workmanship and appearance we offer the best knife we are able to make and we are confident it will please the most fastidious. Length of handle, 3 inches; length with large blade open, 4⅞ inches.
Price..
If by mail, postage extra, 4 cents.

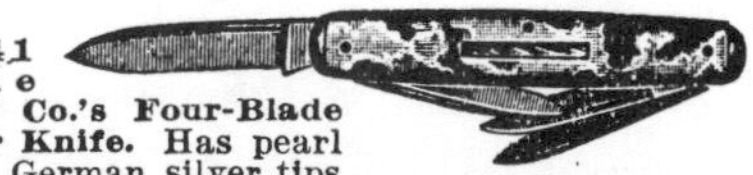

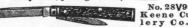

No. 28V941 Keene Cutlery Co.'s Four-Blade Senator Knife. Has pearl handle, German silver tips and shield, German silver lining, satin finish, blades full crocus polished, burnished finish back. Length of handle, 3 inches; length with large blade open, 4¾ inches. Price..
If by mail, postage extra, 4 cents.

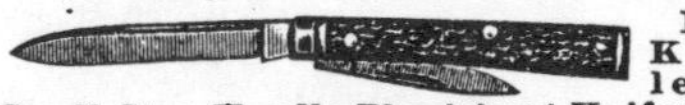

No. 28V985 Keene Cutlery Co.'s Small Stag Handle Physicians' Knife; not only a good physician's knife, but desirable for office and desk use. It has German silver butt, iron bolsters and brass lining. Length of handle, 3¼ inches; length with large blade open, 5⅞ inches. Price..............
If by mail, postage extra, 4 cents.

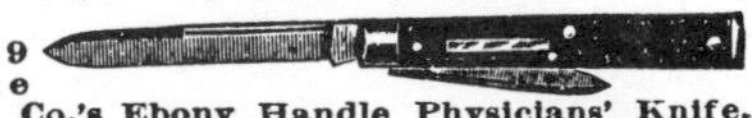

No. 28V989 Keene Cutlery Co.'s Ebony Handle Physicians' Knife, with German silver butt, bolsters and shield, brass lining, finely finished inside and out, blades full crocus polished. Length of handle, 3⅝ inches; length with large blade open, 6⅝ inches. Price..............
If by mail, postage extra, 5 cents.

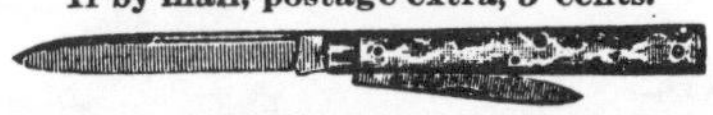

No. 28V990 Keene Cutlery Co.'s Pearl Handle Physicians' Knife. German silver butt, German silver bolster and German silver lining, finely finished inside and out, blades full crocus polished. Length of handle, 3⅝ inches; length with large blade open, 6⅝ inches. Price..............
If by mail, postage extra, 5 cents.

Push Button Knives.

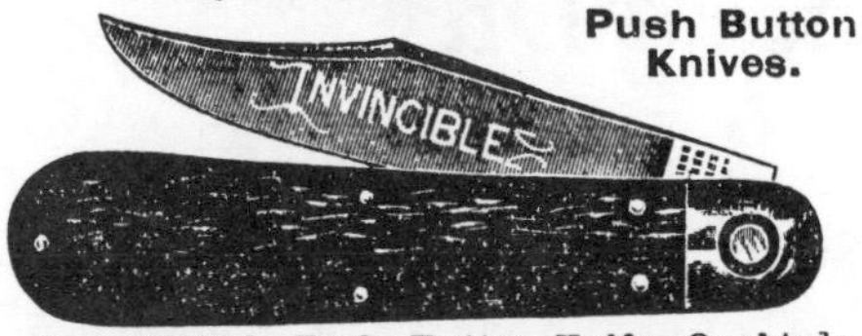

No. 28V1324 Push Button Knife. One blade, clip point, stag handle, single bolster, iron lined. Length of handle, 4¾ inches; length with blade open, 8⅜ inches. Price..........................
If by mail, postage extra, 5 cents.
No. 28V1320 Push Button Knife. One bladé clip point, stag handle, single bolster, iron lined. Length of handle, 3⅞ inches; length with blade open, 6⅞ inches. Price..............................55c
If by mail, postage extra, 5 cents.

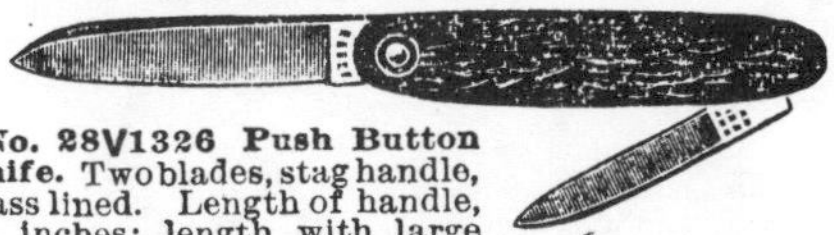

No. 28V1326 Push Button Knife. Two blades, stag handle, brass lined. Length of handle, 3⅜ inches; length with large blade open, 5¾ inches. Price......................

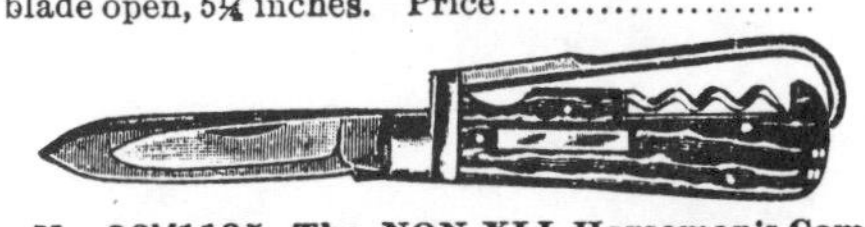

No. 28V1135 The NON-XLL Horseman's Combination Knife. A kit of tools in itself; has large and small blades, fleam, hoof pick, corkscrew, reamer, screwdriver, tweezers and toothpick. Made of the best English steel, with genuine stag handle, and fully warranted. Length of handle, 3¾ inches; length with large blade open, 6½ inches. Price.......

Genuine Joh. Engstrom Swedish Hunting Knife.

Blade can be removed, folded into its frame, and replaced in the handle. This knife is a popular woodworkers' tool, as well as a hunting knife. Has solid boxwood handle. **The blade is best of steel, and the maker's name is a guarantee of cutting qualities and temper.** We have this knife in three sizes.

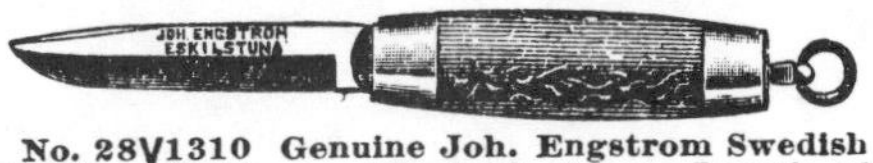

No. 28V1310 Genuine Joh. Engstrom Swedish Hunting Knife, as described above. Length of handle, 2⅞ inches. Price..........................
No. 28V1311 Genuine Joh. Engstrom Swedish Hunting Knife, as described above. Length of handle, 3¼ inches. Price..........................
No. 28V1312 Genuine Joh. Engstrom Swedish Hunting Knife, as described above. Length of handle, 4⅜ inches. Price..........................

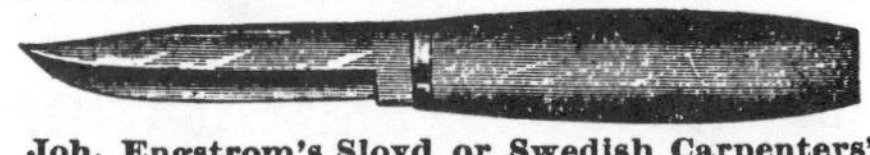

Joh. Engstrom's Sloyd or Swedish Carpenters' Bench Knife. Intended for the tool chest or work bench. Used in manual training schools. Made from the finest quality of Swedish razor steel.
No. 28V1315 Swedish Carpenters' Bench Knife. Length of blade, 2¼ inches. Price..............
If by mail, postage extra, 6 cents.
No. 28V1316 Swedish Carpenters' Bench Knife. Length of blade, 3¼ inches. Price..............
If by mail, postage extra, 6 cents.

IMPORTED KNIVES.

The following pocket knives No. 28V1000 to 28V1332 are imported from Europe and are not guaranteed. In order that our customers may not be misled, we have described them as good, fair and cheap. The cheap grade is good for the price, but the price is not enough for a good knife. Fair grade will usually give satisfaction. The good grades are commonly sold as warranted, but we do not warrant them. Any of these goods will be better value than you can secure elsewhere for the same money.

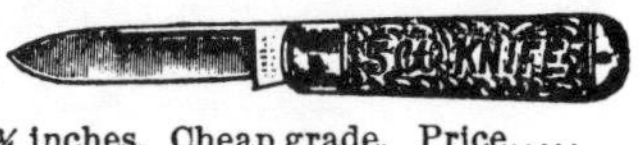

No. 28V1000 Metal Handle Knife, one blade, iron lined; blade, 2⅜ inches. Cheap grade. Price.....
If by mail, postage extra, 4 cents.

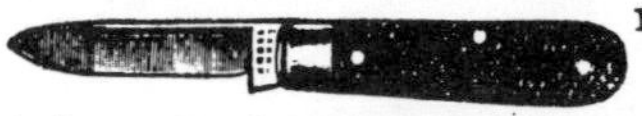

No. 28V1004 Ebony Handle Knife, one blade, iron lined; blade, 2⅝ inches. Cheap grade. Price..
If by mail, postage extra, 4 cents.

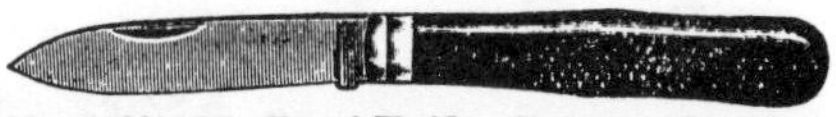

No. 28V1005 Boys' Knife. Cheap grade. Entire length open, 6¾ inches. Length of handle, 3¾ inches. Black japanned handle, bright bolster. A great big knife for the money, and one that will please the boys. Price..

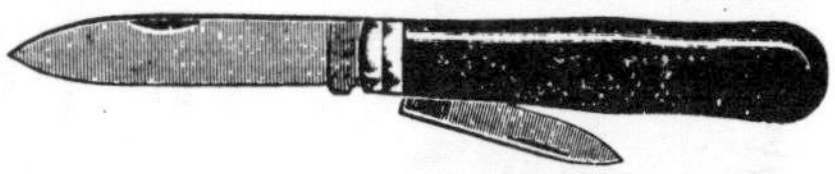

No. 28V1006 Same knife as described under preceding number, with two blades. Price........

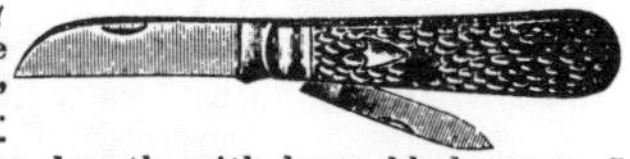

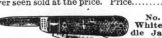

No. 28V1007 Iron Handle Boys' Knife, with two blades. Length of handle, 2⅞ inches; length with large blade open, 5 inches. Cheap grade but much better than we have ever seen sold at the price. Price..................

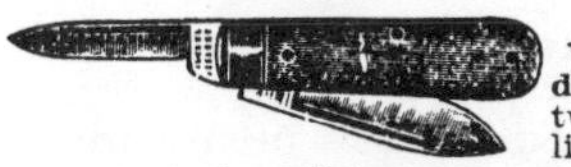

No. 28V1012 White Bone Handle Jack Knife two blades, iron lined. Cheap grade knife, 2¾ inches. Price..........................
If by mail, postage extra, 5 cents.

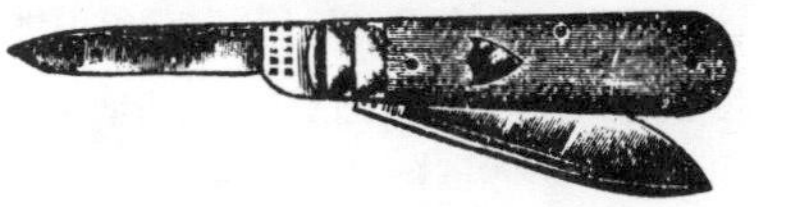

No. 28V1020 White Bone Handle Boys' Knife, with bolster. Two blades, iron lined, 3½ inches. Cheap grade. Price..........................
If by mail, postage extra, 6 cents.

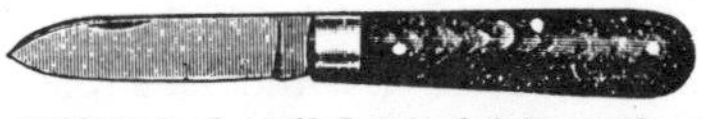

No. 28V1021 A well finished fair grade single blade boys' jack knife. Length of handle, 3⅛ inches; length with large blade open, 5⅝ inches. Rosewood handle, iron lined. Price..............

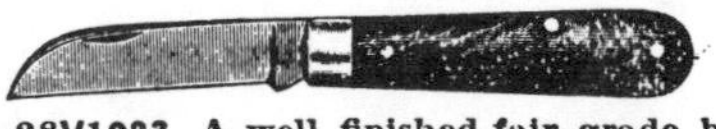

No. 28V1023 A well finished fair grade boys' German jack knife. Same as preceding knife, except it has sheep foot blade. Not warranted.
Price..

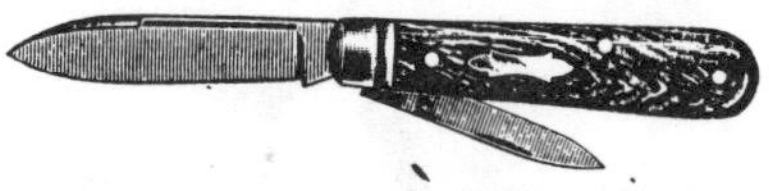

No. 28V1026 A well finished fair grade German jack knife; dogwood handle, two blades. Price..

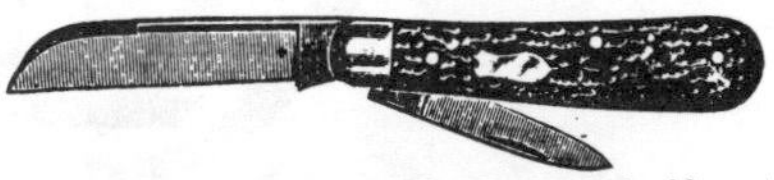

No. 28V1029 A fair grade German knife; stag handle; sheep foot blade. Entire length open, 6¼ inches; length of handle, 3½ inches. Price.....

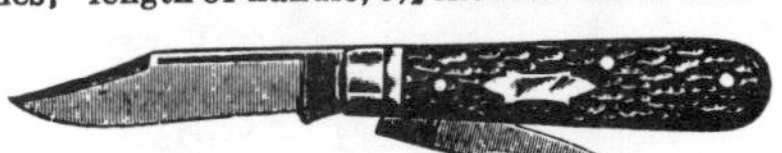

No. 28V1030 Stag clip. A fair grade German knife. Stag handle, clip blade. Entire length open, 6¼ inches; length of handle, 3½ inches. Price..

You'll use
your Remington Camp Knife
a Dozen Times a Day

NO need to tell a camper of the many uses for knives that will do so many things so well.

As you look over their blade equipment—keep in mind that these are *Remington Knives*.

Their handiness has been made *practical* by Remington steel and Remington care in manufacture.

They stand up to their work—in the way people have come to expect of all Remington Pocket Knives.

The Scout Knife is the "Official Knife—Boy Scouts of America"—so designated by the Boy Scout Headquarters. Its quality and workmanship have been approved by the U. S. Government Bureau of Standards.

The Camp Knife is a fit running mate to it.

You should carry one or the other of these Remington Knives with you whether you are out for a day's hike or a whole season's camping.

* * *

There are Remington Pocket-Knives designed to meet the particular needs of every man and woman, boy and girl.

Your dealer can show them to you in every combination of blades and handles. Every one a *real* knife.

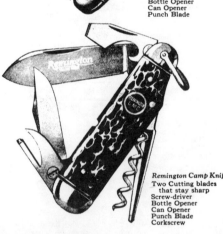

Remington "Official Knife—Boy Scouts of America"
Strong, sharp master blade
Screw-driver
Bottle Opener
Can Opener
Punch Blade

Remington Camp Knife
Two Cutting blades that stay sharp
Screw-driver
Bottle Opener
Can Opener
Punch Blade
Corkscrew

REMINGTON ARMS COMPANY, Inc.
Established 1816
New York City

Remington

THE AUTHORITY IN FIRE ARMS, AMMUNITION AND CUTLERY

Remington Cutlery
America's Highest Quality Workmanship and Finish

R6175
Office *or*
School Knife

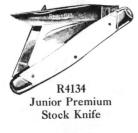

R4134
Junior Premium
Stock Knife

R395
Jack Knife

R3363
Trappers' Knife

R3333
Scout and Camp
Knife

The kind you have always wanted

NEARLY everybody carries a knife—and nearly everybody apologizes for the knife he carries.

"I don't know whether you can find a blade that will cut." You hear it all the time.

Yet America has better steel today than it ever had. Better workmen. Finer and more exact tempering methods.

All it needed was for some one to *apply these resources* to pocket knives—rather than trying to meet some fancied price situation in the trade.

This Company came into the pocket knife business with the purpose of creating a positive standard of pocket knife *quality* and pocket knife *honesty*.

Its responsibility is to the *men* and *women* who are going to *use the knives*.

It brings to the task all the resources of metallurgy; all the equipment—*plus* the initiative, energy and ability that have made Remington one of the outstanding names of American industry.

Here are just a few of the Remington Pocket Knives.

There's a Remington Pocket Knife made to suit your every requirement. So if you don't see here the style you need—ask your hardware dealer for it.

He can get it for you from *Remington*. It will show you what a knife *can* be when made to a positive standard of quality.

Manufactured Exclusively by
REMINGTON ARMS COMPANY, INC.
GENERAL OFFICES: NEW YORK CITY

On Display *at all good* Hardware Stores

R6434
Vest Pocket Knife
(with shackle)

R6244
Pen Knife

R585-M
Jack Knife
(with Punch Blade)

R3053
Premium Stock Knife

R3225-E
Carpenters' Knife

R6823

Carpenters' Knives

SKILLED mechanics of all kinds, for whom sharp knives are a necessity, appreciate the many fine Remingtons made expressly for mechanics' needs. They know they can rely on Remington steel.

Pruning Knives

FOR nurserymen and gardeners—Remington knives with heavy scimitar blades. Their keen, concave edges make clean, shearing cuts on growing things. Useful and practical, too, for cutting oilcloth, linoleum, and rubber.

R698

Buy A Knife You'll be Proud to Own

REMINGTON Pocket Knives are sharp. The blades are made of the finest steel. And Remington's methods of tempering give keen-cutting edges that are durable and uniform from point to heel.

Handles, trim, and linings—every detail of construction—are beautifully fashioned to make each part worthy of the fine steel in the blades.

A Remington knife is built for every purpose a pocket knife may serve. For campers, tourists, fishermen, hunters, trappers, and all outdoor people. Knives for carpenters, plumbers, skilled mechanics, and wood carvers. Pruning knives, and knives for farm and ranch. Knives as fine as the watch on the other end of any chain. Knives to delight men and women, boys and girls. Knives for everyone.

See the various styles at your dealer's and buy a knife you'll be proud to own—a Remington.

Remington Arms Company, Inc.
25 Broadway   Established 1816   New York City

Fishermen's Knives

Disgorger

R1613

HERE'S a fisherman's knife with a disgorger on the handle. An ideal knife for cutting bait, cleaning or scaling fish. In fact, made with the full knowledge of what a fisherman needs. That's the Remington way.

Stockmen's Knives

ALL-ROUND knives with real surgical blades for altering, docking, marking, dewlapping, vaccinating, and all the veterinary work around the farm and ranch. Nickel Silver linings and trim prevent the rust that causes infection.

R4213

Farmers' Knives

THESE solidly built knives have punch blades that will drill holes from ⅟₁₆ to ½ inch in diameter. Fine for repairing harness or belting. Their sturdy, general-utility blades have keen, durable, uniform cutting edges.

R3313

Vest Pocket Knives

A BEAUTIFUL assortment with many combinations of blades and handles—pearl, stag, or gold. Practical knives of graceful design and exquisite workmanship. Gifts that are always welcome.

R7364

Firearms ~ Ammunition ~ Cash Registers

REMINGTON POCKET KNIVES

FULLY WARRANTED

Illustrations Half Size

Green and pearl Pyremite handles; three blades; one large spear blade, crocus polished and etched; one spey blade, glazed finish and one punch blade, blued inside and polished back; nickel silver lined; nickel silver bolsters and shield; length closed 3⅜ inches.

No. R4425E ....

Weight per dozen, 1½ lbs.; one-half dozen in a box.

Stag handle; three blades; one large clip blade, crocus polished and etched; one spey blade, glazed finish; one punch blade, blued inside and polished back; nickel silver lined; nickel silver bolsters and shield; length closed 3⅜ inches.

No. R3413 ....

Weight per dozen, 1½ lbs.; one-half dozen in a box.

Pearl handle; three blades; one large spear blade and one pen blade, both full crocus polished, one nail file; nickel silver lining and tips; length, closed, 3 inches.

No. R6534 ....

Weight per dozen, ⅞ lb.; one-half dozen in a box.

White and blue tinsel Pyremite handles; three blades; one large clip blade, crocus polished and etched; one spey blade, glazed finish; one punch blade, blued inside and polished back; nickel silver lining; nickel silver bolsters and shield; length closed 3⅜ inches.

No. R3415 ....

Weight per dozen, 1½ lbs.; one-half dozen in a box.

Stag handle; three blades; one clip blade, crocus polished and etched; one sheepfoot blade and one pen blade, glazed finish; brass lined; nickel silver bolsters and shield; length closed 3¼ inches.

No. R4653 ....

Weight per dozen, 1¾ lbs.; one-half dozen in a box.

Stag handle; three blades; one clip blade crocus polished and etched; one sheepfoot blade and one pen blade, glazed finish; linings and back made of one piece of nickel silver; nickel silver bolsters and shield; length closed 3⅜ in.

No. R100A ....

Weight per dozen, 1½ lbs.; one-half dozen in a box.

Stag handle; three blades; one clip blade crocus polished and etched; one spey blade; glazed finish and one punch blade blued inside and polished back; linings and back made of one piece of nickel silver; nickel silver bolsters and shield; length closed 3⅜ inches.

No. R100B ....

Weight per dozen, 1½ lbs.; one-half dozen in a box.

Stag handle; three blades; one large clip blade, crocus polished and etched; one punch blade, blued inside and polished back; one spey blade, glazed finish; brass lined; nickel silver bolsters and shield; length closed 3½ in.

No. R3183 ....

Weight per dozen, 2⅝ lbs.; one-half dozen in a box.

Stag handle; three blades; one large clip blade, crocus polished and etched; one sheepfoot blade and one spey blade, glazed finish; brass lined; nickel silver bolsters and shield; length closed 3½ in.

No. R3203 ....

Weight per dozen, 2¼ lbs.; one-half dozen in a box.

Stag handle; three blades; one clip blade, etched; one sheepfoot blade and one spey blade, crocus polished; brass lined; nickel silver bolsters; nickel silver shield; length closed 3⅞ inches.

No. R3553 ....

Weight per dozen, 2½ lbs.; one-half dozen in a box.

REMINGTON POCKET KNIVES
FULLY WARRANTED

Pyremite handles; three blades; one large clip blade; mirror polished and etched; one spey blade, glazed finish; one punch blade, blued inside and polished back; brass lining; nickel silver bolsters and shield; length closed 3⅜ inches.

No. R3415H ....
Weight per dozen, 1½ lbs.; one-half dozen in a box.

Stag handle; three blades; one clip and one spey, both full mirror finished; one punch, blued inside polished back; nickel silver bolsters and shield; brass lined; length closed 3¼ inches.

No. R100B ....
Weight per dozen, 1¾ lbs.; one-half dozen in a box.

Stag handle; three blades; one large clip blade, one spey blade, mirror polished and etched; one punch blade, blued inside and polished back; brass lined; nickel silver bolsters and shield; length closed 3⅜ inches.

No. R3413 ....
Weight per dozen, 1½ lbs.; one-half dozen in a box.

Stag handle; three blades; one large clip and one spey, both mirror finished; one punch blade, blued and polished; brass lined; nickel silver bolsters and shield; length closed, 3¼ inches.

No. R4683 ....
Weight per dozen, 1¾ lbs.; one-half dozen in a box.

Stag handle; three blades; one large clip blade, mirror polished and etched; one punch blade, blued inside and polished back; one spey blade, mirror finish; brass lined; nickel silver bolsters and shield; length closed, 3½ in.

No. R3183 ....
Weight per dozen, 2⅝ lbs.; one-half dozen in a box.

Stag handle; three blades; one large clip blade, one spey blade, mirror polished and etched; one punch blade, blued inside and polished back; brass lined; nickel silver bolsters and shield; length closed 3⅝ inches.

No. R3963 ....
Weight per dozen, 1¾ lbs.; one-half dozen in a box.

Stag handle; 3 blades, one large clip and one spey, mirror finish and one punch blade; blued inside and polished back; brass lined; nickel silver bolsters and shield; length closed, 3⅞ inches.

No. R3063 ....
Weight per dozen, 1½ lbs.; one-half dozen in a box.

Pyremite handle; three blades, one large clip and one spey, mirror finish and one punch blade; blued inside and polished back; brass lined; nickel silver bolsters and shield; length closed 3⅞ inches.

No. R3065 ....
Weight per dozen, 1½ lbs.; one-half dozen in a box.

BOY SCOUT
Official Knife, Boy Scouts of America; Regulation Size

Stag handle; four blades; one large spear blade, mirror polished and etched with Boy Scout insignia; one combination bottle opener and screw-driver, one can opener blade, mirror finish; one punch blade blued inside and polished back; brass lined; nickel silver bolsters, shackle and emblem shield; length closed 3¾ inches.

No. RS3333 ....
Weight per dozen, 2¾ lbs.; one-half dozen in a box.

REMINGTON POCKET KNIVES
FULLY WARRANTED

Stag type handle; two blades; one large clip mirror finish, one small pen mirror finish; brass lined; nickel silver tips and shield; length closed 3¼ inches.

No. RC8 ....
Weight per dozen, 1½ lbs.; one-half dozen in a box.

Pyremite handle; two blades; one large clip mirror finish and etched, one small pen mirror finish; brass lined; nickel silver bolsters and shield, length closed 3⅜ inches.

No. R2605M ....
Weight per dozen, 1½ lbs.; one-half dozen in a box.

Pyremite handle; two blades; one large clip mirror finish and etched; one small pen mirror finish; brass lined; nickel silver bolsters and shield; length closed 3⅜ inches.

No. R2605R ....
Weight per dozen, 1½ lbs.; one-half dozen in a box.

Stag handle; two blades; one large clip mirror finish and etched; one small pen mirror finish; brass lined; nickel silver bolsters and shield; length closed 3⅜ inches.

No. R2603 ....
Weight per dozen, 1½ lbs.; one-half dozen in a box.

Stained bone handle; two blades; one large spear blade, glazed finish; one pen blade, glazed finish; steel lined; polished steel bolster; length closed 3⅜ inches.

No. RB43 ....
Weight per dozen, 2 lbs.; one-half dozen in a box.

Stained bone handle; two blades; one large clip blade and one small pen blade, glazed finish; polished steel lined; polished steel bolster; length closed 3⅜ inches.

No. RB44 ....
Weight per dozen, 1½ lbs.; one-half dozen in a box.

White pyremite handle; two blades; one large clip blade and one pen blade, both mirror polished steel lined; polished steel bolster; length closed 3⅜ inches.

No. RB44W ....
Weight per dozen, 2 lbs.; one-half dozen in a box.

Stag handle; two blades; one large spear and one small pen blade; mirror finished; brass lined; nickel silver cap, bolster and shield; length closed 3⅜ inches.

No. R2203 ....
Weight per dozen, 1¾ lbs.; one-half dozen in a box.

Stag handle; two blades; one large clip and one small pen blade, mirror finished; brass lined; nickel silver cap, bolster and shield; length closed, 3⅜ inches.

No. R2213 ....
Weight per dozen, 1¾ lbs. · one-half dozen in a box.

Pyremite handle; two blades, one large clip and one small pen blade; mirror finished; brass lined; nickel silver cap, bolster and shield; length closed 3⅜ inches.

No. R2215M ....
Weight per dozen, 1¾ lbs.; one-half dozen in a box.

MAIZE

Brass lining; polished steel bolster; full mirror finished.

No. R2043—Stag; lgth 3⅛ ins__

Brass lining; polished steel bolster; full mirror finished.

No. R2053—Stag; lgth 3⅛ ins___

Brass lining; polished steel bolster; full mirror finished.

No. R2073—Stag; lgth 3⅛ ins___

Brass lining; polished steel bolster; full mirror finished.

No. R2045—Pyremite; lgth 3⅛ ins_____

Brass lining; polished steel bolster; full mirror finished.

No. R2055 — Pyremite; lgth 3⅛ ins_____

Brass lining; polished steel bolster; full mirror finished.

No. R2075 — Pyremite; lgth 3⅛ ins_____

Nickel silver lining, bolster, cap and shield; full polished; length 3 inches.

No. R1323—Stag_____

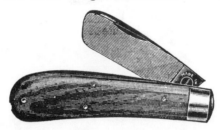

Polished steel lining and bolster; blue glazed blade. Length 4⅛ inches.

No. R921—Rosewood handle___

Brass lining; steel bolster; full polished. Length 3⅜ inches.

No. R33—Stag_____

Polished steel lining and bolster; glazed; length 3⅜ inches.

No. RB43—Brown bone_____

Polished steel lining and bolster; glazed; length 3⅜ inches.

No. RB44—Brown bone_____
No. RB44W—White pyralin___

Polished steel lining and bolster; glazed blades. Length 3⅜ inches.

No. RB45—Brown bone_____

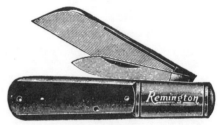

Polished steel lining and bolster; glazed blades. Length 3⅜ inches.

No. RB46—Brown bone_____

Polished steel lining and bolster; glazed.

No. RB040—Brown bone; lgth 3⅜ ins_____

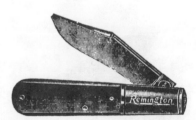

Polished steel lining and bolster; glazed.

No. RB041—Brown bone; lgth 3⅜ ins_____

One-half dozen in glassene wrapped box; two dozen in carton.

POCKET KNIVES, *Remington.*

One piece nickel silver lining, back and bolsters; full polished. Stag handle; length 3⅜ inches.

No. R-100A—Small pen blade ⎫
No. R-100B—Punch blade ⎬
instead of pen blade‑‑‑‑‑‑ ⎭

Brass lining; nickel silver bolsters and shield; full polished.

No. R3123—Stag; lgth 3⅞ ins‑‑‑

Brass lining; nickel silver bolsters and shield; full polished.

No. R3113—Stag; lgth 3⅞ ins‑‑‑

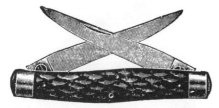

Brass lining; nickel silver bolsters; full polished. Length 3⅞ inches.

No. R4593—Stag‑‑‑‑‑‑‑‑‑‑

Brass lining and rivets; polished steel bolster and cap; glazed. Length 5 inches.

No. R953—Stag‑‑‑‑‑‑‑‑‑ ⎫
No. R955—Pyremite‑‑‑‑‑‑‑ ⎬

Nickel silver lining, bolsters and shield; full polished.

No. R4103—Stag; lgth 3⅜ ins‑‑‑

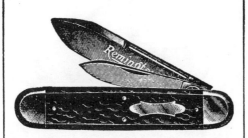

Brass lining; nickel silver bolster, cap and shield; full polished. Length 4¼ inches.

No. R1225W—White pyremite‑

Brass lining; nickel silver bolsters and shield; full polished. Length 4½ inches.

No. R7833—Stag‑‑‑‑‑‑‑‑‑‑

Brass lining; nickel silver bolsters and shield; full polished. Length 3¾ inches.

No. R333—Stag‑‑‑‑‑‑‑‑‑‑

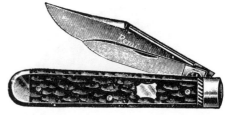

Brass lining; nickel silver bolster, cap and shield; full polished.

No. R1343—Stag; lgth 4¼ ins‑‑‑

Nickel silver lining, bolsters and shield; full polished.

No. R1853—Stag; lgth 3⅜ ins‑‑

Nickel silver lining, bolsters and shield; full polished.
No. R1863—Stag; lgth 3⅜ ins‑‑‑

Nickel silver lining, bolsters and shield; full polished. Length 3¼ inches.

No. R555—Pyralin‑‑‑‑‑‑‑‑‑

Half doz in glassene wrapped box; two doz in carton.

Brass lining; nickel silver bolsters and shield; full polished.   Length 3½ inches.

No. R153—Stag _ _ _ _ _ _ _ _ _ _ _ _ _ _

Brass lining; nickel silver bolster, cap and shield; full polished; length 3⅜ inches.

No. R1065W—White pyremite _

Nickel silver lining, bolsters and shield; full polished; length 3⅝ inches.

No. R1823—Stag _ _ _ _ _ _ _ _ _ _ _ _ _

Brass lining, bolsters and shield; full polished.

No. R1873—Stag; lgth 3⅝ ins _ _

＋

You'll Get The Goods

Brass lining; nickel silver bolster, cap and shield; full polished.   Length 3⅜ inches.

No. R1113—Stag _ _ _ _ _ _ _ _ _ _ _ _

Brass lining; nickel silver bolster, cap and shield; full polished; length 3⅜ inches.

No. R1073—Stag _ _ _ _ _ _ _ _ _ _ }
No. R1075—Pyremite _ _ _ _ _ }

Brass lining; nickel silver bolsters and shield;   full polished.

No. R623—Stag; lgth 3⅞ ins _ _

Nickel silver lining, bolsters and shield; full polished; length 3⅜ inches.

No. R603—Stag _ _ _ _ _ _ _ _ _ _ _ _ _
No. R605—Pyralin _ _ _ _ _ _ _ _ _ _ _

Nickel silver lining, bolsters and shield; full polished.   Length 3⅜ inches.

No. R3533—Stag _ _ _ _ _ _ _ _ _ _ _ _ _

Brass lining; nickel silver cap and bolster.   Full mirror finished blades.

No. R2103—Stag; length 3⅛ ins

Brass lining; nickel silver cap and bolster.   Full mirror finished blades.

No. R2105—Pyremite handle; length 3⅛ ins _ _ _ _ _ _ _ _ _ _ _ _ _ _

Brass lining; nickel silver bolsters and shield; full polished.   Length 3⅜ inches.

No. R2215—Pyremite _ _ _ _ _ _ _ _ _

Brass lining; nickel silver bolsters and shield; full polished.   Length 3⅜ inches.

No. R2213—Stag _ _ _ _ _ _ _ _ _ _ _ _ _

Brass lining; nickel silver bolsters and shield; full polished.   Length 3⅜ inches.

No. R2205—Pyremite _ _ _ _ _ _ _ _ _

Half doz in glassene wrapped box; two doz in carton.

VAN CAMP POCKET KNIVES
FULLY WARRANTED

Stag handle; three blades, large spear, pen and nail; large blade polished one side and etched; brass lining; nickel silver bolsters and shield; length closed 3 ¼ inches.

No. 3358 ....
Weight per dozen, 2½ lbs.; one-half dozen in a box.

Stag handle, three blades, large sheepfoot and spear, small pen; spear blade polished one side and etched; brass lining; nickel silver bolsters and shield; length closed 3⅝ inches.

No. 3553 ....
Weight per dozen, 2½ lbs.; one-half dozen in a box.

Stag handle; three blades, clip, spey and punch; clip blade polished one side and etched; brass lined; nickel silver bolsters and shield; length closed 3½ inches.

No. 3568 ....
Weight per dozen, 2½ lbs.; one-half dozen in a box.

Imitation horn celluloid handle; three blades, spear, and two pens; large blade full crocus finish one side and etched; brass lined, nickel silver tips and shield; length closed 3⅜ inches.

No. 31635M ....
Weight per dozen, 1 lb.; one-half dozen in a box.

Stag handle; four blades, large spear, screw driver and crown seal lifter, can opener and punch blades with ring for fastening to chain; spear blade full crocus finish one side and etched; brass lined; nickel silver bolsters; length closed, 3⅜ inches.

No. 4508 ....
Weight per dozen, 2¼ lbs.; one-half dozen in a box.

REMINGTON POCKET KNIVES
FULLY WARRANTED

Stained bone handle; one large clip blade; glazed finish; steel lined; polished steel bolster; length closed 3⅝ inches.

No. RC091 ....
Weight per dozen, 1½ lbs.; one dozen in a display box.

With Fish Hook Disgorger
Stag type handle; one large clip blade, glazed finish; steel lined; polished steel bolster; length closed 5 inches.

No. RC953 ....
Weight per dozen, 2½ lbs.; one-half dozen in a box.

With Fish Hook Disgorger
Pyremite handle; one large clip blade, glazed finish; steel lined; polished steel bolsters; length closed 5 inches.

No. RC955L ....
Weight per dozen, 2½ lbs.; one-half dozen in a box.

Lock Back
Stag handle; one blade for sticking and skinning; full mirror finish; nickel silver bolsters, shield, rivets and lining; hollow rivet in butt for thong; length closed 4½ inches.

No. R1303 ....
Weight per dozen, 4½ lbs.; one-half dozen in a box.

Stag type handle; two blades; one large clip point mirror finish, one small pen mirror finish; rustless lining; nickel silver shield; length closed 3¼ inches.

No. RC6 ....
Weight per dozen, 1¼ lbs.; one dozen in a display box.

REMINGTON POCKET KNIVES
FULLY WARRANTED
Illustrations Half Size

Gold pearl Pyremite handles; three blades; one clip blade, etched; one sheepfoot blade and one spey blade; glazed finish; brass lined; polished steel bolsters; nickel silver shield; length closed 3⅞ inches.

No. R3555W ....
Weight per dozen, 2½ lbs.; one-half dozen in a box.

Stag handle; three blades; one large clip blade, etched and one spey blade, glazed finished; one punch blade, blued and polished; brass lined; polished steel bolsters; nickel silver shield; length closed 3⅞ inches.

No. R3563 ....
Weight per dozen, 2½ lbs.; one-half dozen in a box.

White pyremite handle; three blades; one large clip, blue glazed finish and etched; one spey blade glazed finish; one punch blade, blued and polished; brass lined; steel bolsters; nickel silver shield; length closed, 3⅞ inches .

No. R3565W ....
Weight per dozen, 2½ lbs.; one-half dozen in a box.

Stag handle; three blades; one large clip blade, crocus polished and etched; one spey and one pen blade, glazed finish; brass lined; nickel silver bolsters and shield; length closed 3⅞ inches.

No. R3873 ....
Weight per dozen, 2½ lbs.; one-half dozen in a box.

Red Pyremite handle; three blades; one slender Turkish clip blade, crocus polished and etched; one spey blade and one pen blade, glazed finish; nickel silver lined; nickel silver bolsters and shield; length closed 3⅜ inches.

No. R4135R ....
Weight per dozen, 1¼ lbs.; one-half dozen in a box.

Stag handle; three blades; one large clip blade, crocus polished and etched; one spey blade, blue glazed; one punch blade, blued inside and polished back; brass lined; nickel silver bolsters and shield; length closed 3⅝ inches.

No. R3963 ....
Weight per dozen, 1¾ lbs.; one-half dozen in a box.

Stag handle; three blades; one large clip blade, crocus polished and etched; one spey blade and one pen blade, glazed finish; brass lined; nickel silver bolsters and shield; length closed 3⅝ inches.

No. R3973 ....
Weight per dozen, 1¾ lbs.; one-half dozen in a box.

Stag handle; three blades; one large clip blade, crocus polished and etched; one sheepfoot blade, one spey blade, glazed finish; brass lined nickel silver bolsters and shield; length closed 3⅝ in.

No. R3993 ....
Weight per dozen, 1¼ lbs.; one-half dozen in a box.

Stag handle; two blades; one large clip blade crocus polished and etched; one punch blued inside with polished back; brass lined; nickel silver cap and bolster; length closed 3½ inches.

No. R1763 ....
Weight per dozen, 2¼ lbs.; one-half dozen in a box.

REMINGTON POCKET KNIVES

FULLY WARRANTED

Illustrations Half Size

Stag handle; two blades; one large spear blade, crocus polished and etched; one pen blade, glazed finish; brass lined; nickel silver bolsters and shield; length closed, 3 ⅛ inches.

No. R6623 . . . .
Weight per dozen, 1 lb.; one-half dozen in a box.

Stag handle; two blades; one large spear blade, crocus polished and etched; file blade glazed finish; brass lined; nickel silver bolsters; length closed 3 inches.

No. R6473 . . . .
Weight per dozen, ¾ lb.; one-half dozen in a box.

White Pyremite handle; two blades; one large spear blade, crocus polished; one erasing blade, glazed finish; brass lined; length closed 3 ⅜ inches.

No. R6785W . . . .
Weight per dozen, 1 lb.; one-half dozen in a box.

White Pyremite handle; spear bladle, crocus polished; eraser blade, glazed finish; brass lined; length closed 3 ¾ inches.

No. R6175W . . . .
Weight per dozen, 1 ¼ lbs.; one-half dozen in a box.

Black handle; two blades; one large spear blade, crocus polished and etched; one pen blade, glazed finish; nickel silver lined; nickel silver bolsters and shield; length closed, 3 ¼ in.

No. R3442 . . . .
Weight per dozen, 1 ½ lbs.; one-half dozen in a box.

Stag handle; two lance blades; glazed finish; polished steel lined; polished steel bolsters; length closed, 3 ⅞ inches.

No. R4593 . . . .
Weight per dozen, 2 lbs.; one-half dozen in a box.

Stag handle; two blades; one large spear blade, crocus polished and etched; one pen blade, glazed finish; brass lined; nickel silver bolsters and shield; length closed 3 inches.

No. R7223 . . . .
Weight per dozen, 1 ¼ lbs.; one-half dozen in a box.

Pearl handle; two blades; one large spear blade, crocus polished and etched; one pen blade, glazed finish; nickel silver lined; nickel silver bolsters; length closed 3 ¼ inches.

No. R6194 . . . .
Weight per dozen, ¾ lb.; one-half dozen in a box.

Shell Pyremite handle; two blades; one large clip blade, crocus polished and etched; one pen blade, glazed finish; nickel silver lined; nickel silver bolster and shield; length closed, 3 ⅜ in.

No. R3535S . . . .
Weight per dozen, 1 ⅛ lbs.; one-half dozen in a box.

Stag handle; three blades, one large spear blade, crocus polished and etched; two pen blades, glazed finish; nickel silver lined; nickel silver bolsters and shield; length closed 3 ⅜ inches.

No. R8023 . . . .
Weight per dozen, 1 ½ lbs.; one-half dozen in a box.

Stag handle; three blades; one clip blade, crocus polished and etched; one spey blade, glazed finish; one punch blade, blued and polished outside; brass lined; nickel silver shield and bolsters; length closed 3 ¼ inches.

No. R4683 . . . .
Weight per dozen, 1 ¾ lbs.; one-half dozen in a box.

REMINGTON POCKET KNIVES

FULLY WARRANTED

Illustrations Half Size

Gold pearl Pyremite handle; two blades; one large clip crocus polished and etched, one pen glazed finish; nickel silver lined; nickel silver bolsters and shield; length closed 3⅝ inches.

No. R605G . . . .
Weight per dozen, 1½ lbs.; one-half dozen in a box.

Candy stripe Pyremite handle; two blades, one large spear blade, etched; one pen blade, glazed finish; nickel silver lining; nickel silver cap, bolster and shield; length closed, 3¼ inches.

No. R555L . . . .
Weight per dozen, 1¾ lbs.; one-half dozen in a box.

Stag handle; two blades; one large clip blade, crocus polished and etched; one small pen blade, glazed finish; nickel silver lined; nickel silver bolsters and shield; length closed 3¼ inches.

No. R573 . . . .
Weight per dozen, 1¾ lbs.; one-half dozen in a box.

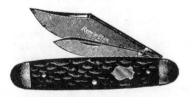

Stag handle; two blades; one large clip blade, crocus polished and etched; one pen blade glazed finish; nickel silver lined; nickel silver cap and bolster; length closed 3⅝ in.

No. R1853 . . . .
Weight per dozen, 1½ lbs.; one-half dozen in a box.

Abalone Pyremite handle; two blades; one large spear blade, crocus polished and etched; one small pen blade, glazed finish; nickel silver lined; nickeled silver cap, bolster and shield; length closed 3¼ inches.

No. R995N . . . .
Weight per dozen, 1½ lbs.; one-half dozen in a box.

Smoked pearl Pyremite handle; two blades; one large spear blade crocus polished and etched; one pen blade, glazed finish; nickel silver lined; nickel silver cap, bolster and shield; length closed 3⅛ inches.

No. R875D . . . .
Weight per dozen, 1 lb.; one-half dozen in a box.

Stag handle; two blades; one large sheep foot blade crocus polished and etched; one screw driver and wire scraper blade, glazed finish; brass lined; nickle silver cap, bolster and shield; length closen 3¾ inches.

No. R1973 . . . .
Weight per dozen 2 lbs.; one-half dozen in a box.

Stag handle; two blades; one large spear blade, crocus polished and etched; one small pen blade, glazed finish; brass lined; nickel silver cap and bolster; length closed 2⅞ inches.

No. R1643 . . . .
Weight per dozen, 1 lb.; one-half dozen in a box.

Stag handle; two blades; one large double sabre clip blade crocus polished and one pen blade, glazed finish; brass lined; nickel silver cap and bolster; length closed 2⅞ in.

No. R1653 . . . .
Weight per dozen, 1 lb.; one-half dozen in a box.

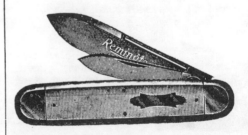

White pyremite handle; two blades; one large spear blade, crocus polished and etched; one pen blade, glazed finish; brass lined; nickel silver cap, bolster and shield; length closed 4¼ in.

No. R1225W . . . .
Weight per dozen, 2½ lbs.; one-half dozen in a box.

REMINGTON POCKET KNIVES

FULLY WARRANTED

Illustrations Half Size

Stag handle; two blades; one sabre clip blade, crocus polished and etched, one pen glazed finish; brass lined; nickel silver cap, bolster and shield; length closed 2 ⅞ inches.

No. R983 . . . .
Weight per dozen, 1 lb.; one-half dozen in a box.

Pyremite handle; two blades; one large sabre Turkish clip blade, crocus polished and etched; one pen blade, glazed finish; brass lined, nickel silver cap, bolster and shield; length closed, 2 ⅞ in.

No. R985 . . . .
Weight per dozen, 1 lb.; one-half dozen in a box.

Pearl handle; two blades; one large spear blade, crocus polished and etched; one small pen blade, glazed finish; brass lined; nickel silver bolsters; length closed 3 inches.

No. R6464 . . . .
Weight per dozen, ¾ lb.; one-half dozen in a box.

Stag handle; three blades; clip blade, crocus polished and etched; one spey blade and one pen blade, glazed finish; milled brass lined; nickel silver bolsters and shield; length closed 3 ¾ in.

No. R3253 . . . .
Weight per dozen, 2 ½ lbs.; one-half dozen in a box.

Stag handle; four blades; one large spear blade, crocus polished and etched; two pen blades, glazed finish; one file blade; brass lined; nickel silver bolsters and shield; length closed 3 inches.

No. R6703 . . . .
Weight per dozen, 1 lb.; one-half dozen in a box.

Black handle; four blades; one Congress blade, crocus polished; one sheepfoot and two pen blades, glazed finish; brass lined; nickel silver bosters; length closed 3 ½ inches.

No. R6032 . . . .
Weight per dozen, 1 ⅝ lbs.; one-half dozen in a box.

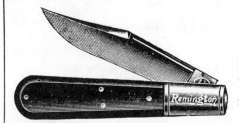

Brown bone handle; one large clip blade, glazed; polished steel bolsters and lining; length closed 5 inches.

No. RB1240 . . . .
Weight per dozen, 3 lbs.; one-half dozen in a box.

BOY SCOUT

Official Knife, Boy Scouts of America; Regulation Size

Stag handle; four blades; one large spear blade, crocus polished and etched with Boy Scout insignia; one combination bottle opener and screw-driver, one can opener blade, glazed finish; one punch blade blued inside and polished back; brass lined; nickel silver bolsters, shackle and emblem shield; length closed 3 ¾ inches.

No. RS3333 . . . .
Weight per dozen, 2 ¾ lbs.; one-half dozen in a box.

Official Knife, Boy Scouts of America; Junior Size

Stag handle; four blades; one large spear blade, crocus polished and etched with Scout insignia; one combination bottle opener and screw-driver blade, and one can opener blade, glazed finish; one punch blade, blued inside and polished back; nickel silver lined; nickel silver bolsters, shackle and emblem shield; length closed 3 ⅜ inches.

No. RS4233 . . . .
Weight per dozen, 2 lbs.; one-half dozen in a box.

POCKET KNIVES, *Remington*

Only one grade of steel is used in making Remington Pocket Knives—the same steel, the same hardening and tempering process is used in all of them.

Remington pocket knives are hand honed just before being cleaned, wrapped and packed. They come to you with a strong, keen edge, ready for use, and this edge lasts.

The accuracy of precision methods enter into the solid construction and fitting of Remington pocket knives—springs of strength and resiliency insure smooth positive action blades.

Handle covers are a wide variety of redwood, black, English cocobolo, American bone stag, genuine English stag, specially selected pearl, gold, nickel silver, Buffalo horn and Pyremite, a durable material produced in many strikingly beautiful colors.

The blade and handle finish is superior in every detail as befits a product of quality—the quality which merits respect and makes friends.

Brass lining; nickel silver bolsters and shield; full polished. Length 3⅞ inches.

No. R-3553—Stag_____
No. R-3555W—White pyralin__

Brass lining; nickel silver bolsters and shield; full polished. Length 3⅞ inches.

No. R3563—Stag _____

Brass lining; nickel silver bolsters and shield; full polished. Length 3⅞ inches.

No. R3555G—Gold mottled pyralin_____

Brass lining; nickel silver bolsters and shield; full polished. Length 3⅞ inches.

No. R3565W—White pyralin____

Nickel silver lining, bolsters and shield; full polished. Length 3⅝ inches.

No. R3973—Stag_____

Nickel silver lining, bolsters and shield; full polished. Length 3⅝ inches.

No. R3975—Pyralin_____

Nickel silver lining, bolsters and shield; full polished. Length 3⅝ inches.

No. R3993—Stag_____

Nickel silver lining, bolsters and shield; half polished. Length 3⅝ inches.

No. R3965—Pyralin_____

Nickel silver lining and trim; mirror finished blades. Length 3⅝ inches.

No. R3963—Stag_____

Nickel silver lining, bolsters and shield; milled center scale; half polished.

No. R4405—Pyremite; lgth 3⅜ ins

Nickel silver lining, bolsters and shield; full polished.

No. R3485—Pyralin; lgth 3⅜ ins

Nickel silver lining, bolsters and shield; full polished. Length 3⅜ inches.

No. R4133—Stag _____
No. R4135—Pyremite _____

Nickel silver lining, bolsters and shield; full polished.
No. R3493—Stag; lgth 3⅜ ins ___

Nickel silver lining, bolsters and shield; full polished. Length 3⅝ inches.

No. R4005—Pyralin_____

One-half doz in glassene wrapped box; two dozen in carton.

POCKET KNIVES, *Remington*

Nickel silver lining, tips and shield; full polished.

No. R6483—Stag; lgth 3 ins

Nickel silver lining and tips; full polished.

No. R6843—Stag; lgth 2¾ ins

Nickel silver lining, tips and shield; full polished.

No. R6643—Stag; lgth 3⅛ ins

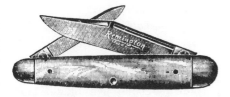

Nickel silver lining and bolsters; full polished.   Length 3⅛ inches.

No. R7425C—Pyralin

Nickel silver lining, bolsters and shield; full polished.   Length 3⅛ inches.

No. R6623—Stag

Steel lining and bolsters; full polished. Length 3⅛ inches.

No. R7773—Stag

Nickel silver lining, bolsters and shield; full polished.
No. R7423—Stag; lgth 3⅛ ins

Nickel silver lining and trim; mirror finished blades.   Length 3 inches.

No. R7233—Stag

Nickel silver lining, tips and shield; full polished.
No. R6653—Stag; lgth 3⅛ ins

Nickel silver lining and trim; mirror finished blades.   Length 3⅛ inches.

No. R6723—Stag

Nickel silver lining and trim; mirror finished blades.   Length 2½ inches.

No. R6904—Genuine pearl

Nickel silver lining and trim; mirror finished blades.   Length 3⅛ inches.

No. R7633—Stag

Steel lining and bolsters; full polished.

No. R7854—Pearl; lgth 3 ins

Steel lining and bolster; blue glazed blades.   Length 3 inches.

No. R1623—Stag

Steel lining and bolster; blue glazed blades.   Length 3 inches.

No. R1573—Stag

Steel lining and bolster; blue glazed blades.   Length 3 inches.

No. R1622—Black pyralin

Steel lining and bolster; blue glazed. Length 3 inches.

No. R1582—Black pyralin

Steel lining and bolster; blue glazed. Length 3 inches.

No. R1882—Black pyralin

One-half dozen in glassene wrapped box; two dozen in carton.

REMINGTON POCKET KNIVES

FULLY WARRANTED

Illustrations Half Size

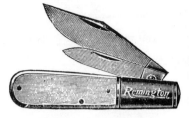

White pyremite handle; two blades; one large clip blade and one pen blade, both blue glazed; polished steel lined; polished steel bolster; length closed 3⅜ inches.

No. RB44W ....
Weight per dozen, 2 lbs.; one-half dozen in a box.

Stag handle; two blades; one large spear blade, crocus polished and etched; one small pen blade, glazed finish; nickel silver lined; nickel silver tips and shield; length closed 3⅛ inches.

No. R6643 ....
Weight per dozen, 1 lb.; one-half dozen in a box.

Pyremite handle; two blades; one large clip blade, crocus polished and etched; one pen blade, blue glazed; nickel silver lined; nickel silver cap, bolster and shield; length closed 3⅝ inches.

No. R1825W ....
Weight per dozen, 1½ lbs.; one-half dozen in a box.

Pearl handle; two blades; one spear blade, crocus polished and etched; one pen blade, blue glazed; nickel silver lined; nickel silver bolsters; lining and bolsters in one piece; length closed 3 inches.

No. R7854 ....
Weight per dozen, ¾ lbs.; one-half dozen in a box.

Pyremite handle; two blades; one large clip blade, crocus polished; one pen blade, blue glazed; brass lined; polished steel cap, bolster and shield; length closed 3⅜ inches.

No. R1075T ....
Weight per dozen, 1⅞ lbs.; one-half dozen in a box.

Pearl handle; two blades; one large spear blade, crocus polished; one pen blade, blue glazed; nickel silver lining, tips and shackle; length closed 2½ inches.

No. R6904 ....
Weight per dozen, ⅞ lb.; one-half dozen in a box.

Pyremite handle; two blades; one master spear blade and one pen blade, both blue glazed; nickel silver lined; nickel silver cap, bolster and shield; cap, bolster and lining in one piece; length closed 3 inches.

No. R1595P ....
Weight per dozen, 1¾ lbs.; one-half dozen in a box.

Smoked pearl Pyremite handle; two blades; one large spear blade, crocus polished and etched; one pen blade, glazed finish; nickel silver lined; nickel silver tips and shield; length closed 3⅛ inches.

No. R6645D ....
Weight per dozen, ¾ lb.; one-half dozen in a box.

White Pyremite handle; two blades; one large spear blade, crocus polished and etched; one pen blade, glazed finish; nickle silver lined; nickle silver bolsters; length closed, 3⅜ inches.

No. R8015W ....
Weight per dozen, 1⅛ lbs.; one-half dozen in a box.

VAN CAMP POCKET KNIVES

FULLY WARRANTED

Illustrations Half Size

Black enameled embossed iron handle; one spey blade, full crocus finish one side and etched; length closed, 3⅜ inches.

No. 102E–Black handle..............

Weight per doz., 1½ lbs.; half dozen in a box.

With Chain

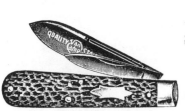

Stag handle; two blades, spear and pen; large blade full crocus finish one side and etched; brass lined; steel bolster; nickel silver shield; 15 inch steel chain with loop on end; length closed, 3½ inches.

No. 272CH–Stag handle..............

Weight per doz., 2 lbs.; half dozen in a box.

Easy Opener

Imitation horn celluloid handle; two blades, spear and pen; large blade full crocus finish one side and etched; brass lined; nickel silver bolster and cap; length closed, 3⅜ inches.

No. 23R–Cocobolo handle ....

Weight per doz., 2¼ lbs.; half dozen in a box.

Ebony handle; three blades, one large spear and two small pens; large blade full crocus finish one side and etched; brass lined; nickel silver bolsters; length closed, 3⅜ inches.

No. 0354E–Ebony handle ....

Weight per dozen, 1½ lbs.; half dozen in a box.

Imitation horn celluloid handle; three blades, large spear, spey and punch blades; spear blade full crocus finish one side and etched; brass lined; nickel silver bolsters; length closed, 3⅞ inches.

No.
7338CH–Imitation horn celluloid handle.......

Weight per dozen, 2 lbs.; half dozen in a box.

With Clip, Sheep's Foot and Spey Blades

Celluloid horn handle; three blades, clip, sheep's foot and spey; clip blade full crocus finish one side and etched; brass lined; nickel silver bolsters; length closed, 3¼ in.

No. 334CH–Celluloid horn handle ....

Weight per doz. 1½ lbs.; half dozen in a box.

Imitation horn celluloid handle; three blades, large clip, spey and punch; clip blade full crocus polished one side and etched; brass lined; nickel silver bolsters; length closed, 3½ inches.

No. 7842CH–Imit. horn celluloid handle..

Weight per doz. 1¾ lbs.; half dozen in a box.

Stag handle; four blades, large spear, screw driver and crown seal lifter, can opener and punch blades with ring for fastening to chain; spear blade full crocus finish one side and etched; brass lined; nickel silver bolsters; length closed, 3⅜ inches.

No. 4100–Stag handle ....

Weight per doz. 2¼ lbs.; half dozen in a box.

Imitation horn celluloid handle; two blades, large sabre clip and spear; clip blade full crocus finish one side and etched; brass lined; iron cap and bolster; length closed, 5 inches.

No. 229½ CH–Imit. horn celluloid handle.

Weight per doz. 3 lbs.; half dozen in a box.

REMINGTON POCKET KNIVES
FULLY WARRANTED
Illustrations Half Size

Stag handle; long clip blade, glazed finish and etched; b r a s s lined; polished steel cap and bolster; length closed 5 inches.

No. R953 ....
Weight per dozen, 2½ lbs.; one-half dozen in a box.

Stag handle; two blades; one large clip blade and one small pen blade, glazed finish; polished steel lined; polished steel bolster; length closed 3⅜ in.

No. R33 ....
Weight per dozen, 1⅝ lbs.; one-half dozen in a box.

Stag handle; one large pruning blade, glazed and etched; polished steel bolster and lining; hole in butt end of handle for l e a t h e r thong; length closed 3⅝ inches.

No. R693 ....
Weight per dozen, 2½ lbs.; one-half dozen in a box.

Stag handle; two blades; one large spear blade and one small pen blade, glazed finish; polished steel lined; polished steel bolster; length closed 3⅜ in.

No. R23 ....
Weight per dozen, 1½ lbs.; one-half dozen in a box.

Stag handle; easy opener; two blades; one large spear blade, etched; one pen blade; glazed finish; steel lined; steel bolster; length closed, 3⅜ in.

No. R1673 ....
Weight per dozen, 1½ lbs.; one-half dozen in a box.

Black handle; t w o blades; one large clip blade, crocus polished; one small pen blade, glazed finish; brass lined; polished steel bolster; nickel s i l v e r shield; length closed 3⅜ inches.

No. R1072 ....
Weight per dozen, 1⅝ lbs.; one-half dozen in a box.

Brown bone handle; two blades; one large spear blade, glazed finish; one pen blade, glazed finish; steel lined; polished steel bolster; length closed 3⅜ inches.

No. RB43 ....
Weight per dozen, 2 lbs.; one-half dozen in a box.

Stag handle; two blades; one large clip blade, crocus polished; one small pen blade, glazed finish; brass lined; polished steel bolster; n i c k e l silver shield; length closed 3⅜ inches.

No. R1073 ....
Weight per dozen, 1⅝ lbs.; one-half dozen in a box.

Brown bone handle; two blades; one large clip blade and one small pen blade, glazed finish; polished steel lined; polished steel bolster; length closed 3⅜ inches.

No. RB44 ....
Weight per dozen, 1½ lbs.; one-half dozen in a box.

Stag handle; two blades; one large spear blade, crocus polished; one pen blade, glazed finish; brass lined; polished steel bolster; nickel silver shield; length closed, 3⅜ in.

No. R1063 ....
Weight per dozen, 1⅝ lbs.; one-half dozen in a box.

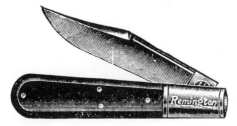

Steel lining and bolster. Length 5 inches.

No. RB1240—Brown bone....

Scout.

Nickel silver lining, bolsters and emblem shield. Snap-on nickel plated shackle.

Large spear full polished and etched with scout insignia; combination bottle opener and screw-driver, can opener, blue glazed finish.

No. RS-4783—Stag; length 3½ ins..................

Scout.

Brass lining, nickel silver bolsters, official emblem shield and belt ring.

Large spear blade, full polished; leather punch, tack puller, bottle opener, can opener and screw driver.

No. RS3333—Stag; lgth 3¾ ins.

Brass lining; nickel silver bolsters and shield; full polished.

No. R6043—Stag; lgth 4³⁄₁₆ ins.

Brass lining; nickel silver bolsters and shield; full polished.

No. R6073—Stag; lgth 3¾ ins.

Nickel silver lining and bolsters; full polished.

No. R6693—Stag; lgth 3 ins....

Brass lining; polished steel rat tail bolsters; full polished.

No. R6163—Stag; lgth 3⅞ ins...

Brass lining; polished steel rat tail bolsters and shield; full polished. Length 3¾ inches.

No. R6093—Stag...........

Brass lining; polished steel rat tail bolsters; full polished.

No. R6143—Stag; lgth 3½ ins.

Brass lining and bolsters; full polished. Length 3 inches.

No. R6103—Stag..........

Nickel silver lining, bolsters and shield; full polished; length 3⅜ inches.

No. R3535—Pyralin..........

Brass lining; full polished; pyralin handle.

No. R6785—Length 3⅜ ins...
No. R6175—Length 3¾ ins...

Polished steel lining and bolsters; full polished.

No. R7853—Stag; lgth 3 ins..

Nickel silver handle; two blades. 1 spear, etched, 1 pen, mirror finished.

No. R6499—Length 3 ins....

Nickel silver lining and bolsters; full polished. Length 3 inches.

No. R6463—Stag............

Nickel silver lining, tips and shield; half polished.

No. R8003—Stag; lgth 3 ins..

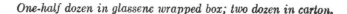

One-half dozen in glassene wrapped box; two dozen in carton.

REMINGTON POCKET KNIVES

FULLY WARRANTED

Illustrations Half Size

White Pyremite handle; two blades, one large spear blade, crocus polished and one small pen blade, glazed finish; brass lined; polished steel cap and bolster; length closed 3 ⅜ inches.

No. R1065W ....
Weight per dozen, 1 ⅞ lbs.; one-half dozen in a box.

Stag handle; two blades; one large spear blade, crocus polished and etched; one pen blade, glazed finish; brass lined; nickel silver cap, bolster and shield; length closed, 3 ½ inches.

No. R1753 ....
Weight per dozen, 2 ¼ lbs.; one-half dozen in a box.

Stag handle; two blades; one large clip blade, crocus polished and etched; one pen blade, glazed finish; brass lined; nickel silver cap, bolster and shield; length closed, 3 ½ inches.

No. R1783 ....
Weight per dozen, 2 ⅛ lbs.; one-half dozen in a box.

Stag handle; two blades; one large spear blade, crocus polished and etched; one small pen blade, glazed finish; nickel silver lining; nickel silver bolsters and shield; length closed 3 in.

No. R1283 ....
Weight per dozen, 1 ¼ lbs.; one-half dozen in a box.

Stag handle; two blades; one large clip blade, crocus polished and etched; one small pen blade, glazed finish; brass lining; nickle silver bolster, cap and shield; length closed 3 ½ inches.

No. R153 ....
Weight per dozen, 2 ⅛ lbs.; one-half dozen in a box.

Stag handle; two blades; one large clip blade, crocus polished and etched; one small pen blade, glazed finish; nickel silver lined; nickel silver cap, bolster and shield; length closed 3 in.

No. R1323 ....
Weight per dozen, 1 ½ lbs.; one-half dozen in a box.

Celluloid stag handles; two blades; one large spear blade and one small pen blade, glazed finish; nickel silver lined; nickel silver cap and bolster; length closed 3 inches.

No. R1903 ....
Weight per dozen, 1 ¾ lbs.; one-half dozen in a box.

Celluloid stag handle; two blades; one large clip blade and one small pen blade, glazed finish; nickel silver lined; nickel silver cap and bolster; length closed 3 in.

No. R1593 ....
Weight per dozen, 1 ¾ lbs.; one-half dozen in a box.

Green pearl Pyremite handles, assorted; two blades; one large clip blade and one small pen blade, glazed finish; nickel silver lined; nickel silver cap and bolster; length closed 3 inches.

No. R1905E ....
Weight per dozen, 1 ¾ lbs.; one-half dozen in a box.

Stag handle; two blades; one large spear blade crocus polished and etched; one small pen blade, glazed finish; brass lined; nickel silver cap, bolster and shield; length closed 3 ⅝ inches.

No. R1833 ....
Weight per dozen, 2 lbs.; one-half dozen in a box.

Stag handle; two blades; one large clip blade, crocus polished and etched; one small pen blade, glazed finish; nickel silver lined; nickel silver bolsters and shield; length closed 3 ⅜ inches.

No. R603 ....
Weight per dozen, 1 ½ lbs.; one-half dozen in a box.

REMINGTON POCKET KNIVES
FULLY WARRANTED

Stag handle; two long lance blades, both full mirror finished; brass lined; nickel silver bolsters; length closed 3 ⅞ inches.

No. R4593 . . . .
Weight per dozen, 2 lbs.; one-half dozen in a box.

Shell Pyremite handle; two blades; one large clip blade, one pen blade, mirror polished and etched; brass lined; nickel silver bolster and shield; length closed, 3 ⅜ inches.

No. R3535S . . . .
Weight per dozen, 1 ⅛ lbs.; one-half dozen in a box.

Pyremite handle; two blades; one large spear blade, one pen blade mirror polished and etched; nickel silver lined; nickel silver tips and shield; length closed 3 ⅛ inches.

No. R6645C . . . .
Weight per dozen, ¾ lb.; one-half dozen in a box.

Stag handle; two blades; one large spear blade, mirror polished and etched; one small pen blade, glazed finish; nickel silver lined; nickel silver tips and shield; length closed 3 ⅛ inches.

No. R6643 . . . .
Weight per dozen, 1 lb.; one -half dozen in a box.

Stag handle; two blades; one large clip and one small pen, both mirror finished; brass lined; nickel silver bolsters and shield; length closed 3 ⅜ inches.

No. R3533 . . . .
Weight per dozen, 1 lb.; one-half dozen in a box.

Stag handle; two blades; one large clip blade, mirror polished and etched; one pen blade, glazed finish; nickel silver lined; nickel silver bolsters and shield; length closed 3 ⅛ inches.

No. R7423 . . . .
Weight per dozen, ¾ lb.; one-half dozen in a box.

Stag handle; two blades; one large spear blade, one pen blade, mirror polished and etched; brass lined; nickel silver bolsters and shield; length closed, 3 ⅛ inches.

No. R6623 . . . .
Weight per dozen, 1 lb.; one-half dozen in a box.

Pyremite handle; two blades; one large clip and one small pen blades, both full mirror finished; one piece brass lined; nickel silver bolsters; length closed 3 ⅛ inches.

No. R7425MW . . . .
Weight per dozen, ¾ lb.; one-half dozen in a box.

Stag handle; two blades; one spear blade and one pen blade, both mirror finish; nickel silver lined; nickel silver tips and shield; length closed, 3 ¼ inches.

No. R7543 . . . .
Weight per dozen, ⅞ lbs.; one-half dozen in a box.

Stag handle; two blades; one spear blade and one pen blade; both mirror finish; nickel silver lined; nickel silver tips and shield; length closed 3 ¼ inches.

No. R7233 . . . .
Weight per dozen, 1 ¼ lbs.; one-half dozen in a box.

Nickel silver handle; two blades, one spear and one pen, both mirror finished; length closed, 3 inches.

No. R6499 . . . .
Weight per dozen, 10 oz.; one-half dozen in a box.

Pearl handle; two blades, one spear and one pen, both mirror finished; nickel silver lined; nickel silver tips; length closed, 2 ½ inches.

No. R6914 . . . .
Weight per dozen, 7 oz.; one-half dozen in a box.

REMINGTON POCKET KNIVES
FULLY WARRANTED

Stag handle; two blades, one large sheepfoot and one small pen blade, mirror finished; brass lined; nickel silver cap bolster and shield; length closed 3⅜ inches.

No. R2223 ....
Weight per dozen, 1¾ lbs.; one-half dozen in a box.

Pyremite handle; two blades, one large clip and one small pen blade, polished; brass lined; polished steel bolster cap and shield; length closed 3½ in.

No. R155 ....
Weight per dozen, 2⅛ lbs.; one-half dozen in a box.

Pyremite handle; two blades, one large spear and one small pen blade, mirror finished; brass lined; nickel silver cap, bolster and shield; length closed 3⅜ inches.

No. R2205B ....
Weight per dozen, 1¾ lbs.; one-half dozen in a box.

Stag handle; two blades; one large clip blade, mirror polished and etched; one small pen blade, glazed finish; brass lining; nickel silver bolster, cap and shield; length closed 3½ inches.

No. R153 ....
Weight per dozen, 2⅛ lbs.; one-half dozen in a box.

Stag handle; two blades, one large clip and one small pen blade; both full mirror finished; brass lining; nickel silver cap and bolster; length closed 3⅛ in.

No. R2103 ....
Weight per dozen, 1 lb.; one-half dozen in a box.

Stag handle; two blades; one large clip blade, mirror polished and etched; one small pen blade, glazed finish; brass lined; nickel silver cap, bolster and shield; length closed 3 inches.

No. R1323 ....
Weight per dozen, 1½ lbs.; one-half dozen in a box.

Pyremite handle; two blades, one large clip and one small pen blade; both full mirror finished; brass lined; nickel silver bolster cap and shield; length closed 3⅛ inches.

No. R2105MW ....
Weight per dozen, 1 lb.; one-half dozen in a box.

Stag handle; two blades; one large clip blade; mirror polished and etched; one small pen blade, glazed finish; brass lined; nickel silver cap, bolster and shield; length closed 3⅜ inches.

No. R603 ....
Weight per dozen, 1½ lbs.; one-half dozen in a box.

Pyremite handle; two blades, one large clip and one small pen blade; both full mirror finished; nickel silver cap, bolster, shield and brass lining; length closed 3⅜ inches.

No. R1855M ....
Weight per dozen, 1½ lbs.; one-half dozen in a box.

Gold pearl Pyremite handle; two blades; one large clip mirror polished and etched, one pen glazed finish; brass lined; nickel silver cap, bolsters and shield; length closed 3⅜ inches.

No. R605G ....
Weight per dozen, 1½ lbs.; one-half dozen in a box.

REMINGTON POCKET KNIVES
FULLY WARRANTED

Pyralin handle; "Zip" construction; two blades; one large spear mirror finish and etched, and one one small pen; by pressing the buttons blades are automatically released and can be locked into position; brass lined; length closed 3⅜ inches.

No. R8065H ....
Weight per dozen, 1 lb.; one-half dozen in a box.

Stag handle, "Zip" construction; two blades; one large spear mirror finish and etched; one small pen; by pressing the buttons blades are automatically released and can be locked into position; brass lined; length closed 3⅜ inches.

No. R8063 ....
Weight per dozen, 1 lb.; one-half dozen in a box.

Pearl handle; two blades; one spear, etched and one pen blade, both mirror finished; one piece nickel silver lining and bolsters; length closed 3 inches.

No. R7854 ....
Weight per dozen, ¾ lb.; one-half dozen in a box.

Pearl handle; two blades, one spear mirror polished and one manicure file blade on back; nickel silver lined; nickel silver tips, rivets and shield; length closed 3⅛ inches.

No. R6244 ....
Weight per dozen, 15 ozs.; one-half dozen in a box.

Pyremite handle; three blades; one large clip, mirror finish and etched; one small pen, mirror finish and one sheep foot mirror finish; brass lined; nickel silver bolsters and shield; length closed 3⅜ inches.

No. R4845M ....
Weight per dozen, 1¾ lbs.; one-half dozen in a box.

Pyremite handle; three blades; one large clip, mirror finish and etched, one small pen mirror finish and one sheep foot mirror finish; brass lined; nickel silver bolsters and shield; length closed 3⅜ inches.

No. R4825R ....
Weight per dozen, 1½ lbs.; one-half dozen in a box.

Stag handle; three blades; one large clip, mirror finish and etched; one small pen and one sheep foot mirror finish; brass lined; nickel silver bolsters and shield; length closed 3⅞ inches.

No. R4843 ....
Weight per dozen, 1¾ lbs.; one-half dozen in a box.

Pyremite handle; three blades; one large clip, etched, one sheepfoot and one spey blades, all mirror finished; brass lined; nickel silver bolsters and shield; length closed 3⅜ inches.

No. R3485H ....
Weight per dozen, 1½ lbs.; one-half dozen in a box.

Pyremite handle; **three blades; one** spear, one spey and one pen blade, all full mirror finish; brass lined; nickel silver bolsters and shield; length closed, 3⅜ inches.

No. R4635G ....
Weight per dozen, 1½ lbs.; one-half dozen in a box.

Pyremite handle; three blades; one clip, one sheeps foot and one pen blade all full mirror finish; solid back, brass lined; nickel silver bolsters; length closed 3¼ inches.

No. R105AMW ....
Weight per dozen, 1¾ lbs.; one-half dozen in a box.

REMINGTON POCKET KNIVES
FULLY WARRANTED

Stag handle; two blades; one large clip blade, mirror polished and etched; one pen blade glazed finish; brass lined; nickel silver cap and bolster; length closed 3⅜ inches.

No. R1853 ....
Weight per dozen, 1½ lbs.; one-half dozen in a box.

Stag handle; two blades; one large clip and one small pen blade, both mirror finished; brass lined; nickel silver cap; bolster and shield; length closed 3⅝ in.

No. R1823 ....
Weight per dozen, 1½ lbs.; one-half dozen in a box.

Stag handle; two blades; one large double sabre clip blade mirror polished and one pen blade, glazed finish; brass lined; nickel silver cap and bolster; length closed 2⅞ in.

No. R1653 ....
Weight per dozen, 1 lb.; one-half dozen in a box.

White pyremite handle; two blades; one large spear blade, mirror polished and etched; one pen blade, glazed finish; brass lined; nickel silver cap, bolster and shield; length closed 4¼ in.

No. R1225W ....
Weight per dozen, 2½ lbs.; one-half dozen in a box.

ELECTRICIANS
Rosewood handle; two blades; one large spear blade; one combination wire scraper and screw driver with lock; both fine blue glazed finish; brass lined; nickel silver bolster, shield and shackle; length closed 3⅜ inches.

No. R2111 ....
Weight per dozen, 2⅝ lbs. one-half dozen in a box.

Stag handle; two blades, one large spear and one small pen, both mirror finished; brass lining; nickel silver bolster, cap and shield; length closed 4⅜ in.

No. R1153 ....
Weight per dozen, 3½ lbs.; one-half dozen in a box.

Stag type handle; two blades; one large spear and one small pen; glazed finish; steel lining and bolsters; length closed, 3 in.

No. RC7853 ....
Weight per dozen, ¾ lb.; one-half dozen in a box.

Stag handle; two blades, one large spear and one small pen blade, both full mirror finished; nickel silver lined; nickel silver bolsters; length closed, 3 in.

No. R6463 ....
Weight per dozen, ¾ lb.; one-half dozen in a box.

Pyremite handle; two blades; one large spear blade, one erasing blade, mirror polished; brass lined; length closed 3⅜ inches.

No. R6785IW ....
Weight per dozen, 1 lb.; one-half dozen in a box.

Pyremite handle; two blades; one large spear blade, etched, and one small pen blade; both mirror finished; nickel silver lining; nickel silver bolsters; length closed 3 inches.

No. R6465MW ....
Weight per dozen, ¾ lbs.; one-half dozen in a box.

Pyremite handle; two blades, one spear and one pen, both mirror finished; nickel silver lined; nickel silver tips; length closed 2½ inches.

No. R6905MW ....
Weight per dozen, 7 oz.; one-half dozen in a box.

SCOUT KNIFE SETS

REMINGTON

Boy Scout Gift Package

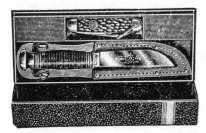

Contains one Official Boy Scout pocket knife and one Official Boy Scout sheath knife packed in an attractive red covered gift box.

No. RS195 ....

Weight per set, 13 oz.; one set in a box.

Girl Scout Gift Package

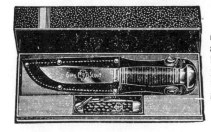

Contains one Official Girl Scout Knife and Official Girl Scout sheath knife packed is an attractive green covered gift box.

No. RS190 ....

Weight per set, 12 oz.; one set in a box.

POCKET KNIFE ASSORTMENTS

JACK MASTER

Hammer Brand

Assortment consists of twelve entirely new designed high grade, precision built, two blade jack knives with beautiful symmetrical handles, perfectly ovalled to fit the grip. Every knife absolutely uniform in design and construction; blades, one clip and one pen made from electrically tempered razor steel, keen edge, full polished smooth easy spring action, exceptionally strong joints; length 3⅛ inches.

Strikingly displayed on a four-color card.

Assorted Celluloid Handles

No. JM3 ....

Imitation Pearl Handles

No. JM4 ....

Weight each, 1½ lbs.; one assortment in a carton.

POCKET KNIFE ASSORTMENTS

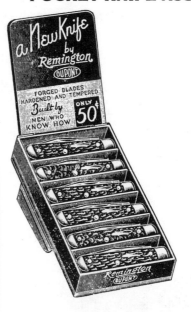

REMINGTON

Contains 12 two blade jack knives assorted stag and blue and red celluloid handles; assorted mirror finished clip and spear large blades and small pen blades; brass lined; German silver caps, bolsters and shields; length closed 3⅝ inches.

Put up in a partitioned display box.

No.	Each
RJ-9	

Wgt. each 1⅞ lbs.; one in a box.

Assortment contains 36 pocket knives with two of each of eighteen patterns, assorted in size from 3¼ to 4 inches in length, some with two and others with three blades including the spear and clip points and the file and spay blades; the handles are also assorted stag, imitation pearl, Pyroxylin and bone; chromium plated shield and bolsters; blades are all highly polished.

Each assortment is packed in a blue steel and glass case with orange plush tray, with price tickets adjoining each knife.

This display case is 10 inches high, 14 inches wide and 6¼ inches deep with space in back for duplicates of knives displayed.

Contents

	Retail Value
16 Knives assorted patterns..............	
10 Knives assorted patterns..............	
10 knives assorted patterns..............	
1 display case	
Total retail value	

No. DC60 ....

One assortment in a carton.

REMINGTON POCKET KNIVES
FULLY WARRANTED

Stag handle; three blades; o n e large spear, one spey and one pen blade; all full mirror finish; brass lined; nickel silver bolster and shield; length closed 3⅜ inches.

No. R4633 ....
Weight per dozen, 1½ lbs.; one-half dozen in a box.

Stag handle; three blades; one clip, o n e sheepfoot and one pen blades, all full mirror finished; brass lined; nickel silver bolsters; length closed 3¼ inches.

No. R100A ....
Weight per dozen, 1¾ lbs.; one-half dozen in a box.

Black pyremite handle; three blades; one large clip blade, one spey, and small pen blade, mirror finish; nickel silver bolsters and shield; b r a s s lined; length closed 3⅜ inches.

No. R4135B ....
Weight per dozen, 1½ lbs.; one-half dozen in a box.

Pyremite handle; three b l a d e s; one large clip, one sheepfoot and one spear blade; mirror finished; brass lined; nickel silver bolsters and shield; length closed 3⅞ inches.

No. R3055 ....
Weight per dozen, 1½ lbs.; one-half dozen in a box.

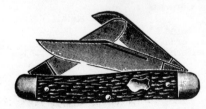

Stag handle; 3 blades; one large clip, one sheepfoot and one spey blade; mirror finish brass lined; nickel silver bolsters and shield; length closed 3⅞ inches.

No. R3053 ....
Weight per dozen, 1½ lbs.; one-half dozen in a box.

Stag handle; three blades; one large clip blade, one spey blade, mirror polished and etched; one sheepfoot blade; brass lined nickel silver bolsters and shield; length closed, 3⅝ inches.

No. R3993 ....
Weight per dozen, 1¼ lbs.; one-half dozen in a box.

Stag handle; three blades; one large spear and one pen blade, both full mirror finish and one nail file blade; nickel silver lined; nickel silver tips and shield; length closed 3¼ inches.

No. R7593 ....
Weight per dozen, 1 lb.; one-half dozen in a box.

Pearl h a n d l e; three blades; one large spear blade and one pen blade, both full mirror polished, one nail file; nickel silver lining and tips; length, closed, 3 inches.

No. R6534 ....
Weight per dozen, ⅞ lb.; one-half dozen in a box.

Pyremite handle; three blades; one large clip, mirror finish and etched; one punch and one spey mirror f i n i s h; brass lined; nickel silver bolsters and shield; length closed 3⅜ inches.

No. R4835M ....
Weight per dozen, 1½ lbs.; one-half dozen in a box.

Stag h a n d l e; three blades; one large clip, mirror finish and etched; one punch and one spey mirror finish; brass lined; nickel silver bolsters and shield; length closed, 3⅞ inches.

No. R4833 ....
Weight per dozen, 1½ lbs.; one-half dozen in a box.

REMINGTON POCKET KNIVES
FULLY WARRANTED

Official Knife, Boy Scouts of America

Stag handle; three blades; one large spear blade, mirror polished and etched with scout insignia; one combination bottle opener and screw driver blade and one can opener blade, both mirror finish; nickel silver lined; nickel silver emblem shield and bolsters; snap-on nickel plated shackle; length closed 3½ inches.

No. RS4783 ....
Weight per dozen, 2⅝ lbs.; one-half dozen in a box.

GIRL SCOUT
Official Knife, Girls Scouts, Inc.

Stag handle; two blades; one large spear and one wood carving blade, mirror polished and etched with Girl Scouts insignia; nickel silver lined; nickel silver bolsters, shackle and emblem shield; length closed 3⅜ inches.

No. R4723 ....
Weight per dozen, 1½ lbs.; one-half dozen in a box.

BARLOW PATTERN

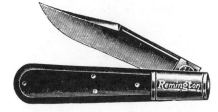

Brown bone handle; one large clip blade, mirror polished; steel lined; polished steel bolster; length closed 5 inches.

No. RB1240 ....
Weight per dozen, 3 lbs.; one-half dozen in a box.

POCKET KNIVES
RUSSELL BARLOW

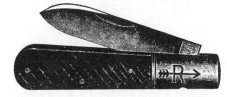

Dark bone handle; one clip blade, glazed; steel lined; steel bolster; length closed 3⅜ inches.

No. 65 ....
Weight per dozen, 1¾ lbs.; one dozen in a box.

POCKET KNIVES
RUSSELL BARLOW

Dark bone handle; one large and one small pen blade, glazed; steel lined; steel bolster; length closed 3⅜ inches.

No. 66—Clip blade ....
No. 62—Spear blade ....
Weight per dozen, 2 lbs.; one dozen in a box.

IMPERIAL

Pyralin handles, assorted colors; one four-inch clip blade full polished; iron lined; iron bolster; length closed 5⅛ inches.

No. 1850C ....
Weight per dozen, 1½ lbs.; one-half dozen in a box.

PRUNING KNIVES

SWORD BRAND
Rosewood handle; one large pruning blade, full mirror polished on both sides; polished steel bolster and lining; length closed 3⅝ inches..

No. 600 .....
Wgt. per doz., 2½ lbs.; one dozen in a display box.

SCOUT KNIFE SETS
IMPERIAL
Kamp King Sets

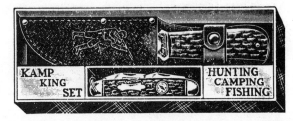

Consists of a standard size Boy Scout knife with nickel silver bolster, stag handle and compass in the handle; length 3⅝ in.; one hunting knife with bone handle and sheath, length 7 in. Put up in an attractive box as shown.

No. KK ....
Wgt. per dozen sets, 6¾ lbs.; one dozen sets in a carton.

4991—Flat spear, screw driver and cap lifter combination, can opener and punch blades. Large blade full polished. Nickel silver bolsters. Nickel silver lining. Stag handle. Crest shield. Shackle.

3 1/2" long

2877—Narrow clip blades. Full polished. Stag handle. Nickel silver bolsters. Nickel silver linings.

4" long

2879—Spear and spey blades. Large blade full polished. Spoon threaded nickel silver bolsters. Brass lining. Stag handle. Crest shield.

4 1/2" long

3963—Long flat clip, sheepfoot and spey stainless steel blades and springs. Blades full polished. Nickel silver round bolsters and lining. Stag handle. Crest shield.

4" long

1613—Spey stainless steel blade and spring. Blade full polished. Nickel silver bolster and lining. Cocobolo handle.

3 3/8" long

2205 — Spear and pen stainless steel blades and spring, full polished. Nickel silver engine turned handle. Skeleton trim. Shackle.

3 1/4" long

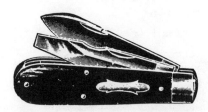

2681—Large spear and screw driver blades. Screw driver blade has two notches for stripping wire. Lock back screw driver. Large blade highly colored. Nickel silver bolster and shield. Brass lining. Ebony handle.

3 3/4" long

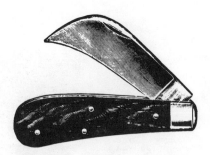

1610—Pruner blade glazed finish. Steel bolster. Steel lining. Cocobolo handle. Hole in butt end of handle for lanyard.

4 1/8" long

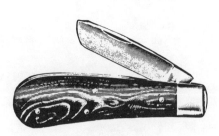

1614—Maize blade. Glazed finish. Cocobolo handle. Steel lining. Steel bolster.

4 1/8" long

3009—Clip, spey and punch blades. Large blade full polished. Nickel silver bolsters and lining. White grain celluloid handle.

3 5/8" long

4950—Flat spear, combination can opener and cap lifter, screw driver and punch blades. Large blade full polished. Nickel silver bolsters. Brass lining. Stag handle. Shackle. Shield.

3 5/8" long

2852—Clip and pen blades. Large blade full polished. Nickel silver bolsters and lining. Stag handle. Crest shield.

3" long

3341—Large spear, small clip and spey blades, full polished. Nickel silver bolsters and lining. Pearl handle. Crest shield.

3 3/8" long

3942—Long spear, small clip and spey blades. Large blade full polished. Nickel silver bolsters and lining. Stag handle. Crest shield.

3 3/8" long

3962—Long flat clip, sheepfoot and spey blades full polished. Nickel silver bolsters and lining. Genuine buffalo horn handle. Crest shield.

4" long

3959—Long flat narrow clip, sheepfoot and spey blades. Large blade full polished. Stag handle. Nickel silver bolsters and lining. Crest shield.

4" long

4963—Short clip, pen, spey and punch blades. Large blade full polished. Nickel silver bolsters and lining. Stag handle. Crest shield.

4" long

3916—Long flat clip, spey and punch blades. Large blade full polished. Stag handle. Nickel silver bolsters and lining. **Crest shield.**

3 1/4" long

WINCHESTER
TRADE MARK

2079—Spear and eraser blades. Large blade full polished. Nickel silver lining. White celluloid handle. Shadow ends.

3 3/8" long

3933—Clip, sheepfoot, and pen blades. Large blade full polished Nickel silver bolsters and lining. Stag handle. Crest shield.

3 3/8" long

Spear, pen and regular file blades. Large blade full polished. Nickel silver bolsters and lining. Crest shield.
3932—Stag handle.
3043—Celluloid handle (red and black).
3044—Celluloid handle (red and green).

3 3/8" long

2842—Spear and pen blades. Large blade full polished. Stag handle. Nickel silver bolsters and lining. Crest Shield.

3 1/4" long

2945—Spear and pen blades. Large blade full polished. Nickel silver tips and lining. Stag handle. Crest shield.

3 1/4" long

3904—Long clip, long spey and pen blades. Clip blade full polished. Stag handle. Nickel silver bolsters and lining. Crest shield.

3 5/8" long

2302—Pen and regular file blade full polished. Nickel silver bolsters and lining. Pearl handle. Shackle.

2 1/4" long

2967—Large spear and flat clip blades. Spear blade full polished. Stag handle. Nickel silver fluted bolsters. Nickel silver lining. Crest shield.

3 5/8" long

3915—Long spear, pen and punch blades. Large blade full polished. Stag handle. Nickel silver bolsters and lining. Crest shield.

3 1/2" long

4931—Two large sheepfoot and two pen blades. Large blades full polished. Stag handle. Nickel silver rat-tail bolsters. Brass lining. Curved bar shield.

3 1/2" long

2996—Large sheepfoot and pen blades. Large blade full polished. Stag handle. Nickel silver rat-tail bolsters. Brass lining. Curved bar shield.

3 3/4" long

2933—Spear and pen blades. Large blade full polished. Nickel silver tips. Nickel silver lining. Stag handle. Crest shield.

3" long

3927—Spear, pen and regular file blades. Large blade full polished. Stag handle. Nickel silver bolsters. Nickel silver lining. Crest shield.

3 3/8" long

2978—Spear and pen blades. Large blade full polished. Nickel silver cap and bolster. Nickel silver lining. Stag handle. Crest shield.

3 3/8" long

2974—Clip and pen blades. Large blade full polished. Steel cap and bolster. Brass lining. Stag handle. Crest shield.

3 1/2" long

Spear and pen blades. Large blade full polished. Nickel silver cap, bolster and lining.
2962—Stag handle.
2086—Silvaleur celluloid handle.
2107—Gold celluloid handle.

2 3/4" long

Long flat clip blade full polished. Nickel silver bolster and cap. Brass lining. Crest shield.
1924—Stag handle.
1051—Celluloid handle (red and black)

4 1/2" long

Large sabre clip blade. Glazed finish. Steel cap and bolster. Brass lining.
1936—Stag handle.
1050—Assorted celluloid handles (2 blue, 2 red, 2 gold).

5" long

One blade, glazed finish. Stag handle. Steel bolster. Steel lining.
1938—Spear blade
1922—Spey blade
1921—Clip blade

3 3/8" long

2983—Clip and pen blades Glazed finish. Steel bolster and lining. Stag handle. Fifteen inch chain with shackle.

3 3/8" long

One blade. Glazed finish. Bone stag handle. Steel bolster. Steel lining.
1701—Spear blade.
1785—Clip blade.

3 1/2" long

1704—Large clip blade. Full polished. Stag handle. Steel bolster. Brass lining.
1703—Large clip blade. Glazed finish. Bone stag handle. Steel bolster. Steel lining.

5" long

Clip and pen blades. Large blade full polished. Nickel silver cap and bolster. Brass lining. Crest shield.
2630—Ebony handle.
2098—Celluloid handle, red and black.
2940—Spear and pen blades. Stag handle.

3 3/8" long

1920—Sabre clip blade glazed finish. Nickel silver cap and bolster. Brass lining. Stag handle. Guimpe shield. Lanyard hole in cap.

5 1/4" long

2851—Spear and pen blades. Large blade full polished. Stag handle. Nickel silver cap and bolster. Brass lining. Crest shield.

3" long

Marble's Pocket Knives

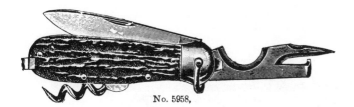

No. 5958,

No. 5294

No. 5206.

No. 6228

No. 8408

No. 8277

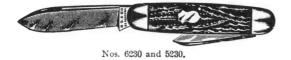

Nos. 6230 and 5230.

No. 5653

No. 5202

POCKET KNIVES.

HIBBARD, SPENCER, BARTLETT & CO'S "OUR VERY BEST," WARRANTED.

No. 411.

No. **157**–1 blade, cocoa handle, iron lined, crocus polished, 3⅛ in.,   · · · · ·
No. **519**–2 blades, cocoa handle, iron lined, crocus polished, 3⅛ in.,   · · · · ·
No. **411**–2 blades, ebony handle, iron lined, crocus polished, 3¼ in.,   · · · · ·
No. **444**–2 blades, cocoa handle, iron lined, crocus polished, 3⅜ in.,   · · · · ·
No. **412**–2 blades, ebony handle, iron lined, crocus polished, 3⅜ in.,   · · · · ·
No. **448**–2 blades, cocoa handle, brass lined, crocus polished, 3⅜ in

No. 153.

No. **153**–1 blade, cocoa handle, iron lined, crocus polished, 3⅝ in., · · · · ·
No. **159**–1 blade, stag handle, iron lined, crocus polished, 3⅝ in., · · · · ·

No. 154.

No. **154**–1 blade, cocoa handle, iron lined, crocus polished, 3⅝ in.,   · · · · ·
No. **160**–1 blade, stag handle, iron lined, crocus polished, 3⅝ in.,   · · · · ·

No. 155.

No. **155**–1 blade, cocoa handle, iron lined, crocus polished, 3⅝ in.,   · · · · ·
No. **161**–1 blade, stag handle, iron lined, crocus polished, 3⅝ in.,   · · · · ·

No. 445.

No. **445**–2 blades, cocoa handle, iron lined, crocus polished, 3⅝ in.,   · · · · ·
No. **413**–2 blades, ebony handle, iron lined, crocus polished, 3⅝ in.,   · · · · ·
No. **449**–2 blades, cocoa handle, brass lined, crocus polished, 3½ in.,   · · · · ·
No. **446**–2 blades, cocoa handle, iron lined, crocus polished, 3¾ in.,   · · · · ·
No. **414**–2 blades, ebony handle, iron lined, crocus polished, 3⅞ in.,   · · · · ·
No. **450**–2 blades, cocoa handle, brass lined, crocus polished, 3¾ in.,   · · · · ·

HALF DOZEN IN A BOX.

POCKET KNIVES.

HIBBARD, SPENCER, BARTLETT' & CO'S "OUR VERY BEST," WARRANTED.

No 460.

No. 458–2 blades, buffalo handle, brass lined, crocus polished, 3⅛ in., · · · · ·
No. 459–2 blades, ivory handle, brass lined, crocus polished, 3⅛ in., · · · · ·
No. 460–2 blades, pearl handle, brass lined, crocus polished, 3⅛ in., · · · · ·

No. 451

No. 451–2 blades, cocoa handle, brass lined, crocus polished, 3⅜ in., · · · ·
No. 452–2 blades, ebony handle brass lined, crocus polished, 3⅜ in., · · · ·

No. 503.

No. 501–2 blades, cocoa handle, brass lined, crocus polished, 3¾ in., · · · · ·
No. 502–2 blades, ebony handle, brass lined, crocus polished, 3¾ in., · · · · ·
No. 503–2 blades, white bone handle, brass lined, crocus polished, 3¾ in., · · · ·
No. 515–2 blades, cocoa handle, iron lined, crocus polished, plain bolster. 3¾ in., · · ·

No. 456.

No. 456–2 blades, cocoa handle, brass lined, crocus polished, 3⅝ in., · · · ·
No. 457–2 blades, ebony handle, brass lined, crocus polished, 3⅝ in., · · · ·

No. 454

No. 453–2 blades, cocoa handle, brass lined, crocus polished, 3⅝ in., · · · ·
No. 454–2 blades, ebony handle, brass lined, crocus polished, 3⅝ in., · · · ·
No. 455 2 blades, white bone handle, brass lined, crocus polished, 3⅝ in., · · · ·

HALF DOZEN IN A BOX.

POCKET KNIVES.

HIBBARD, SPENCER, BARTLETT & CO'S "OUR VERY BEST," WARRANTED.

No. 481.

No. 480–2 blades, cocoa handle, brass lined, crocus polished, 3⅝ in., ·   ·   ·   ·   ·
No. 481–2 blades, ebony handle, brass lined, crocus polished, 3⅝ in. ·   ·   ·   ·   ·
No. 482–2 blades, ivory handle, brass lined, crocus polished, 3⅝ in., ·   ·   ·   ·   ·
No. 483–2 blades, stag   handle, brass lined, crocus polished, 3⅝ in., ·   ·   ·   ·   ·

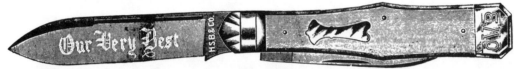

No. 493½

No. 491 –2 blades, cocoa handle, brass lined, crocus polished, 3¾ in., ·   ·   ·   ·
No. 492 –2 blades, ebony handle, brass lined, crocus polished, 3¾ in., ·   ·   ·   ·
No. 493½–2 blades, white bone handle, brass lined, crocus polished, 3¾ in., ·   ·   ·

No. 484–2 blades, stag handle, brass lined. crocus polished, 3⅝ in., ·   ·   ·   ·   ·

No. 521–2 blades, stag handle, brass lined, crocus polished, 3½ in., ·   ·   ·   ·   ·

No. 500–2 blades, stag handle, brass lined, crocus polished. 3⅝ in., ·   ·   ·   ·   ·

HALF DOZEN IN A BOX

POCKET KNIVES.

HIBBARD, SPENCER, BARTLETT & CO'S "OUR VERY BEST," WARRANTED.

No. 447.

No. 447–2 blades, ebony handle, iron lined, crocus polished, 3⅝ in., • • • •
No. 511–2 blades, stag handle, brass lined, crocus polished, hollow bolster, 3⅜ in., • •
No. 514–2 blades, stag handle, brass lined, crocus polished, hollow bolster, 3⅝ in.,

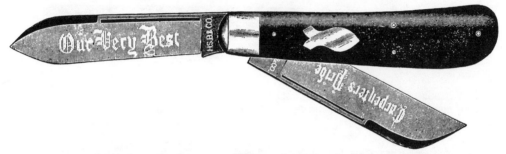

No. 506–2 blades, ebony handle, iron lined, crocus polished, 3⅝ in., • • • •

No. 489.

No. 489–2 blades, cocoa handle, brass lined, crocus polished, 3¾ in., • • • •
No. 490–2 blades, buffalo handle, brass lined, crocus polished, 3¾ in., • • • •

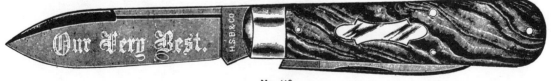

No. 418.

No. 418–2 blades, cocoa handle, brass lined, crocus polished, 3⅞ in., • • • •
No. 419–2 blades, buffalo handle, brass lined, crocus polished, 3⅞ in., • • • •
No. 477–2 blades, cocoa handle, brass lined, crocus polished, 3⅞ in., extra heavy, • •
No. 478–2 blades, ebony handle, brass lined, crocus polished, 3⅞ in., extra heavy, • •

No. 256–2 blades, ebony handle, brass lined, crocus polished, 4 in., • • • •

HALF DOZEN IN A BOX.

POCKET KNIVES.

No. 165.

No. 165–1 blade, iron handle, crocus polished, 3⅜ in., ...
No. 534–2 blades, iron handle, crocus polished, 3⅜ in., ...

No. 509.

No. 509–2 blades, stag handle, brass lined, crocus polished, 3½ in., ...
No. 512–2 blades, stag handle, brass lined, crocus polished, 3⅝ in.,

No. 513.

No. 443–Cocoa handle, iron lined, crocus polished, clip blade, 3½ in., ...
No. 510–Stag handle, brass lined, crocus polished, clip blade, hollow bolster, 3⅜ in., . .
No. 513–Stag handle, brass lined, crocus polished, clip blade, hollow bolster, 3⅝ in.. . .

No. 517–2 blades, ebony handle, iron lined, crocus polished, 3¾ in., ...

No. 479.

No. 158–1 speying blade, cocoa handle, iron lined, crocus polished, 3⅝ in., ...
No. 479–2 blades, cocoa handle, iron lined, crocus polished, 3⅝ in., ...

HALF DOZEN IN A BOX.

POCKET KNIVES.

HIBBARD, SPENCER, BARTLETT & CO'S, WARRANTED.

No. 582P–2 blades, iron handle, large blade crocus polished, 3½ in., · · · · · ·

No. 204P

No. 204P–2 blades, cocoa handle, iron lined, large blade crocus polished, clip   point, 3⅝ in., ·
No. 203P–2 blades, cocoa handle, iron lined, large blade crocus polished, spear point, 3⅝ in., ·

No. 205P–2 blades, cocoa handle, iron lined, large blade crocus polished, 3⅝ in., · · ·

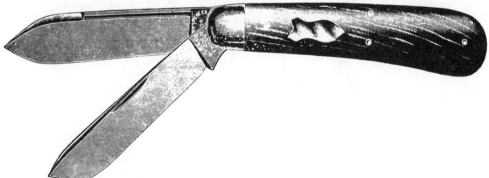

No. 479P–2 blades, cocoa handle, iron lined, large blade crocus polished, 3⅝ in., · · ·

No. 219P.

No. 120P–1 blade,   cocoa handle, iron lined, large blade crocus polished, 3⅞ in., · · ·
No. 219P–2 blades, cocoa handle, iron lined, large blade crocus polished, 3⅞ in., · · ·

HALF DOZEN IN A BOX.

POCKET KNIVES.

HIBBARD, SPENCER, BARTLETT & CO'S. WARRANTED.

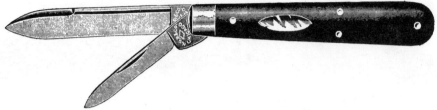

No. 211P–2 blades, ebony handle, brass lined, large blade crocus polished, 3⅛ in., ·   ·   ·

No. 244P–2 blades, ebony handle, brass lined, large blade crocus polished, 3¼ in., ·   ·   ·

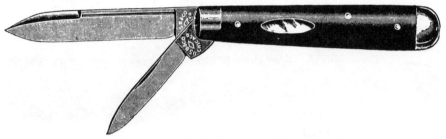

No. 212P–2 blades, ebony handle, brass lined, large blade crocus polished, 3⅛ in., ·   ·   ·

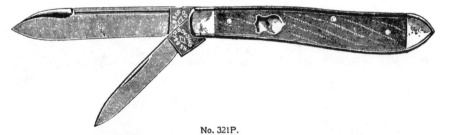

No. 321P.

No. 321P–2 blades, cocoa handle, brass lined, large blade crocus polished, 3⅛ in., ·   ·   ·
No. 322P–2 blades, ebony handle, brass lined, large blade crocus polished, 3⅛ in., ·   ·   ·
No. 323P–2 blades, stag   handle, brass lined, large blade crocus polished, 3⅛ in., ·

No. 571P.

No. 571P 2 blades, ebony handle, brass lined, large blade crocus polished, 3¼ in.,   ·   ·
No. 572P–2 blades, stag   handle, brass lined, large blade crocus polished, 3¼ in., ·

No. 573P–2 blades, stag handle, brass lined, large blade crocus polished, 3¾ in.,   ·   ·

HALF DOZEN IN A BOX.

POCKET KNIVES.

HIBBARD, SPENCER, BARTLETT & CO'S, WARRANTED.

No. 270P.

No. **245P**–2 blades, cocoa handle, brass lined, large blade crocus polished, 3½ in.,   •   •
No. **268P**–2 blades, cocoa handle, brass lined, large blade crocus polished, 3⅝ in.,   •   •
No. **269P**–2 blades, ebony handle, brass lined, large blade crocus polished, 3⅝ in.,   •   •
No. **270P**–2 blades, white bone handle, brass lined, large blade crocus polished, 3⅝ in.,   •
No. **216P**–2 blades, cocoa handle, iron lined, large blade crocus polished, 3¾ in.,

No. 431P.

No. **431P**–2 blades, ebony handle, iron lined, large blade crocus polished, clip point, 3⅝ in.,   •
No. **425P**–2 blades, cocoa handle, iron lined, large blade crocus polished, spear point, 3⅝ in.,   •
No. **426P**–2 blades, ebony handle, iron lined, large blade crocus polished, spear point, 3⅝ in.,   •

No. 430P.

No. **427P**–2 blades, cocoa handle, iron lined, large blade crocus polished, 3⅝ in.,   •   •
No. **428P**–2 blades, ebony handle, iron lined, large blade crocus polished, 3⅝ in.,   •   •
No. **259P**–2 blades, cocoa handle, brass lined, large blade crocus polished, 3⅝ in.,   •   •
No. **260P**–2 blades, ebony handle, brass lined, large blade crocus polished, 3⅝ in.,   •   •
No. **430P**–2 blades, ebony handle, iron lined, large blade crocus polished, 3⅞ in.,   •   •

No. **378P**–2 blades, ebony handle, brass lined, large blade crocus polished, 3⅝ in.,   •   •

No. 272P.

No. **223P**–2 blades, cocoa handle, iron lined, large blade crocus polished, 3⅞ in.,   •   •
No. **272P**–2 blades, cocoa handle, brass lined, large blade crocus polished, 4 in.,   •   •

HALF DOZEN IN A BOX.

POCKET KNIVES.

HIBBARD, SPENCER, BARTLETT & CO'S, WARRANTED.

No. 275P–2 blades, stag handle, brass lined, large blade crocus polished, 3½ in.,   ·   ·   ·

No. 271P.

No. 281P–2 blades, cocoa handle, brass lined, large blade crocus polished, 3½ in.,   ·   ·
No. 282P–2 blades, stag   handle, brass lined, large blade crocus polished, 3½ in.,   ·   ·
No. 271P–2 blades, ebony handle, brass lined, large blade crocus polished, 3¾ in.,   ·   ·

No. 213P.

No. 227P–2 blades, cocoa handle, iron   lined, large blade crocus polished, 3½ in.,   ·   ·
No. 213P–2 blades, cocoa handle, brass lined, large blade crocus polished, 3½ in.,   ·   ·
No. 214P–2 blades, ebony handle, brass lined, large blade crocus polished, 3½ in.,   ·   ·
No. 215P–2 blades, white bone handle, brass lined, large blade crocus polished, 3½ in.,   ·

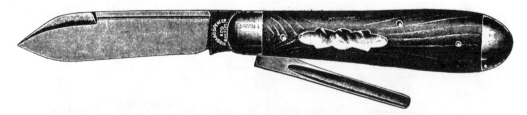

No. 206P–1 blade, with gouge, cocoa handle, brass lined, crocus polished, 3⅝ in.,   ·   ·

No. 349.

No. 348½–2 blades, cocoa handle, brass lined, large blade crocus polished, 3¾ in.,   ·   ·
No. 349 –2 blades, ebony handle, brass lined, large blade crocus polished, 3¾ in.,   ·   ·
No. 374 –2 blades, stag   handle, brass lined, large blade crocus polished, 3¾ in.,   ·   ·

HALF DOZEN IN A BOX.

POCKET KNIVES.

HIBBARD. SPENCER, BARTLETT & CO'S, WARRANTED.

No. 292P.

No. 291P –2 blades, cocoa handle, brass lined, large blade crocus polished, 3½ in.,   ·   ·

No. 291½P–2 blades, ebony handle, brass lined, large blade crocus polished, 3½ in.,   ·   ·

No. 292P –2 blades, stag   handle, brass lined. large blade crocus polished. 3½ in.,   ·   ·

No. 273P–2 blades, stag handle, brass lined, large blade crocus polished, 3⅝ in.,   ·   ·   ·

No. 579P–2 blades, stag handle, brass lined, large blade crocus polished, 4 in.,   ·   ·   ·

No. 581P–2 blades, stag handle, brass lined. large blade crocus polished, 4⅜ in ,   ·   ·   ·

HALF DOZEN IN A BOX.

POCKET KNIVES.

HIBBARD, SPENCER, BARTLETT & 'CO'S. WARRANTED.

No. 277P

No. **277P**–2 blades, ebony handle, brass lined, large blade crocus polished, 3¼ in.,   · ·
No. **278P**–2 blades, stag   handle, brass lined, large blade crocus polished, 3¼ in.,   · ·

No. 285P.

No. **298P**–2 blades, cocoa handle, brass lined, large blade crocus polished, 3¼ in , · ·
No. **285P**–2 blades, ebony handle, brass lined, large blade crocus polished, 3½ in., · ·
No. **286P**–2 blades, stag   handle, brass lined, large blade crocus polished, 3½ in., · ·

No. 373P.

No. **225P**–2 blades, cocoa handle, iron   lined, large blade crocus polished, 3⅝ in., · ·
No. **371P**–2 blades, cocoa handle, brass lined, large blade crocus polished. 3⅝ in., · ·
No. **372P**–2 blades, ebony handle, brass lined, large blade crocus polished, 3⅝ in., · ·
No. **373P**–2 blades, stag   handle, brass lined, large blade crocus polished, 3⅝ in., · ·
No. **308P**–2 blades. white bone handle, brass lined, large blade crocus polished, 3⅝ in., ·

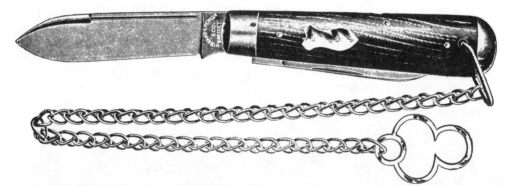

No. **331P**–2 blades, cocoa handle, brass lined, large blade crocus polished, 3½ in., 18 in. nickel plated chain,
    per dozen   · · · · · · · · · · · · · ·

No. 370P.

No. **369P**–2 blades, cocoa handle, brass lined, large blade crocus polished, 4   in.,   · ·
No. **370P**–2 blades, cocoa handle, brass lined, large blade crocus polished, 4¼ in.,   · ·

HALF DOZEN IN A BOX.

70

POCKET KNIVES.

No 0603

No. 0604 2 blades, cocoa handle, brass lined, glazed, 3⅜ in., ...
No. 0603 2 blades, ebony handle, brass lined, glazed, 3⅜ in, ...
No. 0605 2 blades, stag handle, brass lined, glazed, 3⅜ in, ...

No. 0607

No. 0607 2 blades, cocoa handle, brass lined, glazed, 3⅜ in., ...
No. 0606 2 blades, ebony handle, brass lined, glazed, 3⅜ in., ...
No. 0608 2 blades, stag handle, brass lined, glazed, 3⅜ in., ...

No. 0611.

No. 0610 2 blades, cocoa handle, brass lined, glazed, 3⅝ in., ...
No. 0609 2 blades, ebony handle, brass lined, glazed, 3⅝ in., ...
No. 0611 2 blades, stag handle, brass lined, glazed, 3⅝ in., ...

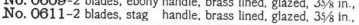

No 0371

No. 0371 2 blades, cocoa handle, brass lined, glazed, 3⅝ in., ...
No. 0372 2 blades, ebony handle, brass lined, glazed, 3⅝ in., ...

No. 0433 2 blades, stag handle, brass lined, glazed 3⅜ in., ...

No 0407.

No. 0406 2 blades, cocoa handle, brass lined, etched, 3⅞ in., ...
No. 0407 2 blades, ebony handle, brass lined, etched, 3⅞ in. . . . .

HALF DOZEN IN A BOX.

POCKET KNIVES.

NEW YORK KNIFE CO'S, WARRANTED.

No. 3208N.

No. 3202N–3 blades, stag   handle, brass lined, large blade crocus polished, 3⅜ in., · · ·
No. 3206N–3 blades, ebony handle, brass lined, large blade crocus polished, 3⅝ in., · · ·
No. 3208N–3 blades, stag   handle, brass lined, large blade crocus polished, 3⅝ in., · · ·

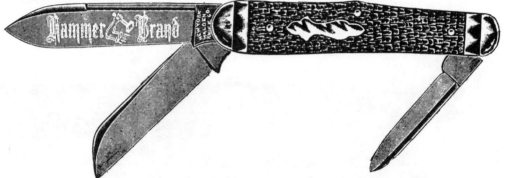

No. 3718N–3 blades, stag handle, brass lined, large blade crocus polished, 3⅝ in., · · ·

No. 3215N–3 blades, stag handle, brass lined, glazed, 4 in., · · · · · · · ·

No. 4215N–4 blades, stag handle, rope milled German silver lining, large blade crocus polished, 3⅞ in.,
per dozen · · · · · · · · · · · · · · · · ·

HALF DOZEN IN A BOX.

POCKET KNIVES.

HIBBARD, SPENCER, BARTLETT & CO'S, WARRANTED.

No. 821P-4 blades, stag handle, brass lined, large blade crocus polished, 2¾ in.,⸱⸱⸱⸱⸱⸱⸱⸱⸱ · ·

No. 818P.

No. 817P-4 blades, buffalo handle, brass lined, large blade crocus polished, 3⅛ in.,⸱⸱⸱ - ·
No. 816P-4 blades, stag handle, brass lined, large blade crocus polished, 3⅛ in.,⸱⸱⸱ - ·
No. 818P-4 blades, pearl handle, brass lined, large blade crocus polished, 3⅛ in.,⸱⸱⸱ - ·

No. 820P.

No. 819P-4 blades, stag handle, brass lined, large blade crocus polished, 3⅛ in.,⸱⸱⸱ · ·
No. 820P-4 blades, pearl handle, brass lined, large blade crocus polished, 3⅛ in.,⸱⸱⸱ · ·

No. 813P.

No. 812P-4 blades, pearl handle, aluminum bolsters, German silver lined, large blade crocus polished,
    3⅛ in.⸱⸱⸱⸱⸱⸱⸱⸱⸱⸱⸱⸱⸱⸱⸱⸱
No. 813P-4 blades, pearl handle, aluminum bolsters, German silver lined, large blade crocus polished,
    3⅜ in.,⸱⸱⸱⸱⸱⸱⸱⸱⸱⸱⸱⸱⸱⸱⸱⸱

HALF DOZEN IN A BOX.

POCKET KNIVES.

HIBBARD, SPENCER, BARTLETT & CO'S, WARRANTED.

No. 799P-3 blades, cocoa handle, brass lined, large blade crocus polished, 3⅝ in.,

No. 623P-3 blades, stag handle, brass lined, large blade crocus polished, 3⅝ in., ·   ·   ·

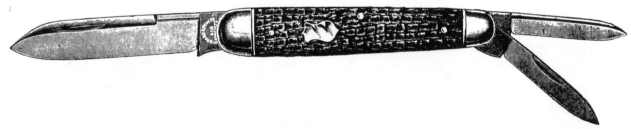

No. 678P

No. 676P-3 blades, cocoa handle, brass lined, large blade crocus polished, 3½ in.,   ·   ·
No. 677P-3 blades, ebony handle, brass lined, large blade crocus polished, 3½ in.,   ·   ·
No. 678P-3 blades, stag   handle, brass lined, large blade crocus polished, 3½ in.,   ·   ·

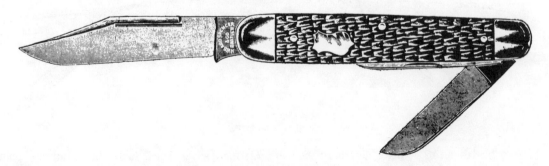

No. 682P-3 blades, stag handle, brass lined, large blade crocus polished, 3¾ in., ·   ·   ·

HALF DOZEN IN A BOX.

POCKET KNIVES.

HIBBARD, SPENCER, BARTLETT & CO'S, WARRANTED.

No. 330P.

No. 329P–2 blades, buffalo handle, brass lined, large blade crocus polished, 2⅞ in.,　·　·
No. 330P–2 blades, pearl　handle, brass lined, large blade crocus polished, 2⅞ in.,　·　·

No. 570P–2 blades, stag handle, brass lined, large blade crocus polished, 3 in.,　·　·　·

No. 295P.

No. 295P–2 blades, ebony handle, brass lined, large blade crocus polished, 3⅜ in.,　·　·
No. 296P–2 blades, stag　handle, brass lined, large blade crocus polished, 3⅜ in.,　·　·

No. 294P.

No. 293P–2 blades, cocoa handle, brass lined, large blade crocus polished, 3½ in.,　·　·
No. 294P–2 blades, stag　handle, brass lined, large blade crocus polished, 3½ in.,　·　·

No. 318P.

No. 317P–2 blades, ebony handle, brass lined, large blade crocus polished, 3¼ in ,　·　·
No. 318P–2 blades, stag　handle, brass lined, large blade crocus polished, 3¼ in.,　·　·

No. 319P.

No. 319P–2 blades, ebony handle, brass lined, large blade crocus polished, 3¾ in.,　·　·
No. 320P–2 blades, stag　handle, brass lined, large blade crocus polished, 3¾ in.,　·　·

HALF DOZEN IN A BOX.

POCKET KNIVES.

HIBBARD, SPENCER. BARTLETT & CO'S, WARRANTED.

No. 620P–3 blades, pearl handle, brass lined, large blade crocus polished, 2¾ in.,

No. 811P–4 blades, pearl handle, aluminum bolsters, German silver lined, large blade crocus polished
2¾ in.,   ·   ·   ·   ·   ·   ·   ·   ·   ·   ·   ·   ·   ·   ·

No. 629P.

No. 628P–3 blades, stag handle, rope milled brass lining, large blade crocus polished, 3⅜ in.,
No. 629P–3 blades, pearl handle, rope milled brass lining, large blade crocus polished, 3⅜ in.,

No. 619P–3 blades, pearl handle, brass lined, large blade crocus polished, 3 in.,   ·   ·   ·

HALF DOZEN IN A BOX.

76

POCKET KNIVES.

HIBBARD, SPENCER. BARTLETT & CO'S, WARRANTED.

No. 300P–2 blades, pearl handle, brass lined, large blade crocus polished 2⅝ in.,   ·   ·   ·

No. 299P–2 blades, pearl handle. brass lined, large blade crocus polished, 2⅝ in.,   ·   ·   ·

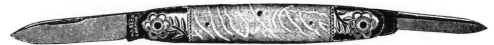

No. 344P.

No. 343P–2 blades, pearl handle, **aluminum bolsters**, German silver lined, large blade crocus polished,
2¾ in.,   ·   ·   ·   ·   ·   ·   ·   ·   ·   ·
No. 344P–2 blades, pearl handle, aluminum bolsters, German silver lined, large blade crocus polished,
3⅛ in.,   ·   ·   ·   ·   ·   ·   ·   ·   ·   ·
No. 345P–2 blades, pearl handle, aluminum bolsters, German silver lined, large blade crocus polished,
3½ in.,   ·   ·   ·   ·   ·   ·   ·   ·   ·   ·

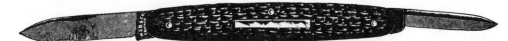

No. 316P–2 blades, stag handle, brass lined, large blade crocus polished, 3⅛ in.,   ·   ·   ·

No. 311P.

No. 309P–2 blades, buffalo handle, brass lined, large blade crocus polished, 3 in.,   ·   ·   ·
No. 310P–2 blades, stag   handle, brass lined, large blade crocus polished, 3 in.,   ·   ·   ·
No. 311P–2 blades, pearl   handle, brass lined, large blade crocus polished, 3 in.,   ·   ·   ·

No. 312P.

No. 313P–2 blades, buffalo handle, brass lined, large blade crocus polished, 3⅜ in.,   ·   ·   ·
No. 312P–2 blades, stag   handle, brass lined, large blade crocus polished, 3⅜ in.,   ·   ·   ·

No. 314P.

No. 315P–2 blades, buffalo handle, brass lined, large blade crocus polished, 3⅜ in.,   ·   ·   ·
No. 314P–2 blades, stag   handle, brass lined, large blade crocus polished, 3⅜ in.,   ·   ·   ·

HALF DOZEN IN A BOX.

POCKET KNIVES.

HIBBARD, SPENCER, BARTLETT & CO'S, WARRANTED.

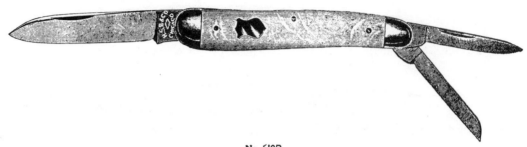

No. 610P.

No. 608P–3 blades, buffalo handle, brass lined, large blade crocus polished, 3 in., · · ·
No. 609P–3 blades, stag   handle, brass lined, large blade crocus polished, 3 in., · · ·
No. 610P–3 blades, pearl handle, brass lined, large blade crocus polished, 3 in., ·

No. 618P.

No. 617P–3 blades, buffalo handle, brass lined, large blade crocus polished, 3⅛ in., · ·
No. 616P–3 blades, stag   handle, brass lined, large blade crocus polished, 3⅛ in., · ·
No. 618P–3 blades, pearl handle, brass lined, large blade crocus polished, 3⅛ in., · ·

No. 613P.

No. 611P–3 blades, buffalo handle, brass lined, large blade crocus polished, 3⅛ in., · ·
No. 612P–3 blades, stag   handle, brass lined, large blade crocus polished, 3⅛ in., · ·
No. 613P–3 blades, pearl handle, brass lined, large blade crocus polished, 3⅛ in., · ·

No. 621P.

No. 621P–4 blades, pearl handle, aluminum bolsters, German silver lined, large blade crocus polished,
    3⅛ in., · · · · · ·
No. 622P–4 blades, pearl handle, aluminum bolsters, German silver lined, large blade crocus polished,
    3½ in., · · · · · ·

HALF DOZEN IN A BOX.

POCKET KNIVES.

HIBBARD, SPENCER, BARTLETT & CO'S, WARRANTED.

No. 109.

No. 109–1 blade, cocoa handle, iron lined, 3¼ in.,
No. 110–1 blade, ebony handle, iron lined, 3¼ in.,
No. 111–1 blade, cocoa handle, iron lined, 3⅜ in.,

No. 231–2 blades, cocoa handle, iron lined, 3¼ in.,

No. 208.

No. 207–2 blades, cocoa handle, iron lined, 3¼ in.,
No. 208–2 blades, cocoa handle, iron lined, 3½ in.,

No. 233.

No. 232–2 blades, ebony handle, iron lined, 3¼ in.,
No. 233–2 blades, cocoa handle, iron lined, 3½ in.,
No. 239–2 blades, cocoa handle, iron lined, with shield, 3½ in.,

No. 209.

No. 112 –1 blade, cocoa handle, iron lined, 3½ in.,
No. 209 –2 blades, cocoa handle, iron lined, 3⅓ in.,
No. 210 –2 blades, ebony handle, iron lined, 3½ in.,
No. 210½–2 blades, white bone handle, iron lined, 3½ in.,
No. 122 –1 extra heavy blade, ebony handle, brass lined, 3⅞ in.,
No. 142 –1 extra heavy blade, ebony handle, iron lined, 4⅛ in.,

HALF DOZEN IN A BOX.

POCKET KNIVES.

HIBBARD, SPENCER, BARTLETT & CO'S "OUR VERY BEST," WARRANTED.

No. 728.

No. **741**—3 blades, stag handle, crocus polished, rope milled German silver lining. 3   in.,   ·
No. **742**—3 blades, pearl handle, crocus polished, rope milled German silver lining, 3   in.,   ·
No. **727**—3 blades, stag handle, crocus polished, rope milled German silver lining, 3¼ in.,   ·
No. **728**—3 blades, pearl handle, crocus polished, rope milled German silver lining, 3¼ in.,   ,

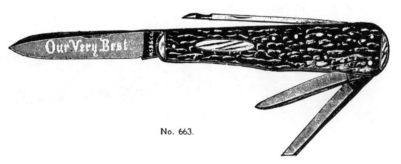

No. 663.

No. **663**—3 blades, stag handle, brass lined, crocus polished, 3⅛ in.,   ·   ·   ·   ·   ·
No. **664**—3 blades, pearl handle, brass lined, crocus polished, 3⅛ in.,   ·   ·   ·   ·   ·

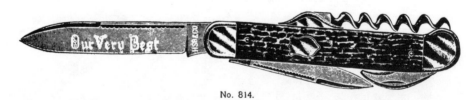

No. 814.

No. **814**—Stag handle, brass lined, crocus polished, 3¼ in.,   ·   ·   ·   ·   ·   ·
No. **815**—Pearl handle, brass lined, crocus polished, 3¼ in.,   ·   ·   ·   ·   ·

No. 756.

No. **755**—3 blades, stag handle, brass lined, crocus polished, 3⅝ in.,   ·   ·   ·   ·
No. **756**—3 blades, pearl handle, brass lined. crocus polished, 3⅝ in.,   ·   ·   ·   ·

HALF DOZEN IN A BOX.

POCKET KNIVES.

HIBBARD, SPENCER, BARTLETT & CO'S, WARRANTED.

No. 222.

No. 119–1 blade, cocoa handle, iron lined, crocus polished, 3⅜ in., · · ·
No. 222–2 blades, cocoa handle, iron lined, crocus polished, 3⅜ in., · · ·
No. 263–2 blades, stag   handle, iron lined, glazed, hollow bolster, 3⅜ in., · · ·
No. 266–2 blades, stag   handle, iron lined, glazed, hollow bolster, 3⅝ in., · · ·

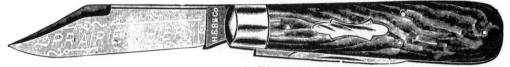

No. 377.

No. 377 –2 blades, cocoa handle, iron lined, glazed, etched "Prairie Chief," 3½ in., · ·
No. 377½–2 blades, ebony handle, iron lined, glazed, etched "Prairie Chief," 3½ in., · ·
No. 366 –2 blades, cocoa handle, brass lined, crocus polished, etched "Rustler," 3⅝ in., ·
No. 367 –2 blades, ebony handle, brass lined, crocus polished, etched "Rustler," 3⅝ in., ·
No. 148 –1 blade, cocoa handle, iron lined, crocus polished, etched "Rustler," 3⅝ in., ·
No. 204 –2 blades, cocoa handle, iron lined, crocus polished, etched "Rustler," 3⅝ in., ·
No. 267 –2 blades, white bone handle, iron lined, crocus polished, etched "Rustler," 3⅝ in., ·
No. 431 –2 blades, ebony handle, iron lined, crocus polished, etched "Rustler." 3¾ in., ·

No. 425.

No. 203–2 blades, cocoa handle, iron lined, crocus polished, 3⅝ in., · · · · ·
No. 243–2 blades, cocoa handle, brass lined, glazed, not etched, 3½ in., · · · ·
No. 147–1 blade, cocoa handle, iron lined, crocus polished, etched "Rustler," 3½ in., ·
No. 425–2 blades, cocoa handle, iron lined, crocus polished, etched "Rustler," 3¾ in., ·
No. 426–2 blades, ebony handle iron lined, crocus polished, etched "Rustler," 3¾ in., · ·

No. 205.

No. 149–1 blade, cocoa handle, iron lined, crocus polished, 3½ in., · · · · ·
No. 205–2 blades, cocoa handle, iron lined, crocus polished, 3⅝ in., · · · · ·
No. 429–2 blades, cocoa handle, brass lined, crocus polished, 3½ in., · · · · ·

No. 230.

No. 229–2 blades, cocoa handle, iron   lined, 3⅝ in., · · · · · ·
No. 230–2 blades, ebony handle, brass lined, 3⅝ in., · · · · · ·
HALF DOZEN IN A BOX.

POCKET KNIVES.

HIBBARD, SPENCER, BARTLETT & CO'S "OUR VERY BEST," WARRANTED.

No. 461½–2 blades, stag handle, brass lined, crocus polished, 3⅛ in.,   ·   ·   ·   ·   ·

No. 462.

No. 461–2 blades, buffalo handle, brass lined, crocus polished, 3⅛ in.,   ·   ·   ·   ·
No. 462–2 blades, ivory   handle, brass lined, crocus polished, 3⅛ in.,   ·   ·   ·   ·
No. 463–2 blades, pearl   handle, brass lined, crocus polished, 3⅛ in.,   ·   ·   ·   ·

No. 441.

No. 439–2 blades, cocoa handle, brass lined, crocus polished, 3⅜ in.,   ·   ·   ·   ·
No. 440–2 blades, ebony handle, brass lined, crocus polished, 3⅜ in.,   ·   ·   ·   ·
No. 441–2 blades, stag   handle, brass lined, crocus polished, 3⅜ in.,   ·   ·   ·   ·
No. 442–2 blades, ivory handle, brass lined, crocus polished, 3⅜ in..   ·   ·   ·   ·

No. 540.

No. 540–2 blades, ebony handle, brass lined, crocus polished, 3⅜ in.,   ·   ·   ·   ·
No. 541–2 blades, stag   handle, brass lined, crocus polished, 3⅜ in.,   ·   ·   ·   ·
No. 542–2 blades, ivory handle, brass lined, crocus polished, 3⅜ in.,   ·   ·   ·   ·

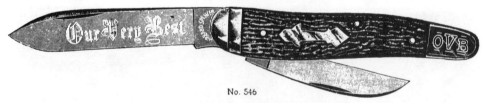

No. 546

No. 546   –2 blades, stag handle, brass lined, crocus polished, 3½ in.,   ·   ·   ·   ·
No. 547½–2 blades, white bone handle, brass lined, crocus polished, 3½ in.,   ·   ·   ·

No. 162–1 blade, budding, buffalo handle, brass lined, ivory end, crocus polished, 4⅞ in.,   ·

HALF DOZEN IN A BOX.

POCKET KNIVES.

HIBBARD, SPENCER, BARTLETT & CO'S, WARRANTED.

No. 241.

No. 240–2 blades, cocoa handle, iron lined, 3½ in., ...
No. 241–2 blades, ebony handle, iron lined, 3½ in., ...

No. 215.

No. 227–2 blades, cocoa handle, iron   lined, glazed, not etched, 3½ in., ...
No. 213–2 blades, cocoa handle, brass lined, crocus polished, etched "Rustler," 3½ in., .
No. 214–2 blades, ebony handle, brass lined, crocus polished, etched "Rustler," 3½ in., .
No. 215–2 blades, white bone handle, brass lined, crocus polished, etched "Rustler," 3½ in.,

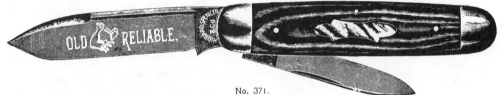

No. 371.

No. 298–2 blades, cocoa handle, brass lined, glazed, not etched, 3¼ in., ...
No. 246–2 blades, cocoa handle, iron   lined, glazed, not etched, 3½ in., ...
No. 247–2 blades, ebony handle, iron   lined, glazed, not etched, 3½ in., ...
No. 248–2 blades, stag   handle, iron   lined, glazed, not etched, 3½ in., ...
No. 225–2 blades, cocoa handle, iron   lined, glazed, not etched, 3⅝ in., ...
No. 371–2 blades, cocoa handle, brass lined, crocus polished, etched, 3⅝ in., ...
No. 372–2 blades, ebony handle, brass lined, crocus polished, etched, 3⅝ in., ...
No. 373–2 blades, stag· handle, brass lined, crocus polished, etched, 3⅝ in., ...

No. 350.

No. 352–2 blades, ebony handle, brass lined, 3⅝ in., ...
No. 350–2 blades, stag   handle, brass lined, 3⅝ in., ...

No. 307.

No. 306–2 blades, cocoa handle, brass lined, 3⅝ in., ...
No. 307–2 blades, ebony handle, brass lined, 3⅝ in., ...
No. 304–2 blades, stag   handle, brass lined, 3⅝ in., ...
No. 308–2 blades, white bone handle, brass lined, 3⅝ in., ...

HALF DOZEN IN A BOX.

POCKET KNIVES.

HIBBARD, SPENCER, BARTLETT & CO'S, WARRANTED.

No. 238.

No. 216–2 blades, cocoa handle, iron lined, 3¾ in., ·   ·   ·   ·   ·   ·
No. 237–2 blades, cocoa handle, brass lined, 3¾ in., ·   ·   ·   ·   ·
No. 238–2 blades, ebony handle, brass lined, 3¾ in., ·   ·   ·   ·   ·

No. 430.

No. 123–1 blade, cocoa handle, brass lined, plain blade, 3⅞ in., ·   ·   ·   ·
No. 340–2 blades, cocoa handle, iron lined, plain blade, 3⅞ in., ·   ·   ·
No. 339–2 blades, ebony handle, iron lined, plain blade, 3⅞ in., ·   ·   ·   ·
No. 430–2 blades, ebony handle, iron lined, crocus polished, etched, 3⅞ in., ·   ·
No. 226–2 blades, ebony handle, brass lined, plain blade, double thick, 3⅞ in.,

No. 341–2 blades, cocoa handle, iron lined, 3⅞ in., ·   ·   ·   ·   ·   ·

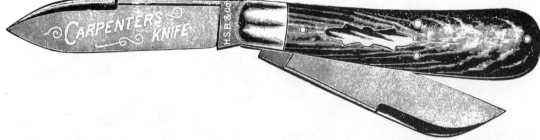

No. 242–2 blades, cocoa handle, iron lined, 3⅞ in., ·   ·   ·   ·   ·

No. 223.

No. 223–2 blades, cocoa handle, iron lined, crocus polished, extra heavy, 3⅞ in., ·   ·
No. 251–2 blades, cocoa handle, iron lined, etched "Hercules," 4⅛ in., ·   ·   ·
No. 563–2 blades, white bone handle, iron lined, crocus polished, extra heavy, etched "Rustler," 3⅞ in
    per dozen ·   ·   ·   ·   ·   ·   ·   ·   ·   ·   ·   ·
HALF DOZEN IN A BOX.

POCKET KNIVES.

HIBBARD, SPENCER, BARTLETT & CO'S, WARRANTED.

No. 211.

No. 211–2 blades, ebony handle, brass lined, crocus polished, 3⅛ in.,　•　‹　•　·
No. 244–2 blades, ebony handle, brass lined, glazed, not etched, 3⅛ in.,　•　·　·　•

No. 212–2 blades, ebony handle, brass lined, crocus polished, 3⅛ in.,　•　·　•　·

No.. 253.

No. 252–2 blades, cocoa handle, brass lined, glazed, 3⅜ in., ·　•　·　·　•　·　·
No. 253–2 blades, stag　handle, brass lined, glazed, 3⅜ in., ·　·　·　·　·

No. 844.

No. 379–2 blades, stag handle, iron　lined, glazed, 3⅜ in., ·　·　•　·　•　·　•
No. 844–4 blades, stag handle, brass lined, glazed, 3⅜ in., ·　·　·　·　·　·

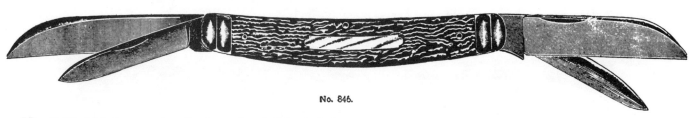

No. 846.

No. 845–4 blades, stag handle, brass lined, glazed, 3½ in., ·　•　·　•　·　•
No. 562–2 blades, stag handle, iron　lined, crocus polished, etched "Rustler," 3¾ in.,　•
No. 846–4 blades, stag handle, brass lined, glazed, 3⅞ in., ·　·　·　·　·　·
No. 847–4 blades, stag handle, brass lined, glazed, 4¼ in.; ·　·　·　·　·　·
HALF DOZEN IN A BOX.

POCKET KNIVES.

HIBBARD, SPENCER, BARTLETT & CO'S, WARRANTED.

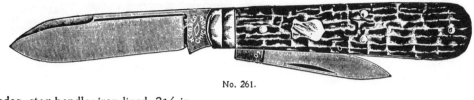

No. 261.

No. 261–2 blades, stag handle, iron lined, 3⅜ in., · · · · · · · ·
No. 264–2 blades, stag handle, iron lined, 3⅝ in.. · · · · · · · ·

No. 265.

No. 262–2 blades, stag handle, iron lined, 3⅜ in., · · · · · · ·
No. 265–2 blades, stag handle, iron lined, 3⅝ in., · · · · · · ·

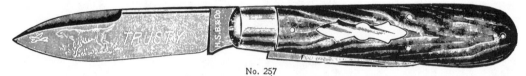

No. 257

No. 257–2 blades, cocoa handle, iron lined, etched "Trusty," 3⅝ in., · · · ·
No. 258–2 blades, ebony handle, iron lined, etched "Trusty," 3⅝ in., · · · ·
No. 259–2 blades, cocoa handle, brass lined, etched "Trusty," 3⅝ in., · · · ·
No. 260–2 blades, ebony handle, brass lined, etched "Trusty," 3⅝ in., · · · ·
No. 427–2 blades, cocoa handle, iron lined, crocus polished, etched "Rustler," 3⅝ in., ·
No. 428–2 blades, ebony handle, iron lined, crocus polished, etched "Rustler," 3⅝ in., ·

No. 276.

No. 274–2 blades, cocoa handle, brass lined, beveled blade, 3¾ in., · · · ·
No. 276–2 blades, ebony handle, brass lined, beveled blade, 3¾ in., · · · ·

No. 120.

No. 120–1 blade, cocoa handle, iron lined, 3⅞ in., · · · · · · ·
No. 219–2 blades, cocoa handle, iron lined, 3⅞ in., · · · · · · ·

HALF DOZEN IN A BOX.

POCKET KNIVES.

HIBBARD, SPENCER, BARTLETT & CO'S, WARRANTED.

No. 666.

No. 605–3 blades, cocoa handle, iron lined, glazed, not etched, 3¾ in.,   ·   ·   ·   ·

No. 666–3 blades, ebony handle. brass lined. crocus polished, etched "Rustler," 3¾ in.,   ·

No. 601.

No. 601–3 blades, cocoa handle, brass lined, glazed, 3¾ in., ·   ·   ·   ·   ·   ·

No. 604–3 blades, ebony handle, brass lined, glazed, 3¾ in., ·   ·   ·   ·   ·   ·

No. 683.

No. 606–3 blades, cocoa handle, iron lined, glazed, not etched, 3⅝ in.,   ·   ·   ·   ·

No. 683–3 blades, ebony handle, brass lined, glazed, etched, 3⅝ in.,   ·   ·   ·   ·

No. 684–3 blades, stag handle, brass lined, glazed, etched, 3⅝ in.,   ·   ·   ·   ·

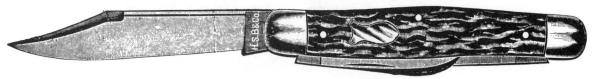

No. 687.

No. 686–3 blades, stag handle, brass lined, clip, marking and speying blades, 4⅛ in.,   ·   ·

No. 687–3 blades, stag handle, brass lined, clip, marking and pen blades, 4⅛ in.,   ·   ·

HALF DOZEN IN A BOX.

POCKET KNIVES.

HIBBARD, SPENCER, BARTLETT & CO'S, WARRANTED.

No. 228–2 blades, stag handle, iron lined, full crocus polished, 4 in., ...

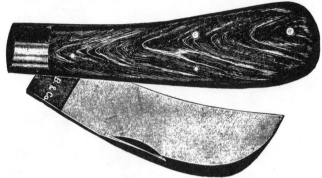

No. 128–1 blade, pruner. cocoa handle, iron lined, 4 in., ...

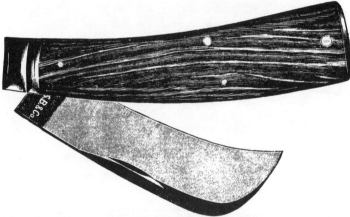

No. 129–1 blade, pruner, cocoa handle, iron lined, seal cap, 4½ in., ...

No. 164–1 blade. pruner, stag handle, iron lined, seal cap crocus polished, 4½ in., . . .

HALF DOZEN IN A BOX.

POCKET KNIVES.

HIBBARD, SPENCER, BARTLETT & CO'S, WARRANTED.

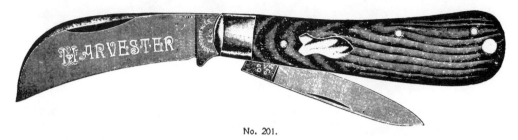

No. 201.

No. 101–1 blade, cocoa handle, iron lined, 3¾ in., for binder twine, ...

No. 201–2 blades, cocoa handle, iron lined, 3¾ in., for binder twine, ...

No. 691–3 blades, stag handle, brass lined, crocus polished, 4¼ in., ...

No. 561–2 blades, stag handle, iron lined, crocus polished, 4⅜ in., ...

No. 370–2 blades, cocoa handle, brass lined, 4¼ in., ...

HALF DOZEN IN A BOX.

POCKET KNIVES.

HIBBARD, SPENCER, BARTLETT & CO'S, WARRANTED.

No. 250.

No. 249–2 blades, ebony handle, iron lined, 3⅝ in., ...
No. 250–2 blades, stag   handle, iron lined, 3⅝ in., ...

No. 349.

No. 348½–2 blades, cocoa handle, brass lined, 3¾ in., ...
No. 349 –2 blades, ebony handle, brass lined, 3¾ in., ...
No. 374 –2 blades, stag   handle, brass lined, 3¾ in., ...

No. 676

No. 676–3 blades, cocoa handle, brass lined, crocus polished, 3½ in., ...
No. 677–3 blades, ebony handle, brass lined, crocus polished, 3½ in., ...
No. 678–3 blades, stag   handle, brass lined, crocus polished, 3½ in., ...

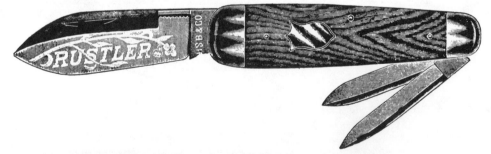

No. 667–3 blades, cocoa handle, brass lined, extra heavy blade, crocus polished, 3½ in.,   .

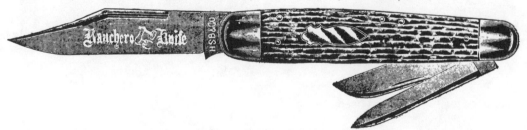

No. 682–3 blades, stag handle, brass lined, 3¾ in., ...
HALF DOZEN IN A BOX.

POCKET KNIVES.

HIBBARD, SPENCER, BARTLETT & CO'S, WARRANTED.

No. 574P–2 blades, ebony handle, brass lined, large blade crocus polished. 3¾ in.,　·　·

No. 251P.

No. 237P–2 blades, cocoa　handle, brass lined, large blade crocus polished, 3¾ in.,　·　·
No. 238P–2 blades, ebony handle, brass lined, large blade crocus polished, 3¾ in.,　·　·
No. 251P–2 blades, cocoa　handle, iron　lined, large blade crocus polished, 4　in.,　·　·
No. 280P–2 blades, ebony　handle, brass lined, large blade crocus polished, 3⅞ in.,　·　·

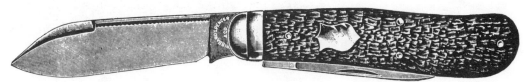

No. 575P.

No. 575P–2 blades, stag　handle, iron　lined, large blade crocus polished, 3¾ in.,　·　·
No. 576P–2 blades, ebony handle, brass lined, large blade crocus polished, 3¾ in.,　·　·

No. 578P.

No. 578P–2 blades, cocoa handle, iron lined, large blade crocus polished, 3¾ in.,　·　·　·
No. 577P–2 blades, stag　handle, iron lined, large blade crocus polished, 3¾ in.,　·　·

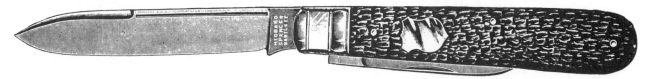

No. 580P–2 blades, stag handle, brass lined, large blade crocus polished, 4⅜ in.,　·　·

HALF DOZEN IN A BOX.

POCKET KNIVES.

HIBBARD, SPENCER, BARTLETT & CO'S, WARRANTED.

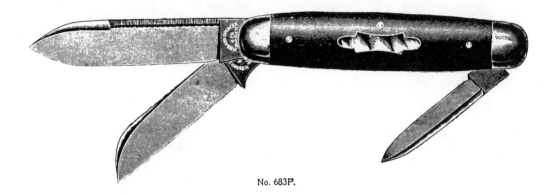

No. 683P.

No. 683P–3 blades, ebony handle, brass lined, large blade crocus polished, 3⅝ in., • • •
No. 684P–3 blades, stag   handle, brass lined, large blade crocus polished, 3⅝ in., • • •

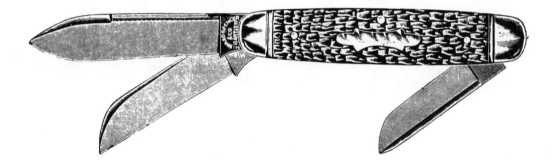

No. 685P–3 blades, stag handle, brass lined, large blade crocus polished, 3⅝ in., • • •

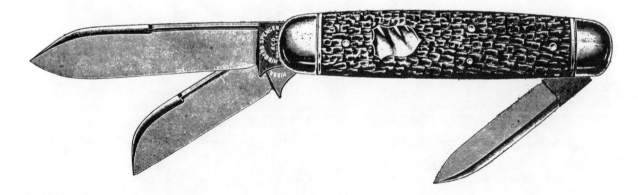

No. 691P–3 blades, stag handle, brass lined, large blade crocus polished, 4¼ in., • • •

HALF DOZEN IN A BOX.

POCKET KNIVES.

HIBBARD, SPENCER, BARTLETT & CO'S, WARRANTED

No. 328P

No. 252P--2 blades, cocoa handle, brass lined, large blade crocus polished, 3⅜ in.,   ·   ·
No. 254P--2 blades, buffalo handle, brass lined, large blade crocus polished, 3⅜ in.,   ·   ·
No. 253P--2 blades, stag   handle, brass lined, large blade crocus polished, 3⅜ in.,   ·   ·
No. 327P--2 blades, ebony handle, brass lined, large blade crocus polished, 3⅝ in.,   ·   ·
No. 328P--2 blades, stag   handle, brass lined, large blade crocus polished, 3⅝ in.,   ·   ·

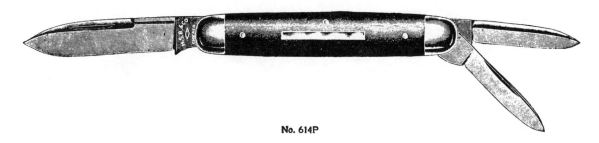

No. 614P

No. 614P-3 blades, buffalo handle, brass lined, large blade crocus polished, 3¼ in.,   ·   ·
No. 615P-3 blades, stag   handle, brass lined, large blade crocus polished, 3¼ in.,   ·   ·

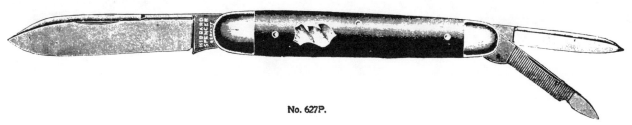

No. 627P.

No. 627P-3 blades, buffalo handle, brass lined, large blade crocus polished, 3⅝ in.,   ·   ·
No. 626P-3 blades, stag   handle, brass lined, large blade crocus polished, 3⅝ in.,   ·   ·

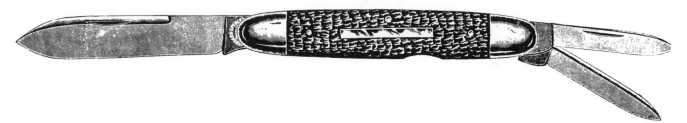

No. 625P-3 blades, stag handle, brass lined, large blade crocus polished, 3⅞ in.,   ·   ·   ·

HALF DOZEN IN A BOX.

POCKET KNIVES.

HIBBARD, SPENCER, BARTLETT & CO'S, WARRANTED.

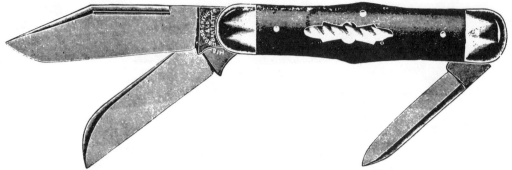

No. 604P–3 blades, ebony handle, brass lined, large blade crocus polished, 3¾ in.,   ·   ·

No. 666P–3 blades, ebony handle, brass lined, large blade crocus polished, 3¾ in.,   ·   ·

No. 667P–3 blades, cocoa handle, brass lined, large blade crocus polished, 3¾ in.,   ·

No. 631P.

No. 624P–3 blades, stag handle, iron lined, large blade crocus polished, 3⅝ in.,   ·   ·
No. 631P–3 blades, stag handle, brass lined, large blade crocus polished, 4   in.,   ·   ·

HALF DOZEN IN A BOX.

POCKET KNIVES.

HIBBARD, SPENCER, BARTLETT & CO'S "OUR VERY BEST," WARRANTED.

No. 783

No. **782**—3 blades, ebony handle, brass lined, crocus polished, 3⅝ in., ·   ·   ·   ·   ·
No. **783**—3 blades, stag   handle, brass lined, crocus polished, 3⅝ in., ·   ·   ·   ·   ·
No. **784**—3 blades, ivory handle, brass lined, crocus polished, 3⅝ in., ·   ·   ·   ·   ·
No. **785**—3 blades, pearl handle, brass lined, crocus polished, 3⅝ in., ·   ·   ·   ·   ·

No. **743**—3 blades, stag handle, crocus polished, 4 in., ·   ·   ·   ·   ·   ·   ·   ·

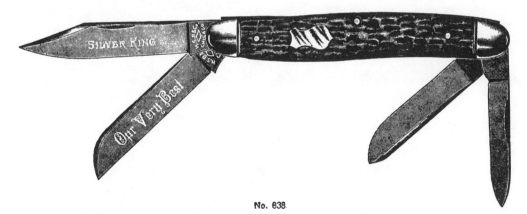

No. 838

No. **838**—4 blades, stag handle, rope milled German silver lining, crocus polished, 3⅞ in.,   ·   ·
No. **843**—4 blades, pearl handle, rope milled German silver lining, crocus polished, 3⅞ in.,   ·

No. **828**—4 blades, stag handle, brass lined, crocus polished, 3⅞ in., ·   ·   ·   ·   ·

HALF DOZEN IN A BOX.

POCKET KNIVES.

HIBBARD, SPENCER, BARTLETT & CO'S "OUR VERY BEST," WARRANTED.

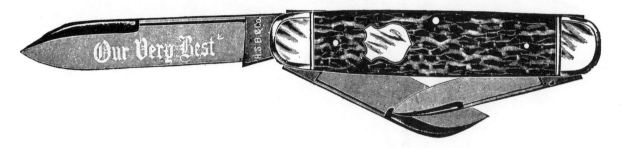

No. 724–3 blades, stag handle, brass lined, crocus polished, 4¼ in.,　·　·　·　·　·

No. 723–3 blades, stag handle, brass lined, crocus polished, 4¼ in.,　·　·　·　·　·

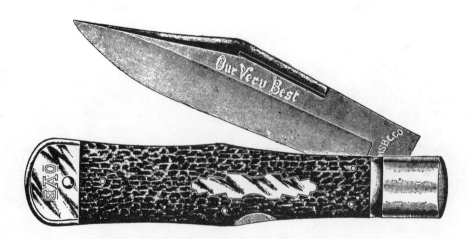

No. 156–1 blade, stag handle, brass lined, crocus polished, lock back, 5½ in. handle, 4⅝ in. blade,

HALF DOZEN IN A BOX.

POCKET KNIVES.

HIBBARD, SPENCER, BARTLETT & CO'S "OUR VERY BEST." WARRANTED.

No. 707–3 blades, stag handle, brass lined, crocus polished, 3¾ in.,　·　·　·　·　·

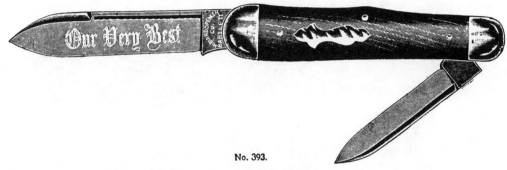

No. 393.

No. 393–2 blades, cocoa handle, brass lined, crocus polished, 3⅝ in.,　·　·　·　·
No. 394–2 blades, ebony handle, brass lined, crocus polished, 3⅝ in.,　·　·　·　·
No. 406–2 blades, cocoa handle, brass lined, crocus polished, single spring, 3⅝ in.,　·　·
No. 407–2 blades, stag　handle, brass lined, crocus polished, single spring, 3⅝ in.,　·　·

No. 703.

No. 700–3 blades, cocoa handle, brass lined, crocus polished, 3⅝ in.,　·　·　·　·
No. 701–3 blades, ebony handle, brass lined, crocus polished, 3⅝ in.,　·　·　·　·
No. 702–3 blades, stag　handle, brass lined, crocus polished, hollow bolsters, 3⅝ in.,　·　·
No. 703–3 blades, pearl handle, brass lined, crocus polished, 3⅝ in.,　·　·　·　·

No. 718.

No. 794–3 blades, ebony handle, brass lined, crocus polished, large blade clip point, 3⅝ in.,　·
No. 718–3 blades, stag　handle, brass lined, crocus polished, large blade spear point, 3⅝ in.,　·

HALF DOZEN IN A BOX.

POCKET KNIVES.

HIBBARD, SPENCER, BARTLETT & CO'S "OUR VERY BEST," WARRANTED.

No. 432.

No. 432 –2 blades, cocoa handle, brass lined, crocus polished, 3½ in .   •   •   •   •
No. 433 –2 blades, ebony handle, brass lined, crocus polished, 3½ in.,   •   •   •   •
No. 434 –2 blades, stag   handle, brass lined, crocus polished, 3½ in.,   •   •   •   •
No. 434½–2 blades, white bone handle, brass lined, crocus polished, 3½ in., -   •   •   •
No. 435 –2 blades, pearl handle brass lined, crocus polished, 3½ in.,   •   •   •   •

No. 422.

No. 422–2 blades, cocoa handle, brass lined, crocus polished, 3½ in.,   •   •   •   •
No. 423 2 blades, ebony handle, brass lined, crocus polished, 3½ in ,   •   •   •   •
No. 424–2 blades, stag   handle, brass lined, crocus polished, 3½ in.,   •   •   •   •

No. 388.

No. 387–2 blades, cocoa handle, brass lined, crocus polished, 3½ in.,   •   •   •   •
No. 388–2 blades, ebony handle, brass lined, crocus polished, 3½ in.,   •   •   •   •
No. 389–2 blades, stag   handle, brass lined, crocus polished, hollow bolsters, 3½ in.,   •

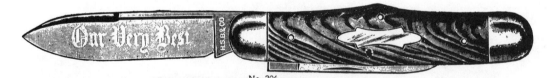

No. 396.

No. 396–2 blades, cocoa handle, brass lined, crocus polished, 3⅞ in.,   •   •   •   •
No. 397–2 blades, ebony handle, brass lined, crocus polished, 3⅞ in.,   •   •   •   •
No. 398–2 blades, stag   handle, brass lined, crocus polished, hollow bolsters, 3⅞ in.,   •   •

No. 408–2 blades, pearl handle, brass lined, crocus polished, 3⅞ in.,   •   •   •   •

HALF DOZEN IN A BOX.

POCKET KNIVES.

HIBBARD, SPENCER, BARTLETT & CO'S, WARRANTED.

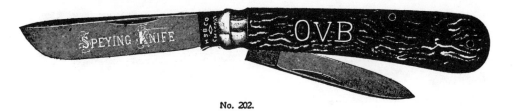

No. 202.

No. 102–1 blade, iron handle, speying knife, 3½ in., · · · · · ·
No. 202–2 blades, iron handle, speying knife, 3½ in., · · · · ·

No. 104–1 blade, speying, cocoa handle, iron lined, 3½ in., · · · · ·

No. 220.

No. 111½–1 blade, cocoa handle, iron lined, glazed, not etched, 3½ in., , · · ·
No. 234 –2 blades, cocoa handle, iron lined, glazed, not etched, 3½ in., · · · ·
No. 117 –1 blade, cocoa handle, iron lined, crocus polished, etched "Old Hickory," 3⅜ in., ·
No. 220 –2 blades, cocoa handle, iron lined, crocus polished, etched "Old Hickory," 3⅜ in., ·

No. 221.

No. 118–1 blade, cocoa handle, iron lined, crocus polished, 3⅜ in., · · · · ·
No. 221–2 blades, cocoa handle, iron lined, crocus polished, 3⅜ in., · · · · ·
No. 236–2 blades, cocoa handle, iron lined, glazed, not etched, 3½ in., · · · · ·

No. 218.

No. 235–2 blades, cocoa handle, iron lined, 3½ in., · · · · · ·
No. 116–1 blade, ebony handle, iron lined, 3¾ in., · · · · · ·
No. 217–2 blades, cocoa handle, iron lined, 3⅞ in., · · · · · ·
No. 218–2 blades, ebony handle, iron lined, 3⅞ in., · · · · · ·

HALF DOZEN IN A BOX.

POCKET KNIVES.

HIBBARD, SPENCER, BARTLETT & CO'S "OUR VERY BEST," WARRANTED.

No. 469–2 blades, stag handle, brass lined, crocus polished, 3½ in., · · · · ·

No .499.

No. 496–2 blades, cocoa handle, brass lined, crocus polished, 3¾ in., · · · · ·
No. 497–2 blades, ebony handle, brass lined, crocus polished, 3¾ in., · · · · ·
No. 499–2 blades, stag   handle, brass lined, crocus polished, 3¾ in., · · · · ·
No. 498–2 blades, ivory   handle, brass lined, crocus polished, 3¾ in., · · · · ·

No. 392.

No. 392–2 blades, stag handle, brass lined, crocus polished, 3½ in., · · · · ·
No. 402–2 blades, stag handle, brass lined, crocus polished, 3⅞ in., · · · · ·

No. 400.

No. 390–2 blades, cocoa handle, brass lined, crocus polished, 3½ in., · · · · ·
No. 391–2 blades, ebony handle, brass lined, crocus polished, 3½ in., · · · · ·
No. 400–2 blades, cocoa handle, brass lined, crocus polished, 3⅞ in., · · · · ·
No. 401–2 blades, ebony handle, brass lined, crocus polished, 3⅞ in., · · · · ·

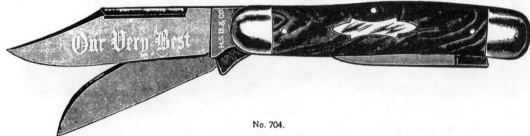

No. 704.

No. 704–3 blades, cocoa handle, brass lined, crocus polished, 3⅞ in., · · · · ·
No. 705–3 blades, ebony handle, brass lined, crocus polished, 3⅞ in., · · · · ·
No. 706–3 blades, stag   handle, brass lined, crocus polished, hollow bolsters, 3⅞ in., · ·

HALF DOZEN IN A BOX.

POCKET KNIVES.

HIBBARD, SPENCER, BARTLETT & CO'S "OUR VERY BEST," WARRANTED.

No. 325–1 blade, with button hook, pearl handle, brass lined, 2⅝ in..   · · · ·

No. 409.

No. 409–2 blades, shell handle, brass lined, crocus polished, 2⅝ in.,   · · · ·
No. 410–2 blades, pearl handle, brass lined, crocus polished, 2⅝ in.,   · · · ·

No. 585.

No. 583–2 blades, buffalo handle, brass lined, crocus polished, 3 in.,   · · · · ·
No. 584–2 blades, stag   handle, brass lined, crocus polished, 3 in.,   · · · · ·
No. 585–2 blades, pearl   handle, brass lined, crocus polished, 3 in.,   · · · · ·

No. 505.

No. 504–2 blades, stag   handle, brass lined, crocus polished, 3 in.,   · · · · ·
No. 505–2 blades, pearl handle, brass lined, crocus polished, 3 in.,   · · · · ·

No. 495–2 blades, pearl handle, German silver lined, crocus polished, 2⅝ in.,   · · ·

No. 744.

No. 744–3 blades, pearl handle, German silver lined, crocus polished, 2⅝ in.,   · · ·
No. 776–3 blades, pearl handle, German silver lined, crocus polished, 2⅞ in.,   · · ·

HALF DOZEN IN A BOX.

POCKET KNIVES.

HIBBARD, SPENCER, BARTLETT & CO'S "OUR VERY BEST," WARRANTED.

No. 740–3 blades, pearl handle, German silver lined, crocus polished, 2¼ in., ·   ·   ·   ·

No. 745–3 blades, pearl handle, German silver lined, crocus polished, with tortoise shell nail cleaner, 2⅝ in.,
per dozen ·   ·   ·   ·   ·   ·   ·   ·   ·   ·   ·   ·   ·   ·   ·   ·

No. 761–3 blades, pearl handle, German silver lined, crocus polished, 3 in., ·   ·   ·   ·

No. 380–2 blades, stag handle, brass lined, crocus polished, 3 in., ·   ·   ·   ·   ·

No. 362.

No. 528–2 blades, ivory handle, brass lined, crocus polished, 2¾ in., ·   ·   ·   ·   ·
No. 530–2 blades, pearl handle, brass lined, crocus polished, 2¾ in., ·   ·   ·   ·   ·
No. 363–2 blades, stag handle, brass lined, crocus polished, 3   in., ·   ·   ·   ·   ·
No. 360–2 blades, ivory handle, brass lined, crocus polished, 3   in., ·   ·   ·   ·   ·
No. 362–2 blades, pearl handle, brass lined, crocus polished, 3   in., ·   ·   ·   ·   ·

HALF DOZEN IN A BOX.

POCKET KNIVES.

HIBBARD, SPENCER, BARTLETT & CO'S "OUR VERY BEST," WARRANTED.

No. 798.

No. **798**–3 blades, ebony handle, brass lined, crocus polished, 3⅝ in., ·   ·   ·   ·   per dozen

No. **757**–3 blades, stag   handle, rope milled German silver lining, crocus polished, lock back, 3⅞ in.,
per dozen   ·   ·   ·   ·   ·   ·   ·   ·   ·   ·   ·   ·   ·   ·   ·

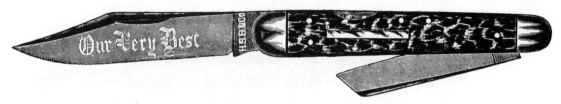

No. **527**–2 blades, stag handle, brass lined, crocus polished, lock back, 3⅞ in.,   ·   ·   ·

No. **127**–1 blade, cocoa handle, brass lined, lock back, crocus polished, 4½ in.,   -   -   -

No. **143**–1 blade, stag handle, brass lined, lock back, crocus polished, 4½ in.,   -   -   -

HALF DOZEN IN A BOX.

POCKET KNIVES.

HIBBARD, SPENCER, BARTLETT & CO'S "OUR VERY BEST," WARRANTED.

No. 793–3 blades, pearl handle, German silver lined, crocus polished, 2⅝ in.,   ·   ·   ·

No. 753.

No. 753–3 blades, stag handle, German silver lined, crocus polished, 2¾ in.,   ·   ·   ·
No. 754–3 blades, pearl handle, German silver lined, crocus polished, 2¾ in.,   ·   ·   ·

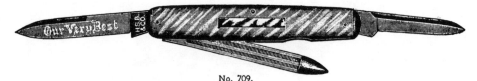

No. 709.

No. 709–3 blades, pearl handle, brass lined, crocus polished, 2¾ in.,   ·   ·   ·   ·
No. 822–4 blades, pearl handle, brass lined, crocus polished, 2¾ in.,   ·   ·   ·   ·

No. 837.

No. 531–2 blades, ivory handle, German silver lined, crocus polished, 2¾ in.,   ·   ·   ·
No. 532–2 blades, shell handle, German silver lined, crocus polished, 2¾ in.,   ·   ·   ·
No. 533–2 blades, pearl handle, German silver lined, crocus polished, 2¾ in.,   ·   ·   ·
No. 837–4 blades, pearl handle, German silver lined, crocus polished, 2¾ in.,   ·   ·   ·

No. 839.

No. 520–2 blades, stag handle, brass lined, crocus polished, 3 in.,   ·   ·   ·   ·   ·
No. 839–4 blades, stag handle, brass lined, crocus polished, 3 in.,   ·   ·   ·   ·   ·

HALF DOZEN IN A BOX.

POCKET KNIVES.

HIBBARD, SPENCER, BARTLETT & CO'S "OUR VERY BEST," WARRANTED.

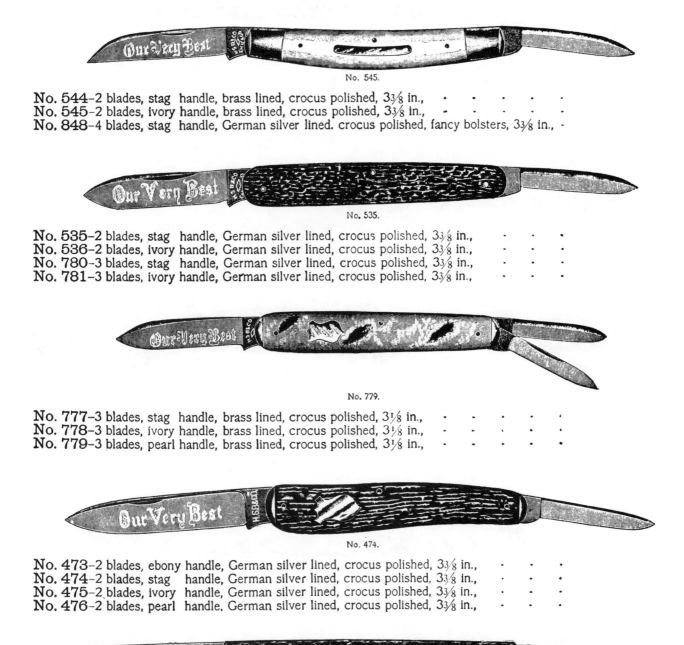

No. 545.

No. 544–2 blades, stag handle, brass lined, crocus polished, 3⅜ in.,   ·   ·   ·   ·
No. 545–2 blades, ivory handle, brass lined, crocus polished, 3⅜ in.,   ·   ·   ·   ·
No. 848–4 blades, stag handle, German silver lined. crocus polished, fancy bolsters, 3⅜ in., ·

No. 535.

No. 535–2 blades, stag handle, German silver lined, crocus polished, 3⅜ in.,   ·   ·   ·
No. 536–2 blades, ivory handle, German silver lined, crocus polished, 3⅜ in.,   ·   ·   ·
No. 780–3 blades, stag handle, German silver lined, crocus polished, 3⅜ in.,   ·   ·   ·
No. 781–3 blades, ivory handle, German silver lined, crocus polished, 3⅜ in.,   ·   ·   ·

No. 779.

No. 777–3 blades, stag handle, brass lined, crocus polished, 3⅛ in.,   ·   ·   ·   ·   ·
No. 778–3 blades, ivory handle, brass lined, crocus polished, 3⅛ in.,   ·   ·   ·   ·   ·
No. 779–3 blades, pearl handle, brass lined, crocus polished, 3⅛ in.,   ·   ·   ·   ·   ·

No. 474.

No. 473–2 blades, ebony handle, German silver lined, crocus polished, 3⅜ in.,   ·   ·   ·
No. 474–2 blades, stag   handle, German silver lined, crocus polished, 3⅜ in.,   ·   ·   ·
No. 475–2 blades, ivory handle, German silver lined, crocus polished, 3⅜ in.,   ·   ·   ·
No. 476–2 blades, pearl handle. German silver lined, crocus polished, 3⅜ in.,   ·   ·   ·

No. 842–4 blades, stag handle, German silver lined, crocus polished, 3¾ in.,   ·   ·   ·
HALF DOZEN IN A BOX.

POCKET KNIVES.

HIBBARD, SPENCER, BARTLETT & CO'S "OUR VERY BEST," WARRANTED.

No. 759

No. **759**-3 blades, ebony handle, brass lined, crocus polished, 3⅛ in.,   ·   ·   ·   ·
No. **760**-3 blades, stag   handle, brass lined, crocus polished, hollow bolsters, 3⅛ in., ·   ·
No. **769**-3 blades, pearl handle, brass lined, crocus polished, 3⅛ in.,   ·   ·   ·

No. **762**-3 blades, stag handle, brass lined, crocus polished, 3⅜ in.,   ·   ·   ·   ·

No. 791.

No. **791**-3 blades, ebony handle, German silver lined, crocus polished, 3⅜ in.,   ·   ·   ·
No. **792**-3 blades, stag   handle, German silver lined, crocus polished, 3⅜ in.,   ·   ·

No. 735.

No. **729**-3 blades, stag handle, brass lined, crocus polished, 3⅛ in., · · · · ·
No. **730**-3 blades, ivory handle, brass lined, crocus polished, 3⅛ in., · · · · ·
No. **731**-3 blades, pearl handle, brass lined, crocus polished, 3⅛ in., · · · · ·
No. **735**-3 blades, pearl handle, brass lined, crocus polished, 3⅜ in., · · · · ·

HALF DOZEN IN A BOX.

POCKET KNIVES.

HIBBARD, SPENCER, BARTLETT & CO'S "OUR VERY BEST," WARRANTED.

No. 736.

No. **736**–3 blades, stag handle, brass lined, crocus polished, 3⅛ in, · · · ·
No. **739**–3 blades, pearl handle, brass lined, crocus polished. 3⅛ in., · · · ·

No. 569.

No. **567**–2 blades, stag handle, brass lined, crocus polished, 3⅛ in., · · · ·
No. **568**–2 blades, ivory handle, brass lined, crocus polished, 3⅛ in., · · · ·
No. **569**–2 blades, pearl handle, brass lined, crocus polished, 3⅛ in., · · · ·
No. **537**–2 blades, stag handle, brass lined, crocus polished, 3½ in., · · · ·
No. **538**–2 blades, ivory handle, brass lined, crocus polished, 3½ in., · · · ·
No. **539**–2 blades, pearl handle, brass lined, crocus polished, 3½ in., · · · ·

No. 851.

No. **849**–4 blades, stag handle, brass lined, crocus polished, 3½ in., · · · ·
No. **850**–4 blades, ivory handle, brass lined, crocus polished, 3½ in., · · · ·
No. **851**–4 blades, pearl handle, brass lined, crocus polished, 3½ in., · · · ·

No. 763.

No. **790**–3 blades, ebony handle, brass lined, crocus polished, 3½ in., · · · ·
No. **763**–3 blades, stag handle, brass lined, crocus polished, 3½ in., · · · ·
No. **775**–3 blades, ivory handle, brass lined, crocus polished, 3½ in., · · · ·

No. **908**–5 blades, pearl handle, rope milled German silver lining, crocus polished, 3⅜ in.,
HALF DOZEN IN A BOX.

POCKET KNIVES.

HIBBARD, SPENCER, BARTLETT & CO'S "OUR VERY BEST," WARRANTED.

No. 827.

No. 827–4 blades, stag handle, brass lined, crocus polished, hollow bolsters, 3¼ in.,   ·
No. 833–4 blades, pearl handle, brass lined, crocus polished, German silver bolsters, 3⅜ in.,

No. 713.

No. 712–3 blades, stag handle, brass lined, crocus polished, 3⅜ in.,   ·   ·   ·   ·   ·
No. 713–3 blades, shell handle, brass lined, crocus polished, 3⅜ in.,   ·   ·   ·   ·   ·
No. 714–3 blades, pearl handle, brass lined, crocus polished, 3⅜ in.,   ·   ·   ·   ·   ·

No. 717.

No. 787–3 blades, stag handle, brass lined, crocus polished, patent nail blade, 3 in.,   ·   ·
No. 788–3 blades, ivory handle, brass lined, crocus polished, patent nail blade, 3 in.,   ·   ·
No. 789–3 blades, pearl handle, brass lined, crocus polished, patent nail blade, 3 in.,   ·   ·
No. 715–3 blades, stag handle, rope milled German silver lining, crocus polished, 3¼ in.,   ·
No. 716–3 blades, shell handle, rope milled German silver lining, crocus polished, 3¼ in.,   ·
No. 717–3 blades, pearl handle, rope milled German silver lining, crocus polished, 3¼ in.,   ·
No. 830–4 blades, stag handle, rope milled German silver lining, crocus polished, 3⅛ in.,   ·
No. 831–4 blades, shell handle, rope milled German silver lining, crocus polished, 3⅛ in.,   ·
No. 832–4 blades, pearl handle, rope milled German silver lining, crocus polished, 3⅛ in.,   ·

No. 719.

No. 719–3 blades, stag handle, German silver lined, crocus polished, 3⅜ in.,   ·   ·
No. 720–3 blades, pearl handle, German silver lined, crocus polished, 3⅜ in.,   ·   ·

No. 747.

No. 746–3 blades, stag handle, rope milled German silver lining, crocus polished, 3⅜ in.,   ·
No. 747–3 blades, pearl handle, rope milled German silver lining, crocus polished, 3⅜ in.,   ·

HALF DOZEN IN A BOX.

POCKET KNIVES.

HIBBARD, SPENCER, BARTLETT & CO'S "OUR VERY BEST," WARRANTED.

No. 797. (Style of No. 796.)

No. 553. (Style of Nos. 553 and 554.)

No. 796—3 blades, stag   handle, German silver lined, crocus polished, patent nail file, 3   in.,
No. 797—3 blades, pearl   handle, German silver lined, crocus polished, patent nail file, 3   in.,
No. 552—2 blades, stag   handle, German silver lined, crocus polished, patent nail file, 2⅞ in.,
No. 553—2 blades, ivoride handle, German silver lined, crocus polished, patent nail file, 2⅞ in.,
No. 554—2 blades, pearl   handle, German silver lined, crocus polished, patent nail file, 2⅞ in.,

No. 559. (Style of Nos. 558 and 560.)

No. 556. (Style of Nos. 555 and 557.)

No. 558—2 blades, stag   handle, German silver lined, crocus polished, patent nail file, 3 in., ·
No. 559—2 blades, ivoride handle, German silver lined, crocus polished, patent nail file, 3 in., ·
No. 560—2 blades, pearl   handle, German silver lined, crocus polished, patent nail file, 3 in., ·
No. 555—2 blades, stag   handle, German silver lined, crocus polished, patent nail file, 3 in., ·
No. 556—2 blades, ivoride handle, German silver lined, crocus polished, patent nail file, 3 in., ·
No. 557—2 blades, pearl   handle, German silver lined, crocus polished, patent nail file, 3 in., ·

No. 786—3 blades, pearl handle, German silver lined, crocus polished, patent nail file, 3 in.,

HALF DOZEN IN A BOX.

POCKET KNIVES.

HIBBARD, SPENCER, BARTLETT & CO'S "OUR VERY BEST," WARRANTED

No. 551.

No. 550–2 blades, ivory handle, German silver lined, crocus polished, 2¾ in., · · ·
No. 551–2 blades, pearl handle, German silver lined, crocus polished, 2¾ in.,

No. 381–2 blades, pearl handle, brass lined, crocus polished, 3⅛ in., · · ·

No. 399–2 blades, pearl handle, brass lined, crocus polished, 3 in., · · ·

No. 824.

No. 823–4 blades, pearl handle, rope milled brass lining, crocus polished, 2¾ in., · ·
No. 825–4 blades, stag handle, rope milled brass lining, crocus polished, 3⅛ in., · ·
No. 824–4 blades, pearl handle, rope milled brass lining, crocus polished, 3⅛ in., ·

No. 133.

No. 131–1 blade, spatula, easy opener, cocoa handle, brass lined, 3⅜ in., · · ·
No. 133–1 blade, spatula, easy opener, pearl handle, brass lined, aluminum bolsters, 3⅜ in.,

No. 152–1 blade, ivory handle, brass lined, crocus polished, 3¼ in., · · · ·

HALF DOZEN IN A BOX.

POCKET KNIVES.

HIBBARD, SPENCER, BARTLETT & CO'S "OUR VERY BEST," WARRANTED.

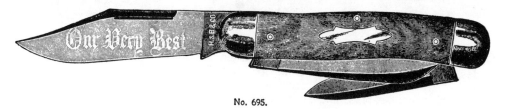

No. 695.

No. 695 –3 blades, cocoa handle, brass lined, crocus polished, 3½ in.,   •   •   •   •
No. 696 –3 blades, ebony handle, brass lined, crocus polished, 3½ in.,   •   •   •
No. 696½–3 blades, stag   handle, brass lined, crocus polished, hollow bolsters, 3½ in.,   •
No. 695½–3 blades, ivory   handle, brass lined, crocus polished, 3½ in.,   •   •   •   •

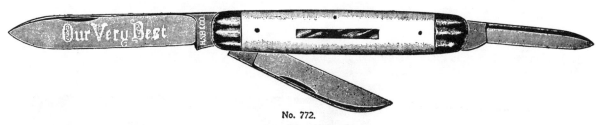

No. 772.

No. 770–3 blades, ebony handle, brass lined, crocus polished, 3⅜ in., •   •   •   •
No. 771–3 blades, stag   handle, brass lined, crocus polished, 3⅜ in., •   •   •   •
No. 772–3 blades, ivory   handle, brass lined, crocus polished, 3⅜ in., •   •   •   •

No. 766.

No. 764–3 blades, cocoa handle, brass lined, crocus polished, 3⅜ in., •   •   •   •   •
No. 765–3 blades, ebony handle, brass lined, crocus polished, 3⅜ in., •   •   •   •   •
No. 766–3 blades, stag   handle, brass lined, crocus polished, 3⅜ in., •   •   •   •   •
No. 768–3 blades, pearl   handle, brass lined, crocus polished, 3⅜ in., •   •   •   •   •

No. 774.

No. 773–3 blades, stag handle, brass lined, crocus polished, 3⅝ in., •   •   •   •
No. 774–3 blades, pearl handle, brass lined, crocus polished, 3⅝ in., •   •   •   •

HALF DOZEN IN A BOX.

POCKET KNIVES.

HIBBARD, SPENCER, BARTLETT & CO'S "OUR VERY BEST," WARRANTED.

No. 465

No. 464   –2 blades, buffalo handle, brass lined, crocus polished, 3¼ in., ...
No. 464½–2 blades, stag   handle, brass lined, crocus polished, 3¼ in., ...
No. 465   –2 blades, ivory   handle, brass lined, crocus polished, 3¼ in., ...
No. 466   –2 blades, pearl   handle, brass lined, crocus polished, 3¼ in., ...

No. 522–1 spear and 1 spatula blade, stag handle, brass lined, crocus polished, 3⅜ in..   .

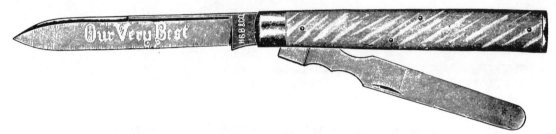

No. 523–1 spear and 1 spatula blade, pearl handle, brass lined, crocus polished. 3¾ in.,   .

No. 375.

No. 467–2 blades, ebony handle, brass lined, crocus polished, 3¾ in., ...
No. 375–2 blades, stag   handle, brass lined, crocus polished, 3¾ in., ...
No. 468–2 blades, pearl   handle, brass lined, crocus polished, 3¾ in., ...

No. 437.

No. 436–2 blades, ebony handle, brass lined, crocus polished, 3⅞ in., ...
No. 437–2 blades, stag   handle, brass lined, crocus polished, 3⅞ in., ...

HALF DOZEN IN A BOX.

POCKET KNIVES.

HIBBARD, SPENCER, BARTLETT & CO'S, "OUR VERY BEST," WARRANTED.

No. 854.

No. 852–4 blades, stag handle, German silver lined, crocus polished, 3⅛ in.,　·　·　·
No. 854–4 blades, pearl handle, German silver lined, crocus polished, 3⅛ in.,　·　·　·

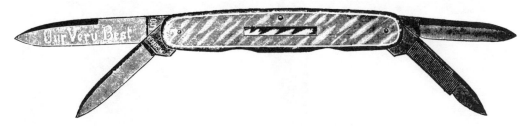

No. 841–4 blades, pearl handle, German silver lined, crocus polished, 3⅛ in.,　·　·　·

No. 835.

No. 834–4 blades, stag handle, German silver lined, crocus polished, 3¼ in.,　·　·　·
No. 835–4 blades, pearl handle, German silver lined, crocus polished, 3⅜ in.;　·　·　·

No. 829–4 blades, pearl handle, German silver lined, crocus polished, 3⅜ in.,　·　·　·

HALF DOZEN IN A BOX.

POCKET KNIVES.

HIBBARD, SPENCER, BARTLETT & CO'S "OUR VERY BEST," WARRANTED.

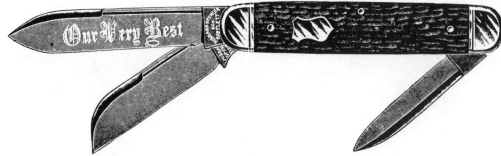

No. 749–3 blades, stag handle, brass lined, crocus polished, 3⅝ in.,　.　.　.　.　.

No. 840–4 blades, stag handle, brass lined, crocus polished. 3⅝ in.,　.　.　.　.　.

No. 751–3 blades, stag handle, brass lined, crocus polished, 3¾ in.,　.　.　.　.

No. 630–3 blades, stag handle, rope milled brass lining, crocus polished, 4 in.,　.　.　.　.

HALF DOZEN IN A BOX.

POCKET KNIVES.

HIBBARD, SPENCER, BARTLETT & CO'S "OUR VERY BEST," WARRANTED.

No. 487½.

No. 485 —2 blades, cocoa handle, brass lined, crocus polished, 3½ in.,   ·   ·   ·   ·
No. 486 —2 blades, ebony handle, brass lined, crocus polished, 3½ in.,   ·   ·   ·   ·
No. 487½—2 blades, white bone handle, brass lined, crocus polished, 3½ in., ·   ·   ·
No. 488 —2 blades, stag handle. brass lined, crocus polished, 3½ in.,   ·   ·   ·   ·

No. 525.

No. 301—2 blades, ebony handle, brass lined, crocus polished, 3⅜ in.,   ·   ·   ·   ·
No. 524—2 blades, cocoa handle, brass lined, crocus polished, 3½ in.,   ·   ·   ·   ·
No. 525—2 blades, ebony handle, brass lined, crocus polished, 3½ in.,   ·   ·   ·   ·
No. 526—2 blades, stag handle, brass lined, crocus polished, 3½ in.,   ·   ·   ·   ·

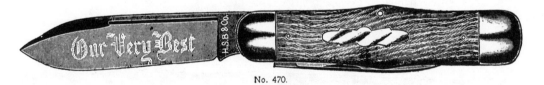

No. 470.

No. 470—2 blades, cocoa handle, brass lined, crocus polished, 3¾ in.,   ·   ·   ·   ·
No. 471—2 blades, ebony handle, brass lined, crocus polished, 3¾ in.,   ·   ·   ·   ·
No. 472—2 blades, white bone handle, brass lined, crocus polished, 3¾ in., ·   ·   ·

No. 421.

No. 420—2 blades, cocoa handle, brass lined, crocus polished, 3½ in.,   ·   ·   ·   ·
No. 421—2 blades, ebony handle, brass lined, crocus polished, 3½ in.,   ·   ·   ·   ·

No. 416.

No. 416—2 blades, cocoa handle, brass lined, crocus polished, 3¾ in.,   ·   ·   ·   ·
No. 417—2 blades, ebony handle, brass lined, crocus polished, 3¾ in.,   ·   ·   ·   ·

HALF DOZEN IN A BOX.

POCKET KNIVES.

HIBBARD, SPENCER, BARTLETT & CO'S, WARRANTED.

No 337P.

No. 289P-2 blades, ebony handle, brass lined, large blade crocus polished, 3½ in.,⠀⠀⠀⠀⠀·⠀⠀·
No. 290P-2 blades, stag   handle, brass lined, large blade crocus polished, 3½ in,⠀⠀⠀⠀⠀·⠀⠀·
No. 337P-2 blades, cocoa handle, brass lined, large blade crocus polished, 3¾ in.,⠀⠀⠀⠀·⠀⠀·
No. 338P-2 blades, ebony handle, brass lined, large blade crocus polished, 3¾ in⠀⠀⠀⠀⠀·⠀⠀·

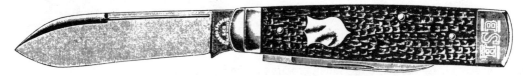

No 284P

No. 287P-2 blades, cocoa handle, brass lined, large blade crocus polished, 3½ in.,⠀⠀⠀·⠀⠀·
No. 288P-2 blades, stag   handle, brass lined, large blade crocus polished, 3½ in.,⠀⠀⠀·⠀⠀·
No. 283P-2 blades, ebony handle, brass lined, large blade crocus polished, 3⅝ in.,⠀⠀⠀·⠀⠀·
No. 284P-2 blades, stag   handle, brass lined, large blade crocus polished, 3⅝ in.,⠀⠀⠀·⠀⠀·

No. 306P.

No. 306P-2 blades, cocoa handle, brass lined, large blade crocus polished, 3¾ in.,⠀⠀⠀·⠀⠀·
No. 307P-2 blades, ebony handle, brass lined, large blade crocus polished, 3¾ in.,⠀⠀⠀·⠀⠀·
No. 304P-2 blades, stag   handle, brass lined, large blade crocus polished, 3¾ in.,⠀⠀⠀·⠀⠀·

No. 350P.

No. 352P-2 blades, ebony handle, brass lined, large blade crocus polished, 3¾ in.,⠀⠀⠀·⠀⠀·
No. 350P-2 blades, stag   handle, brass lined, large blade crocus polished, 3¾ in.,⠀⠀⠀·⠀⠀·

HALF DOZEN IN A BOX.

JOHN PRIMBLE POCKET KNIVES

Brass lining; nickel silver tips; half polished. Length 3⅛ inches.

No. 5745MP—Mottled pyralin...
No. 5745PP—Pearl pyralin....

Stainless Steel Blades.

Nickel silver lining and handle; half polished, with shackle. Length 3¹⁄₁₆ inches.

No. 5754SSC—Metal handle....

Brass lining; nickel silver tips and shackle; half polished.

No. 5755C—Celluloid..........

Brass lining; nickel silver tips and shield; half polished.

No. 5232S—Stag; lgth 3⁵⁄₁₆ ins...

Brass lining; nickel silver bolsters and shield; half polished.

No. 5264S—Stag; lgth 3⅝ ins....

Nickel silver lining; nickel silver bolsters and shield; full polished. Length 3⅞ inches.

No. 5478JP—Japanese Pearl pyralin...................

Office Knife.

Brass lining; half polished.
No. 5600I—White celluloid lgth 3¾ ins...............

Brass lining; nickel silver bolsters and shield; half polished. Per Doz
No. 5751SP—Shell pyralin; lgth 3⅜ ins...............

Brass lining; nickel silver bolsters; full polished. Length 2⅞ inches.
No. 5344P—Pearl..............

Brass lining; nickel silver tips; full polished.
Length 2¾ inches.
No. 5030P—Pearl..............

Brass lining; nickel silver bolsters and shield; full polished. Length 2⅞ inches.

No. 5332P—Pearl.............

Half doz in attractive cardboard box.

Budding Knife.
Stag scale lining; half polished.

No. 5231S—Stag; lgth 3⅞ ins...

Budding.

Brass lining; steel bolster. Special shaped blade for use by nurserymen. Length 3¼ inches.

No. 4806S—Stag..............

Electricians Knife.

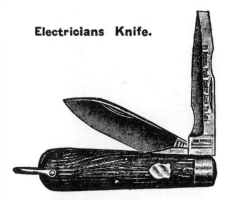

Brass lining, nickel silver bolsters and shackle, spear blade and screw driver blade (with locking device), glazed finish.

No. JPEK—Cocobolo handle; lgth 3½ ins....................

Pruning Knife.
Steel lining and bolster; highly glazed.

No. 5106R—Rosewood; lgth 4 ins...................

JOHN PRIMBLE POCKET KNIVES
Made In America

PEN

HANDLE—Bone stag.
BLADES—Two: clip and pen.
BOLSTERS—Nickel silver.
SHIELD—Nickel silver.
LINING—Brass, milled.
LENGTH—3⅜ inches.

C1-5279S

Half doz in box;
wt doz 2 lbs.

PEN

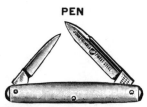

HANDLE—Genuine pearl.
BLADES—Two: spear and pen.
TIPS—Nickel silver.
LINING—Brass, milled.
LENGTH—2¾ inches.

C1-5763P

Half doz in box;
wt doz 1 lb.

PEN

HANDLE—Bone stag.
BLADES—Two: spear and pen. Full
polished and etched.
BOLSTERS—Nickel silver tips.
LINING—Brass, milled.
LENGTH—2¾ inches.

C1-5763S

Half doz in box;
wt doz 1 lb.

SERPENTINE PEN

HANDLE—Bone stag.
BLADES—Two: clip and pen. Large
blade polished on one side.
BOLSTERS—Nickel silver.
SHIELD—Nickel silver.
LINING—Brass.
LENGTH—2¾ inches.

C1-902S

Half doz in box;
wt doz 1 lb.

PEN

HANDLE—Bone stag.
BLADES—Two: spear and pen. Full
polished and etched.
BOLSTERS—Nickel silver.
LINING—Brass, milled.
LENGTH—2¾ inches.

C1-5344S

Half doz in box;
wt doz 1 lb.

PEN

HANDLE—Bone stag.
BLADES—Two: clip and pen.
BOLSTERS—Nickel silver.
SHIELD—Nickel silver.
LINING—Brass.
LENGTH—2¾ inches.

C1-5323S

Half doz in box;
wt doz ½ lb.

SLIM SENATOR PATTERN

HANDLE—New pearl.
BLADES—Two: spear and flexible
nail file. Large blade polished on one
side.
TIPS—Nickel silver.
LINING—Nickel silver.
LENGTH—2⅞ inches.

C1-901NP

Half doz in box;
wt doz ½ lb.

TEXAS JACK

HANDLE—Bone stag.
BLADES—Two: clip and spear. Full
polished and etched. French nail mark
on master blade.
BOLSTERS—Nickel silver.
SHIELD—Nickel silver.
LINING—Brass.
LENGTH—4 inches.

C1-4987S

Half doz in box;
wt doz 3 lbs.

LARGE JACK

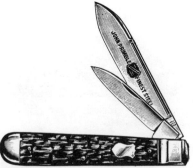

HANDLE—Bone stag.
BLADES—Two: spear and pen.
BOLSTERS—Nickel silver.
SHIELD—Nickel silver.
LINING—Brass.
LENGTH—4½ inches.

C1-4942S

Half doz in box;
wt doz 4 lbs.

JOHN PRIMBLE POCKET KNIVES

Brass lining; nickel silver bolsters; half polished. Congress pattern.

No. 5224S—Stag; lgth 3 ins ____

Brass lining; nickel silver bolsters; full polished. Length 3 inches. Congress pattern.

No. 5222S—Stag ____
No. 5222 P—Pearl ____

Brass lining; nickel silver bolsters and shield; half polished.

No. 5433S—Stag; lgth 4³⁄₁₆ ins ____

Brass lining; nickel silver bolsters and shield; half polished. Length 3⅝ inches.

No. 5409S—Stag ____

No. 5278S

Catch side; nickel silver lining; nickel silver bolsters and shield; half polished. Stag handle. Per Doz

No. 5278S—Two Blade. Spear; length 3⁵⁄₁₆ ins ____

No. 5279S—Two Blade. Clip; length 3⅜ ins ____

No. 5280S—Three Blade. Pen spear and clip; length 3⅛ ins ____

Flexible Manicure File.

Brass lining; nickel silver tips and shield. Length 2⅞ inches.

No. 5755S—Stag ____

Nickel silver lining, bolsters and shield; mirror finished blades. Length 3⅛ inches.

No. 5736S—Stag ____
No. 5736 P P—Pearl pyralin ____

Brass lining; nickel silver tips and shield; half polished. Length 3⅛ inches.

No. 5130S—Stag ____

Brass lining; nickel silver bolsters and shield; half polished. Length 3⅜ inches.

No. 5330S—Stag ____

Brass lining; flat nickel silver bolsters and shield; half polished.

No. 5408S—Stag; length 3⅛ ins
Half doz in attractive cardboard box.

Brass lining; nickel silver bolsters and shield; half polished. Length 3⁷⁄₁₆ inches.

No. 5410S—Stag ____

Brass lining; nickel silver bolsters and shield; half polished.

No. 5652S—Stag, length 3⅝ ins

Brass lining; nickel silver bolsters; half polished. Length 2⅞ inches.

No. 5344S—Stag ____

Brass lining; nickel silver tips, polished. Length 3⁵⁄₁₆ inches.

No. 5230S—Stag ____
No. 5230P—Pearl ____

Stainless Steel Blades and Back.

Brass lining; nickel silver tips and shield; half polished. Length 3⁵⁄₁₆ inches.

No. 3000S P—Pearl pyralin ____
No. 3000SS—Stag ____

Brass lining; nickel silver bolster and shield; half polished.

No. 5444S—Stag; lgth 3¼ ins ____

JOHN PRIMBLE POCKET KNIVES

Punch Knife.

Nickel silver lining; nickel silver bolsters and shield; half polished.   Length 3⅝ inches.

No. 5286S—Stag; spear_____
No. 5285M P — Mottled pyralin; spear_____

Punch Knife.

Brass lining; nickel silver bolsters and shield; half polished.   Length 3¼ inches.

No. 5269S—Stag_____

Punch Knife.

Brass lining; nickel silver bolsters and shield; half polished.
Length 3⅜ inches.

No. 5270S—Stag_____

Nickel silver lining; plain bolsters and shield; half polished.

No. 5373S—Stag; lgth 3⅜ ins __

Brass lining; nickel silver bolsters and shield; half polished.

No. 4988S—Stag; lgth 4¼ ins _____

Brass lining; nickel silver bolsters and shield; half polished.
Length 4 inches.

No. 5389S—Stag_____

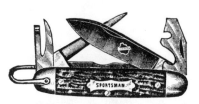

Sportsman.

Brass lining; stag handle; nickel silver bolsters, shield and belt ring.
Large spear blade, leather punch, can opener, bottle opener, tack puller and screw driver.

No. 5283S—Length 3⅝ ins_____

Brass lining; nickel silver bolsters and shield; half polished.

No. 4989S—Stag; lgth 4 ins_____

Brass lining; nickel silver bolsters and shield; half polished.
No. 4987S—Stag; lgth 4 ins_____

Brass lining; nickel silver bolsters and shield; half polished. Japanese pearl pyralin.

No. 4983J P—Length 4 ins___
No. 5751 P P—Length 3⅜ ins_
Half doz in attractive cardboard box.

Brass lining; nickel silver bolsters and shield; half polished.   Length 3⅜ inches.

No. 4994S—Stag_____

Brass lining; nickel silver bolsters and shield; half polished.   Length 3⅜ inches.

No. 4994S P—Shell pyralin_____

Brass lining; nickel silver bolster and cap; polished metal shield; blade highly glazed and etched.   Length 5 inches.

No. 4815S—Stag _____
No. 4815R—Red pyralin_____

Brass lining; nickel silver bolster and cap; half polished.   Length 4¼ inches.

No. 5727W—White bone_____
No. 52046S—Genuine Stag____

Brass lining; nickel silver bolster, cap and shield. Half polished.

No. 5180S—Stag; lgth 4¼ ins _____

JOHN PRIMBLE POCKET KNIVES

Brass lining; nickel silver bolster, cap and shield; length 4¼ inches.
No. 5190S—Stag - - - - - - - - - -

Brass lining; nickel silver bolster, cap and shield; half polished. Stag; length 3⅜ inches.
No. 4860S—Spear blade - - - - - }
No. 4861S—Clip blade - - - - - - }

Brass lining; nickel silver bolster, cap and shield; half polished. Length 3¼ inches.

No. 4955S—Stag; spear blade instead of clip blade - - - - - - -

Brass lining; nickel silver bolster, cap and shield. Length 3¼ inches.

No. 4961JP—Japanese pearl pyralin - - - - - - - - - - - - - - - - - -

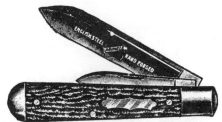

Brass lining; nickel silver bolster, cap and shield; half polished. Length 4½ inches.
No. 5035S—Stag; spear blade - - - - - - - - - - - - - - - -
No. 5037S—Stag; clip blade

Brass lining; nickel silver bolster, cap and shield; half polished. Stag.

No. 4942S—Length 4¼ ins - - - - -
No. 4941S—Length 3⅞ ins - - - - -

Nickel silver lining; nickel silver bolster, cap and shield; half polished.

No. 5140S—Stag; lgth 3¾ ins -

Brass lining; flat nickel silver bolster, cap and shield; half polished.
No. 5132S—Stag; lgth 3¹³⁄₁₆ ins -

Brass lining; nickel silver bolster, cap and shield; half polished.
No. 5134S—Stag; lgth 3⅞ ins -

Brass lining; nickel silver bolster, cap and shield; mirror finished. 3⅝ inches.
No. 4984S—Stag - - - - - - - - - - - -

Brass lining; nickel silver bolster, cap and shield; half polished. Stag. Length 3⅝ inches.
No. 5072S—Spear blade - - - - - }
No. 5073S—Clip blade - - - - - - }

Brass lining; steel bolster and cap; nickel silver shield; half polished. Stag. Length 3¾ inches.
No. 5123S—Spear blade - - - - -
No. 5124S—Sheep foot blade -
No. 5125S—Clip blade - - - - - -

Brass lining; nickel silver cap and bolster; full polished.

No. 4845S—Stag; lgth 3½ ins - -

Punch Knife.
Brass lining; nickel silver bolster, cap and shield; half polished.

No. 05670S—Stag; lgth 3⁷⁄₁₆ ins - -

Brass lining; nickel silver bolster, cap and shield; half polished.

No. 5175S—Stag; lgth 3⅝ ins - - -

Half doz in attractive cardboard box.

JOHN PRIMBLE POCKET KNIVES

Brass lining; nickel silver bolster, cap and shield; half polished.   Length 3⁵⁄₁₆ inches.

No. 57390 P—Opal pyralin; spear
No. 4844S—Stag; spear _____
No. 4855S—Stag; clip _____

Brass lining; nickel silver bolster and cap; half polished.   Length 3⁵⁄₁₆ inches.

No. 5147S—Stag_____

Brass lining; nickel silver Washington bolster, flat cap and shield; half polished. Length 3 inches.

No. 4938G P—Gold pyralin; spear blade_____
No. 4938S—Stag; spear blade__

Brass lining; nickel silver bolster, cap and shield; half polished.   Length 3¹⁄₁₆ inches.

No. 4937S—Stag _____

Nickel silver lining; nickel silver bolster and shield; half polished. Length 3¼ inches.

No. 4992S—Stag _____

Nickel silver lining; nickel silver bolster and shield; half polished.   Two blade, clip and spear. Length 3⅜ inches.

No. 4993S—Stag_____

Brass lining; nickel silver bolster, cap and shield; half polished.   Length 3⅛ inches.

No. 5746G P—Gold pyralin_____

Switch Knife.
Brass lining; nickel silver bolster, cap and shield; half polished.

No. 5726S—Stag, lgth 3⅝ ins___

Brass lining; nickel silver bolster, cap and shield; half polished.   Length 3⁵⁄₁₆ inches.
No. 4950J P—Jap. pearl pyralin__
No. 4950S—Stag_____

Brass lining; nickel silver bolster and cap; half polished.   Thumb notch in handle; spear and pen blades. Length 3⅛ inches.

No. 5753S—Stag_____

Half doz in attractive cardboard box.

Brass lining; nickel silver bolsters and shield; half polished.

No. 4920S—Stag; lgth 3 ins____

Brass lining; nickel silver bolster and cap; full polished.   Length 2¾ inches.

No. 4927GS—Genuine stag _____
No. 4927S— Stag_____
No. 4927 P—Pearl_____

Brass lining; nickel silver bolster and cap; full polished.   Length 2¾ inches.

No. 4923S—Stag___ _____
No. 4923 P P—Pearl pyralin____

Brass lining; nickel silver bolsters, cap and shield; half polished.
Length 3 inches.

No. 4933M P—Mottled pyralin__

Brass lining; nickel silver bolster and cap; half polished.
Length 3 inches.
No. 5715S—Stag; clip and pen blade_____

Brass lining; steel bolster and cap; nickel silver shield; half polished.

No. 5749S—Stag; lgth 3⁵⁄₁₆ ins__

POCKET KNIVES

TWO BLADE JACK

12 two-blade jack knives with assorted colored handles.
Good quality steel blades, polished.

No. 1751—Length knives 2¾ ins
One doz in cardboard box.

—PINE KNOT—
Three Blade.

Twelve 3-blade knives with nickel silver bolsters, brass linings; fully polished blades. Assorted horn, celluloid and imitation pearl handles. Blading consisting of master, clip, spey and pen and master, spear, spey and pen.

(Sold only in full assortments).

No. 3450 — Length assorted 3⅜, 3¼ and 3½ ins
One doz in display box; wt ass't 1⅝ lbs.

—PINE KNOT—
Premium Stock Knife.
Three Blade.

12 three blade knives with nickel silver bolsters, full polished blades; brass lining. Assorted stag and colored celluloid handles. Blading-clip, spey and pen and clip, spey and punch.

No. 370-1 — Length knives 4 ins
Half doz in cardboard box; wt ass't 1 lbs.

—PINE KNOT—
Two Blade.

Brass lining; nickel silver bolsters and shield. Spear and pen blades. Length knives 4¼ inches.

No. 53W — White ivory celluloid handles
Half doz in cardboard box.

—PINE KNOT—
Two Blades. Congress Knife.

Iron lining; iron bolsters; full polished blades. Sheepfoot and pen blades. Length 3⅛ inches.

No. 22S—Stag handles
One doz in cardboard box; wt doz 1 lb.

—PINE KNOT—
Four Blades.
Congress Knife.

Steel lining; steel bolsters; full polished blades. Two large sheepfoot blades and 2 small pen blades. Length 3¾ inches.

No. 24S—Stag handles
One doz in cardboard box; wt doz 1⅞ lbs.

IMPERIAL
SCOUT

Scout, brass lining; polished steel bolsters; nickel silver shield and belt ring.
Spear blade, punch, tack puller, screw driver, bottle and can opener. Length 3¾ inches.

No. 27S—Stag handles
Half doz in cardboard box.

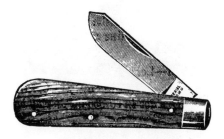

IMPERIAL MAIZE

One blade. Iron lining, single iron bolster. Sheepfoot blade full polished. Length 4 inches.

No. 850—Wood handle
One doz in cardboard box.

Although a piece of cutlery bearing the John Primble trade mark may cost a little more, it is the cheapest in the end. There is none finer than John Primble. Look for the Primble Shield.

123

JOHN PRIMBLE POCKET KNIVES

Brass lining; steel bolster and cap; nickel silver shield; half polished. Length 3⅜ inches.

No. 5748S—Stag _____

Brass lining; steel bolster and cap nickel silver shield; half polished.

No. 5750S—Stag; lgth 3⁵⁄₁₆ ins ___

Brass lining; nickel silver bolsters, cap and shield; half polished. Length 3⅜ inches. Stag.

No. 5758S—Spear _____
No. 5759S—Clip _____

Steel lining; nickel silver bolster; half polished. Length 3⁷⁄₁₆ inches. Stag handle.
No. 5010S—Spear blade _____
No. 5012S—Sheep foot blade ___
No. 5008S—Clip blade _____

Brass lining; nickel silver bolsters, cap and shield; half polished.
No. 4952S—Stag; lgth 3¼ ins __

Steel lining and bolster; glazed shield; half polished.

No. 4813R—Redwood; lgth 3⁷⁄₁₆ ins _____

Brass lining; nickel silver bolsters; nickel silver shield; half polished. Length 4¼ inches. Congress pattern.

No. 5516S—Stag _____
No. 5394GS—Genuine stag ____

Brass lining; nickel silver bolsters; nickel silver shield; half polished. Length 3⅞ inches. Congress pattern; stag handle.

No. 5512S—Tobacco blade _____

Brass lining; nickel silver bolsters and shield; half polished. Congress pattern.

No. 5324GS—Genuine stag; lgth 3¼ ins _____

Brass lining; nickel silver bolsters, nickel silver shield; half polished. Congress pattern.

No. 5369GS—Genuine stag; lgth 3½ ins _____

Half doz in attractive cardboard box.

Brass lining; nickel silver bolsters; nickel silver shield; half polished. Congress pattern.

No. 5509S—Stag; lgth 3¼ ins ____

Brass lining; nickel silver shield and bolsters; half polished. Congress pattern.

No. 5432S—Stag; lgth 4 ins ____

Brass lining; nickel silver bolsters; nickel silver shield; half polished. Length 3¾ inches. Congress pattern.

No. 5228S—Stag _____

Brass lining; flat nickel silver bolsters and shield; half polished. Congress pattern.

No. 5437S—Stag; length 3⅛ ins __

Brass lining; nickel silver bolsters and shield; half polished. Length 3¼ inches. Congress pattern.

No. 5223S—Stag _____

Brass lining; nickel silver bolsters and shield; half polished. Congress pattern.

No. 5458S—Stag; lgth 3½ ins ___

The Blades—There positively are no finer Pocket Knives made than "John Primble". The blades are carefully forged from the very finest quality India Steel.

Workmanship—In the manufacture of John Primble Pocket Knives only the very latest modern methods, combined with the most skilled workmanship are employed. Such detail as hardening, tempering, grinding and finishing is done with perfect accuracy which insures uniform excellence.

Stag Handles—The Stag Handles on John Primble Pocket Knives are genuine, made from finest quality stag horns. This stag is carefully inspected for choice stock making it impossible to apply imperfect handles to the knives.

Pearl Handles—Only shells of the first water are selected for use on John Primble Pearl Handle Pocket Knives, possessing perfect skin of delicate texture, free from specks or flaws. They are clear translucent and of beautiful color.

Inspection—Every John Primble Pocket Knife after having been made goes through a rigid inspection which makes the general excellence so superior that John Primble Pocket Knives have grown steadily in popularity for over 50 years. Every user of a Pocket Knife recognizes and appreciates quality. That is what you get in a John Primble. The quality of these knives is backed by the reputation of the Belknap Hardware and Manufacturing Company, protecting the dealers and consumers from defects and flaws incident to manufacture or faulty material.

Proper Care of Pocket Knives—They should be sharpened on oil stone holding the back of blade slightly elevated so that only the cutting edge rests on stone. Do not lay the blade flat like honing a razor. Never put a Pocket Knife blade on the stone or emery wheel. Never carry a Pocket Knife in a sweaty pocket as this will cause the linings of the knife to rust.

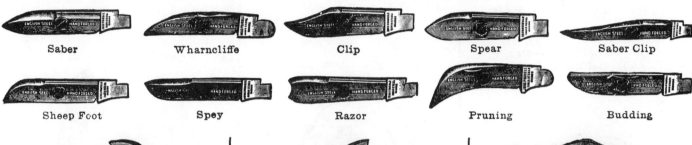

Saber	Wharncliffe	Clip	Spear	Saber Clip

Sheep Foot	Spey	Razor	Pruning	Budding

Brass lining; nickel silver bolsters and shield; half polished. Length 4 inches.

No. 5371JP—Japanese p e a r l pryalin, with spey blade _ _ _ _ _ _
No. 05371JP—Japanese p e a r l pryalin, with punch blade _ _ _ _ _
No. 5378JP—P e a r l pyralin, pen blade instead of spey blade

No. 3001SJP—S a m e as No. 5371JP except has stainless steel blades and back spring _ _ _

No. 5370JP
Brass lining; nickel silver bolsters and shield; half polished. Length 3¾ inches.

No. 5370JP—Japanese pearl _ _ _ _

Nickel silver lining; nickel silver bolsters and shield; half polished.
No. 5386S—Stag; length 3½ ins.

Brass lining; nickel silver bolsters and shield; half polished. Length 3⅜ inches.

No. 5380S P—Shell pyralin _ _ _ _ _

Premier Stock Knife.
Brass lining; nickel silver bolsters and shield; half polished.
No. 5385S—Stag; length 4 ins _ _ _

Brass lining; nickel silver bolsters and shield. Mirror finished.
No. 5385NH—Imitation h o r n pyremite handle; length 4 ins_
Half doz in atttractive cardboard box.

Brass lining; nickel silver bolsters and shield; half polished.
No. 5374S—Stag; length 3⅞ ins_

Nickel silver lining; nickel silver bolsters and shield; half polished.

No. 5381S—Stag; length 3¹¹⁄₁₆ ins

Punch Knife.
Brass lining; nickel silver bolsters and shield; half polished.

No. 5383S—Stag; length 4 ins _ _ _

JOHN PRIMBLE POCKET KNIVES
Made In America

SMALL SIZE PREMIUM STOCK

BLADES—Three: clip, spey and sheepfoot.
BOLSTERS—Nickel silver.
SHIELD—Nickel silver.
LINING—Brass.
LENGTH—2 5/8 inches.

Bone Stag Handle
C1-708S__   Doz **$63 00**

New Pearl Handle
C1-708NP__   Doz **$63 00**
Half doz in box;
wt doz 1 lb.

SMALL PREMIUM STOCK

BLADES—Three: master clip, pen, and sheepfoot.
BOLSTERS—Nickel silver.
SHIELD—Nickel silver.
LINING—Brass, milled center.
LENGTH—2 3/4 inches.

Bone Stag Handle
C1-5390S__   Doz **$81 90**

New Pearl Handle
C1-5390NP__   Doz **$81 90**
Half doz in box;
wt doz 1 lb.

The name and **Primble** Trade Mark on a piece of cutlery is absolutely assurance of excellent quality. John Primble cutlery is guaranteed to give entire satisfaction. **No finer made.**

CONGRESS

HANDLE—Bone stag.
BLADES—Four: two pen, two sheepfoot. Full polished and etched.
BOLSTERS—Nickel silver.
SHIELD—Nickel silver.
LINING—Brass.
LENGTH—4 1/4 inches.

C1-5617S__   Doz **$100 80**
Half doz in box;
wt doz 2 lbs.

CONGRESS

HANDLE—Bone stag.
BLADES—Four: two pen, two sheepfoot.
BOLSTERS—Nickel silver.
SHIELD—Nickel silver.
LINING—Brass, milled center.
LENGTH—3 11/16 inches.

C1-5514S__   Doz **$94 50**
Half doz in box;
wt doz 2 lbs.

CONGRESS

HANDLE—Bone stag.
BLADES—Four: two pen, two sheepfoot.
BOLSTERS—Nickel silver.
SHIELD—Nickel silver.
LINING—Brass, center milled.
LENGTH—3 11/16 inches.

C1-5511S__   Doz **$88 20**
Half doz in box;
wt doz 2 lbs.

CONGRESS

HANDLE—Bone stag.
BLADES—Four: two pen, two sheepfoot.
BOLSTERS—Nickel silver.
SHIELD—Nickel silver.
LINING—Brass, center milled.
LENGTH—3 11/16 inches.

C1-5512S__   Doz **$88 20**
Half doz in box;
wt doz 1 lb.

CONGRESS PATTERN

HANDLE—Bone stag.
BLADES—Four: 2 pen, 2 sheepfoot.
BOLSTERS—Nickel silver.
LINING—Brass.
LENGTH—3 1/2 inches.

C1-711S__   Doz **$66 15**
Half doz in box;
wt doz 1 lb.

PREMIUM STOCK

HANDLE—Bone stag.
BLADES—Four: saber clip, pen, spey and sheepfoot.
BOLSTER—Nickel silver.
LINING—Brass.
LENGTH—3 5/16 inches.

C1-732S__   Doz **$69 30**
Half doz in box;
wt doz 2 lbs.

JOHN PRIMBLE POCKET KNIVES
Made In America

LARGE EQUAL END JACK

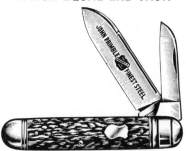

HANDLE—Bone stag.
BLADES—Two: spear and pen.
BOLSTERS—Nickel silver.
SHIELD—Nickel silver.
LINING—Brass.
LENGTH—4 3/16 inches.
C1-5727S
Half doz in box;   Doz **$88 20**
wt doz 3 lbs.

LARGE JACK

HANDLE—Bone stag.
BLADES—Two: half saber clip and pen.
BOLSTER AND CAP—Nickel silver.
SHIELD—Nickel silver.
LINING—Brass.
LENGTH—3 7/8 inches.
C1-913S
Half doz in box;   Doz **$88 20**
wt doz 2 lbs.

LARGE AND MEDIUM SERPENTINE JACK

HANDLE—Bone stag.
BLADES—Two: swedged clip and pen. Full polished and etched.
BOLSTERS—Nickel silver.
SHIELD—Nickel silver.
LINING—Brass.
LENGTH—3 7/8 inches.
C1-5133S
Half doz in box;   Doz **$75 60**
wt doz 4 lbs.

MEDIUM EQUAL END JACK

HANDLE—Bone stag.
BLADES—Two: clip and pen. Full polished and etched.
BOLSTERS—Nickel silver.
SHIELD—Nickel silver.
LINING—Brass.
LENGTH—3 5/8 inches.

C1-4861S
Half doz in box;   Doz **$75 60**
wt doz 3 lbs.

MEDIUM EQUAL END JACK

HANDLE—Bone stag.
BLADES—Two: spear and pen. Full polished and etched.
BOLSTERS—Nickel silver.
SHIELD—Nickel silver.
LINING—Brass.
LENGTH—3 5/8 inches.

C1-4860S
Half doz in box;   Doz **$75 60**
wt doz 2 lbs.

MEDIUM SERPENTINE JACK

HANDLE—Bone stag.
BLADES—Two: clip and pen. Full polished and etched.
BOLSTERS—Nickel silver.
SHIELD—Nickel silver.
LINING—Brass.
LENGTH—3 1/2 inches.

C1-4984S
Half doz in box;   Doz **$63 00**
wt doz 2 lbs.

MEDIUM SERPENTINE—JACK

HANDLE—Bone stag.
BLADES—Two: clip and pen. Master blade polished mark side only, other blade glazed on both sides.
LINING—Brass.
BOLSTERS—Nickel silver.
LENGTH—3 1/2 inches.

C1-701S
Half doz in box;   Doz **$63 00**
wt doz 2 lbs.

SERPENTINE—JACK

HANDLE—Bone stag.
BLADES—Two: clip and pen. Large blade polished on one side.
BOLSTERS—Nickel silver.
SHIELD—Nickel silver.
LINING—Brass.
LENGTH—3 5/16 inches.

C1-910S
Half doz in box;   Doz **$75 60**
wt doz 2 lbs.

MEDIUM JACK

HANDLE—Bone stag.
BLADES—Two: clip and pen.
BOLSTER AND SHIELD—Nickel silver.
LINING—Brass.
LENGTH—3 5/16 inches.

C1-4952S
Half doz in box;   Doz **$63 00**
wt doz 2 lbs.

JOHN PRIMBLE POCKET KNIVES
Made In America

PREMIUM STOCK

HANDLE—New pearl.
BLADES—Four: saber clip, pen, spey, and sheepfoot, nickel plated.
BOLSTER—Nickel silver.
LINING—Brass.
LENGTH—3 5/16 inches.

   C1-732NP__   Doz **$69 30**
Half doz in box:
wt doz 2 lbs.

BOY SCOUT TYPE

HANDLE—Bone stag.
BLADES—Four: pen, spear, can opener, screw driver and cap puller combination.
   All blades fully polished. Master blade etched. Ring for attaching chain.
LINING—Brass.
BOLSTERS—Nickel silver.
SHIELD—Nickel silver.
LENGTH—Closed 3 3/4 inches.

   C1-3335S__   Doz **$81 90**
Half doz in box;
wt doz 3 lbs.

CONGRESS PEN

HANDLE—Bone stag.
BLADES—Two: pen and sheepfoot.
Full polished and etched.
BOLSTERS—Nickel silver.
SHIELD—Nickel silver.
LINING—Brass, milled.
LENGTH—3 3/4 inches.

   C1-5228S__   Doz **$63 00**
Half doz in box;
wt doz 1 lb.

CONGRESS PEN

HANDLE—Bone stag.
BLADES—Two: pen and sheepfoot.
Full polished and etched.
BOLSTERS—Nickel silver.
LINING—Brass, milled.
LENGTH—3 inches.

   C1-5222S__   Doz **$56 70**
Half doz in box;
wt doz 1 lb.

CONGRESS PEN

HANDLE—Bone stag.
BLADES—Two: pen and sheepfoot.
Etched. Large blade polished on one side.
BOLSTERS—Nickel silver.
LINING—Brass.
LENGTH—3 inches.

   C1-900S _____ Doz **$63 00**
Half doz in box; wt doz 1 lb.

CONGRESS PEN

HANDLE—Bone stag.
BLADES—Two: pen and sheepfoot.
BOLSTERS—Iron.
LINING—Brass.
LENGTH—3 inches.

   C1-5224S__   Doz **$50 40**
Half doz in box;
wt doz 2 lbs.

LARGE SERPENTINE PENS

HANDLE—Bone stag.
BLADES—Two: clip and spey; full polished. French nail mark on master blade.
BOLSTERS—Nickel silver.
SHIELD—Nickel silver.
LINING—Brass.
LENGTH—4 inches.

   C1-4983S__   Doz **$85 05**
Half doz in box;
wt doz 2 lbs.

HANDLE—Pearl pyralin.
BLADES—Two: clip and spey, full polished. French nail mark on master blade.
BOLSTERS—Nickel silver.
SHIELD—Nickel silver.
LINING—Brass.
LENGTH—4 inches.

   C1-4983JP__   Doz **$85 05**
Half doz in box;
wt doz 2 lbs.

PEN KNIVES STOCK PATTERN

HANDLE—Bone stag.
BLADES—Two: clip and pen. Full polished and etched. Stainless steel.
BOLSTERS—Nickel silver.
LINING—Brass, milled.
LENGTH—3 1/2 inches.

   C1-4995S__   Doz **$63 00**
Half doz in box;
wt doz 2 lbs.

JOHN PRIMBLE POCKET KNIVES
Made In America

MEDIUM JACK

HANDLE—Bone stag.
BLADE—Two: spear and pen. Mirror polished and etched.
BOLSTER AND SHIELD—Nickel silver.
LINING—Brass.
LENGTH—3⁵⁄₁₆ inches.

C1-4953S

Half doz in box;   Doz **$63 00**
wt doz 2 lbs.

MEDIUM EQUAL END JACK

HANDLE—Bone stag.
BLADES—Two: clip and pen.
BOLSTER AND SHIELD—Nickel silver.
LINING—Brass.
LENGTH—3⁵⁄₁₆ inches.

C1-4992S

Half doz in box;   Doz **$63 00**
wt doz 2 lbs.

SLIM SERPENTINE JACK

HANDLE—Bone stag.
BLADES—Two: clip and pen, master blade polished mark side only, other blade glazed on both sides.
LINING—Brass.
BOLSTERS—Nickel silver.
LENGTH—3¼ inches.

C1-702S

Half doz in box;   Doz **$50 40**
wt doz 1 lb.

MEDIUM DOUBLE END PEN

BLADES—Two: spear and pen. Full polished and etched.
BOLSTERS—Nickel silver.
SHIELD—Nickel silver.
LINING—Nickel silver.
LENGTH—3⅛ inches.

New Pearl Handle

C1-5733NP
                              Doz **$63 00**

Bone Stag Handle

C1-5733S
Half doz in box;   Doz **$63 00**
wt doz 2 lbs.

JACK KNIFE

BLADES—Two: clip and pen.
BOLSTER—Nickel silver.
LINING—Brass.
Full polished blades.   Length 2⅞ in.

Stag Handle

C1-728S
                              Doz **$50 40**

New Pearl Handle

C1-728NP
Half doz in box;   Doz **$50 40**
wt doz 1 lb.

MEDIUM AND SMALL JACK

HANDLE—Bone stag.
BLADES—Two: spear and pen. Mirror polished and etched.
BOLSTER—Nickel silver.
SHIELD—Nickel silver.
LINING—Brass.
LENGTH—3¼⁄₁₆ inches.

C1-5100S

Half doz in box;   Doz **$63 00**
wt doz 1 lb.

DOG LEG—JACK

HANDLE—Bone stag.
BLADES—Two: Clip and pen.
BOLSTERS—Nickel silver.
SHIELD AND CAPS—Nickel silver.
LINING—Brass.
LENGTH—2⅞ inches.

C1-908S   Doz **$69 30**
Half doz in box;
wt doz 1 lb.

MEDIUM AND SMALL JACK

BLADES—Two: swedged saber clip and pen.
BOLSTER—Nickel silver.
LINING—Brass.
LENGTH—2⅞ inches.

Bone Stag Handle
C1-4927S
                              Doz **$50 40**

New Pearl Pyralin Handle

C1-4927NP
Half doz in box;   Doz **$50 40**
wt doz 1 lb.

MEDIUM AND SMALL JACK

BLADES—Two: spear and pen. Mirror polished and etched.
BOLSTER—Nickel silver.
LINING—Brass.
LENGTH—2⅞ inches.

Bone Stag Handle
C1-4923S
                              Doz **$50 40**

New Pearl Pyralin Handle

C1-4923NP
Half doz in box;   Doz **$50 40**
wt doz 2 lbs.

JOHN PRIMBLE POCKET KNIVES
Made In America

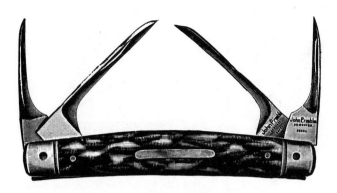

"OLD JOHN"

Actual photograph of a John Primble pocket knife, still in perfect condition after 32 years of daily use!

Original cost to owner $1 50, less than 5c per year!

THE BLADES—The blades are carefully forged from the very finest quality steel.

WORKMANSHIP—Only the very latest modern methods, combined with the most skilled workmanship are employed. Hardening, tempering, grinding and finishing are done with perfect accuracy to insure uniform excellence.

BONE STAG HANDLES—Accurately cut to size; from chemically treated shin-bone.

PEARL HANDLES—Only shells of the first water are selected for use on John Primble Pearl Handle Pocket Knives.

INSPECTION—Every John Primble Pocket Knife after having been made goes through a rigid inspection which makes the general excellence so superior that John Primble Pocket Knives have grown in popularity for over 75 years.

PROPER CARE OF POCKET KNIVES—They should be sharpened on oil stone, holding the back of blade slightly elevated so that only the cutting edge rests on stone. Do not lay the blade flat like honing a razor. Never put a pocket knife blade on the stone or emery wheel. Never carry a pocket knife in a sweaty pocket as this will cause the blades of the knife to rust.

All John Primble knives are guaranteed against defective workmanship and materials. Not guaranteed against abuse.

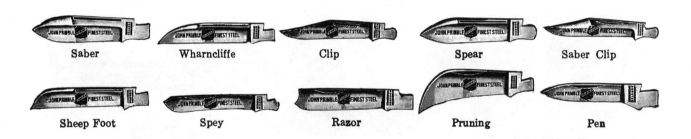

| Saber | Wharncliffe | Clip | Spear | Saber Clip |

| Sheep Foot | Spey | Razor | Pruning | Pen |

PREMIUM STOCK

HANDLE—See below.
BLADES—Three: clip, spey and sheepfoot. Full polished and etched. French nail mark on master blade.
DIAGONAL BOLSTERS—Nickel silver.
SHIELD—Nickel silver.
LINING—Brass, milled center.
LENGTH—4 inches.

Pearl Pyralin
C1-5371JP

Yellow Pyralin
C1-5371Y
Half doz in box;
wt doz 2 lbs.

PREMIUM STOCK

HANDLE—Bone stag.
BLADES—Three: clip, spey and sheepfoot. Full polished and etched. French nail mark on master blade
DIAGONAL BOLSTERS—Nickel silver.
SHIELD—Nickel silver.
LINING—Brass, milled center.
LENGTH— 4 inches.

C1-5371S
Half doz in box;
wt doz 2 lbs.

STANDARD PREMIUM STOCK

HANDLE—Bone stag.
BLADES—Three: clip, spey and sheepfoot. Full polished and etched. French nail mark on master blade.
BOLSTERS—Nickel silver.
SHIELD—Nickel silver.
LINING—Nickel silver, milled center.
LENGTH—4 inches.

C1-5385S
Half doz in box;
wt doz 2 lbs.

JOHN PRIMBLE DISPLAY SHIELDS

POCKET KNIVES

Suggested list of items to be sold with No. C4-1957-1 display shield.
Selection includes ¼ dozen each of the following items:

	Cost Per Doz	Total Cost
C1-728S	$16 00	4 00
C1-4923S	16 00	4 00
C1-4952S	20 00	5 00
C1-5222S	18 00	4 50
C1-5224S	16 00	4 00
C1-5323S	22 00	5 50
C1-5344S	19 00	4 75
C1-5370S	24 00	6 00
C1-5371JP	28 00	7 00
C1-5373S	24 00	6 00
C1-5380S	26 00	6 50
C1-5385S	27 00	6 75
C1-5514S	30 00	7 50
C1-5733S	20 00	5 00
C1-5763S	18 00	4 50
C1-5922	16 00	4 00

C4-1957-1 — As described with display shield _____Ass't **$255 00**

NOTE—In writing orders please be certain to itemize completely specifying quantities and stock numbers (either the list above or others of yours or your dealer selection), and prices. The suggested lists are offered as a guide in quoting and selling.

ORIGINAL

BELKNAP

JOHN PRIMBLE CUTLERY DISPLAY DEALER CONTRACT

THIS AGREEMENT, between BELKNAP HARDWARE AND MFG. COMPANY, 111 East Main St., Louisville, Kentucky, hereinafter referred to as "BELKNAP", and

JOHN DOE—Cross Roads—Ky.

_____, hereinafter referred to as the DEALER.

In consideration of BELKNAP selling the DEALER____1____only_____John Primble Cutlery Case amounting to $_____X X X_____BELKNAP will allow for a period not to exceed one year from date listed below, but not in excess of the above purchase price of Display Case only, a credit in the amount of 10% on all John Primble Cutlery, including Pocket Knives, Kitchen and Table Cutlery, Scissors and Shears, and all other John Primble Goods purchased by the DEALER from BELKNAP during the life of this contract as outlined above.

It is also agreed the DEALER will pay for the John Primble Cutlery Case at the price and at the terms shown on the invoice.

This agreement entered into on this_____day of_____, 196_____.

Salesman_____

BELKNAP HARDWARE AND MFG. COMPANY

BY_____

DEALER_____

BY_____

ADDRESS_____

CITY AND STATE_____

NOTE: This agreement is to be filled out in duplicate and both copies sent to BELKNAP attached to the order for the John Primble Cutlery Case and the Cutlery then purchased. BELKNAP, upon acceptance will complete the signature, retain the duplicate copy and return the original to the DEALER for his file and record.

DISPLAY CASE FREE

Includes free display case (value $20 00) and 48 knives assorted, ⅓ dozen each of 12 most popular sellers, not just with Belknap, but nationwide with cutlery manufacturers.   Hardwood construction case smooth sanded and waxed light natural finish; glass-covered front; panel board with knife clips for easy mounting and removal; stock numbers printed under each knife; storage space in back of case for overstock, fitted with hasp for locking.   Quantity stock number and dealer cost of each knife listed on packing slip in every carton.

Consists of ⅓ dozen each of the following John Primble pocket knives:

C1-3335S	C1-5370S	C1-5373S	C1-5517S
C1-4992S	C1-5371JP	C1-5390S	C1-5922
C1-4927S	C1-5371S	C1-5514S	C1-711S

(See Numerical Page for Catalog Page 2612 on which these Nos. are described.)

C2-1975—Size case 17½ ins high; 14 ins wide; depth 8¾ ins _ Ass't **$311 07**
One ass't in shp ctn; wt ass't 22 lbs.

JOHN PRIMBLE POCKET KNIFE GUARANTEE

All John Primble Pocket Knives are thoroughly inspected at various stages of production for grinding, temper, workmanship and finish. Any imperfections, therefore, are usually detected before the knives leave the factory.

All John Primble Pocket Knives, therefore, can be fully guaranteed to be of the best material, proper temper and hardness of blades and free from manufacturing flaws.

If any imperfections should develop, they would show up immediately after knife is put into use.

Under the circumstances, no replacements can be made on knives that have been in daily use for several years.

No longer will replacements be made on knives that have been abused or worn out by use.

To sharpen Quality Pocket Knives, use an oil stone. Do not use a grindstone or emery wheel. Such stones cut too fast, grind the edge too thin and remove the temper from the blade thru overheating.

Hold blade at about a 20° angle, not flat, and draw it across oil stone towards the edge, from heel to point

No claims can be allowed on knives on which the blades have been improperly ground.

A Pocket Knife is strictly a cutting tool—not a screwdriver, wedge or pry bar.

Pocket knives cannot be guaranteed against breaking out a blade since this is not caused from cutting.

No claims for broken handles can be recognized. They will not break in ordinary usage and we cannot be held responsible for damage caused as a result of dropping knife on hard pavement or due to other careless mishandling.

A drop of oil should be inserted at the joints where the hinge of the blade meets the spring at the end of the knife. Do this at least once a week. This preserves the spring action of the blade and prevents rust. Rust is what causes most springs to break.

Salesmen are not to tell dealers that all knives returned to them will be replaced. If dealer and salesman are in doubt as to what is or is not defective, knives can be returned for our inspection.

No claims will be allowed for rusted, broken back springs.

CUTLERY DISPLAY CASES

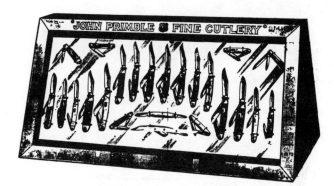

Selected hardwood and plywood.
Display portion of case with glass top with removable display panel, large enough to display 25 pocket knives of your own selection. Rear of case designed with drop door permitting easy access to 10x27 inch storage space. Fitted with brass lock. Sold with dealer's own selection of John Primble cutlery items amounting to $100.00 in value. We mount all items, lacquer all blades and place price buttons with stock numbers and selling prices under each item free.
Length 28 7/8 inches; width 14 1/2 inches; height 13 1/4 inches. Panel size 1/4x27 1/2x11 3/16 inches.

C4-1950N-N—Natural finish __Each $78 75
With an order for $100 00 of John Primble Cutlery Min. Amt.
One in shipping carton; wt each 27 1/2 lbs.

SUGGESTED LIST OF ITEMS TO BE SOLD WITH C4-1950N-N CUTLERY CASE SELECTION INCLUDES 1/2 DOZEN EACH OF THE FOLLOWING POCKET KNIVES

	Doz		Doz		Doz		Doz
C1-708NP	$60 00	C1-908S	$66 00	C1-4923NP	$48 00	C1-5371JP	$ 84 00
C1-731S	60 00	C1-914S	90 00	C1-4952S	60 00	C1-5373S	72 00
C1-900S	60 00	C1-915S	90 00	C1-4992S	60 00	C1-5365S	81 00
C1-901NP	60 00	C1-916S	96 00	C1-5222S	54 00	C1-5386S	78 00
C1-902S	66 00	C1-917S	96 00	C1-5323S	66 00	C1-5514S	90 00
C1-910S	72 00	C1-921S	84 00	C1-5344S	57 00	C1-5763P	105 00
						C1-5763S	54 00

In writing orders please be certain to itemize completely, specifying quantities and stock numbers (either the above or others of yours or your dealer's selection) and prices.

Note—The above selection with one each of the items lacquered and mounted on the display panels.

CUTLERY DISPLAY CASES

JOHN PRIMBLE

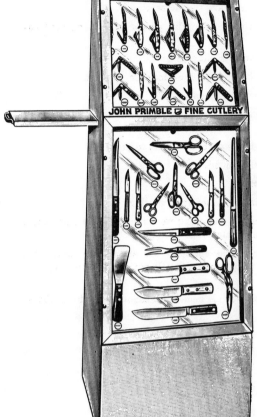

The perfect storage and display cabinet.

Specially designed to attractively display John Primble fine cutlery for greatly increased sales.

Sturdily built of hardwoods and plywoods.

Two storage spaces.

Drawers fitted with Corbin locks.   Easy roll casters.

Built in no-tilting stops and brass drawer pulls.

Pull out shelf for writing orders and laying merchandise.

The items selected will be mounted on this case, all blades will be lacquered and price buttons placed under each item with stock number and retail price shown on each item given to us on order form.

4 Drawers { 2—18x20 inches. {br} 2—14x20 inches.   Panels { Upper 19¾x16¾ inches. {br} Lower 19¾x28½ inches.

Upper display panel holds 19 items.   Height 60 inches.

Lower display panel holds 19 items.   Width 22 inches.

C4-87WN-N—Natural finish_____ Each **$299 25**

One in shp ctn; wt each 104 lbs.

SUGGESTED LIST OF ITEMS TO BE SOLD WITH C4-87WN-N CUTLERY CASE

SELECTION INCLUDES ½ DOZEN EACH OF THE FOLLOWING ITEMS:

Pocket Knives

	Doz
C1-5514S _____	$90 00
C1-4923NP _____	48 00
C1-5100S _____	60 00
C1-5373S _____	72 00
C1-5385S _____	81 00
C1-916S _____	96 00
C1-5371JP _____	84 00
C1-914S _____	90 00
C1-4927NP _____	48 00
C1-4861S _____	72 00
C1-4992S _____	60 00
C1-5722 _____	36 00
C1-5763S _____	54 00
C1-5222S _____	54 00
C1-921S _____	84 00
C1-901NP _____	60 00
C1-902S _____	66 00
C1-900S _____	60 00
C1-5733S _____	66 00
C1-910S _____	57 00
C1-5344S _____	54 00
C1-4952S _____	60 00
C1-4984S _____	60 00

Slicers

	Doz
C5-35SL _____	$36 00
C5-6-4H _____	28 50

Butcher Knives

C5-35-7 _____	$36 00
C5-35-6 _____	32 40
C5-35-8 _____	39 60
C5-6-6H _____	28 50
C5-6-7H _____	31 50
C5-6-8H _____	34 50

Paring Knives

C5-35-1 _____	$16 50
C5-35-2 _____	18 00
C5-6-CH _____	15 00
C5-6-5H _____	15 00

Boning Knives

C5-35B-6 _____	$32 40
C5-6-1-H _____	27 00

Bent Shears

	Doz
C9-40-7 _____	$99 00
C9-440-7 _____	90 00

Shears

C9-20-7 _____	$99 00
C9-220-7 _____	78 00

Pocket or Dry Goods Scissors

C9-31-6 _____	$66 00

Barber Shears

C9-54-7½ _____	$81 00

Scissors

C9-31-5 _____	$60 00
C9-31-4 _____	54 00
C9-32-4 _____	54 00

1 ONLY No. C4-87WN-N Cutlery Case_____ $ 299 25

The above selection with one each of the items lacquered and mounted on the display panels.

Approximate value of case and knives_____ 1665 25

In writing orders please be certain to itemize completely specifying quantities and stock numbers (either the list above or others of yours or your dealer's selection), and prices.

JOHN PRIMBLE POCKET KNIVES
Made In America

SMALL JACK

HANDLE—Bone stag.
BLADES—Two: Pen and sabre clip.
Full polished and etched.
LINING—Brass.
BOLSTERS—Nickel silver.
SHIELD—Nickel silver.
LENGTH—2 ⅝ inches.

C1-707S
Half doz in box;   Doz **$50 40**
wt doz 1 lb.

SMALL SERPENTINE JACK KNIFE

HANDLE—New Pearl.
BLADES—Two: clip and pen, fully mirror polished.
BOLSTER AND SHIELD—Nickel silver.
LINING—Brass.
LENGTH—2⁹⁄₁₆ inches.

C1-707NP
Half doz in box;   Doz **$50 40**
wt doz 1 lb.

MUSKRAT

HANDLE—Bone stag.
BLADES—Two: Narrow clip. Polished.
BOLSTER AND SHIELD—Nickel silver trim.
LINING—Brass.
LENGTH—4 inches.

C1-20S
Half doz in box;   Doz **$75 60**
wt doz 2 lbs.

SERPENTINE PATTERN

HANDLE—Bone stag.
BLADES—Half saber clip and long spey.
BOLSTER AND SHIELDS—Nickel silver.
LENGTH—3 ⅞ inches.

C1-923S_ _ _ _ _ _ _ _ _ _ _ _ _ _ _ _ _ _   Doz **$88 20**
One doz in box; wt doz 3 lbs.

LARGE SKINNING

BLADES—Two: Heavy saber clip and skinning, full polished.
BOLSTERS AND CAPS—Nickel silver.
LINING—Brass.
LENGTH—5¼ inches.

BONE STAG HANDLE
C1-7007S_ _ _ _ _ _ _ _ _ _ _ _ _ _ _ _   Doz **$119 70**
Half doz in box; wt doz 3 lbs.

NEW PEARL HANDLE
C1-7007NP_ _ _ _ _ _ _ _ _ _ _ _ _ _ _   Doz **$119 70**
Half doz in box; wt doz 3 lbs.

JOHN PRIMBLE POCKET KNIVES
Made In America

PREMIUM AND JR. STOCK

HANDLE—Bone stag.
BLADES—Three: clip, spey and sheep-
foot. Full polished and etched.
BOLSTERS—Nickel silver.
SHIELD—Nickel silver.
LINING—Brass, center milled.
LENGTH—3 ⅜ inches.

C1-5373S

Half doz in box;   Doz $75 60
wt doz 2 lbs.

PREMIUM STOCK

HANDLE—Bone stag.
BLADES—Three: clip, spey and pen.
Large blade polished on one side.
BOLSTERS—Nickel silver.
SHIELD—Nickel silver.
LINING—Brass.
LENGTH—3⁵⁄₁₆ inches.

C1-914S

Half doz in box;   Doz $94 50
wt doz 2 lbs.

PREMIUM STOCK

HANDLE—Bone stag.
BLADES—Three: clip, pen and sheep-
foot.
BOLSTERS—Nickel silver.
SHIELD—Nickel silver.
LINING—Brass.
LENGTH—3⁵⁄₁₆ inches.

C1-915S

Half doz in box;   Doz $94 50
wt doz 3 lbs.

PREMIUM STOCK

HANDLES—Yellow plastic.
BLADES—Three: clip, spey and pen.
LINING—Brass.
SHIELD AND ROSETTES—Nickel
silver.
BOLSTER—Nickel silver.
LENGTH—3⁵⁄₁₆ inches.

C1-932Y

Half doz in box;   Doz $94 50
wt doz 1 lb.

PREMIUM STOCK

HANDLE—New pearl.
BLADES—Three: clip, spey and pen.
BOLSTERS—Nickel silver.
LINING—Brass.
LENGTH—3⁵⁄₁₆ inches.

C1-731NP

Half doz in box;   Doz $63 00
wt doz 1 lb.

PREMIUM STOCK

HANDLE—Bone stag.
BLADES—Three: clip, pen and sheep-
foot.
BOLSTERS—Nickel silver.
LINING—Brass.
LENGTH—3⁵⁄₁₆ inches.

C1-731S

Half doz in box;   Doz $63 00
wt doz 2 lbs.

PREMIUM STOCK

HANDLE—Bone stag.
BLADES—Clip, spey and punch.
LINING—Brass.
Steel high carbon cutlery.
BLADE FINISH—Mirror polish.
LENGTH—Closed 3½ inches.

C1-786S

Half doz in box;   Doz $63 00
wt doz 2 lbs.

SLIM PREMIUM STOCK

LINING—Brass.
BLADES—Three: clip, spey and sheep-
foot, etched.
BOLSTERS—Nickel silver.
LENGTH—3¼ inches.

Bone Stag Handle
C1-703S
                            Doz $63 00

Yellow Pyralin Handle
C1-703Y

Half doz in box;   Doz $56 70
wt doz 2 lbs.

SMALL SIZE STOCK KNIFE

HANDLE—Bone stag.
BLADES—Three: clip, pen and sheep-
foot.
BOLSTERS—Nickel silver.
SHIELD—Nickel silver.
LINING—Brass, milled backs.
LENGTH—2¾ inches.

C1-921S

One doz in box;   Doz $88 20
wt doz 1 lb.

JOHN PRIMBLE POCKET KNIVES
Made In America

SPORT SABER CLIP

HANDLE—Pyralin.
BLADE—Single. Saber clip. Full polished and etched.
BOLSTERS—Nickel silver.
LINING—Brass.
LENGTH—4 7/8 inches.

C1-713Y—Yellow_____   Doz **$50 40**
Half doz in box; wt doz 2 lbs.

SPORT KNIFE

Saber Clip Blade
Bone stag handle. Carbon steel blade; brass lining; nickel silver bolsters. Length 3 7/8 inches.

C1-5019S_____   Doz **$63 00**
Half doz in box; wt doz 2 lbs.

PRUNING

HANDLE—Black stagged with hole in handle for lanyard.
BLADE—One large pruning, full mirror finish.
BOLSTER—Nickel silver.
LINING—Brass.
LENGTH—4 inches.

C1-700S_____   Doz **$37 80**
Half doz in box; wt doz 2 lbs.

BARLOW HEAVY GAUGE

HANDLE—Bone.
BLADES—Two: clip and pen. Full polished and etched.
BOLSTER—Steel, flat.
LINING—Brass.
LENGTH—3 3/8 inches.

C1-5922
Doz **$50 40**

Half doz in box; wt doz 2 lbs.

BARLOW HEAVY GAUGE

HANDLE—Bone.
BLADE—Two: spear and pen. Full polished.
BOLSTER—Steel.
LINING—Brass, flat.
LENGTH—3 3/8 inches.

C1-5921
Doz **$50 40**

Half doz in box; wt doz 3 lbs.

BARLOW HEAVY GAUGE

HANDLE—Bone.
BLADES—Two: sheepfoot and pen. Full polished.
BOLSTER—Steel.
LINING—Brass, flat.
LENGTH—3 3/8 inches.

C1-5924
Doz **$50 40**

Half doz in box; wt doz 2 lbs.

Although a piece of cutlery bearing the John Primble trade mark may cost a little more, it is the cheapest in the end. There is none finer than John Primble. Look for the Primble Shield.

JOHN PRIMBLE POCKET KNIVES
Made In America

PREMIUM STOCK

HANDLE—Bone stag.
BLADES—Three: clip, spey and pen.
DIAGONAL BOLSTERS—Nickel silver.
SHIELD—Nickel silver.
LINING—Brass, milled.
LENGTH—4 inches.

C1-5372S

Half doz in box;   Doz **$88 20**
wt doz 2 lbs.

SLIM PREMIUM STOCK

HANDLE—Bone stag.
BLADES—Three: Turkish clip, sheepfoot, pen.
BOLSTERS—Nickel silver.
SHIELD—Nickel silver.
LINING—Brass.
LENGTH—3 9/16 inches.

C1-917S

Half doz in box;   Doz **$100 80**
wt doz 2 lbs.

PREMIUM STOCK

HANDLES—Yellow plastic.
BLADES—Three: clip, spey and sheepfoot.
LININGS—Brass.
SHIELD—Nickel silver.
LENGTH—4 inches.

C1-933Y

Half doz in box;   Doz **$94 50**
wt doz 2 lbs.

SLIM PREMIUM STOCK

HANDLE—See below.
BLADES—Three: clip, spey and sheepfoot.
BOLSTERS—Nickel silver.
SHIELD—Nickel silver.
LINING—Brass.
LENGTH—3 9/16 inches.

Bone Stag Handle

C1-916S

Half doz in box;   Doz **$100 80**
wt doz 2 lbs.

Yellow Pyralin Handle

C1-916Y

Half doz in box;   Doz **$100 80**
wt doz 2 lbs.

PREMIUM STOCK

HANDLE—Bone stag.
BLADES—Three: Turkish clip, spey and sheepfoot.
BOLSTERS—Nickel silver.
SHIELD—Nickel silver.
LINING—Brass, center milled.
LENGTH—3 1/2 inches.

C1-5386S

Half doz in box;   Doz **$81 90**
wt doz 2 lbs.

PREMIUM AND JR. STOCK

HANDLE—Bone stag.
BLADES—Three: Turkish clip, spey and pen.
BOLSTERS—Nickel silver.
SHIELD—Nickel silver.
LINING—Brass, center milled.
LENGTH—3 1/2 inches.

C1-5380S

Half doz in box;   Doz **$81 90**
wt doz 2 lbs.

CARPENTER'S KNIFE

HANDLE—Bone stag.
BLADES—Three: saber clip, cut off spey and pen.
BOLSTERS—Nickel silver.
SHIELD—Nickel silver.
LINING—Brass.
LENGTH—3 1/2 inches.

C1-5264S

Half doz in box;   Doz **$85 05**
wt doz 2 lbs.

JUNIOR—PREMIUM STOCK

HANDLE—Bone stag.
BLADES—Three: clip, spey and pen.
BOLSTERS—Nickel silver square.
SHIELD—Nickel silver.
LINING—Brass.
LENGTH—3 1/2 inches.

C1-769S

Half doz in box;   Doz **$63 00**
wt doz 2 lbs.

SLIM PREMIUM STOCK

HANDLE—Bone stag.
BLADES—Three: clip, spey and pen, full polished.
BOLSTERS—Nickel silver.
SHIELD—Nickel silver.
LINING—Brass, center milled.
LENGTH—3 3/8 inches.

C1-5370S

Half doz in box;   Doz **$75 60**
wt doz 2 lbs.

POCKET KNIVES
—BLUE GRASS—BARLOW

HANDLE—Bone.
BLADES—Two: clip and pen. Full polished.
BOLSTER—Steel.
LINING—Steel.
LENGTH—3⁵⁄₁₆ inches.

C1-5722
Half doz in box;
wt doz 2 lbs.

Doz $37 80

—BLUE GRASS—BARLOW

HANDLE—Bone.
BLADES—Two: spear and pen. Full polished.
BOLSTER—Steel.
LINING—Steel.
LENGTH—3⁵⁄₁₆ inches.

C1-5721
Half doz in box;
wt doz 2 lbs.

Doz $37 80

—BLUE GRASS—BARLOW

HANDLE—Bone.
BLADES—Two: sheepfoot and pen.
BOLSTER—Steel.
LINING—Steel.
LENGTH—3⁵⁄₁₆ inches.

C1-5724
Half doz in box;
wt doz 2 lbs.

Doz $37 80

JOHN PRIMBLE POCKET KNIVES
Made In America
NUMERICAL LIST

Catalog No.	Page	Doz
C1-20S	2610	$ 75 60
C1-700S	2611	37 80
C1-701S	2608	63 00
C1-702S	2609	50 40
C1-703S	2604	63 00
C1-703Y	2604	56 70
C1-707S	2610	50 40
C1-707NP	2610	50 40
C1-708S	2605	63 00
C1-708NP	2605	63 00
C1-711S	2605	66 15
C1-713Y	2611	50 40
C1-728NP	2609	50 40
C1-728S	2609	50 40
C1-731NP	2604	63 00
C1-731S	2604	63 00
C1-732NP	2606	69 30
C1-732S	2605	69 30
C1-769S	2603	63 00
C1-786S	2604	63 00
C1-900S	2606	63 00
C1-901NP	2607	63 00
C1-902S	2607	69 30
C1-908S	2609	69 30
C1-910S	2608	75 60
C1-913S	2608	88 20
C1-914S	2604	94 50
C1-915S	2604	94 50
C1-916S	2603	100 80
C1-916Y	2603	100 80
C1-917S	2603	100 80
C1-921S	2604	88 20
C1-923S	2610	88 20
C1-932Y	2604	94 50
C1-933Y	2603	94 50
C1-3335S	2606	81 90
C1-4860S	2608	75 60
C1-4861S	2608	75 60
C1-4923NP	2609	50 40
C1-4923S	2609	50 40
C1-4927NP	2609	50 40
C1-4927S	2609	50 40
C1-4942S	2607	88 20
C1-4952S	2608	63 00
C1-4953S	2609	63 00
C1-4983JP	2606	85 05
C1-4983S	2606	85 05
C1-4984S	2608	63 00
C1-4987S	2607	81 90
C1-4992S	2609	63 00
C1-4995S	2606	63 00
C1-5019S	2611	63 00
C1-5100S	2609	63 00
C1-5133S	2608	75 60
C1-5222S	2606	56 70
C1-5224S	2606	50 40
C1-5228S	2605	63 00
C1-5264S	2603	85 05

Catalog No.	Page	Doz
C1-5279S	2607	$ 63 00
C1-5323S	2607	69 30
C1-5344S	2607	59 85
C1-5370S	2603	75 60
C1-5371JP	2602	88 20
C1-5371S	2602	88 20
C1-5371Y	2602	88 20
C1-5372S	2603	88 20
C1-5373S	2604	75 60
C1-5380S	2603	81 90
C1-5385S	2602	85 05
C1-5386S	2603	81 90
C1-5390S	2605	81 90
C1-5390NP	2605	81 90
C1-5511S	2605	88 20
C1-5512S	2605	88 20
C1-5514S	2605	94 50
C1-5517S	2605	100 80
C1-5727S	2608	88 20
C1-5733NP	2609	63 00
C1-5733S	2609	63 00
C1-5763P	2607	110 25
C1-5763S	2607	56 70
C1-5921	2611	50 40
C1-5922	2611	50 40
C1-5924	2611	50 40
C1-7007NP	2610	119 70
C1-7007S	2610	119 70

KNIFE PURSES
OPEN END

Made of finest suede lamb skin with stitched edges.
Brown and gray color.
C3-1F—Length 3 inches.
C3-3F—Length 3½ inches.
C3-4F—Length 4 inches.
Loose.   Doz $3 30

GIFT BOXES
INDIVIDUAL

Made of heavy cardboard, with gold top and cream bottom, ideal for knife gift boxes.
Fits Jack or Pen knives.
C3-300
Fits Scout and 3-bladed knives.
C3-301
For 3 or 4-bladed knives.
C3-302
Loose.   Doz $1 89

JOHN PRIMBLE CUTLERY DISPLAY CASE

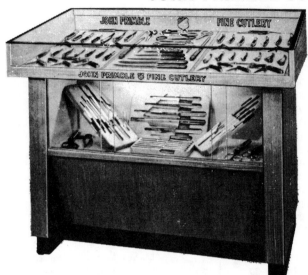

THREE PANELS

Solid oak and plywood construction. All corners mortised, clamp-nailed, and glued for extra strength. Light oak finish. Base black.

Overall length 45½ inches; width 26 inches; rear height 36 inches; front height 33½ inches; with ¼-inch plate glass top 26¼x45½ inches. Front lighted display area in base with 20 watt fluorescent lamp with five foot cord with 2-sliding glass doors with glass door lock.

At rear under glass top, 2 hinged doors, finished with chrome pulls.

At bottom rear, storage area with three stationary shelves with two sliding doors with lock. Panel size ³⁄₁₆x13¹¹⁄₁₆x23¼₁₆ in.

C4-1960-N_____ Each **$472 50**
One in shp crate; wt each, 200 lbs.

See Opposite Page for Color Illustration

SUGGESTED LIST OF ITEMS TO BE SOLD WITH C4-1960-N CUTLERY CASE
SELECTION INCLUDES ½ DOZEN EACH OF THE FOLLOWING ITEMS

Pocket Knives.	Doz	Pocket Knives	Doz	Scissors	Doz
C1-702S	$48 00	C1-4992S	$ 60 00	C9-32-4	$54 00
C1-703S	60 00	C1-5100S	60 00	C9-32-5	60 00
C1-708NP	60 00	C1-5222S	54 00	C9-54-7½—Barber	
C1-711S	63 00	C1-5224S	48 00	Shears	81 00
C1-728NP	48 00	C1-5264S	81 00	C9-33-5	48 00
C1-731NP	60 00	C1-5323S	66 00	**Shears**	
C1-732NP	66 00	C1-5344S	57 00	C9-20-7	$99 00
C1-732S	66 00	C1-5370S	72 00	C9-220-7	78 00
C1-900S	60 00	C1-5371JP	84 00	C9-40-7—Bent Shears	99 00
C1-901NP	60 00	C1-5372S	84 00	C9-440-7	90 00
C1-902S	66 00	C1-5373S	72 00	**Paring Knife**	
C1-908S	66 00	C1-5380S	78 00	C5-420	$22 50
C1-910S	72 00	C1-5386S	78 00	**Utility Knife**	
C1-913S	84 00	C1-5390NP	78 00	C5-120	$34 50
C1-914S	90 00	C1-5390S	78 00	**Sandwich Knife**	
C1-916S	96 00	C1-5512S	84 00	C5-920	$45 00
C1-917S	96 00	C1-5514S	90 00	**Narrow Slicer**	
C1-921S	84 00	C1-5722	36 00	C5-220	$60 00
C1-4861S	72 00	C1-5727S	84 00	**Regular Slicer**	
C1-4923S	48 00	C1-5733NP	60 00	C5-820	$60 00
C1-4927NP	48 00	C1-5733S	60 00	**Ham Slicer**	
C1-4952S	60 00	C1-5763P	105 00	C5-230	$60 00
C1-4983S	81 00	C1-5763S	54 00	**Butcher Knife**	
C1-4984S	60 00	**Scissors**		C5-930	$60 00
C1-4987S	78 00	C9-31-4	$54 00		
		C9-31-6	66 00		

Approximate value of case and knives_____ $2764 13

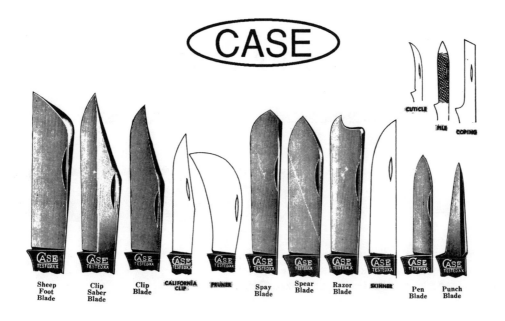

CASE

| Sheep Foot Blade | Clip Saber Blade | Clip Blade | California Clip | Pruner | Spay Blade | Spear Blade | Razor Blade | Skinner | Pen Blade | Punch Blade |

CUTICLE   FILE   COPING

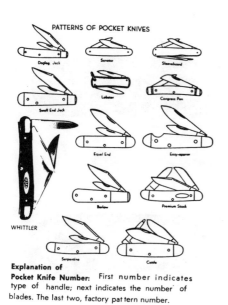

PATTERNS OF POCKET KNIVES

Daylag Jack
Senator
Sleeveboard
Lobster
Congress Pen
Swell End Jack
Equal End
Easy-opener
WHITTLER
Barlow
Premium Stock
Serpentine
Castle

Explanation of Pocket Knife Number: First number indicates type of handle; next indicates the number of blades. The last two, factory pattern number.

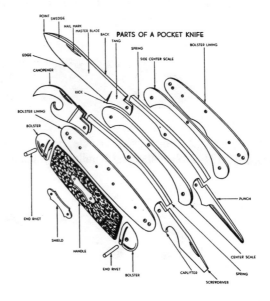

PARTS OF A POCKET KNIFE

POINT, SWEDGE, NAIL MARK, MASTER BLADE, BACK, TANG, SPRING, SIDE CENTER SCALE, BOLSTER LINING, EDGE, CANOPENER, KICK, BOLSTER LINING, BOLSTER, END RIVET, SHIELD, HANDLE, END RIVET, BOLSTER, CAPLIFTER, SCREWDRIVER, SPRING, CENTER SCALE, PUNCH

POCKET KNIVES.

NEW YORK KNIFE CO'S. WARRANTED.

No. 226N.

No. 125N–1 blade, cocoa handle, iron lined, glazed, 3¼ in., · · · · ·
No. 226N–2 blades, cocoa handle, iron lined, glazed, 3⅜ in., · · · · ·
No. 209N–2 blades, cocoa handle, iron lined, glazed, 3⅜ in., clip point, · · · · ·

No. 2430N–2 blades, cocoa handle, iron lined, glazed, 3¼ in., · · · · ·

No. 2451N.

No. 2450N–2 blades, cocoa handle, iron lined, glazed, 3½ in., · · · · ·
No. 2451N–2 blades, ebony handle, iron lined, glazed, 3½ in., · · · ·

No. 2461N.

No. 2460N–2 blades, cocoa handle, iron lined, large blade crocus polished, 3⅝ in., · ·
No. 2461N–2 blades, ebony handle, iron lined, large blade crocus polished. 3⅝ in., · ·

No. 138N–1 blade, cocoa handle, iron lined, glazed, 3¾ in., · · · · ·

HALF DOZEN IN A BOX.

POCKET KNIVES.

NEW YORK KNIFE CO'S, WARRANTED.

No. 241N-2 blades, ebony handle, brass lined, crocus polished, 3⅛ in., · · · · · ·

No. 2449N.

No. 2449N-2 blades, stag handle, brass lined, glazed, 3½ in., clip point. · · · ·
No. 2444N-2 blades, stag handle, brass lined, glazed, 3½ in., spear point. · · · ·

No. 2225N.

No. 2222N-2 blades, cocoa handle, iron lined, glazed, 3½ in., · · · · · · ·
No. 2223N-2 blades, ebony handle, iron lined, glazed, 3½ in., · · · · · · ·
No. 2225N-2 blades, stag   handle, iron lined, glazed, 3½ in., · · · · · · ·
No. 2334N-2 blades, white bone handle, brass lined, glazed, 3½ in., · · · · ·

No. 2672N-2 blades, cocoa handle, iron lined, large blade crocus polished, 3⅝ in., · · ·

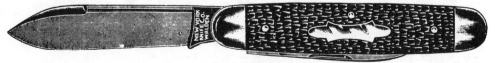

No. 2628N.

No. 2625N-2 blades, cocoa handle, iron   lined, glazed, 3½ in., · · · · · ·
No. 2628N-2 blades, stag   handle, iron   lined, glazed, 3½ in., · · · · · ·
No. 228N-2 blades, cocoa handle, iron   lined, glazed, 3⅝ in., · · · · · ·
No. 2420N-2 blades, cocoa handle, brass lined, glazed, 3¼ in., · · · · · ·
No. 2525N-2 blades, cocoa handle, brass lined, glazed, 3½ in., · · · · · ·
No. 2526N-2 blades, ebony handle, brass lined, glazed, 3½ in., · · · · · ·
No. 2528N-2 blades, stag   handle, brass lined, glazed, 3½ in., · · · · · ·

HALF DOZEN IN A BOX.

POCKET KNIVES.

NEW YORK KNIFE CO'S, WARRANTED.

No. 2348N–2 blades, ebony handle, brass lined, glazed, 3¼ in., ...

No. 2755N.

No. 2755N–2 blades, cocoa handle, iron lined, large blade crocus polished, etched "Ranchero," 3½ in.,
    per dozen . . . .
No. 2965N–2 blades, cocoa handle, iron lined, large blade crocus polished, etched "Rustler," 3⅝ in.,
    per dozen . . . .

No. 2743N.

No. 2742N–2 blades, cocoa handle, iron lined, large blade crocus polished, etched "Rustler," 3⅝ in.,
    per dozen . . . .
No. 2743N–2 blades, ebony handle, iron lined, large blade crocus polished, etched "Rustler," 3⅝ in.,
    per dozen . . . .
No. 2762N–2 blades, cocoa handle, iron lined, large blade crocus polished, etched "Old Reliable," 3¾ in.,
    per dozen . . . .
No. 2339N–2 blades, stag handle, brass lined, large blade crocus polished, not etched, 3½ in.,

No. 2294N–2 blades, cocoa handle, brass lined, large blade crocus polished, 3⅝ in., . . .

No. 2872N–2 blades, ebony handle, brass lined, large blade crocus polished, 3⅞ in., . . .

No. 275N–2 blades, cocoa handle, brass lined, large blade crocus polished, extra heavy, 3⅞ in.,
HALF DOZEN IN A BOX.

POCKET KNIVES.

NEW YORK KNIFE CO'S, WARRANTED.

No. 2425N–2 blades, cocoa handle. brass lined, large blade crocus polished, 3½ in., ·

No. 2731N–2 blades, ebony handle. brass lined, large blade crocus polished, 3½ in., ·   ·

No. 2403N–2 blades, stag handle, brass lined, large blade crocus polished, 3½ in., ·   ·

No. 2738N–2 blades, stag handle, brass lined, large blade crocus polished, 3½ in., ·   ·

No. 2434N–2 blades, stag handle, brass lined, large blade crocus polished, 3½ in., ·   ·

No. 2813N.

No. 2811N–2 blades, ebony handle, brass lined, large blade crocus polished, 3⅝ in., ·   ·
No. 2813N–2 blades, stag   handle, brass lined, large blade crocus polished, 3⅝ in., ·   ·

HALF DOZEN IN A BOX.

POCKET KNIVES.

NEW YORK KNIFE CO'S. WARRANTED.

No. 242N–2 blades, ebony handle, brass lined, large blade crocus polished, 3⅛ in., · · ·

No. 2299N.

No. 2288N–2 blades, stag handle, brass lined, large blade crocus polished, 3⅛ in., · · ·
No. 2299N–2 blades, pearl handle, brass lined, large blade crocus polished, 3⅛ in., · · ·

No 2301N

No. 2301N–2 blades, ebony handle, brass lined, large blade crocus polished, 3½ in., · ·
No. 2303N–2 blades, stag handle, brass lined, large blade crocus polished, 3¼ in., · ·

No. 2522N

No. 2521N–2 blades, ebony handle, brass lined, crocus polished, 3¼ in., · · · ·
No. 2522N–2 blades, stag handle, brass lined, crocus polished, 3¼ in., · · · ·

No. 2543N.

No. 2540N–2 blades, ebony handle, brass lined, crocus polished, 3¾ in., · · · ·
No. 2542N–2 blades, stag handle, brass lined, crocus polished, 3¾ in., · · · ·
No. 2543N–2 blades, pearl handle, brass lined, crocus polished, 3¾ in., · · · ·

HALF DOZEN IN A BOX:

POCKET KNIVES.

NEW YORK KNIFE CO'S, WARRANTED.

No. 2333N.

No. 2358N–2 blades, ebony handle, brass lined, glazed, not etched, 3¼ in., ·   ·   ·   ·
No. 2333N–2 blades, ebony handle, brass lined, large blade crocus polished, etched, 3½ in., ·
No. 2335N–2 blades, stag   handle, brass lined, large blade crocus polished, etched, 3½ in., ·

No. 2705N–2 blades, cocoa handle, brass lined, large blade crocus polished, 3½ in.,   ·   ·

No. 2205N

No. 2205N–2 blades, cocoa handle, brass lined, large blade crocus polished, 3⅝ in.,   ·   ·
No. 2208N–2 blades, stag   handle, brass lined, large blade crocus polished, 3⅝ in.,   ·

No. 2602N.

No. 2601N–2 blades, cocoa handle, brass lined, large blade crocus polished, 3⅝ in ,   ·   ·
No. 2602N–2 blades, ebony handle, brass lined, large blade crocus polished, 3⅝ in.,

No. 2535N.

No. 2636N–2 blades, ebony handle, iron   lined, glazed, spear point, 3½ in.,   ·   ·
No. 2431N–2 blades, cocoa handle, brass lined, large blade crocus polished, clip   point, 3½ in.,
No. 2535N–2 blades, cocoa handle, brass lined, large blade crocus polished, spear point, 3¾ in.,

HALF DOZEN IN A BOX

POCKET KNIVES.

NEW YORK KNIFE CO'S WARRANTED.

No. 4057N.

No. 4054N-4 blades, stag handle, rope milled brass lining, crocus polished. 3⅛ in., · · ·
No. 4037N-4 blades, pearl handle, rope milled brass lining, crocus polished. 2¾ in., · · ·
No. 4057N-4 blades, pearl handle, rope milled brass lining, crocus polished, 3⅛ in., · ·

No. 4999N-4 blades, stag handle, brass lined, crocus polished, 3⅜ in., · · · ·

No. 4167N.

No. 4164N 4 blades, stag handle, brass lined, crocus polished, 3⅜ in., · · · ·
No. 4167N-4 blades, pearl handle, brass lined, crocus polished, 3⅜ in., · · ·

No. 4417N.

No. 4415N-4 blades, stag handle, rope milled brass lining, crocus polished, 3 in., · ·
No. 4417N 4 blades, pearl handle, rope milled brass lining, crocus polished, 3 in., · ·

No. 4772N-4 blades, pearl handle, German silver lined, aluminum bolsters, crocus polished, 3⅛ in.,

HALF DOZEN IN A BOX.

POCKET KNIVES.

NEW YORK KNIFE CO'S, WARRANTED.

No. 291N–2 blades, stag handle, brass lined, glazed, 3 in., · · · · ·

No. 2045N–2 blades, stag handle, brass lined, glazed, 3¼ in., · · · ·

No. 2022N.

No. 2621N–2 blades, buffalo handle, brass lined, large blade crocus polished, 3⅜ in., · ·
No. 2022N–2 blades, stag   handle, brass lined, large blade crocus polished, 3⅜ in., · ·

No. 2369N.

No. 2369N–2 blades, ebony handle, brass lined, large blade crocus polished, 3⅜ in., · ·
No. 2370N–2 blades, stag   handle, brass lined, large blade crocus polished, 3⅜ in., · ·

No. 2167N.

No. 2355N–2 blades, stag handle, brass lined, glazed, 3¼ in., · · · ·
No. 2164N–2 blades, stag handle, brass lined, crocus polished, 3⅜ in., · · · ·
No. 2382N–2 blades, pearl handle, brass lined, crocus polished, 3⅛ in., · · · ·
No. 2167N–2 blades, pearl handle, brass lined, crocus polished, 3⅜ in., · · · ·

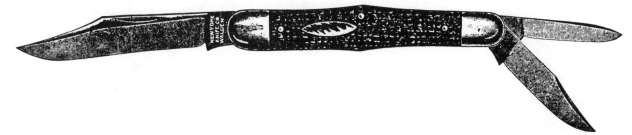

No. 807N–3 blades, stag handle, brass lined, glazed, 3⅝ in., · · · · · ·

HALF DOZEN IN A BOX.

POCKET KNIVES.

NEW YORK KNIFE CO'S, WARRANTED.

No. 304N–3 blades, pearl handle, brass lined. crocus polished, 2⅞ in., ·   ·   ·   ·

No. 3157N

No. 3154N–3 blades, stag handle, brass lined, crocus polished, 3⅛ in., ·   ·   ·   ·
No. 3157N–3 blades, pearl handle, brass lined, crocus polished, 3⅛ in., ·   ·   ·   ·

No. 3053N.

No. 3051N–3 blades, stag handle, German silver lined, crocus polished, 2⅞ in., · ·   ·
No. 3053N–3 blades, pearl handle, German silver lined. crocus polished, 2⅞ in., · ·   ·

No. 3381N.

No. 3378N–3 blades, stag handle, brass lined, crocus polished, 3⅛ in., ·   ·   ·   ·
No. 3381N–3 blades, pearl handle, brass lined, crocus polished, 3⅛ in., ·   ·   ·   ·

No. 3081N–3 blades, pearl handle, brass lined, crocus polished, 3⅛ in., ·   ·   ·   ·
HALF DOZEN IN A BOX.

POCKET KNIVES.

NEW YORK KNIFE CO'S. WARRANTED.

No. 2010N–2 blades, pearl handle, brass lined, crocus polished, 2⅝ in.,   ·   ·   ·   ·

No. 2395N–2 blades, pearl handle, brass lined, crocus polished, 2¾ in.,   ·   ·   ·   ·

No. 2771N–2 blades, pearl handle, German silver lined, fancy bolsters, crocus polished, 2¾ in.,

No. 253N–2 blades, pearl handle, brass lined, crocus polished, 2⅞ in.,   ·   ·   ·   ·

No. 2307N.

No. 2991N–2 blades, pearl handle, brass lined, crocus polished, 2⅝ in.,   ·   ·   ·   ·
No. 2307N–2 blades, pearl handle, brass lined, crocus polished, 3⅛ in.,   ·   ·   ·   ·

No. 263N.

No. 260N–2 blades, ebony handle, brass lined, crocus polished, 3¼ in.,   ·   ·   ·   ·
No. 261N–2 blades, stag   handle, brass lined, crocus polished, 3¼ in.,   ·   ·   ·   ·
No. 263N–2 blades, pearl handle, brass lined, crocus polished, 3¼ in.,   ·   ·   ·   ·

POCKET KNIVES
GEO. WOSTENHOLM & SONS' I. X. L. BRAND.

BARLOWS

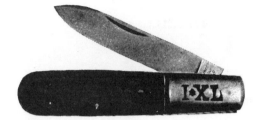

No. 1S—One blade, spear point_____

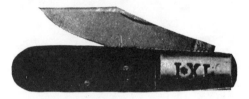

No. 1C—One blade, clip point_____

No. 1SF—One blade, sheep foot point_____

No. 1R—One blade, razor point_____

TWO BLADE
No. 2S—Large blade, spear point_____
No. 2C—Large blade, clip point_____
No. 2SF—Large blade, sheep foot point___

ONE BLADE—IRON HANDLE
No. 50SF—3¼-inch embossed iron handle, with sheep foot blade_____

ONE BLADE—STAG HANDLE
No. 8094—4-inch genuine stag handle; hollow steel bolsters; long spear blade_____

ONE BLADE—STAG HANDLE
No. 7681—4½-inch stag handle; hollow steel bolsters; sheep foot blade_____

TWO BLADE—IRON HANDLE
No. 11169—3½-inch embossed iron handle; hollow steel bolsters. Has one spey and one pen blade.

Per Dozen_____

TWO BLADE—PATENT STAG HANDLE
No. 7001—3¾-inch patent stag handle; steel bolsters. Has one large spear and one pen blade.

Per Dozen_____

POCKET KNIVES
GEO. WOSTENHOLM & SONS' I. X. L. BRAND.

TWO BLADE

No. 2294—3½-inch patent stag handle; German silver shield and bolsters; brass lined. Has one large spear and one pen blade_____

TWO BLADE

No. 2060—3¼-inch patent stag handle; brass lined. Has one large spear and one pen blade.

Per Dozen_____

TWO BLADE

No. 2148—3½-inch patent stag handle; German silver shield and bolsters; brass lined. Has one large spear and one pen blade_____Per Dozen,

TWO BLADE

No. 2289—3⅝-inch patent stag handle; German silver shield and bolsters; brass lined. Has one large spear and one pen blade_____

TWO BLADE

No. 2408—3¼-inch patent stag handle; polished hollow steel bolsters; brass lined. Has one large sheep foot and one pen blade_____

TWO BLADE

No. 2152—3-inch patent stag handle; polished hollow steel bolsters; brass lined. Has one large sheep foot and one pen blade_____

No. 2154—Same as No. 2152, except has 3½-inch handle. Per Dozen_____

No. 2156—Same as No. 2152, except has 4-inch handle. Per Dozen_____

THREE BLADE

No. 2061—3⅜-inch patent stag handle; brass lined. Has one large spear, one manicure and one pen blade_____

THREE BLADE

No. 2065—3½-inch patent stag handle; German silver tips; brass lined. Has one large spear and two pen blades_____

FOUR BLADE

No. 16157—3¾-inch patent stag handle; German silver grooved bolsters; brass lined. Has one large sheep foot, one tobacco and two pen blades. Per Dozen_____

No. 15523—Same as No. 16157, except has 4¼-inch handle. Per Dozen_____

POCKET KNIVES
GEO. WESTENHOLM & SONS' I. X. L. BRAND.

TWO BLADE

No. **6917**—3¼-inch genuine stag handle; hollow steel bolsters. Has one large sheep foot and one pen blade..

No. **6920**—Same as No. 6917, except has 3½-inch handle. Per Dozen...

No. **6926**—Same as No. 6917, except has 3¾-inch handle. Per Dozen...

No. **6974**—Same as No. 6917, except has 4-inch handle. Per Dozen...

No. **6988**—Same as No. 6917, except has 4½-inch handle. Per Dozen...

TWO BLADE—CAP AND BOLSTER

No. **17009**—3¾-inch patent stag handle; hollow steel bolsters; German silver shield and cap. Has one large spear and one pen blade...

TWO BLADE—CAP AND BOLSTER

No. **17003**—3½-inch patent stag handle; German silver shield, cap and bolsters. Has one large spear and one pen blade........................

TWO BLADE—PHYSICIAN'S KNIFE

No. **17005**—3¾-inch patent stag handle; German silver cap; brass lined. Has large spear and one pen blade......................................Per Dozen,

TWO BLADE—LOCK BACK

No. **17015**—4⅝-inch patent stag handle. Has one large spear blade.........................

ONE BLADE—PRUNING KNIFE

No. **14151**—4-inch embossed iron handle; hollow polished steel bolsters....................

ONE BLADE—PRUNING KNIFE

No. **7696**—4½-inch cocobola wood handle; polished hollow steel bolsters..................

TWO BLADE—PRUNING KNIFE

No. **8049**—4-inch genuine stag handle; polished hollow steel bolsters; German silver shield; brass lined. Has one pruning and one budding blade.
Per Dozen...

154

POCKET KNIVES
GEO. WOSTENHOLM & SONS' I. X. L. BRAND.

FOUR BLADE—CONGRESS PATTERN

No. 2191—3½-inch patent stag handle; polished hollow
    steel bolsters; brass lined. Has one large sheep
    foot, one tobacco, and two pen blades.
Per Dozen...

No. 2192—Same as No. 2191, except has 3¾-inch handle.
    Per Dozen.................................

No. 2193—Same as No. 2191, except has 4-inch handle.
    Per Dozen.................................

No. 2160—3½-inch patent stag handle; polished hollow
    steel bolsters; brass lined. Has one large sheep
    foot, one manicure and two pen blades.
Per Dozen...

No. 2163—Same as No. 2160, except has 4¼-inch handle.
    Per Dozen.................................

FOUR BLADE—STAG HANDLE

No. 2402S—3-inch genuine stag handle; German silver
    shield and tips; brass lined. Has one large spear
    one manicure and two pen blades...

TWO BLADE—PEARL HANDLE

No. 2044—3¼-inch pearl hande; brass lined. Has one
    large spear and one pen blade.......

THREE BLADE—PEARL HANDLE

No. 2045—3½-inch pearl handle; brass lined. Has one
    large spear and two pen blades.......

TWO BLADE—IVORY HANDLE

No. 2018—3¼-inch ivory handle; brass lined. Has one
    large spear and one pen blade.......

FOUR BLADE—PEARL HANDLE

No. 2401—3-inch pearl handle; German silver shield;
    brass lined. Has one large spear, one manicure
    and two pen blades.................

FOUR BLADE—PEARL HANDLE

No. 2402P—3-inch pearl handle; German silver shield
    and tips; brass lined. Has one large spear, one
    manicure and two pen blades.......

POCKET KNIVES.

GEORGE WOSTENHOLM & SON'S CELEBRATED I★XL.

No 306W

No. 305W–1 blade, bone handle, iron lined, 3¼ in.,　·　·　·　·　·　·　·
No. 306W–2 blades, bone handle, iron lined, 3¼ in.,　·　·　·　·　·　·　·

No. 8019.

No. 8018–1 blade, iron handle, iron lined, 3⅜ in.,　·　·　·　·　·
No. 8019–2 blades, iron handle, iron lined, 3⅜ in.,　·　·　·　·　·
No. 7967–2 blades, iron handle, iron lined, large blade sheep foot, 3⅜ in.,　·　·　·
No. 11169–2 blades, iron handle, iron lined, large blade speying,　3⅜ in.,　·　·　·

No. 2000

No. 2000–2 blades, cocoa handle, iron　lined, glazed, 3⅜ in.,　·　·　·　·　·　·
No. 2001–2 blades, ebony handle, iron　lined, glazed, 3⅜ in.,　·　·　·　·　·　·
No. 2036–2 blades, stag　handle, iron　lined, glazed, 3⅜ in.,　·　·　·　·　·　·
No. 2164–2 blades, cocoa handle, brass lined, glazed, 3⅜ in.,　·　·　·　·　·　·
No. 2165–2 blades, ebony handle, brass lined, glazed, 3⅜ in.,　·　·　·　·　·　·
No. 2167–2 blades, stag　handle; brass lined, glazed, 3⅜ in.,　·　·　·　·　·　·

No. 2172.

No. 2168–2 blades, cocoa handle, iron　lined, glazed, 3⅝ in.,　·　·　·　·　·　·
No. 2169–2 blades, ebony handle, iron　lined, glazed, 3⅝ in.,　·　·　·　·　·　·
No. 2171–2 blades, stag　handle, iron　lined, glazed, 3⅝ in.,　·　·　·　·　·　·
No. 2172–2 blades, cocoa handle, brass lined, glazed, 3⅝ in.,　·　·　·　·　·　·
No. 2173–2 blades, ebony handle, brass lined, glazed, 3⅝ in.,　·　·　·　·　·　·
No. 2175–2 blades, stag　handle, brass lined, glazed, 3⅝ in.,　·　·　·　·　·　·

HALF DOZEN IN A BOX.

POCKET KNIVES.

GEORGE WOSTENHOLM & SON'S CELEBRATED I✶XL.

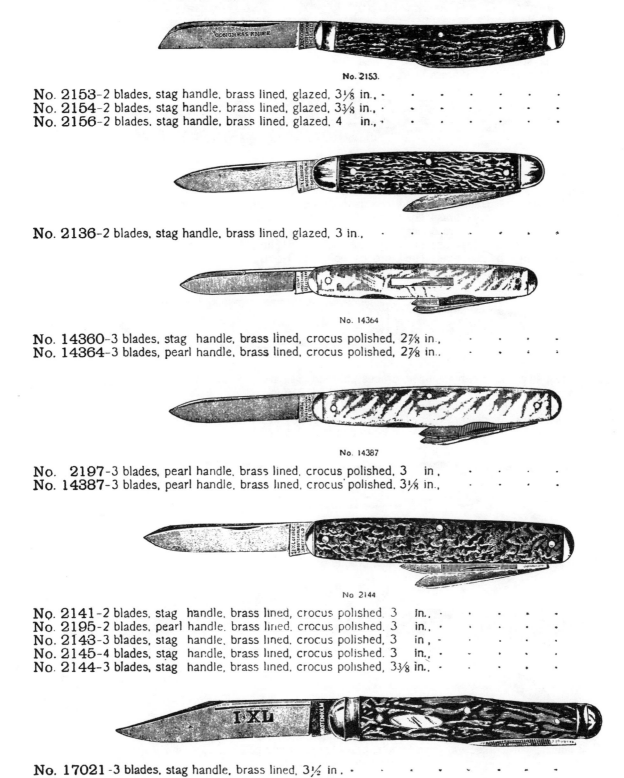

No. 2153.

No. 2153-2 blades, stag handle, brass lined, glazed, 3⅛ in., · - · - · - · - ·
No. 2154-2 blades, stag handle, brass lined, glazed, 3⅜ in., · - · - · - · - ·
No. 2156-2 blades, stag handle, brass lined, glazed, 4 in., · - · - · - · - ·

No. 2136-2 blades, stag handle, brass lined, glazed, 3 in., · - · - · - · - ·

No. 14364

No. 14360-3 blades, stag handle, brass lined, crocus polished, 2⅞ in., · - · - · - ·
No. 14364-3 blades, pearl handle, brass lined, crocus polished, 2⅞ in., · - · - · - ·

No. 14387

No. 2197-3 blades, pearl handle, brass lined, crocus polished, 3 in, · - · - · - ·
No. 14387-3 blades, pearl handle, brass lined, crocus polished, 3⅛ in., · - · - · - ·

No 2144

No. 2141-2 blades, stag handle, brass lined, crocus polished, 3 in., · - · - · - ·
No. 2195-2 blades, pearl handle, brass lined, crocus polished, 3 in., · - · - · - ·
No. 2143-3 blades, stag handle, brass lined, crocus polished, 3 in , · - · - · - ·
No. 2145-4 blades, stag handle, brass lined, crocus polished, 3 in., · - · - · - ·
No. 2144-3 blades, stag handle, brass lined, crocus polished, 3⅜ in., · - · - · - ·

No. 17021 -3 blades, stag handle, brass lined, 3½ in ., · - · - · - · - ·

HALF DOZEN IN A BOX.

POCKET KNIVES.

GEORGE WOSTENHOLM & SON'S CELEBRATED I★XL.

No. 17023.

No. 17023–3 blades, stag handle, brass lined, glazed, 3⅜ in., · · · · ·
No. 13401–3 blades, pearl handle, brass lined, crocus polished, 3 in., · · · · ·

No. 2061.

No. 2017–2 blades, buffalo handle, brass lined, crocus polished, 3¼ in., · · · ·
No. 2018–2 blades, ivory handle, brass lined, crocus polished, 3¼ in., · · · ·
No. 2060–2 blades, stag   handle, brass lined, crocus polished, 3¼ in., · · · ·
No. 2044–2 blades, pearl handle, brass lined, crocus polished, 3¼ in., · · · ·
No. 2020–3 blades, buffalo handle, brass lined, crocus polished, 3¼ in., · · · ·
No. 2015–3 blades, ivory handle, brass lined, crocus polished, 3¼ in., · · · ·
No. 2061–3 blades, stag   handle, brass lined, crocus polished, 3¼ in., · · · ·
No. 2045–3 blades, pearl handle, brass lined, crocus polished, 3¼ in., · · · ·

No. 2069.

No. 2064–2 blades, stag handle, brass lined, crocus polished, 3⅜ in., · · · · ·
No. 2067–2 blades, ivory handle, brass lined, crocus polished, 3⅜ in., · · · · ·
No. 2065–3 blades, stag handle, brass lined, crocus polished, 3⅜ in., · · · · ·
No. 2069–3 blades, ivory handle, brass lined, crocus polished, 3⅜ in., · · · · ·
No. 2070–3 blades, pearl handle, brass lined, crocus polished, 3⅜ in., · · · · ·

No. 14284–4 blades, fine pearl handle, brass lined, crocus polished, 3⅝ in., · · ·

No. 15713.

No. 15712–3 blades, with corkscrew, ivory handle, brass lined, crocus polished, 3⅝ in., ·
No. 15713–3 blades, with corkscrew, pearl handle, brass lined, crocus polished, 3⅝ in., ·

HALF DOZEN IN A BOX.

POCKET KNIVES.

GEORGE WOSTENHOLM & SON'S CELEBRATED I★XL.

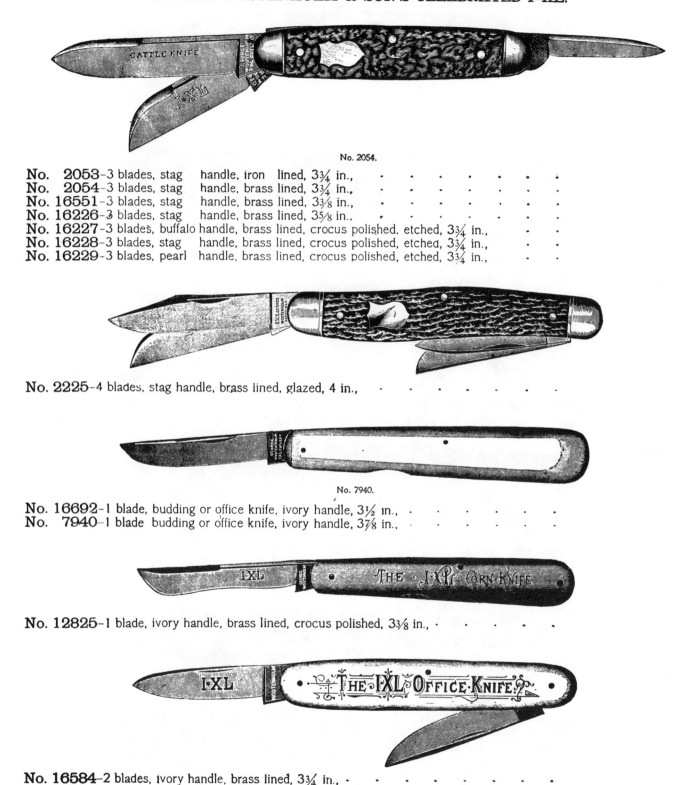

No. 2054.

No. 2053–3 blades, stag handle, iron lined, 3¾ in., · · · · · ·

No. 2054–3 blades, stag handle, brass lined, 3¾ in., · · · · · ·

No. 16551–3 blades, stag handle, brass lined, 3⅜ in., · · · · · ·

No. 16226–3 blades, stag handle, brass lined, 3⅝ in., · · · · · ·

No. 16227–3 blades, buffalo handle, brass lined, crocus polished, etched, 3¾ in., ·

No. 16228–3 blades, stag handle, brass lined, crocus polished, etched, 3¾ in., ·

No. 16229–3 blades, pearl handle, brass lined, crocus polished, etched, 3¾ in., ·

No. 2225–4 blades, stag handle, brass lined, glazed, 4 in., · · · · · ·

No. 7940.

No. 16692–1 blade, budding or office knife, ivory handle, 3½ in., · · · ·

No. 7940–1 blade budding or office knife, ivory handle, 3⅞ in., · · · ·

No. 12825–1 blade, ivory handle, brass lined, crocus polished, 3⅜ in., · · · ·

No. 16584–2 blades, ivory handle, brass lined, 3¾ in., · · · · · ·

HALF DOZEN IN A BOX.

POCKET KNIVES.

GEORGE WOSTENHOLM & SON'S CELEBRATED I★XL.

No. 2122–3 blades, pearl handle, brass lined, crocus polished, 3 in.,　·　·　·　·　·

No. 2160.

No. 2160–4 blades, stag handle, brass lined, glazed, 3½ in.,　·　·　·　·　·　·
No. 2161–4 blades, stag handle, brass lined, glazed, 3¾ in.,　·　·　·　·　·　·
No. 2162–4 blades, stag handle, brass lined, glazed, 4　in.,　·　·　·　·　·　·

No. 16580.

No. 16711–3 blades, pearl handle, brass lined, crocus polished, 3 in.,　·　·　·　·
No. 16580–4 blades, pearl handle, brass lined, crocus polished, 3 in.,　·　·　·　·

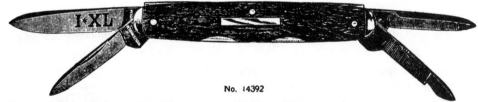

No. 14392.

No. 14392–4 blades, stag　handle, brass lined, crocus polished, 3⅛ in.,　·　·　·
No.　2199–4 blades, pearl handle, brass lined, crocus polished, 3　in.,　·　·　·
No.　2210–4 blades, stag　handle, brass lined, crocus polished, 3½ in.,　·　·　·
No.　2216–4 blades, pearl handle, brass lined, crocus polished, 3½ in.,　·　·　·

No. 16573–4 blades, pearl handle, brass lined, crocus polished, 3⅜ in.,　·　·　·

No. 2055–3 blades, stag handle, brass lined, glazed, 3⅝ in.,　·　·　·　·　·
HALF DOZEN IN A BOX.

POCKET KNIVES.

GEORGE WOSTENHOLM & SON'S CELEBRATED IXL.

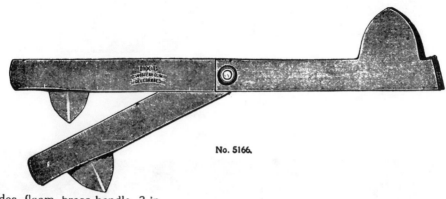

No. 5166.

No. **5166**–2 blades, fleam, brass handle, 3 in., ...

No. **5167**–3 blades, fleam, brass handle, 3 in., ...

ONE DOZEN IN A BOX.

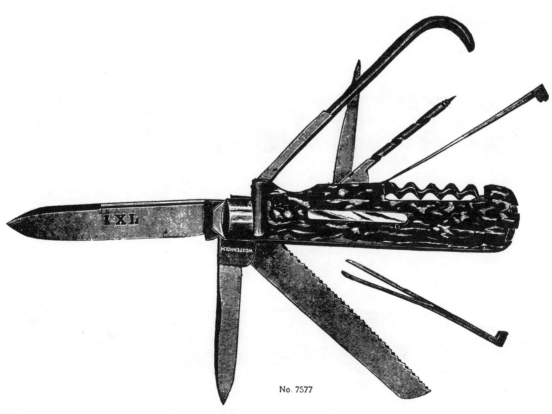

No. 7577

No. **1335**–2 blades, sportsmen's, stag handle, iron lined, 5 tools, 3⅝ in., ...

No. **13950**–3 blades, sportsmen's, stag handle, iron lined 6 tools, 3⅝ in., "IXL," . .

No. **2998**–4 blades, sportsmen's, stag handle, iron lined, 9 tools, 3⅝ in., ...

No. **7577**–4 blades, sportsmen's, stag handle, iron lined, 9 tools, 3⅝ in., "IXL," . .

HALF DOZEN IN A BOX.

POCKET KNIVES.

GEORGE WOSTENHOLM & SON'S CELEBRATED I★XL.

No. 7691–1 blade, buffalo handle, brass lined, ivory budder, 4⅞ in.,　·　·　·　·　·

No. 14151–1 blade, iron handle, glazed, 3¾ in.,　·　·　·　·　·　·　·

No. 11270–1 blade, cocoa handle, iron lined, 3⅝ in.,　·　·　·　·　·　·

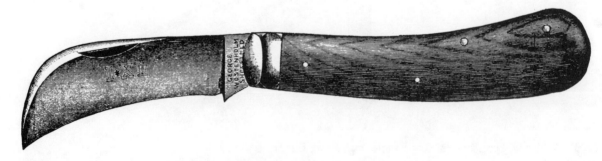

No. 11950–1 blade, cocoa handle, iron lined, glazed, 4½ in.,　·　·　·　·　·　·

HALF DOZEN IN A BOX.

POCKET KNIVES.

GEORGE WOSTENHOLM & SON'S CELEBRATED I✶XL.

No. 12056—2 blades, buffalo handle, brass lined, crocus polished, 3⅛ in.,   ·   ·   ·   ·

No. 2004.

No. 2004—2 blades, ebony handle, iron lined, glazed, 3⅝ in.,   ·   ·   ·   ·   ·
No. 2038—2 blades, stag   handle, iron lined, glazed, 3⅝ in.   ·   ·   ·   ·   ·

No. 9890.

No. 9890—2 blades, cocoa   handle, brass lined, crocus polished, 3¾ in.,   ·   ·   ·
No. 8926—2 blades, buffalo handle, brass lined, crocus polished, 3¾ in.,   ·   ·   ·
No. 9881—2 blades, white bone handle, brass lined, crocus polished, 3¾ in.   ·   ·   ·

No. 14958.

No. 17009—2 blades, stag handle, iron lined, 3⅝ in ,   ·   ·   ·   ·   ·
No. 14958—2 blades, stag handle, iron lined, crocus polished, 3⅝ in.,   ·   -   ·

No. 16148.

No. 16145—2 blades, cocoa   handle, brass lined, glazed, 3⅞ in ,   ·   ·   ·   ·
No. 16148—2 blades, ebony   handle, brass lined, glazed, 3⅞ in.,   ·   ·   ·   ·
No. 16144—2 blades, buffalo handle, brass lined, glazed, 3⅞ in.,   ·   ·   ·   ·
No. 16485—2 blades, stag   handle, brass lined, crocus polished, 3⅞ in..   '   ·   ·   ·

HALF DOZEN IN A BOX.

POCKET KNIVES.

GEORGE WOSTENHOLM & SON'S CELEBRATED I★XL.

No. 13575–2 blades. buffalo handle. brass lined, crocus polished 3 in., · · · · · ·

No. 17095–2 blades, stag handle, brass lined, crocus polished, 3½ in., · · · · ·

No 2013.

No. 2013–2 blades, ebony handle, brass lined, glazed, 35/8 in., · · · · · ·
No. 2040–2 blades, stag   handle, iron lined, glazed, 35/8 in., · · · · · ·

No. 2043.

No. 2033–2 blades, ebony handle, brass lined, glazed, 35/8 in., · · · · · ·
No. 2043–2 blades, stag   handle, brass lined, glazed, 35/8 in., · · · · · ·

No. 17011.

No. 14126–2 blades, cocoa handle, brass lined, glazed, 35/8 in., · · · · · ·
No. 12044–2 blades, buffalo handle, brass lined, glazed, 35/8 in., · · · · · ·
No. 17011–2 blades, stag   handle, brass lined, glazed, 35/8 in., · · · · · ·

HALF DOZEN IN A BOX.

POCKET KNIVES

CELEBRATED BOKER "TREE BRAND."

TWO BLADE.   No. 6202P.   PEARL HANDLE.

No. 6202P—3-inch pearl handle. German silver hollow bolsters, brass lined. Has one large sheep foot and one pen blade. _____

THREE BLADE.   No. 7234.   PEARL HANDLE.

No. 7234—3-inch pearl handle, German silver bolsters, brass lined.   Has one large spear and two pen blades, Per Dozen. _

THREE BLADE.   No. 11615.   PEARL HANDLE.

No. 11615—3-inch pearl handle, German silver shield and tips, brass lined. Has one large spear, one manicure and one pen blade. _ _

THREE BLADE.   No. 11618.   PEARL HANDLE.

No. 11618—3-inch pearl handle, German silver shield and bolsters, brass lined.   Has one large spear, one manicure and one pen blade. _

THREE BLADE.   No. 6157.   PEARL HANDLE.

No. 6157—3¼-inch pearl handle, German silver tips, brass lined. Has one large spear, one manicure and one pen blade. _

POCKET KNIVES

CELEBRATED BOKER "TREE BRAND."

FOUR BLADE.   No. 5839.   PEARL HANDLE.

No. 5839—3-inch pearl handle, brass lined. Has one large sheep foot, one manicure and two pen blades.
Per Dozen_____

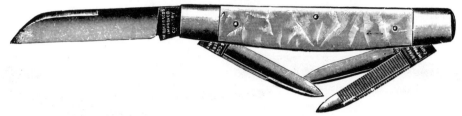

FOUR BLADE.   Nos. 7236 and 6228.   PEARL HANDLE

No. 7236—3-inch pearl handle, German silver bolsters, brass lined.   Has one large sheep foot, one maincure
and two pen blades_____

No. 6228—Same as No. 7236, except has 3½-inch handle_____

FOUR BLADE.   No. 6204.   PEARL HANDLE.

No. 6204—3¾-inch pearl handle, polished hollow steel bolsters, brass lined.   Has one large sheep foot, one manicure, and two pen blades_____

FOUR BLADE.   No. 6911.   PEARL HANDLE.

No. 6911—3½-inch two-piece pearl handle, German silver bands and bolsters, brass lined.   Has one large sheep
foot, one manicure and two pen blades_____

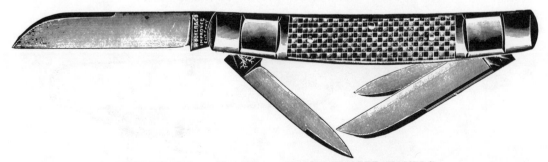

FOUR BLADE.   No. 6189.   BLACK RUBBER HANDLE.

No. 6189—3¾-inch checkered hard rubber handle, German silver bolsters, brass lined.   Has one large sheep
foot, one tobacco, and two pen blades_____

POCKET KNIVES

CELEBRATED BOKER "TREE BRAND"

FOUR BLADE Nos. 6554, 5950 and 5595

No. 6554—3½-inch patent stag handle, **German silver** shield and bolsters, brass lined. Has one large sheep foot, one manicure and two pen blades--

No. 5950—Same as No. 6554, except has 3-inch handle--

No. 5595—Same as No. 6554, except has 3¾-inch handle, and **Tobacco Blade** instead of manicure blade. Per Dozen--

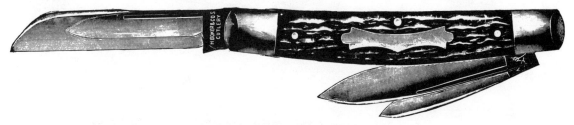

FOUR BLADE No. 6007

No. 6007—3¾-inch patent stag handle, German silver shield and bolsters, brass lined. Has one large sheep foot, one large spear and two pen blades--

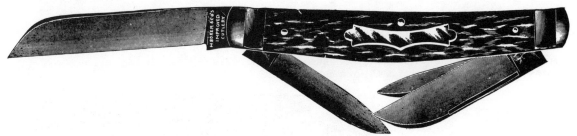

FOUR BLADE Nos. 6006, 6243 and 5753

No. 6006—3¾-inch patent stag handle, German silver shield, polished hollow steel bolsters, brass lined. Has one large sheep foot, one tobacco and two pen blades--

No. 6243—Same as No. 6006, except has 3½-inch handle and is steel lined and without shield on handle. Per Dozen--

No. 5753—Same as No. 6006, except has 3¼-inch handle, manicure instead of tobacco blade and without shield on handle--

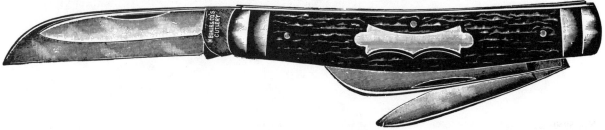

FOUR BLADE No. 5973

No. 5973—4-inch patent stag handle, German silver shield, polished hollow steel bolsters, brass lined. **Has** one large sheep foot, one tobacco, and two pen blades--

POCKET KNIVES
CELEBRATED BOKER "TREE BRAND."

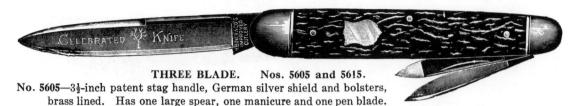

THREE BLADE.   Nos. 5605 and 5615.

No. 5605—3½-inch patent stag handle, German silver shield and bolsters, brass lined.   Has one large spear, one manicure and one pen blade.

Per Dozen

No. 5615—Same as No. 5605, except large blade is not etched and has two pen blades instead of manicure blade as shown in cut

THREE BLADE. No. 6005. WHARNCLIFFE PATTERN.

No. 6005—3¾-inch stag handle, German silver shield and bolsters, brass lined. Has one large Wharncliffe and two pen blades.

Per Dozen

FOUR BLADE.   Nos. 6153, 5613 and 5614.

No. 6153—3-inch patent stag handle, German silver shield and tips, brass lined. Has one large spear, one manicure, and two pen blades

No. 5613—Same as No. 6153, except has 3¼-inch handle

No. 5614—Same as No. 6153, except has 3½-inch handle

FOUR BLADE.   No. 5639.

No. 5639—3½-inch patent stag handle, German silver shield and bolsters, brass lined.   Has one large spear, one manicure and two pen blades

FOUR BLADE. Nos. 5960 and 6597.

No. 5960—3¼-inch stag handle, German silver shield and bolsters, brass lined.   Has one large sheep foot, one manicure and two pen blades

No. 6597—Same as No. 5960, except is steel lined, steel bolsters, and has one large sheep foot, one tobacco and two pen blades

POCKET KNIVES
CELEBRATED BOKER "TREE BRAND"

TWO BLADE Nos. 7069 and 6598 **CONGRESS PATTERN**

No. 7069—3-inch patent stag handle, hollow steel bolsters, brass lined. Has one large sheep foot and one
  pen blade.

No. 6598—3½-inch patent stag handle, hollow steel bolsters, steel lined. Has one large sheep foot and one
  pen blade.

TWO BLADE Nos. 6512 and 5738

No. 6512—3⅝-inch patent stag handle, German silver bolsters, brass lined. Has one large spear and one pen
  blade.

No. 5738—3½-inch patent stag handle, German silver bolsters, brass lined. Has one large spear and one pen
  blade.

TWO BLADE No. 6453 **PHYSICIAN'S KNIFE**

No. 6453—3¾-inch patent stag handle, German silver cap, steel bolsters, brass lined. Has one large spear
  and one pen blade.

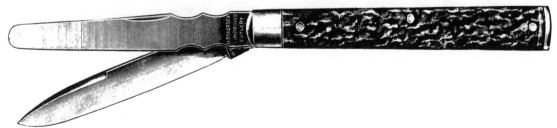

WITH SPATULA No. 6835 **PHYSICIAN'S KNIFE**

No. 6835—3½-inch patent stag handle, German silver cap and bolsters, brass lined. Has large spear blade and
  spatula.

THREE BLADE No. 6111

No. 6111—3¼-inch patent stag handle, German silver shield and bolsters, brass lined. Has one large spear and
  two pen blades.

POCKET KNIVES

CELEBRATED BOKER "TREE BRAND."

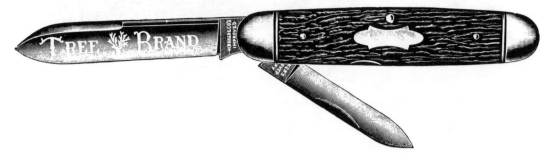

TWO BLADE. No. 9817. CAP AND BOLSTER.

3¼-inch patent stag handle, German silver shield, cap and bolsters, brass lined.

No. 9817SF—Large blade, sheep foot point...

No. 9817SP—Large blade, spear point...

TWO BLADE. No. 9722. CAP AND BOLSTER.

No. 9722—3½-inch patent stag handle, German silver shield, brass lined. Has one large spear and one pen
blade...

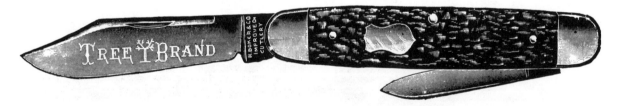

TWO BLADE. No. 9335. BOLSTERED.

No. 9335—3⅝-inch patent stag handle, German silver shield and bolsters, brass lined. Has one large clip and
one pen blade...

THREE BLADE. No. 6720. BOLSTERED.

No. 6720—3½-inch red wood handle, German silver shield and bolsters, brass lined. Has one large heavy
spear and two pen blades..

POCKET KNIVES

CELEBRATED BOKER "TREE BRAND."

No. 201—Boker—one blade Barlow, spear blade_____

No. 202—Boker—two blade Barlow, large blade, spear point_____ _____

TWO BLADE.   No. 9732.   BOLSTERED.

3¾-inch patent stag handle, German silver shield, brass lined.

No. 9732SF—Large blade, sheep foot point_____ _____

No. 9732SP—Large blade, spear point_____

TWO BLADE.   No. 9830.   CAP AND BOLSTER.

3½-inch patent stag handle, German silver shield, cap and bolsters, brass lined.

No. 9830SF—Large blade, sheep foot point_____

No. 9830SP—Large blade, spear point_____

No. 9830C—Large blade, clip point_____

CELEBRATED BOKER "TREE BRAND."

FOUR BLADE.   No. 7238.   PEARL HANDLE.

No. 7238—3-inch two-piece pearl handle, German silver bands and bolsters, brass lined.   Has one large spear, one manicure and two pen blades_____

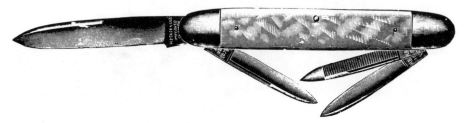

FOUR BLADE.   Nos. 7251 and 7237.   PEARL HANDLE.

No. 7251—3-inch pearl handle, German silver bolsters, brass lined.   Has one large spear, one manicure and two pen blades_____

No. 7237—Same as No. 7251, except has only **Three Blades**_____

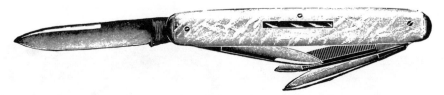

FOUR BLADE.   Nos. 11617 and 11611.   PEARL HANDLE.

No. 11617—3-inch pearl handle, German silver shield and tips, brass lined.   Has one large spear, one manicure and two pen blades_____

No. 11617—Same as No. 11617, except has only **Three Blades**_____

FOUR BLADE.   Nos. 6292 and 4998.   PEARL HANDLE.

No. 6292—3¼-inch pearl handle, German silver shield and tips, brass lined.   Has one large spear, one manicure and two pen blades_____

No. 4998—Same as No. 6292, except has only **Three Blades**_____

FOUR BLADE.   No. 7391.   PEARL HANDLE.

No. 7381—3¼-inch pearl handle, German silver shield and bolsters, brass lined.   Has one large sheep foot, one manicure and two pen blades_____

BOKER POCKET KNIVES
IMPORTED—TREE BRAND
Made In Germany

PREMIUM STOCK

HANDLE—Pearl.
BLADES—One each clip, spey and sheepfoot.
   TRIM—Nickel silver.
   LINING—Nickel silver.
   LENGTH—4 inches.

C3-6089_____Doz **$113 40**
Half doz in box;   *$54 00*
wt doz 3 lbs.

JR. PREMIUM STOCK

HANDLE—Genuine stag.
BLADES—Three: clip, spey, sheepfoot. Hand forged from English bar steel. Hand ground and honed to a razor keen edge.
   BOLSTERS—Nickel silver.
   LINING—Nickel silver.
   LENGTH—3⅜ inches.

C3-7585_____Doz **$113 40**
Half doz in box;   *$54 00*
wt doz 2 lbs.

PREMIUM STOCK

HANDLE—Stag.
BLADES—Three: long spey, spey and sheepfoot. Attractive frosted etching on master blade.
   LINING—Nickel silver.
   LENGTH—Closed 4 inches.

C3-7367_____Doz **$113 40**
Half doz in box;   *$54 00*
wt doz 2 lbs.

PREMIUM STOCK

HANDLE—Genuine deer horn stag.
BLADES—1 clip, 2 pens.
   SHIELD—Nickel silver.
   LINING—Nickel silver.
   LENGTH—3½ inches.

C3-285_____Doz **$119 70**
Half doz in box;   *$57 00*
wt doz 2 lbs.

PREMIUM STOCK

HANDLE—Genuine stag.
BLADES—One each clip, spey and sheepfoot.
   SHIELD—Nickel silver.
   LINING—Nickel silver.
   LENGTH—4 inches.

C3-6085_____Doz **$132 30**
Half doz in box;   *$63 00*
wt doz 8 lbs.

HANDLE—Genuine bone stag.
BLADES—Three: clip, spey, sheepfoot. Large blade etched. Mirror polished and hand honed.
   BOLSTERS—Nickel silver.
   LINING—Nickel silver.
   LENGTH—4 inches.

C3-7474_____Doz **$113 40**
Half doz in box;   *$54 00*
wt doz 2 lbs.

CONGRESS

HANDLES—Bone stag.
LINING—Brass.
SHIELD—Nickel silver.
BLADES—2 sheepfoot, 2 pen.
LENGTH—3¼ inches.

C3-5452_Doz **$100 80**
Half doz in box;   *$48 00*
wt doz 9 ozs.

CONGRESS

HANDLES—Bone stag.
LINING—Brass.
TRIM—Nickel silver.
BLADES—2 sheepfoot, 2 pen.
LENGTH—3¾ inches.

C3-5464_Doz **$113 40**
Half doz in box;   *$54 00*
wt doz 1 lb.

CONGRESS

HANDLES—Bone stag.
LINING—Brass.
TRIM—Nickel silver.
BLADES—1 spear, 1 sheepfoot, 2 pen.
LENGTH—4 inches.

C3-5474_Doz **$126 00**
Half doz in box;   *$60 00*
wt doz 2 lbs.

BOKER POCKET KNIVES
IMPORTED—TREE BRAND
Made In Germany
SPORTSMEN'S KNIFE

HANDLE—Genuine bone stag.

BLADES—Large spear, small clip, screwdriver and cap lifter, can opener, corkscrew, punch blade and shackle.

BOLSTERS—Nickel silver.

LINING—Nickel silver.

LENGTH—3⅝ inches.

C3-7593 _____Doz **$126 00**
Half doz in box; wt doz 4 lbs.   *$60 00*

GIFT BOXES FOR TREE BRAND POCKET KNIVES
BOKER

Presentation gift boxes are brown, pink and gold. Pocket knife can be securely mounted on an attractive pink velour insert.
A black elastic cord holds the knife in place.

(Knife not included)

C3-GB—Size 4x3x1¼ in. _____Doz **$3 15**
Loose.

POCKET KNIVES
IMPERIAL—JACK-MASTER—BARLOW
TWO BLADES

BLADES — Two: clip and pen.
HANDLES—Imitation pearl, assorted colors, red, white and black.
LINING—Brass.
BOLSTERS—Full nickel type.
LENGTH—3⅛ in.

C3-435 _____   Doz **$18 90**
One doz on display card; wt doz 2 lbs.

POCKET KNIVES
IMPERIAL—SPORTSMASTER—SINGLE BLADE

HANDLE—Assorted colored celluloid. Shields and cover pins.
BLADE—One clip. High carbon cutlery steel full polished.
BOLSTERS—Full nickel type.
LINING—Brass.
LENGTH—4¼ inches.

C3-N1499 _____   Doz **$18 90**
One doz on display card; wt doz 1 lb.

BOKER POCKET KNIVES
IMPORTED—TREE BRAND
Made In Germany

PEN

HANDLE—Genuine deer horn stag.
BLADES—Two: spear and pen. Attractive frosted etching on master blade.
BOLSTERS—Nickel silver.
SHIELD—Tree brand.
LINING—Nickel silver.
LENGTH—3 inches.

C3-225 _ _ _ Doz **$88 20**
Half doz in box;   *$42 00*
wt doz 1 lb.

ALL STAINLESS STEEL PEN

HANDLE—Stainless steel, engraved.
BLADES—Two: large spear and pen, mirror polished and hand honed.
LENGTH—3⅜ inches.

C3-7614 _ _ Doz **$81 90**
Half doz in box;   *$39 00*
wt doz 1 lb.

SERPENTINE PEN

HANDLES—Bone stag.
LINING—Brass.
SHIELD—Nickel silver.
BLADES—1 clip, 2 pen.
LENGTH—3½ inches.

C3-280 _ _ Doz **$100 80**
Half doz in box;   *$48 00*
wt doz 1 lb.

HANDLE—Genuine bone stag.
BLADES—Two clips.
LINING—Brass.
SHIELD—Nickel silver.
LENGTH—5¼ inches.

C3-2020 _ _ _ _ _ Doz **$138 60**
Half doz in box;   *$66 00*
wt doz 2 lbs.

HANDLE—Genuine bone stag.
BLADES—Three: pen, clip, sheepfoot.
LINING—Brass.
TRIM—Nickel silver.
LENGTH—2¾ inches.

C3-8388 _ _ _ _ _ _ Doz **$81 90**
Half doz in box;   *$39 00*
wt doz 1 lb.

JR. PREMIUM STOCK

HANDLE—Genuine stag.
BLADES—Three: clip, spey, sheepfoot. Hand forged from English bar steel. Hand ground and honed to a razor keen edge.
BOLSTERS—Nickel silver.
LINING—Nickel silver.
LENGTH—3⅜ inches.

C3-7588 _ _ _ _ _ _ Doz **$100 80**
Half doz in box;   *$48 00*
wt doz 2 lbs.

PREMIUM STOCK

HANDLE—Genuine bone stag.
BLADES — Three: clip, spey and sheepfoot, large blade, etched. Mirror polished, hand honed.
BOLSTERS—Nickel silver.
LINING—Nickel silver.
LENGTH—4 inches.

C3-6066 _ _ _ _ _ _ Doz **$113 40**
Half doz in box;   *$54 00*
wt doz 2 lbs.

IMPORTED—TREE BRAND

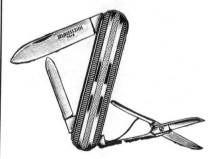

HANDLE—Machined turned stainless steel.
BLADES—One each, spear blade, nail file, scissors.
LINING—Stainless steel.
TRIM—Stainless steel.
LENGTH—3 inches.

C3-7616 _ _ _ _ _ _ Doz **$157 50**
Half doz in box;   *$75 00*
wt doz 1 lb.

BLUE GRASS

175

BOKER POCKET KNIVES
IMPORTED—TREE BRAND
Made In Germany
SERPENTINE PEN

HANDLE—Genuine bone stag.
BLADES—Two—one pen, one clip.
LINING—Brass.
SHIELD—Nickel silver.
LENGTH—2¾ inches.
C3-8288_____Doz **$69 30**
Half doz in box;   *$33 00*
wt doz 1 lb.

CONGRESS

HANDLE—Bone stag.
LINING—Brass.
SHIELD—Nickel silver.
BLADING—1 pen, 1 sheepfoot.
LENGTH—3¼ inches.
C3-5252_____Doz **$71 82**
Half doz in box;   *$34 20*
wt doz 1 lb.

SERPENTINE PEN KNIFE

HANDLE—Bone stag.
LINING—Brass.
SHIELD—Nickel silver.
BLADES—1 clip, 1 pen.
LENGTH—3⅛ inches.
C3-240_____Doz **$71 82**
Half doz in box;   *$34 20*
wt doz 1 lb.

IMPORTED TREE BRAND

BLADES—One clip.
LINING—Brass.
SHIELD—Nickel silver.
LENGTH—4 inches.
BONE STAG HANDLE
C3-93_____Doz **$56 70**
                          $27 00
NEW PEARL HANDLE
C3-93NP_____Doz **$56 70**
Half doz in box;   *$27 00*
wt doz 2 lbs.

HANDLE—Imitation bone stag.
BLADES—Two—1 clip, 1 pen.
LINING—Nickel silver.
SHIELD—Nickel silver.
STEEL—High carbon.
LENGTH—3¼ inches.

C3-7288_____Doz **$75 60**
                          $36 00
Half doz in box;
wt doz 2 lbs.

PEN

HANDLE—Bone stag.
BLADES — Two: spear and pen,
frosted etching on master blade.
BOLSTERS—Nickel silver.
SHIELD—Tree brand.
LINING—Milled brass.
LENGTH—2¾ inches.

C3-230_____Doz **$71 82**
Half doz in box;   *$34 20*
wt doz 1 lb.

PEN

HANDLE—Bone stag.
BLADES—Two: spear and pen. Master blade etched with tree brand insignia
on handle.
BOLSTERS—Nickel silver.
LINING—Brass.

C3-220—3 in.
C3-210—3¼ in.
Half doz in box;   Doz **$71 82**
wt doz 2 lbs.   *$34 20*

PEN

HANDLE—Stainless steel, engine
turned.
BLADES—Two: spear and pen, mirror polished.
LINING—Stainless steel.
BOLSTERS—Stainless steel.
LENGTH—3 inches.
          C3-7612_____Doz **$75 60**
Half doz in box;   *$36 00*
wt doz 1½ lbs.

PEN

HANDLE—Genuine deer horn, stag.
BLADES—Two: large spear and pen,
mirror polished.
LINING—Nickel silver.
BOLSTERS—Nickel silver.
LENGTH—3¼ inches.

          C3-215_____Doz **$88 20**
Half doz in box;   *$42 00*
wt doz 2 lbs.

PEN

HANDLE—Genuine deer horn stag
covering.
BLADES—Two: spear and pen. Attractive frosted etching on master blade.
BOLSTERS—Nickel silver.
LINING—Nickel silver.
LENGTH—2¾ inches.

          C3-235_____Doz **$88 20**
Half doz in box;   *$42 00*
wt doz 9 ozs.

POCKET KNIVES.

JOSEPH ALLEN & SONS' CELEBRATED NON-XLL.

No. 02063–4 blades, pearl handle, brass lined, crocus polished, 3⅛ in.,   ·   ·   ·   ·

No. 02064–4 blades, pearl handle, brass lined, crocus polished, 3⅜ in.,   ·   ·   ·   ·

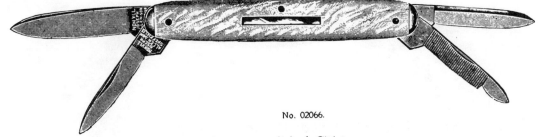

No. 02066.

No. 02065–4 blades, stag   handle, brass lined, crocus polished, 3½ in.,   ·   ·   ·   ·
No. 02066–4 blades, pearl handle, brass lined, crocus polished, 3½ in.,   ·   ·   ·   ·

No. 02067–4 blades, stag handle, brass lined, crocus polished, 3½ in.,   ·   ·   ·   ·

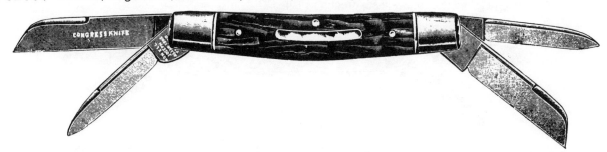

No. 02068–4 blades, stag handle, brass lined, crocus polished, 3⅝ in.,   ·   ·   ·
HALF DOZEN IN A BOX

POCKET KNIVES.

JOSEPH ALLEN & SONS' CELEBRATED NON-XLL.

No. 02054.

No. 02053–3 blades, stag handle, brass lined, crocus polished, 3⅜ in., ...
No. 02054–3 blades, pearl handle, brass lined, crocus polished, 3⅜ in., ...

No. 02055–3 blades, pearl handle, brass lined, crocus polished, 3⅜ in., ...

No. 02057.

No. 02056–4 blades, stag handle, brass lined, crocus polished, 3⅛ in., ...
No. 02058–4 blades, stag handle, iron lined, crocus polished, 3½ in., ...
No. 02057–4 blades, pearl handle, brass lined, crocus polished, 3⅛ in., ...

No. 02060.

No. 02059–4 blades, stag handle, brass lined, crocus polished, 3⅜ in., ...
No. 02060–4 blades, pearl handle, brass lined, crocus polished, 3 in., ...

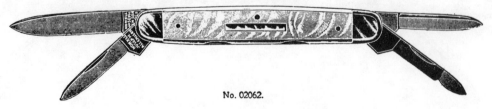

No. 02062.

No. 02061–4 blades, stag handle, brass lined, crocus polished, 3⅛ in., ...
No. 02062–4 blades, pearl handle, brass lined, crocus polished, 3⅛ in., ...
HALF DOZEN IN A BOX.

POCKET KNIVES.

JOSEPH ALLEN & SONS' CELEBRATED NON-XLL.

No. 02027.

No. 02026–2 blades, stag handle, brass lined, crocus polished, single bolster, 3⅝ in.; · ·
No. 02027–2 blades, stag handle, brass lined, crocus polished, double bolster, 3⅝ in., · ·

No. 02028.

No. 02028–2 blades, buffalo handle, brass lined, crocus polished, 3¾ in., · · ·
No. 02029–2 blades, stag handle, brass lined, crocus polished, 3¾ in., · · ·

No. 0326.

No. 0326–1 blade, ivory handle, brass lined, crocus polished, NON-XLL, 3¼ in., · ·
No. 0146–1 blade, ivory handle, brass lined, crocus polished, Morley, 2⅞ in., · ·

No. 0467–2 blades, ivory handle, brass lined, crocus polished, 3¾ in., · ·

No. 02033.

No. 02031–2 blades, buffalo handle, brass lined, crocus polished, 3 in., · · ·
No. 02032–2 blades, stag handle, brass lined, crocus polished, 3 in., · · ·
No. 02033–2 blades, pearl handle, brass lined, crocus polished, 3 in., · · ·

No. 02037.

No. 02034–2 blades, buffalo handle, brass lined, crocus polished, 3⅜ in., · · ·
No. 02035–2 blades, stag handle, brass lined, crocus polished, 3⅜ in., · · ·
No. 02036–2 blades, ivoride handle, brass lined, crocus polished, 3⅜ in., · · ·
No. 02037–2 blades, pearl handle, brass lined, crocus polished, 3⅜ in., · · ·
No. 02038–2 blades, pearl handle, brass lined, crocus polished, 3⅛ in., · · ·

HALF DOZEN IN A BOX.

POCKET KNIVES.

JOSEPH ALLEN & SONS' CELEBRATED NON-XLL.

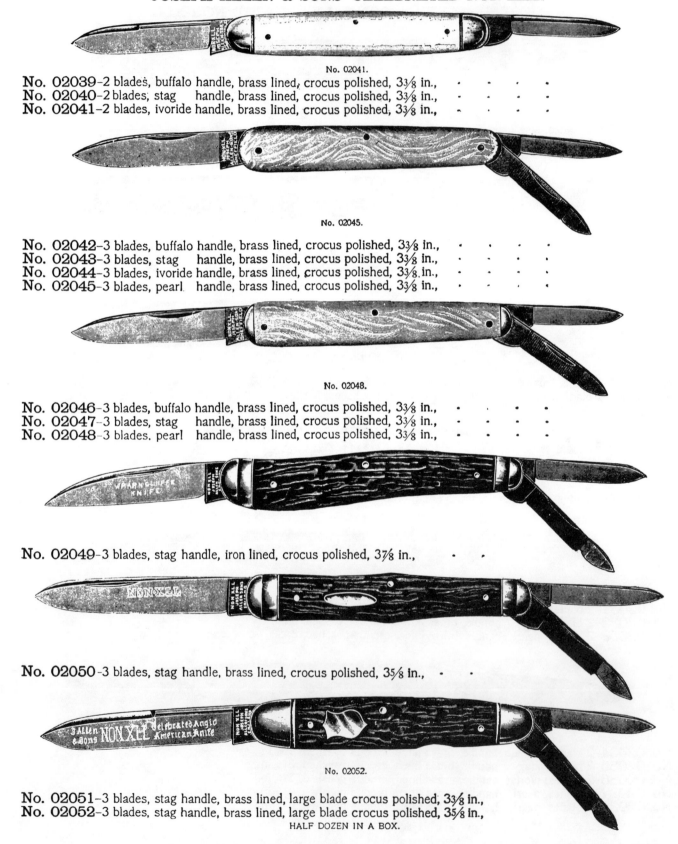

No. 02041.

No. 02039–2 blades, buffalo handle, brass lined, crocus polished, 3⅜ in.,　·　·　·　·　·
No. 02040–2 blades, stag　　handle, brass lined, crocus polished, 3⅜ in.,　·　·　·　·　·
No. 02041–2 blades, ivoride handle, brass lined, crocus polished, 3⅜ in.,　·　·　·　·　·

No. 02045.

No. 02042–3 blades, buffalo handle, brass lined, crocus polished, 3⅜ in.,　·　·　·　·
No. 02043–3 blades, stag　　handle, brass lined, crocus polished, 3⅜ in.,　·　·　·　·
No. 02044–3 blades, ivoride handle, brass lined, crocus polished, 3⅜ in.,　·　·　·　·
No. 02045–3 blades, pearl　handle, brass lined, crocus polished, 3⅜ in.,　·　·　·　·

No. 02048.

No. 02046–3 blades, buffalo handle, brass lined, crocus polished, 3⅜ in.,　·　·　·　·
No. 02047–3 blades, stag　　handle, brass lined, crocus polished, 3⅜ in.,　·　·　·　·
No. 02048–3 blades, pearl　handle, brass lined, crocus polished, 3⅜ in.,　·　·　·　·

No. 02049–3 blades, stag handle, iron lined, crocus polished, 3⅞ in.,　·　·

No. 02050–3 blades, stag handle, brass lined, crocus polished, 3⅝ in.,　·　·

No. 02052.

No. 02051–3 blades, stag handle, brass lined, large blade crocus polished, 3⅜ in.,
No. 02052–3 blades, stag handle, brass lined, large blade crocus polished, 3⅝ in.,
HALF DOZEN IN A BOX.

POCKET KNIVES.

JOSEPH ALLEN & SONS' CELEBRATED NON-XLL.

No. 02019–2 blades, stag handle, brass lined, large blade crocus polished, 3⅝ in., · · ·

No. 02020–3 blades, stag handle, brass lined, crocus polished, 3⅞ in., · · · ·

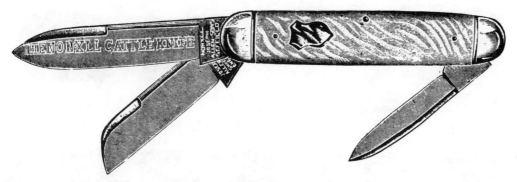

No. 02023

No. 02021–3 blades, buffalo handle, brass lined, crocus polished, 3⅝ in., · · · ·
No. 02022–3 blades, stag   handle, brass lined, crocus polished, 3⅝ in., · · · ·
No. 02023–3 blades, pearl handle, brass lined, crocus polished, 3⅝ in., · · ·

No. 02024–2 blades, stag handle, iron lined, large blade crocus polished, 4 in., · ·

No. 02025–1 blade, iron handle glazed, 4¼ in., · · · · · · · · ·

HALF DOZEN IN A BOX.

POCKET KNIVES.

JOSEPH ALLEN & SONS' CELEBRATED NON-XLL.

No. 02001.

No. 02000–1 blade, iron handle, glazed, 3⅜ in., · · · · · · · ·
No. 02001–2 blades, iron handle, glazed, 3⅜ in., · · · · · · · ·

No. 02002–2 blades, stag handle, iron lined, glazed, 3½ in., · · · · · ·

No. 02004.

No. 02003–2 blades, stag handle, iron lined, glazed, 3¼ in., · · · · ·
No. 02004–2 blades, stag handle, iron lined, large blade crocus polished, 3⅝ in.,

No. 02006.

No. 02005–2 blades, stag handle, iron lined, large blade crocus polished, 3⅝ in., · · ·
No. 02006–2 blades, stag handle, iron lined, large blade crocus polished, 3⅞ in., · · ·

No. 02007–2 blades, stag handle, iron lined, large blade crocus polished, 3⅞ in., · ·

No. 02008.

No. 02008–2 blades, ebony handle, brass lined, large blade crocus polished, 4 in., · ·
No. 02009–2 blades, buffalo handle, brass lined, large blade crocus polished, 4 in., · ·
No. 02010–2 blades, stag   handle, brass lined, large blade crocus polished, 4 in., · ·

HALF DOZEN IN A BOX.

POCKET KNIVES.

JOSEPH ALLEN & SONS' CELEBRATED NON-XLL.

No. 02011.

No. 02011–2 blades, stag handle, iron lined, large blade crocus polished, clip point, 3⅝ in.,
No. 02012–2 blades, stag handle, iron lined, large blade crocus polished, spear point, 3⅝ in.,

No. 02013–2 blades, stag handle, brass lined, large blade crocus polished, 3⅝ in., -   ·   ·

No. 02014.

No. 02014–2 blades, buffalo handle, brass lined, large blade crocus polished, 3½ in,   ·   ·
No. 02015–2 blades, stag   handle, brass lined, large blade crocus polished, 3½ in.,   ·   ·

No. 02016–2 blades, stag handle, brass lined, large blade crocus polished, 3⅝ in.,   ·   ·

No. 02017–2 blades, stag handle, iron lined, large blade crocus polished, 3⅝ in.,   ·   ·

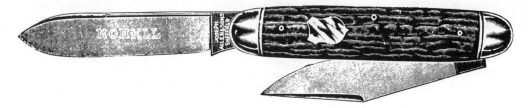

No. 02018 2 blades, stag handle, brass lined, large blade crocus polished, 3⅝ in.,   ·   ·

HALF DOZEN IN A BOX.

SCHRADE WALDEN POCKET KNIVES

CONGRESS PATTERN

HANDLE—Bone stag.
BLADES—Two: sheepfoot and pen.
Large blade polished on one side.
LINING—Brass.
BOLSTERS—Nickel silver.
LENGTH—3 inches.

C3-774

Half doz in box;   Doz **$63 00**
wt doz 11 ozs.

SERPENTINE PEN KNIFE

HANDLE—Stag.
BLADES—Two: clip and pen. Large
blade polished on one side.
LINING—Brass.
BOLSTERS—Nickel silver.
SHIELD—Nickel silver.
LENGTH—2¾ inches.

C3-708

Half doz in box;   Doz **$69 30**
wt doz 10 ozs.

SERPENTINE JACK KNIFE

HANDLE—K-Horn plastic.
BLADES—Two: clip and pen.
LINING—Brass.
BOLSTERS—Nickel silver.
SHIELD—Nickel silver.
LENGTH—3⁵⁄₁₆ inches.

C3-234K

Half doz in box;   Doz **$75 60**
wt doz 1 lb.

SERPENTINE JACK PATTERN

HANDLE—Bone stag.
BLADES—Two: pen and clip.
BOLSTERS—Steel.
SHIELD—Nickel silver.
LINING—Brass.
LENGTH—3⁹⁄₁₆ inches.

C3-236

Half doz in box;   Doz **$75 60**
wt doz 3 lbs.

SERPENTINE JACK KNIFE

HANDLE—Stag.
BLADES—Two: clip and pen. Large
blade polished on one side.
LINING—Brass.
BOLSTERS—Nickel silver.
SHIELD—Nickel silver.
LENGTH—2⅞ inches.

C3-272

Half doz in box;   Doz **$69 30**
wt doz 1 lb.

SERPENTINE JACK KNIFE

HANDLE—Stag.
BLADES—Two: clip and pen.
BOLSTERS AND SHIELD—Nickel
silver.
LENGTH—3⁵⁄₁₆ inches.

C3-233

Half doz in box;   Doz **$75 60**
wt doz 2 lbs.

EQUAL END JACK KNIFE
Slim Pattern

HANDLE—Bone stag.
BLADES—Two: spear and pen.
LINING—Brass.
BOLSTERS—Nickel silver.
SHIELD—Nickel silver.
LENGTH—3⅛ inches.

C3-242

Half doz in box;   Doz **$69 30**
wt doz 1 lb.

WHARNCLIFFE PATTERN

HANDLE—Black celluloid.
BLADES—Two: clip and pen. Large
blade polished on one side.
LINING—Brass.
BOLSTERS—Nickel silver.
SHIELD—Nickel silver.
LENGTH—3¼₆ inches.

C3-766

Half doz in box: Doz **$69 30**
wt doz 1 lb.

MUSKRAT SKINNING

HANDLE—Bone stag.
BLADES—Two skinning, one side
polished.
BOLSTERS—Nickel silver.
SHIELD—Nickel silver.
LINING—Brass.
LENGTH—4 inches.

C3-787

Half doz in box;   Doz **$81 90**
wt doz 2 lbs.

STOCKMAN'S KNIFE

HANDLE—Bone stag.
BLADES—Two: large half saber clip
and large spey.
BOLSTER CAPS AND SHIELD—
Nickel silver.
LINING—Brass.
LENGTH—3⅞ inches.

C3-293

Half doz in box;   Doz **$88 20**
wt doz 3 lbs.

HANDLE—Yellow plastic.
BLADES—Hand-honed stainless steel
cutting blade; multi-purpose blade for
scaler, ruler, bottle cap lifter, hook disgorger, magnetic tip.
Sharpening stone and hook straightener
on handle.
LENGTH—5 inches.

C3-208

Half doz in box;   Doz **$113 40**
wt doz 3 lbs.

POCKET KNIVES

RUSSELL BARLOW

(Illustration No. 60)

Steel lining and bolster; bone handle. Length 3⅜ inches.

No. 60—Spear blade_____
No. 65—Clip blade_____

(Illustration No. 62)

Steel lining and bolster; bone handle. Length 3⅜ inches.

No. 62—Spear blade_____
No. 66—Clip blade_____

(Illustration No. 601)

Steel lining and bolster; bone handle. Length 5 inches.

No. 601—Spear blade_____
No. 600—Clip blade_____

Steel lining and bolster, bone handle. Length 5 inches.

No. 6000—Clip blade_____

SCHRADE SAFETY PUSH BUTTON KNIVES WITH LOCKING DEVICE

Steel lining and bolster; glazed.

No. 1553¾—Stag; length 4¼ ins.

SCHRADE SAFETY PUSH BUTTON KNIVES WITH LOCKING DEVICE

Steel lining and bolster; glazed.

No. 1543¾—Stag; length 4⅞ ins.

SCHRADE
Two Blade—Push Button.

Nickel silver lined; crucible s t e e l blades, full crocus polished.
Safety push button. Length blade 2⅞ inches.

No. 7444-K—B r o w n l i n e d cream Pyralin handle _____

Brass lining, nickel silver tips.

No. 7503 T—Stag; length 3¾ ins.

Brass lining; shadow pattern. Length 3⅜ inches.

No. 7404-O—Opal pyralin__ ⎫
No. 7404-H—Horn_____ ⎪
No. 7404-G P—Pyralin_____ ⎬
No. 7403—Stag_____ ⎪
No. 7404-S T—Gold shelled____ ⎭

Half doz in attractive cardboard box.

GEORGE WOLSTENHOLM AND SON

Brass lining; nickel silver bolster, cap and shield; highly glazed.

No. 17003G—Stag; length 3⅜ ins.

Congress Knife.

Brass lining; polished steel bolsters; highly glazed.

No. 2154—Stag; length 3⅞ ins__

Tobacco Knife.

Brass lining; polished steel bolsters; highly glazed.

No. 2191—Stag; length 3½ ins__

Tobacco Knife.

Brass lining; polished steel bolsters; highly glazed.

No. 2193—Stag; length 4 ins ___

Office Knife.

Brass lining; highly glazed.

No. 16584—White c e l l u l o i d length 3¾ ins_____

POCKET KNIVES
SCHRADE—WALDEN

Length Closed 2-7/8 Inches

Two blades; 1 clip, 1 pen; brass linings; nickel silver caps and bolsters. Stagged handle. Packed six in a box.

No. 272—   44.00   doz.

Length Closed 3-5/16 Inches

Two blades; 1 clip, 1 pen; brass linings; nickel silver bolsters and shield. K-horn plastic handles. Packed six in a box.

No. 234K—   48.00   doz.

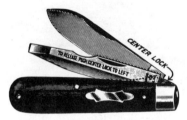

ELECTRICIANS KNIFE
Length Closed 3-3/4 Inches

Two blades; 1 spear, 1 screwdriver. Brass linings, nickel silver bolsters and shield. Screwdriver blade locks open. Wonda-Wood handle. Packed six in a box.

No. 204—   52.20   doz.

ULSTER

BARLOW KNIFE
Length Closed 3-3/8 Inches

Polished Genuine BONE Handles; 2 Blades (Clip & Pen); Brass Linings; Iron Bolsters; Blades Full Mirror Polished. Packed 12 in a box.

No. 10G—   24.00   doz.

Same as above except with spear and pen blades. Packed 1 dozen in a box.

No. 11G—   24.00   doz.

POCKET KNIVES
ULSTER

Premium Stock Knife, 3-1/2 inches long; Genuine BONE STAG Handles; 3 blades (Clip, Spey & Pen); Brass linings; Nickel Silver Bolsters; Blades Full Mirror Polished; Master Blade Etched. Packed six in a box.

No. 45G—   36.00 doz.

Medium Serpentine Jack Knife, 3-1/2 inches long; Genuine BONE STAG handles; 2 blades (Clip & Pen); Brass Linings; Nickel Silver Bolsters; Master Blade Polished Mark Side Only, Other Blades glazed on both sides. Packed six in a box.

No. 40G—   28.80   doz.

General Utility Knife, 3-3/4 inches long; Black Stagged Handles; 4 blades (Spear, Canopener, Screwdriver — Caplifter and Punch); Brass Linings; Nickel Silver •Bolsters, Shackle. Blades Full Mirror Polished. Packed six in a box.

No. 114S—   36.00   doz.

Slim Serpentine Jack Knife, 3-1/4 inches long; Genuine BONE STAG handles; 2 Blades (Clip & Pen); Brass Linings; Nickel Silver Bolsters; Master Blade Polished Mark Side Only and Etched; Other Blade Glazed on Both Sides. Packed six in a box.

No. 50G—   28.80   doz.

POCKET KNIFE
IMPERIAL

6 IN 1

A 4 blade special Handy Man's Knife with wire scraper, recessed head screw driver, can opener, cap lifter and cutting blade. Each knife Blister packed on attractive individual pilfer proof card. 12 cards to a box.

No. RJ-619—   19.00   doz.

ULSTER

Slim serpentine jack knife. Genuine STAG HEAD handles; 2 blades (Clip & Pen); Brass Linings; Nickel Silver Bolsters; Blades Full Mirror Polished. Length closed 3¼". Packed 6 in a carton. Weight per dozen 1¼ lbs.

No. 50-D—   2.40   each

Small serpentine jack knife. Blades: (2) Clip and Pen handles; Simulated Pearl. Length closed: 2-9/16". Packed 1/2 dozen in a boxl Weight er dozen 3/4 pounds.

No. 81-P—   2.40   each

Small serpentine jack knife. Blades: (2) Clip and pen. Handles: Maize (yellow) plastic. Length closed: 2-9/16 inches. Packed 1/2 dozen in box. Weight per dozen 3/4 pounds.

No. 81-Y—   2.40   each

SCHRADE WALDEN POCKET KNIVES

HUNTERS AND TRAPPERS KNIFE

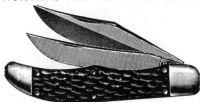

HANDLE—Stagged.
BLADES—Two: large saber clip and skinning.
LINING—Brass.
BOLSTERS—Nickel silver.
LENGTH—5¼ inches.

C3-225SW
Half doz in box;   Doz **$113 40**
wt doz 6 lbs.

SHADOW SERPENTINE PATTERN

HANDLE—Yellow plastic.
BLADES—Clip, spey and pen.
LINING—Solid brass.
BOLSTER—Nickel silver.
LENGTH—3⁵⁄₁₆ inches.

C3-835Y
Half doz in box;   Doz **$94 50**
wt doz 1 lb.

SERPENTINE PATTERN

HANDLE—Bone stag.
BLADES—Three: clip, spey and pen. Large blade polished on one side.
LINING—Brass.
BOLSTERS—Nickel silver.
SHIELD—Nickel silver.
LENGTH—3⁵⁄₁₆ inches.

C3-834
Half doz in box;   Doz **$94 50**
wt doz 1 lb.

SERPENTINE PATTERN

BLADES—Three: clip, sheepfoot and pen. Large blade polished on one side.
LINING—Brass. Milled back.
BOLSTERS—Nickel silver.
SHIELD—Nickel silver.
LENGTH—2¾ inches.

C3-808—Stag Handle

Yellow Plastic Handle
C3-808Y
One doz in box;   Doz **$88 20**
wt doz 1 lb.

PREMIUM STOCK

HANDLE—Yellow plastic.
BLADES—Three: clip, sheepfoot and spey.
LINING—Brass.
SHIELD—Nickel silver.
LENGTH—4 inches.

C3-882Y
Half doz in box;   Doz **$100 80**
wt doz 3 lbs.

PREMIUM STOCK KNIFE

HANDLE—Bone stag.
BLADES—Three: clip, sheepfoot and spey. Large blade polished on one side.
LINING—Brass.
BOLSTERS—Nickel silver.
SHIELD—Nickel silver.
LENGTH—3½ inches.

C3-890
Half doz in box;   Doz **$100 80**
wt doz 1 lb.

PREMIUM STOCK TEXAS PATTERN

BLADES—Three: clip, spey and sheep foot. Large blade polished one side.
LINING—Brass.
BOLSTERS AND SHIELD—Nickel silver.
LENGTH—4 inches.

C3-881—Stag Handle

Yellow Plastic Handle
C3-881Y
Half doz in box;   Doz **$100 80**
wt doz 2 lbs.

SLIM PREMIUM STOCK

HANDLE—K-Horn plastic.
BLADES—Three: Turkish clip, sheepfoot and spey.
LINING—Brass.
BOLSTERS—Nickel silver.
LENGTH—3⁹⁄₁₆ inches.

C3-896K
Half doz in box;   Doz **$100 80**
wt doz 2 lbs.

PREMIUM STOCK

HANDLE—Bone stag.
BLADES—Three: Turkish clip, spey, leather punch.
LINING—Brass.
BOLSTERS—Nickel silver.
SHIELD—Nickel silver.
LENGTH—3⁹⁄₁₆ inches.

C3-899
Half doz in box;   Doz **$100 80**
wt doz 2 lbs.

POCKET KNIVES
SCHRADE—WALDEN

Length Closed 3-1/16 Inches

Two blades; 1 clip, 1 pen; brass linings; nickel silver bolsters and shield. Black plastic handle. Packed six in a box.

No. 766   **44.00** doz.

Length Closed 3-9/16 Inches

Three blades; 1 clip, 1 sheepfoot, 1 spey; brass linings; nickel silver bolsters and shield, K-horn Plastic handle. Packed six in a box.

No. 896K—   **64.00** doz.

Length Closed 3-9/16 Inches

Three blades; 1 clip, 1 sheepfoot, 1 spey. Brass linings. Nickel silver bolsters and shield.   stay handle. Packed six in a box.

No. 895—   **64.00** doz.

POCKET KNIVES
SCHRADE—WALDEN

Length Closed 2-3/4 Inches

Three blades; 1 clip, 1 sheepfoot, 1 pen. Brass linings, nickel silver bolsters and shield, milled back. Stagged handle. Packed six in a box.

No. 808—   **56.00** doz.

Length Closed 3-3/8 Inches

Three blades; 1 clip, 1 sheepfoot, 1 spey; nickel silver bolsters. Bone stag handle. Packed six in a box.

No. 856—   **64.00** doz.

Lenches Closed 3-7/8 Inches

Three blades; 1 large sabre clip, 1 small clip, 1 coping pen; brass linings; nickel silver bolsters and shield. Stagged handle. Packed one in a box with leather purse.

No. 804—   **7.20** doz.

Length Closed 2-3/4 Inches

Two blades; 1 clip, 1 pen; brass linings; nickel silver bolsters and shield. Bone stag handle. Packed six in a box.

No. 708—   **44.00** doz.

POCKET KNIVES
SCHRADE—WALDEN

Length Closed 2-1/2 Inches

Two blades; 1 spear, 1 pen; nickel silver linings, and tips. Marine pearl handle. Packed six in a box.

No. 793—   **40.00** doz.

Length Closed 3-7/8 Inches

Two blades; alf sabre clip, 1 pen; brass lining nickel silver bolsters, caps and s ld. Bone stag handle. Packed six in a box.

No. 294—   **56.00** doz.

Length Closed 3-9/16 Inches

Two blades; 1 clip, 1 pen; brass linings; nickel silver bolsters and shield. Stagged handle. Packed six in a box.

No. 236—   **48.00** doz.

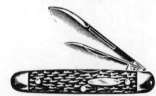

Length Closed 3-1/8 Inches

Two blades; 1 spear, 1 pen; brass linings; nickel silver bolsters and shield. Bone stag handle. Packed six in a box.

No. 242—   **44.00** doz.

SCHRADE WALDEN POCKET KNIVES

PREMIUM STOCK

HANDLE—Bone stag.
BLADE—Three: Turkish clip, sheepfoot and spey.
LINING—Nickel silver.
BOLSTERS—Nickel silver.
LENGTH—4 inches.

C3-861
Half doz in box;   Doz **$113 40**
wt doz 2 lbs.

CONGRESS PATTERN

HANDLE—Bone stag.
BLADES—Four: two sheepfoot, and two pen blades.
LINING—Brass.
BOLSTERS—Nickel silver.
LENGTH—3 inches.

C3-974
Half doz in box;   Doz **$100 80**
wt doz 1 lb.

SCHRADE WALDEN— "OLD TIMER"

HANDLE—Genuine bone stag.
BLADES—Three: clip, sheepfoot and spey.
LINING—Brass.
BOLSTERS—Nickel silver.
SHIELD—Nickel silver.
LENGTH—4 inches.

C3-80T_____Doz **$113 40**
$66 00

Attractively gift packaged in a redwood, hinged box size 5x2x¼ inches; wt doz 5 lbs.

ELECTRICIAN'S AND HANDY MAN KNIFE
ULSTER

HANDLE — R o s e w o o d with ring shackle attached.
BLADES—Two: one spear cutting blade and one screwdriver blade locking when open, released by pressing center lining; high carbon steel, polished finish; screwdriver blade etched.

C3-TL29
Half doz in box;   Doz **$56 70**
wt doz 3 lbs.

CASTRATING KNIVES
ULSTER

HANDLE—Stainless steel.
BLADE—Cutlery steel, spey and hoe shape.
LENGTH—3½ inches.

C3-13C   Doz **$44 10**
Half doz in box;
wt box 2 lbs.

PRUNING OR HORTICULTURAL KNIVES

PRUNING—SCHRADE WALDEN

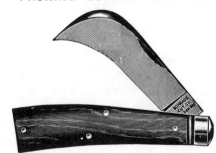

HANDLE—Cocobolo.   LINING—Steel.
BLADE—Pruning.   BOLSTER—Steel.
     LENGTH—4⁷⁄₁₆ inches.

C3-186_____   Doz **$69 30**
Half doz in box; wt doz 4 lbs.

BUDDING SCHRADE WALDEN

HANDLE—Imported cocobolo wood.
BLADE—One carbon steel budding, 2⅛ inches long.
RIVETS—Two compression.
LENGTH—6 inches.

C3-174_____   Doz **$31 50**
One doz in box; wt doz 1 lb.

Belknap Is Recognized By Thousands Of Merchants As Their
"MOST DEPENDABLE SOURCE OF SUPPLY"

VAN CAMP POCKET KNIVES

FULLY WARRANTED

Illustrations Half Size

Imitation tortoise shell handle; two blades, large spear and pen; large blade full crocus finish one side and etched; brass lined; nickel silver bolsters; length closed, 3 inches.

No. 0272CS—Imit. tortoise shell handle..

Weight per doz. ½ lb.; half dozen in a box.

Stag Handle

Large spear blade full crocus finish one side and etched; file blade glazed; milled nickel silver lined; nickel silver tips and shield; length closed, 3 inches.

No. 0259S—Stag handle..............

Weight per doz. 1 lb.; half dozen in a box.

Pearl handle; three blades, large spear, pen and file; all blades full crocus finish both sides; large blade etched; milled nickel silver lined; length closed, 3⅛ inches.

No. 0392P—Pearl handle ....

Weight per dozen, ¾ lb.; half dozen in a box.

Pearl handle; three blades, large sheep foot, pen and file; all blades full crocus finish both sides; large blade etched; milled brass lined; nickel silver shield; length closed, 3⅛ inches.

No. 0389P—Pearl handle ....

Weight per dozen, 1 lb.; half dozen in a box.

Pearl Handle

Pearl handle; three blades, large spear, pen and cut-off pen; all full crocus finish both sides; large blade etched; brass lined; nickel silver bolsters and shield; length closed, 3⅝ inches.

No. 0363P—Pearl handle ....

Weight per dozen, 1 lb.; half dozen in a box.

Pearl handle; three blades, large spear, pen and file, all full crocus finish both sides; large blade etched; nickel silver lined; nickel silver tips and shield; length closed, 3⅜ inches.

No. 0396P—Pearl handle ....

Weight per dozen, 1¼ lbs.; half dozen in a box.

Pearl handle; four blades, large spear, two pens and file; all blades full crocus finish both sides; large blade etched; milled nickel silver lined; nickel silver tips and shield; length closed, 3¼ inches.

No. 04100P—Pearl handle ....

Weight per dozen, 1¼ lbs.; half dozen in a box.

Pearl handle; three blades, large spear, pen and file; all blades full crocus finish both sides; large blade etched; milled nickel silver lined; length closed, 2¾ inches.

No. 0397P—Pearl handle ....

Weight per dozen, ⅞ lb.; half dozen in a box.

Pearl handle; three blades, large spear, pen and file; all blades full crocus finish both sides; milled nickel silver lined; nickel silver shield; length closed, 3 inches.

No. 0393P—Pearl handle ....

Weight per dozen, 1 lb.; half dozen in a box.

Pearl handle; four blades, large spear, two pens and file; full crocus finish both sides; large blade etched; milled nickel silver lined; nickel silver shield; length closed, 3 inches.

No. 0499P—Pearl handle ....

Weight per dozen, 1 lb.; half dozen in a box.

Pearl handle; four blades, large spear, two pens and file; all blades full crocus finish both sides; large blade etched; nickel silver lined; nickel silver shield; length closed, 3 inches.

No. 0498P—Pearl handle ....

Weight per dozen, 1 lb.; half dozen in a box.

Pearl handle; four blades, large spear, two pens and file; all blades full crocus finish both sides; large blade etched; nickel silver lining tips and shield; length closed, 3 inches.

No. 04101P—Pearl handle ....

Weight per dozen, 1⅛ lbs.; half dozen in a box.

VAN CAMP POCKET KNIVES

FULLY WARRANTED

Illustrations Half Size

Stag handle; two blades, clip and pen; clip blade full crocus finish one side and etched; brass lined; nickel silver cap and bolster; length closed, 4½ in.

No. 228½S–Stag handle ....

Weight per doz. 3½ lbs.; half dozen in a box.

With Lock Back

Stag handle; one clip blade glazed finished and etched; brass lined; nickel silver bolster; blade locks open and is released by thumb pressure on the back; length closed, 4½ inches.

No. 130½S–Stag handle ....

Weight per doz. 2½ lbs.; half dozen in a box.

Celluloid black handle; three blades, spear, pen and file; large blade full crocus finish one side and etched, brass lined; nickel silver bolsters and shield; length closed, 3 inches.

No. 0365CB–Celluloid handle ....

Weight per doz. ¾ lb.; half dozen in a box.

Three Blade

Stag handle; three blades, spear, pen and file; large blade full crocus finish one side and etched; brass lined; nickel silver tips and shield; length closed, 3 inches.

No. 0364S–Stag handle ....

Weight per doz. ¾ lb.; half dozen in a box.

Stag handle; three blades, spear and two pens; large blade full crocus finish one side and etched; brass lined; nickel silver tips and shield; length closed, 3⅜ inches.

No. 0355S–Stag handle ....
No. 0355CH–Imit. horn celluloid handle..

Weight per doz. 1 lb.; half dozen in a box.

Stag handle; four blades, large sheep foot, one small sheep foot, small pen and file; large blade full crocus finish one side and etched; brass lined, nickel silver bolsters and shield; length closed, 3¼ inches.

No. 0476S–Stag handle ....

Weight per doz. 1¼ lbs.; half dozen in a box.

Genuine stag handle; four blades, large spear, two pens and file; large blade full crocus finish one side and etched; brass lined; nickel silver tips and shield; length closed, 3¼ inches.

No. 0479GS–Genuine stag handle ....

Weight per doz. 1¾ lbs.; half dozen in a box.

Stag handle; four blades, two large sheep foot and two small pen; one large blade full crocus finish one side and etched; brass lined; nickel silver bolsters and shield; length closed, 4 inches.

No. 0480S–Stag handle ....

Weight per doz. 2 lbs.; half dozen in a box.

Stag handle; four blades, large sheep foot, small sheep foot, pen and file; all blades full crocus finish both sides; large blade etched; brass lining with milled edges; nickel silver bolsters and shield; length closed, 3¼ inches.

No. 0481S–Stag handle ....

Weight per doz. 1 lb.; half dozen in a box.

Stag handle; four blades, large sheep foot, two small pen and file; all blades full crocus finish both sides; large blade etched; milled nickel silver lining; nickel silver tips and shield; finely fitted and finished; length closed, 3⅝ inches.

No. 0482S–Stag handle ....

Weight per doz. 1½ lbs.; half dozen in a box.

VAN CAMP POCKET KNIVES
FULLY WARRANTED

Stag handle; large clip and pen; glaze finish; brass lining; steel bolster; length closed 3⅜ inches.

No. 26618V . . . .
Weight per dozen, 2 lbs.; one-half dozen in a box.

Stag handle; two blades, large spear and small pen; large blade polished one side and etched; nickel silver bolster, cap and shield; brass lining; length closed 3 in.

No. 25663 . . . .
Weight per dozen, 1½ lbs.; one-half dozen in a box.

Stag handle; two blades, large spear and pen; glaze finish; brass lining; steel bolster; length closed 3⅜ inches.

No. 25613 . . . .
Weight per dozen, 1½ lbs.; one-half dozen in a box.

Stag handle; two blades, large clip half sabre ground and small pen; large blade polished one side and etched; brass lining; nickel silver bolster and cap; no shield; length closed 2¾ inches.

No. 29763 . . . .
Weight per dozen, 1 lb.; one-half dozen in a box.

With Chain
Stag handle; two blades, spear and pen; large blade full crocus finish one side and etched; brass lined; steel bolster; nickel silver shield; 15 inch steel chain with loop on end; length closed, 3½ inches.

No. 2683S . . . .
Weight per dozen, 2 lbs.; one-half dozen in a box.

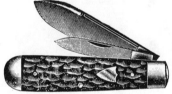

Two blades, large spear and pen; large blade polished one side and etched; brass lining; nickel silver bolster, cap and shield; length closed 3½ in.

No. 2888—Stag handle . . . .
No. 2680RM—Red grained celluloid handle . . . .
Weight per dozen, 2½ lbs.; one-half dozen in a box.

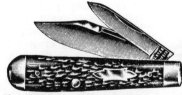

Stag handle; two blades, large clip and small pen; large blade polished one side and etched; brass lining; nickel silver bolster, cap and shield; length closed 3⅜ inches.

No. 2688 . . . .
Weight per dozen, 2 lbs.; one-half dozen in a box.

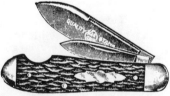

Stag handle; two blades, large spear and pen; large blade polished one side and etched; brass lining; easy opener; nickel silver bolster, cap and shield; length closed 3⅜ inches.

No. 22243 . . . .
Weight per dozen, 1½ lbs.; one-half dozen in a box.

Two blades, large spear and pen; large blade polished one side and etched; brass lining; nickel silver bolster, cap and shields; length closed 3¼ in.

No. 2055BP—Blue Pearl celluloid handle
No. 2058—Stag handle . . . .
Weight per dozen, 1½ lbs.; one-half dozen in a box.

Stag handle; two blades, large spear and pen; large blade polished one side and etched; brass lining; nickel silver bolster, cap and shield; length closed 3⅜ inches.

No. 2243 . . . .
Weight per dozen, 1½ lbs.; one-half dozen in a box.

VAN CAMP POCKET KNIVES
FULLY WARRANTED

Two blades, clip and pen; clip blade polished one side and etched; brass lining; nickel silver bolsters and shield; length closed, 3⅜ inches.

No. 24478—Stag handle . . . .
No. 21475M—Razor horn celluloid handle
Weight per dozen, 2 lbs.; one-half dozen in a box.

Stag handle; two blades; large spear and small pen; spear blade polished one side and etched; brass lining; nickel silver bolsters and shield; length 3 in.

No. 21348 . . . .
Weight per dozen, 1 lb.; one-half dozen in a box.

Stag handle; two blades, spear and pen; spear blade polished one side and etched; brass lined; nickel silver tips and shield; length closed 3 inches.

No. 21318 . . . .
Weight per dozen, ½ lb.; one-half dozen in a box.

Stag handle; two blades, clip and pen; large blade polished one side and etched; nickel silver bolsters and shield; brass lining; length closed 3¼ inches.

No. 23878 . . . .
Weight per dozen, 1 lb.; one-half dozen in a box.

White celluloid handle; two blades, large spear and spey; one side of spear blade polished and etched; brass lining; length closed 3¾ in.

No. 21710W . . . .
Weight per dozen, 1½ lbs.; one-half dozen in a box.

Horn celluloid handle; two blades, large spear and small pen; spear blade polished one side and etched; brass lining; nickel silver bolsters and shield; length 3¼ inches.

No. 21645H . . . .
Weight per dozen, 1 lb.; one-half dozen in a box.

Stag handle; three blades, plain clip, sheepfoot and spey; clip blade polished one side and etched; brass lined; nickel silver bolsters and shield; length closed, 3⅝ inches.

No. 34578 . . . .
Weight per dozen, 2 lbs.; one-half dozen in a box.

Stag handle; three blades, clip, sheepfoot and pen; clip blade polished one side and etched; brass lined; nickel silver bolsters and shield; length 3¼ inches.

No. 33788 . . . .
Weight per dozen, 1½ lbs.; one-half dozen in a box.

Razor horn celluloid handle; three blades, clip, sheepfoot and spey; clip blade polished one side and etched; nickel silver lining and bolsters; length 3¼ inches.

No. 33885M . . . .
Weight per dozen, 1½ lbs.; one-half dozen in a box.

Stag handle; three blades, spear, spey and punch; spear blade half polished and etched; brass lined; nickel silver bolsters and shield; length closed 3⅜ inches.

No. 34473 . . . .
Weight per dozen, 2 lbs.; one-half dozen in a box.

Stag handle; three blades, clip, spey and punch; clip blade polished one side and etched; brass lined; nickel silver bolster and shield; length closed 3⅜ inches.

No. 34478 . . . .
Weight per dozen, 2 lbs.; one-half dozen in a box.

VAN CAMP POCKET KNIVES
FULLY WARRANTED

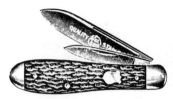

Stag handle; two blades, large spear and pen; large blade polished one side and etched; brass lining; nickel silver bolster, cap and shield; length closed 3½ inches.

No. 2263 ....

Weight per dozen, 2½ lbs.; one-half dozen in a box.

Stag handle; two blades, large spear and pen; large blade polished one side and etched; brass lining; nickel silver bolster cap and shield; length closed 3 inches.

No. 22433 ....

Weight per dozen, 1½ lbs.; one-half dozen in a box.

Stag handle; two blades, large spear and small pen; spear blade polished one side and etched; brass lining; nickel silver bolster, cap and shield; length 3 inches.

No. 22348 ....

Weight per dozen, 1 lb.; one-half dozen in a box.

Razor horn celluloid handle; two blades, large clip and small pen; large blade polished one side and etched; brass lining; nickel silver bolster and cap; length closed 3 in.

No. 29345M ....

Weight per dozen, 1 lb.; one-half dozen in a box.

Stag handle; two blades, large spear and small pen; spear blade polished one side and etched; brass lining; nickel silver bolster, cap and shield; length 3¾ inches.

No. 288 ....

Weight per dozen, 2½ lbs.; one-half dozen in a box.

Razor horn celluloid handle; two blades, large clip half sabre ground and sheepfoot large blade polished one side and etched; brass lining; nickel silver bolster, cap and shield; length closed 3½ inches.

No. 24330M ....

Weight per dozen, 2 lbs.; one-half dozen in a box.

Imitation horn celluloid handle; two blades, large sabre clip and spear; clip blade full crocus finish one side and etched; brass lined; iron bolster and cap; length closed, 5 inches.

No. 22110M ....

Weight per dozen, 3 lbs.; one-half dozen in a box.

Stag handle; two blades, large spear and small pen; large blade polished one side and etched; brass lining; nickel silver bolster, cap and shield; length closed, 3 inches.

No. 21333 ....

Weight per dozen, 1 lb.; one-half dozen in a box.

Razor horn celluloid handle; two blades, large spear and small pen; large blade polished one side and etched; brass lining; nickel silver tips; length closed 3 inches.

No. 21315M ....

Weight per dozen, ½ lb.; one-half dozen in a box.

Stag handle; two blades, large spear and small pen; large blade polished one side and etched; brass lining; nickel silver tips and shield.

Length Closed 3 Inches

No. 21538 ....

Weight per dozen, ½ lb.; one-half dozen in a box.

Length Closed 3¼ Inches

No. 21638 ....

Weight per dozen, 1 lb.; one-half dozen in a box.

POCKET KNIVES

WATAUGA

Blades forged from best grade English Cutlery Steel.   Carefully tempered and sharpened.   Highly finished throughout.

TWO BLADE—CAP AND BOLSTER

No. 201—3½-inch patent stag handle; German silver shield; large spear blade_____
No. 535—Same as No. 201, except has large sheep foot blade_____

TWO BLADE—CAP AND BOLSTER

No. 595—3½-inch patent stag handle; German silver shield; brass lined; large sheep foot blade.
Per Dozen_____
No. 587—Same as No. 595, except has large spear blade.
Per Dozen_____

TWO BLADE—CAP AND BOLSTER

No. 241—3¾-inch patent stag handle; German silver shield, cap and bolsters; brass lined; large spear blade_____

TWO BLADE—BOLSTERED

No. 224—4-inch patent stag handle; German silver shield and bolsters; brass lined; large blade, double beveled, with clip point_____
No. 584—Cap and Bolster. 3½-inch patent stag handle; German silver shield; brass lined; large clip point blade_____

TWO BLADE—CONGRESS PATTERN

No. 565—3⅝-inch patent stag handle; German silver shield and bolsters; brass lined_____

TWO BLADE—CAP AND BOLSTER

No. 251—4-inch gray buff handle; German silver shield, cap and bolsters; brass lined; large spear blade_____
No. 250—Same as No. 251, except has patent stag handle_____

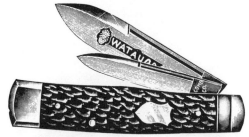

TWO BLADE—CAP AND BOLSTER

No. 240—3¾-inch patent stag handle; German silver shield and cap; brass lined; large spear blade.
Per Dozen_____
No. 213—Same as No. 240, except has gray buff handle.
Per Dozen_____
No. 524—Same as No. 240, except has gray buff handle and large clip blade_____

TWO BLADE—CAP AND BOLSTER

No. 212—4-inch flat patent stag handle; German silver shield, cap and bolsters; brass lined; large spear blade_____
No. 575—Same as No. 212, except has large sheep foot blade_____
No. 221—3⅝-inch patent stag handle; German silver shield, cap and bolsters; brass lined; large spear blade_____

POCKET KNIVES

WATAUGA

Blades forged from best grade English Cutlery Steel.   Carefully tempered and sharpened.   Highly finished throughout.

TWO BLADE—CONGRESS PATTERN

No. 605—4¼-inch patent stag handle; German silver
   shield; hollow steel bolsters; brass lined. Has
   one large sheep foot and one pen blade.
Per Dozen

No. 585—4¼-inch patent stag handle; German silver
   shield; grooved hollow steel bolsters; brass
   lined. Has one large sheep foot and one pen
   blade

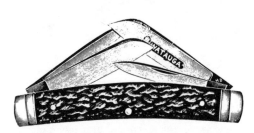

FOUR BLADE—CONGRESS PATTERN

No. 245—3½-inch patent stag handle; hollow steel bolsters; brass lined. Has two large sheep foot
   and two pen blades_____

No. 265—3¼-inch patent stag handle; hollow steel bolsters; brass lined. Has one large sheep foot,
   one manicure and two pen blades___

TWO BLADE—PEARL HANDLE

No. 410—3-inch pearl handle; brass lined. Has one
   large spear and one pen blade_____

TWO BLADE—PEARL HANDLE

No. 400—3-inch pearl handle; German silver tipped
   ends; brass lined. Has one large spear and one
   pen blade_____

TWO BLADE—PEARL HANDLE

No. 415—Congress pattern; 3-inch pearl handle; steel
   hollow bolsters; brass lined. Has one large
   sheep foot and one pen blade_____

FOUR BLADE—PEARL HANDLE

No. 405—Congress pattern; 3¼-inch pearl handle; German silver hollow bolsters; brass lined. Has
   two large sheep foot and two pen blades.
Per Dozen_____

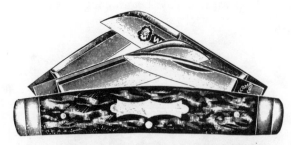

FOUR BLADE—CONGRESS PATTERN

No. 505—4-inch patent stag handle; German silver
   shield; hollow steel bolsters; brass lined. Has
   two large sheep foot and two pen blades.
Per Dozen

No. 345—4-inch genuine stag handle; hollow steel bolsters; steel lined. Has two large sheep foot and
   two pen blades

33

POCKET KNIVES

WATAUGA

Blades forged from best grade English Cutlery Steel.   Carefully tempered and sharpened.   Highly finished throughout.

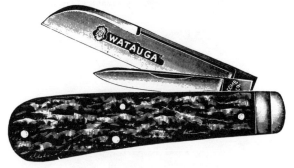

TWO BLADE—BOLSTERED

No. 315—4¼-inch genuine stag handle; hollow bolsters; large sheep foot blade................

No. 305—3¾-inch genuine stag handle; German silver shield; grooved bolsters; brass lined; large sheep foot blade.

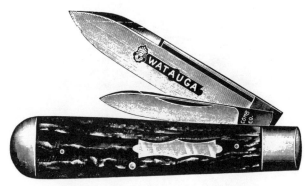

TWO BLADE—CAP AND BOLSTER

No. 300—3¾-inch genuine stag handle; German silver shield; brass lined; large spear blade.

Per Dozen........

TWO BLADE—CAP AND BOLSTER

No. 208—3⅝-inch patent stag handle; German silver shield; brass lined; large spear blade.

Per Dozen....

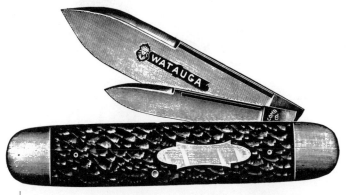

TWO BLADE—CAP AND BOLSTER

No. 207—4¼-inch patent stag handle; German silver shield, cap and bolsters; brass lined; large spear blade. Handles attached to sides of knife with brass screws. A knife of great strength.
Per Dozen..........

ONE BLADE—LOCK BACK

No. 254—4¾-inch patent stag handle; polished hollow steel bolster; clip point blade........

No. 252—Same as No. 254, except has spear point blade.
Per Dozen..........

Cut of No. 227.
WITH LEATHER PUNCH BLADE

No. 226—3¾-inch patent stag handle; German silver shield, cap and bolsters; brass lined. Has one large spear point and one punch blade for punching holes in harness, belting, etc....

No. 227—3¾-inch patent stag handle; German silver shield and bolsters; brass lined; Has one large spear, one short heavy sheep foot, and one punch blade for punching holes in harness, belting, etc..........Per Dozen, 18.00

POCKET KNIVES

WATAUGA

Blades forged from best grade English Cutlery Steel.   Carefully tempered and sharpened.   Highly finished throughout.

TWO BLADE—BOLSTERED

No. 210—3¾-inch patent stag handle; German silver shield; grooved hollow steel bolsters; one large spear and one pen blade............

TWO BLADE

No. 234—4¼-inch patent stag handle; German silver shield. Has one large spear and one large clip blade..............................

THREE BLADE FARMERS' KNIFE

No. 244—4-inch patent stag handle; German silver shield and bolsters; brass lined. Has one large clip, one large sheep foot and one budding blade.

Per Dozen...

TWO BLADE PRUNING KNIFE

No. 306—4-inch genuine stag handle; German silver shield; hollow steel bolsters. Has one pruning and one budding blade.............

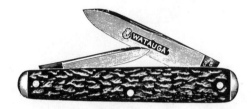

TWO BLADE

No. 230—3¼-inch patent stag handle; German silver tipped ends; brass lined. Has one large **spear** and one pen blade...................

TWO BLADE

No. 220—3½-inch patent stag handle; German silver bolsters; brass lined. Has one large spear and one pen blade...................

TWO BLADE—CONGRESS PATTERN

No. 235—3½-inch patent stag handle; hollow steel bolsters; brass lined. Has one large sheep foot and one pen blade...................

No. 275—3½-inch patent stag handle; smooth German silver bolsters; brass lined. Has one large sheep foot and one pen blade.............

POCKET KNIVES

WATAUGA

Blades forged from best grade English Cutlery Steel.   Carefully tempered and sharpened.   Highly finished throughout.

TWO BLADE—BOLSTERED

No. 202—3⅜-inch patent stag handle; German silver shield and bolsters; brass lined; large spear blade------------------------------------

TWO BLADE—CAP AND BOLSTER

No. 219—3⅝-inch patent stag handle; German silver shield, cap and bolsters; brass lined; large spear blade------------------------------------

TWO BLADE—CAP AND BOLSTER

No. 215—3¼-inch patent stag handle; German silver shield; brass lined; large sheep foot blade.
Per Dozen------------------------------------

No. 218—3¼-inch patent stag handle; German silver shield; brass lined; large spear blade.
Per Dozen------------------------------------

PHYSICIAN'S KNIFE—CAP AND BOLSTER

No. 211—3¾-inch patent stag handle; German silver cap and bolsters; brass lined------

PHYSICIAN'S KNIFE—CAP AND BOLSTER

No. 206—3¾-inch patent stag handle; German silver shield, cap and bolsters; brass lined.   Has large spear point blade and spatula------

TWO BLADE—BOLSTERED

No. 301—3⅞-inch genuine stag handle; German silver shield and bolsters; brass lined; large spear blade------------------------------

TWO BLADE—BOLSTERED

No. 302—4⅛-inch genuine stag handle; German silver shield; hollow bolsters; brass lined; large spear blade------------------------------

No. 303—3¾-inch genuine stag handle; German silver shield; grooved bolsters; brass lined; large spear blade------------------------

No. 304—3⅝-inch genuine stag handle; German silver shield; grooved bolsters; brass lined; large clip blade------------------------

POCKET KNIVES

WATAUGA

Blades forged from best grade English Cutlery Steel.   Carefully tempered and sharpened.   Highly finished.

ONE BLADE—BOLSTERED

No. 130—3¾-inch red wood handle, spear blade.
   Per Dozen_____
No. 135—Same as No. 130, except has sheep foot blade.
   Per Dozen_____

TWO BLADE—BOLSTERED

No. 120—3½-inch red wood handle; large spear blade.
   Per Dozen_____
No. 124—Same as No. 120, except has large clip blade.
   Per Dozen_____
No. 125—Same as No. 120, except has large sheep foot
   blade_____

TWO BLADE—BOLSTERED

No. 205—3¾-inch inch patent stag handle; large sheep
   foot blade_____
No. 200—Same as No. 205, except has large spear blade.
   Per Dozen_____
No. 204—Same as No. 205, except has large clip blade.
   Per Dozen_____

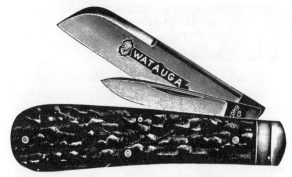

TWO BLADE—BOLSTERED

No. 525—3⅝-inch patent stag handle; hollow bolsters;
   large sheep foot blade_____
No. 285—4⅜-inch patent stag handle; hollow bolsters;
   German silver shield; brass lined; large sheep
   foot blade_____

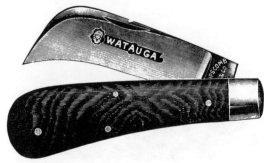

ONE BLADE PRUNING KNIFE

No. 105—4-inch red wood handle, with heavy pruning
   blade_____

TWO BLADE—BOLSTERED

No. 545—4-inch patent stag handle; grooved bolsters;
   German silver shield; large sheep foot blade.
   Per Dozen_____

TWO BLADE—LONG BOLSTER

No. 209—4-inch patent stag handle, brass lined; German silver shield; large spear blade____
No. 100—3¾-inch red wood handle; German silver
   shield; large spear blade_____

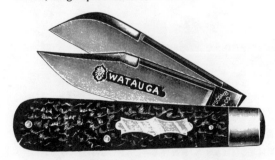

TWO LARGE BLADES—BOLSTERED

No. 515—3¾-inch patent stag handle; German silver
   bolsters and shield; brass lined; one large sheep
   foot blade, other large clip blade____

POCKET KNIVES.

No. 0455

No. 0454–2 blades, cocoa handle, brass lined, crocus polished, 3 in.,   · · · · ·
No. 0455–2 blades, buffalo handle, brass lined, crocus polished, 3 in.,   · · · · ·

No. 0496–2 blades, ebony handle, brass lined, crocus polished, 3 in.,   · · · · ·

No. 0497–2 blades, buffalo handle, brass lined, crocus polished, 3⅛ in.,   · · · · ·

No. 0574–2 blades, stag handle, brass lined, crocus polished, 3¾ in.,   · · · · ·

No. 0573–2 blades, stag handle, brass lined, crocus polished, 3½ in.,   · · · · ·

No. 0589.

No. 0589–2 blades, ebony handle, brass lined, crocus polished, 3½ in.,   · · · · ·
No. 0590–2 blades, stag handle, brass lined, crocus polished, 3½ in.,   · · · · ·

No. 1622.

No. 1622–2 blades, buffalo handle, brass lined, crocus polished, 3⅞ in.,   · · · · ·
No. 1632–2 blades, stag handle, brass lined, crocus polished, 3⅞ in.,   · · · · ·
No. 1662–2 blades, pearl handle, brass lined, crocus polished, 3⅞ in.,   · · · · ·

HALF DOZEN IN A BOX.

POCKET KNIVES.

0570.

No. 0570–2 blades, cocoa handle, brass lined, crocus polished, 3½ in., · · · · ·
No. 0571–2 blades, ebony handle, brass lined, crocus polished, 3½ in., · · · · ·
No. 0572–2 blades. stag handle, brass lined, crocus polished, 3½ in., · · · · ·

No. 0657

No. 0657 2 blades, cocoa handle, brass lined, crocus polished, 3½ in., · · · · ·
No. 0656 2 blades, stag handle, brass lined, crocus polished, 3½ in., · · · · ·

No. 0660

No. 0661–2 blades, cocoa handle, brass lined, crocus polished, 3½ in., · · · ·
No. 0662–2 blades, ebony handle, brass lined, crocus polished, 3½ in., · · · ·
No. 0660–2 blades, stag handle, brass lined crocus polished, 3½ in., · · · ·

No. 0493.

No. 0492–2 blades, cocoa handle, brass lined, crocus polished, 3½ in., · · · ·
No. 0493–2 blades, ebony handle, brass lined, crocus polished, 3½ in., · · · ·
No. 0491–2 blades, stag handle, brass lined, crocus polished, 3½ in., · · · ·

No. 0333.

No. 0331–2 blades, cocoa handle, brass lined, glazed, 3⅝ in., · · · · ·
No. 0332–2 blades, ebony handle, brass lined, glazed, 3⅝ in., · · · · ·
No. 0333–2 blades, stag handle, brass lined, glazed. 3⅝ in., · · · · ·

No. 0598–1 blade and gouge, cocoa handle. brass lined, crocus polished, 3½ in. · · ·
HALF DOZEN IN A BOX.

2801. Farmer's Pride Jack Knife.

Stag, White Bone and Ebony Handle, Strongly Riveted. One Large Blade and One Pen Blade. Well Polished Steel Bolster and Shield. Metal Lined. Length, 3¼ inches.

. . . .

2703. Celebrated Mechanic's Jack Knife.

Stag Handle, Double Spring. Extra Heavy Embossed Bolster. One Large and One Pen Blade, Well Ground and Full Polished. Adapted for Heavy Use. Length, 3⅝ inches.

. . . .

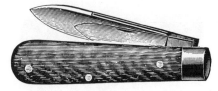

2804. Gem Boy's Jack Knife.

One Strong Polished Spear Blade and One Pen Blade. Metal Lined and Steel Bolster. Stag and Dogwood Handles. Length, 3¼ inches.

. . . .

2104. Imported Physician's Pocket Knife.

Steel Lined, Polished Bolster. One Long, Slender and One Medium Pen Blade, Well Set and Full Polished. Stag, Ebony and Dogwood Handles. Length, 3⅝ inches.

. . . .

2101. Popular NOX-ALL Jack Knife.

Genuine Dogwood Handle. Metal Lined. German Silver Bolster and Shield. Two Extra Strong Steel Blades, Full Polished. Length, 3¼ inches.

. . . .

2102. Extra Heavy Hardware Knife.

Two Strong, Well Tempered Blades. Metal Lined. German Silver Name Plate and Bolster. Stag, White and Dogwood Handles. Length, 4 inches.

. . . .

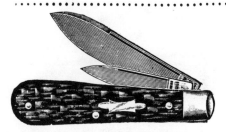

2107. American Pattern Jack Knife.

Steel Lined and Steel Bolster, with German Silver Name Plate. Stag, White, Ebony and Cocoa Handles. Two Extra Well Ground, Serviceable Blades. Length, 3½ inches.

. . . .

2111. Patent Easy Opener Jack Knife.

Stag, White, Bone and Dogwood Handles. Steel Lined. Polished Bolster and German Silver Shield. Large Blade Etched "Easy Opener." One of Our Best Leaders. Length, 3½ inches.

. . . .

3101. Special Cattle Knife.

Imitation Stag Handle. Extra Strong Spear Blade. One Blade for Cleaning Hoofs, and One Medium Pen Blade. Polished Bolsters and Shield. Adapted for Heavy Cutting. Length, 3½ inches.

½ Dozen in a Box.

2113. Popular Gentleman's Jack Knife.

Polished Stag and Buffalo Horn Handle. Full Crocus Finish Blades, Shield and Back. Steel Lined. Triple Riveted. Guaranteed. Length, 3 inches.

½ Dozen in a Box.

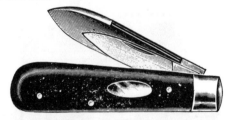

2112. American Model Jack Knife.

Stag, White Bone and Ebony Handles. Refined English Steel Blades. Crocus Finish Back. German Silver Shield, and Flush Bolster. Has always given Satisfaction, and is Warranted. Length, 3⅝ inches.

½ Dozen in a Box.

2109. Celebrated "Razor Steel" Jack Knife.

German Silver Shield and Bolster; Crocus Finish Back. Gunstock Shape. Extra well Ground Blades. Large Blade Etched **"Razor Steel, Price 50c."** Exceptional Value. Length, 3⅝ inches.

½ Dozen in a Box.

2116. Popular Handy Shape Jack Knife.

Stag, White Bone and Ebony Handles. Brass Lined and Division Scale. Fancy German Silver Shield and Flush Bolster. One Large Strong Clip Blade, and one Pen Blade. Fully Polished. Length, 3½ inches.

2117. Extra Carpenters' Jack Knife.

Stag, Ebony, Dogwood and White Bone Handles. Brass Lined. German Silver Heavy Bolster and Shield. Two Strong Refined Steel Blades. Fully Polished and adapted for Heavy Cutting. Length, 4 inches.

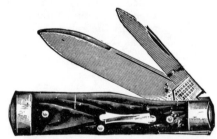

2114. English Gunstock Shape Jack Knife.

Stag, White Bone and Dogwood Handles. Two Refined Steel Blades, well Polished. German Silver Cap, Bolster and Shield; Brass Lined. First Grade in every respect. Length, 3½ inches.

2212 Fancy Wharncliffe Jack Knife.

Stag, White and Ebony Handle. German Silver Bolsters and Shield. Brass Lined. One Large Clip Blade, Etched **"None Better,"** and one Pen Blade. Length, 3½ inches.

1500. Boys' School Jack Knife.
New and Useful. 1 Well Ground Steel Blade.
Fancy Lacquered Handle. Embossed "School Knife." 15 inch Nickel Plated Chain Attached.
Length, 3 inches. 1 Dozen in a Package.

2403. Celebrated S. E. Oates & Son Sheffield (Eng.) Barlow Jack Knife.
Finely Tempered Steel Blade and 1¼ inch Strong Bolster, Triple Riveted. Patent Bone Handles.
Length, 3 inches.

1602. Single Blade Gentlemen's Jack Knife.
Fancy Embossed Bright Metal Handles. Full Polished Steel Blade and Bolster. Length, 3½ inches. 1 Dozen in a Box.

2900. Popular Gun Stock Jack Knife.
Lacquered Handle, with Nickel Cap, Bolster and Shield. Steel Lined. 1 Strong Blade and 1 Pen Blade. Length, 3¼ inches.

7250. Combination Glass Cutter and Pocket Knife.
Fitted with following Attachments: Corkscrew, Glass Cutter; Cigar Cutter, Pen Blade and Large Jack Blade. Imitation Shell Handle. Special Novelty. Length. 3¾ inches. 1 Dozen in a Box.

2610. Boys' Pride Jack Knife.
White Bone Handle, with Double Spring, Steel Lined and Bolster. Two Strong Blades Well Set, Nicely Polished.

2704. Two-Blade Farmers' Jack Knife.
One Large Spear Blade and 1 Pen Blade. Ebony or Dogwood Handle. Fancy Metal Shield, Steel Lined. Length, 3⅛ inches.

2800. Dewey Easy Opener Jack Knife.
Lacquered Metal Handle, Nickeled Bolster. Steel Lined. Length 3½ inches. "The Dewey Opener" Embossed on Handle.

2803. English Pattern Jack Knife.
One Large Strong Clip Blade and One Pen Blade, Fully Polished. Handsomely Embossed, Nickel Handle. Very Strong and Durable. Length, 4½ inches.

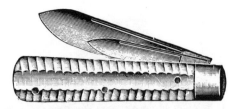

2702. Special Jack Knife.
White Bone and Ebony Corrugated Handle, Plain Bolster, Iron Lined. 1 Large and 1 Pen Blade, Nicely Polished, Triple Riveted. Length, 3 inches.

2115. Heavy Cattle Shaped Jack Knife.
Heavy German Silver Bolsters and Shield. 2 Strong and Well-Tempered Steel Blades. Full Brass Lined and Division Scale. Stag, White and Dogwood Handles, Length, 3½ inches

100. Jos. Warren & Sons Celebrated Pruning Knife.
Razor Tempered Steel. Dogwood Handle. Metal Lined, Full Polished Bolster. A most useful Article for Farmers or Florists. Length, 4¼ inches.

2103. Our American Pattern Jack Knife.
Two Strong, Durable Blades, Well Ground and Full Polished. German Silver Shield and Bolster. Metal Lined. Stag, Ebony, Dogwood and White Bone Handles. Length, 3½ inches.

2110. Novelty Two-Bladed Key Chain Knife
Stag Handle. Hollow Bolster. Steel Lined. Full Polished Back. 18 inch Nickel Plated Key Chain Securely Fastened to Knife. Length, 3½ inches.

POCKET KNIVES.

No. 0613.

No. 0613–2 blades, pearl handle, brass lined, crocus polished, 2¼ in., · · · ·
No. 0614–2 blades, pearl handle, brass lined, crocus polished, with nail file 2¼ in., · · ·

No. 0533–2 blades, pearl handle, brass lined, crocus polished, 2 in., · · · ·

No. 0308–2 blades, pearl handle, brass lined, crocus polished, 2⅜ in., · · · ·

No. 0186–2 blades, pearl handle, brass lined, crocus polished, 2½ in., · · · ·

No. 0409–2 blades, pearl handle, brass lined, crocus polished, 2½ in., · · · ·

No. 0306–2 blades, pearl handle, brass lined, crocus polished, 2½ in., · · · ·

No. 0309–2 blades, pearl handle, brass lined, crocus polished, 2⅝ in., · · · ·

No. 0413.

No. 0307–2 blades, fancy pearl handle, crocus polished, 2½ in., · · · · ·
No. 0413–3 blades, fancy pearl handle, crocus polished, 2¾ in., · · · ·

HALF DOZEN IN A BOX.

POCKET KNIVES.

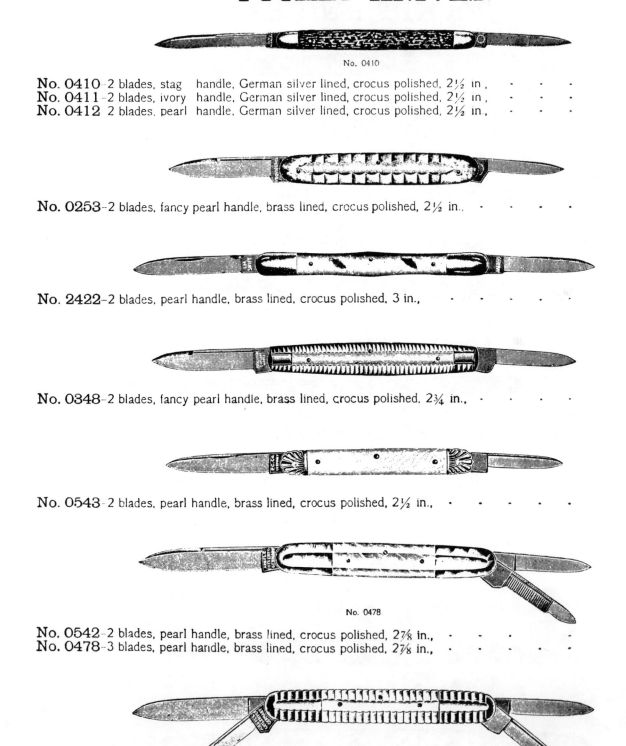

No. 0410

No. 0410—2 blades, stag   handle, German silver lined, crocus polished, 2½ in,   ·   ·   ·
No. 0411—2 blades, ivory handle, German silver lined, crocus polished, 2½ in,   ·   ·   ·
No. 0412 2 blades, pearl handle, German silver lined, crocus polished, 2½ in.,   ·   ·   ·

No. 0253—2 blades, fancy pearl handle, brass lined, crocus polished, 2½ in.,   ·   ·   ·

No. 2422—2 blades, pearl handle, brass lined, crocus polished, 3 in.,   ·   ·   ·

No. 0348—2 blades, fancy pearl handle, brass lined, crocus polished, 2¾ in.,   ·   ·   ·

No. 0543—2 blades, pearl handle, brass lined, crocus polished, 2½ in.,   ·   ·   ·

No. 0478

No. 0542—2 blades, pearl handle, brass lined, crocus polished, 2⅞ in.,   ·   ·   ·
No. 0478—3 blades, pearl handle, brass lined, crocus polished, 2⅞ in.,   ·   ·   ·

No. 0479—4 blades, pearl handle, brass lined, crocus polished, 3 in.,   ·   ·   ·

HALF DOZEN IN A BOX.

POCKET KNIVES.

No. 1392 2 blades, white bone handle, brass lined, crocus polished, 2⅜ in.,

No. 0674

No. 0674–2 blades, ivory celluloid handle, brass lined, crocus polished, 2¾ in.,
No. 0675–2 blades, pearl handle, brass lined, crocus polished, 2¾ in.,

No. 092.

No. 092–2 blades, German silver bound, inlaid with ivory celluloid, crocus polished, 2⅝ in.,
No. 091–2 blades, German silver bound, inlaid with shell celluloid, crocus polished, 2⅝ in.,

No. 0673–2 blades, pearl handle, brass lined, crocus polished, 2¾ in.,

No. 0693 2 blades, pearl handle, brass lined, crocus polished, 2¾ in.,

No. 1502 2 blades, pearl handle, brass lined, crocus polished, 3 in.,

No. 0557 2 blades, pearl handle, brass lined, crocus polished, 2½ in.,

No. 0703–3 blades, pearl handle, brass lined, crocus polished, 2½ in.,

HALF DOZEN IN A BOX.

POCKET KNIVES
—PINE KNOT—

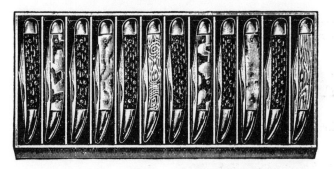

12 large switch blade knives with nickel silver bolsters, fully polished clip blade; assorted celluloid handles.

(Sold only in full assortments.)

No. 52—Length knives 5 ins_____
  One doz in cardboard display box; wt doz 2 lbs.

—PINE KNOT—

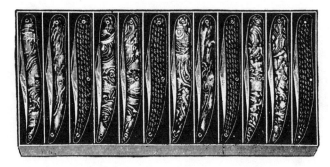

12 large switch blade knives with steel lining and full polished blade.
Assorted: 8 colored and 4 stag handles.

(Sold only in full assortments.)

No. 57—Length knives 5 ins_____
  One doz in cardboard display box; wt doz 1¾ lbs.

—PINE KNOT—

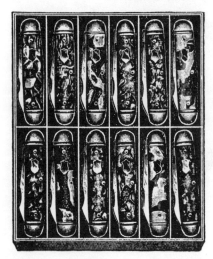

One Blade.
Polished iron lining and bolster; nickel silver shield; polished blade. Assorted colored celluloid handles.

(Sold only in full assortments.)

No. 55 — Length 3⅝ ins___
One doz in cardboard display box; wt doz 1½ lbs.

POCKET KNIVES
—PINE KNOT—

BARLOW
High quality polished cutlery steel blade. Iron bolster and lining. Imitation bone slab handle. Length 3⅜ inches.

No. 8920—Spear blade _____
No. 8921—Clip blade_____
  Loose; wt doz 1¼ lbs.

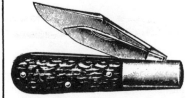

—PINE KNOT—
BARLOW
Polished iron lining and bolster. Full polished blades. Length 3⅜ inches.

Stag Handle.
No. 6721—Spear and pen blades_____ }
No. 6722—Clip and pen blades_____ }

Pearl Pyralin Handle.
No. 7721—Spear and pen blades_____ }
No. 7722—Clip and pen blades_____ }
  One doz in cardboard box.

—BLUE GRASS—BARLOWS

(Illustration No. BG5717)

Bone handle; steel lining and bolster; length 3½ inches.

No. BG5717—Spear blade _____ }
No. BG5718—Clip blade _____ }

—BLUE GRASS—BARLOW

(No. BG5721)

Bone handle; steel lining and bolster; length 3½ inches.

No. BG5721—Spear blade _____
No. BG5722—Clip blade _____
No. BG5723—Spey blade _____ }
No. BG5724—Sheep foot blade _____
No. BG5725—Razor blade _____

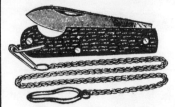

—PINE KNOT—
One Blade.
Steel lining. With 14 inch chain.

No. 10CH—Stag handle; length 2¾ ins_____
  One doz in cardboard box.

210

POCKET KNIVES.

No. 0643–2 blades, stag handle, brass lined, crocus polished, 3 in.,

No. 0524–2 blades, stag handle, brass lined, glazed, 3½ in.,

No. 0513.

No. 0448–2 blades, pearl handle, brass lined, crocus polished, 2⅝ in.,
No. 0513–2 blades, pearl handle, brass lined, crocus polished, 3 in.,

No. 0509–2 blades, pearl handle, brass lined, crocus polished, 3 in.,

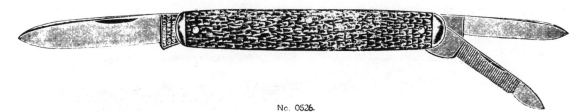

No. 0526.

No. 0525 2 blades, stag handle, brass lined, glazed, 3⅜ in.,
No. 0526 3 blades, stag handle, brass lined, glazed, 3⅜ in.,

No 0500.

No. 0500–3 blades, buffalo handle, brass lined, glazed, 3½ in.,
No. 0501–3 blades, stag handle, brass lined, glazed, 3½ in.,

No. 0691.

No. 0690–2 blades, ebony handle, brass lined, crocus polished, 3¾ in.,
No. 0691–2 blades, stag handle, brass lined, crocus polished, 3¾ in.,

HALF DOZEN IN A BOX.

POCKET KNIVES.

No. 0489.

No. 0489–2 blades, cocoa handle, brass lined, crocus polished, 3¼ in.,   ·   ·   ·   ·
No. 0490–2 blades, stag   handle, brass lined, crocus polished, 3¼ in.,   ·   ·   ·   ·

No. 0488.

No. 0486–2 blades, cocoa   handle, brass lined, crocus polisned, 3¼ in.,   ·   ·   ·
No. 0487–2 blades, ebony   handle, brass lined, crocus polished, 3¼ in.,   ·   ·   ·
No. 0488–2 blades, stag   handle, brass lined, crocus polished, 3¼ in.,   ·   ·   ·

No. 0659.

No. 0659–2 blades, cocoa   handle, brass lined, crocus polished, 3⅝ in.,   ·   ·   ·
No. 0658–2 blades, ebony   handle, brass lined, crocus polished, 3⅝ in.,   ·   ·   ·

No. 0582.

No. 0582–2 blades, cocoa handle, brass lined, crocus polished, 3½ in.,   ·   ·   ·
No. 0581–2 blades, stag   handle, brass lined, crocus polished, 3½ in.,   ·   ·   ·

No. 0334.

No. 0334–2 blades, cocoa   handle, brass lined, glazed, 3½ in.,   ·   ·   ·   ·
No. 0335–2 blades, ebony   handle, brass lined, glazed, 3½ in.,   ·   ·   ·   ·

No. 0482.

No. 0482–2 blades, cocoa handle, brass lined, crocus polished, 3⅜ in.,   ·   ·   ·   ·
No. 0483–2 blades, stag   handle, brass lined, crocus polished, 3⅜ in.,   ·   ·   ·   ·

HALF DOZEN IN A BOX.

POCKET KNIVES.

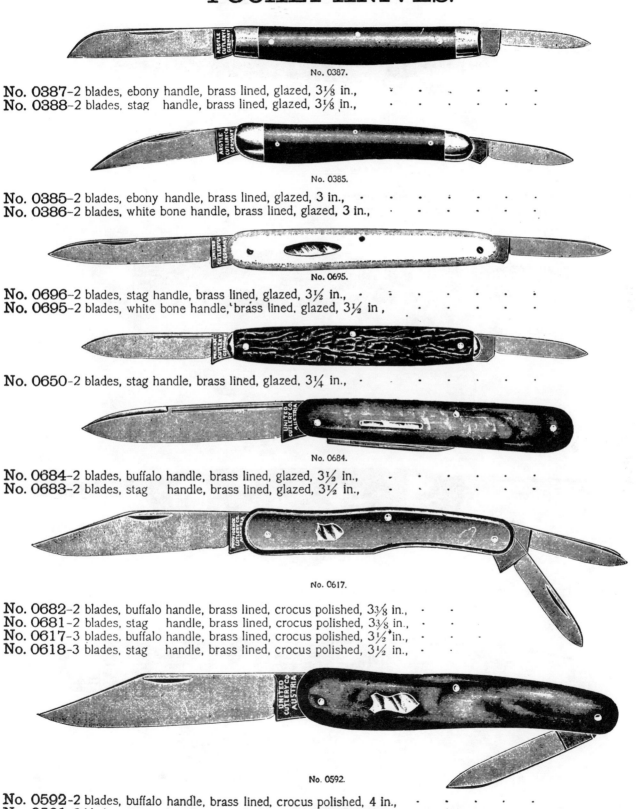

No. 0387.

No. 0387–2 blades, ebony handle, brass lined, glazed, 3⅛ in.,
No. 0388–2 blades, stag handle, brass lined, glazed, 3⅛ in.,

No. 0385.

No. 0385–2 blades, ebony handle, brass lined, glazed, 3 in.,
No. 0386–2 blades, white bone handle, brass lined, glazed, 3 in.,

No. 0695.

No. 0696–2 blades, stag handle, brass lined, glazed, 3½ in.,
No. 0695–2 blades, white bone handle, brass lined, glazed, 3½ in,

No. 0650–2 blades, stag handle, brass lined, glazed, 3¼ in.,

No. 0684.

No. 0684–2 blades, buffalo handle, brass lined, glazed, 3½ in.,
No. 0683–2 blades, stag handle, brass lined, glazed, 3½ in.,

No. 0617.

No. 0682–2 blades, buffalo handle, brass lined, crocus polished, 3⅜ in.,
No. 0681–2 blades, stag handle, brass lined, crocus polished, 3⅜ in.,
No. 0617–3 blades, buffalo handle, brass lined, crocus polished, 3½ in.,
No. 0618–3 blades, stag handle, brass lined, crocus polished, 3½ in.,

No. 0592.

No. 0592–2 blades, buffalo handle, brass lined, crocus polished, 4 in.,
No. 0591–2 blades, stag handle, brass lined, crocus polished, 4 in.,

HALF DOZEN IN A BOX.

213

POCKET KNIVES.

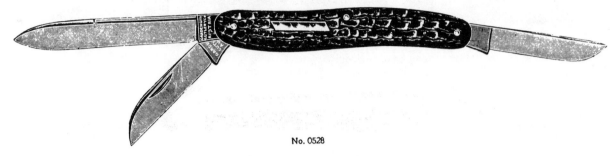

No. 0528

No. 0529 3 blades, buffalo handle, brass lined, crocus polished, 3¼ in., · · · · · ·
No. 0528–3 blades. stag　handle, brass lined, crocus polished, 3¼ in., · · · · · ·

No. 0469–3 blades. stag handle, brass lined, glazed, 3⅝ in., · · · · · ·

No. 0285–3 blades, stag handle, brass lined, crocus polished, 3½ in., · · · · · ·

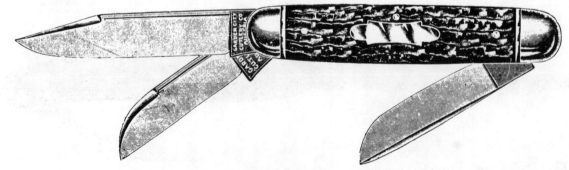

No. 0577–3 blades, stag handle, brass lined, crocus polished, 4 in., · · · · ·

HALF DOZEN IN A BOX.

BARLOWS.

No. 2.

No. 1–1 blade, black bone handle, iron lined, glazed, 3⅜ in., ...
No. 2–2 blades, black bone handle, iron lined, glazed, 3⅜ in., ...

No. 0160.

No. 0160–1 blade, horn handle, iron lined, 3⅛ in., ...
No. 0161–2 blades, horn handle, iron lined, 3⅛ in., ...

No. 10–1 blade, iron handle, 3⅜ in., ...

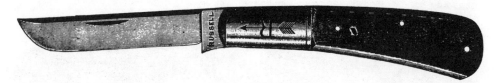

No. 603R–1 blade, black bone handle, iron lined, 3⅜ in., ...

No. 62.

No. 60–1 blade, black bone handle, iron lined, 3⅜ in., ...
No. 62–2 blades, black bone handle, iron lined, 3⅜ in., ...

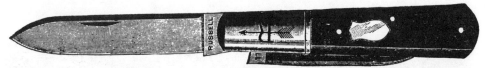

No. 52.

No. 52 –2 blades, polished horn handle, iron lined, 3⅜ in., ...
No. 062R–2 blades, stag handle, iron lined, 3⅜ in., ...
No. 42 –2 blades, white bone handle, iron lined, 3⅜ in., ...

ONE DOZEN IN A BOX.

BARLOWS.

No. 0354.

No. 0354-1 blade,   horn handle, iron lined, 3½ in.,   · · · · · · · ·
No. 0355-2 blades, horn handle, iron lined, 3½ in.,   · · · · · · · ·

No. 0360.

No. 0359-1 blade,   horn handle, iron lined, 3⅜ in.,   · · · · · · · ·
No. 0360-2 blades, horn handle, iron lined, 3⅜ in.,   · · · · · · · ·

No. 0312-2 blades, stag handle, iron lined, crocus polished, 3⅜ in.,   · · · · · ·

No. 0313-2 blades, stag handle, iron lined, crocus polished, 3⅜ in.,   · · · · ·

No. 0665-2 blades, stag handle, iron lined, crocus polished, 3⅜ in.,   · · · · ·

No. 0315-2 blades, stag handle, iron lined, crocus polished, 3⅜ in.,   · · · · ·

ONE DOZEN IN A BOX.

POCKET HUNTING KNIVES.

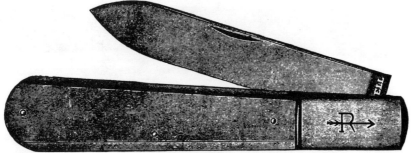

No. 0601.

No. 0593–5 in., "Rivington," 1 blade, black horn handle, iron lined, clip point, · · · · · ·
No. 0594–5 in., "Rivington," 1 blade, black horn handle, iron lined, spear point, · · · · ·
No. 0600–5⅛ in., Russell's, 1 blade, black horn handle, iron lined, clip point, · · · · · ·
No. 0601–5⅛ in., Russell's, 1 blade, black horn handle, iron lined, spear point, · · · · ·

No. 944.

No. 943–4 in., 1 blade, stag handle, iron lined, crocus polished and etched, clip point · · ·
No. 944–4⅞ in., 1 blade, stag handle, iron lined, crocus polished and etched, clip point, · ·

By pressing the button shown in bolster the blade will fly open and become firmly locked in place. To close the blade it is necessary first to press the button.

No. 0278–4⅝ in., NON·XLL, 1 blade, spring back, iron lined, clip point, · · · · ·

No. 7619.

No. 7619–4⅝ in., Wostenholm's, 1 blade, spring back, stag handle, iron lined, crocus polished, spear point, · · · · · · · · · · · ·
No. 7633–4⅝ in., Wostenholm's, 1 blade, spring back, stag handle, iron lined, crocus polished, hollow bolster, clip point, · · · · · · · · · ·

HALF DOZEN IN A BOX.

CAMPING KNIVES.

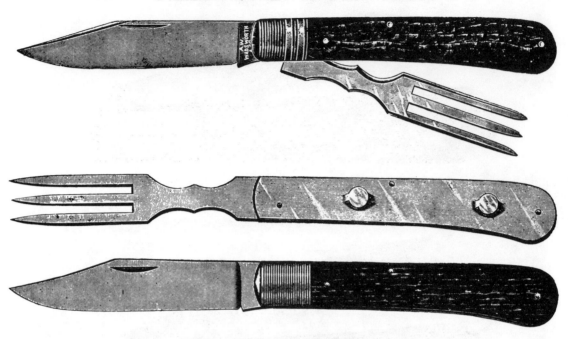

No. 0602–2 pieces, knife and fork, brass lined, stag handle, joins and closes like an ordinary pocket knife, fine quality steel blade and fork, polished, German silver bolster, 3⅞ in.,   ·   ·   ·

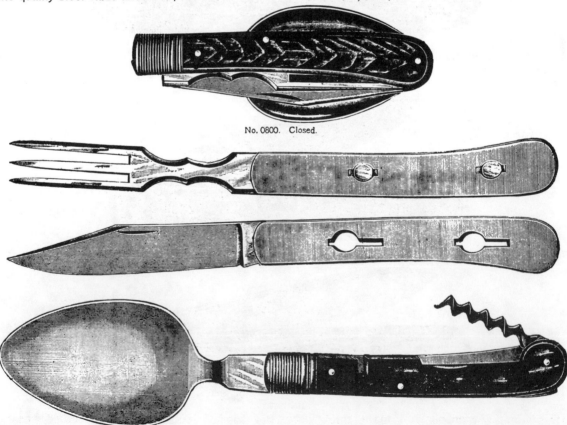

No. 0800. Closed.

No. 0800–3 pieces, knife, fork and spoon, with corkscrew, crocus polished steel knife and fork, with German silver spoon, German silver bolster, brass lined, buffalo horn handle, a splendid article for camp use, 4 in.,   ·   ·   ·   ·   ·

HALF DOZEN IN A BOX.

HUNTING KNIVES.

No. 02.

No. 03–Swedish, 1 blade, solid boxwood handle, 2⅞ in., ...
No. 02–Swedish, 1 blade, solid boxwood handle, 3¼ in., ...
No. 01–Swedish, 1 blade, solid boxwood handle, 4⅜ in., ...

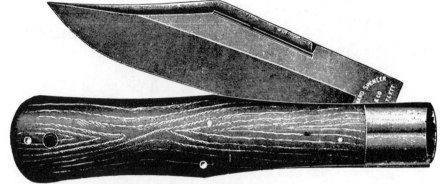

No. 144–H., S., B. & Co's, 1 blade, cocoa handle, iron lined, 5¾ in .   .   .   .   .   .

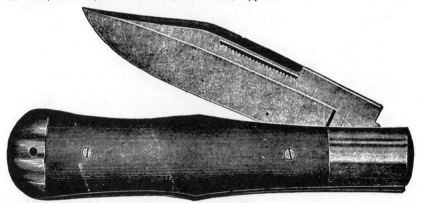

No 145.

No. 145–H., S., B. & Co's, 1 blade, cocoa handle, iron lined, 5⅜ in .   .   .   .   .   .
No. 146–H., S., B. & Co's, 1 blade, stag   handle, iron lined, 5⅜ in., ...
No. 156–"Our Very Best," 1 blade, stag   handle, brass lined, lock back. 5⅜ in., .   .

No. 0156–1 blade, deerfoot handle, brass lined, lock back, crocus polished, 4¾ in.
No. 4839–1 blade, deerfoot handle, brass lined, lock back, crocus polished, 5⅜ in .   .
HALF DOZEN IN A BOX.

POCKET KNIVES.

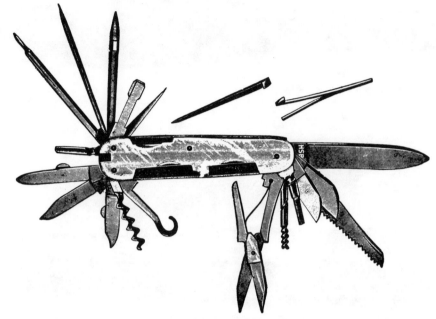

Pearl Handle, Rope Milled German Silver Lining, Crocus Polished.

No. 3025–11 tools, comprising 3 blades, 1 scissors, 1 corkscrew, 1 button hook, 1 file, 2 awls, 2 picks, 3⅛ in., · · · · · · · · · · ·

No. 3028–7 tools, comprising 2 blades, 1 scissors, 1 corkscrew, 1 file, 2 picks, 3⅛ in., ·

No. 6217–7 tools, comprising 2 blades, 1 scissors, 1 corkscrew, 1 file, 2 picks, 3 in., ·

No. 7203–7 tools, comprising 2 blades, 1 scissors, 1 corkscrew, 1 file, 2 picks, 2⅞ in., ·

No. 6741–6 tools, comprising 2 blades, 1 scissors, 1 file, 2 picks, 3 in., · · · ·

No. 6891–6 tools, comprising 2 blades, 1 scissors, 1 file, 2 picks, 2½ in., · · · ·

No. 3836–3 tools, comprising 2 blades, 1 scissors, 2⅝ in., · · · · · ·

No. 22068–Watch charm, 5 tools, comprising 3 blades, 1 scissors, 1 corkscrew, 1½ in., with ring,

No. 1984–2 blades, with corkscrew and champagne opener, gray buffalo handle, brass lined, crocus polished, 3¾ in., · · · · · · · · · · ·

No. 1784–2 blades, with corkscrew and champagne opener, pearl handle, brass lined, crocus polished, 3⅝ in., · · · · · · · · · ·

HALF DOZEN IN A BOX.

POCKET KNIVES.

No. 3001–1 blade, cocoa handle, iron lined, 2¾ in.,   ·   ·   ·   ·   ·   ·   ·

No. 0714.

No. 0713–1 blade, nickel handle, iron lined, 2¾ in.,   ·   ·   ·   ·   ·   ·
No. 0714–2 blades; nickel handle, iron lined, 2¾ in.,   ·   ·   ·   ·   ·   ·

No. 0217.

No. 0217–1 blade, nickel handle, 2⅝ in.,   ·   ·   ·   ·   ·   ·   ·   ·
No. 0218–2 blades, nickel handle, 2⅝ in.,   ·   ·   ·   ·   ·   ·   ·

No. 0402–1 blade, nickel handle, 2¾ in.,   ·   ·   ·   ·   ·   ·   ·   ·

No. 0403–2 blades, nickel handle, 2⅞ in.,   ·   ·   ·   ·   ·   ·   ·

No. 16–1 blade, iron handle, 2¾ in.,   ·   ·   ·   ·   ·   ·   ·   ·

ONE DOZEN IN A BOX.

POCKET KNIVES.

No. 011

No. 010-1 blade, scored ebony handle, iron lined, glazed, 2⅝ in., · · · · · · ·
No. 011-2 blades, scored ebony handle, iron lined, glazed, 2⅝ in., · · · · · · ·

No. 0356-1 blade, cocoa handle, iron lined, glazed, 2¾ in · · · · · · · ·

No. 0357-1 blade, ebony handle, iron lined, glazed, 2⅞ in., · · · · · · · ·

No. 0210.

No. 0105-1 blade, ebony handle, iron lined, glazed, 3 in., · · · · · · · ·
No. 0210-2 blades, ebony handle, iron lined, glazed, 2⅞ in., · · · · · · · ·

No. 0634-2 blades, japanned tin handle, iron lined, glazed, 3⅜ in · · · ·

No. 0686

No. 0687-2 blades, cocoa handle, iron lined, glazed, 3¼ in., · · · · · · ·
No. 0686-2 blades, ebony handle, iron lined, glazed, 3¼ in., · · · · · · ·
No. 0639-2 blades, cocoa handle, iron lined, glazed, 3¼ in., · · · · · · ·
No. 0640-2 blades, ebony handle, iron lined, glazed, 3¼ in., · · · · · · ·

No. 0296-2 blades, ebony handle, iron lined, glazed, 3¼ in., · · · · · · ·

ONE DOZEN IN A BOX.

POCKET KNIVES.

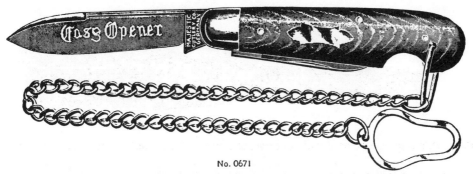

No. 0671

No. 0671-2 blades, cocoa handle, iron lined, glazed, 3½ in., with 18 in. nickel plated chain, ·
No. 0670-2 blades, ebony handle, iron lined, glazed, 3½ in., with 18 in. nickel plated chain, ·
No. 0672-2 blades, stag handle, iron lined, glazed, 3½ in., with 18 in. nickel plated chain, ·

No. 0667

No. 0667-2 blades, cocoa handle, iron lined, glazed, 3½ in., ·   ·   ·   ·   ·   ·
No. 0668-2 blades, ebony handle, iron lined, glazed, 3½ in., ·   ·   ·   ·   ·   ·
No. 0669-2 blades, stag handle, iron lined, glazed, 3½ in., ·   ·   ·   ·   ·   ·

No. 0361.

No. 0361-2 blades, cocoa handle, iron lined, glazed, 3½ in., ·   ·   ·   ·   ·   ·
No. 0362-2 blades, ebony handle, iron lined, glazed, 3½ in., ·   ·   ·   ·   ·   ·

No. 0337.

No. 0337-2 blades, cocoa handle, iron lined, glazed, 3½ in., ·   ·   ·   ·   ·   ·
No. 0338-2 blades, ebony handle, iron lined, glazed, 3½ in., ·   ·   ·   ·   ·   ·

No. 0575.

No. 0576-2 blades, ebony handle, brass lined, crocus polished, 3⅝ in., ·   ·   ·   ·   ·
No. 0575-2 blades, stag handle, brass lined, crocus polished, 3⅝ in., ·   ·   ·   ·   ·

No. 0663.

No. 0663-2 blades, cocoa handle, brass lined, glazed, 3⅞ in., ·   ·   ·   ·   ·   ·
No. 0664-2 blades, ebony handle, brass lined, glazed, 3⅞ in., ·   ·   ·   ·   ·   ·

HALF DOZEN IN A BOX.

POCKET KNIVES.

No. 0505–2 blades, with cork screw, hoof pick and harness reamer, stag handle, brass lined, crocus polished, 2⅞ in., ...

No. 1655–2 blades, with cork screw, stag handle, brass lined, crocus polished, 3⅞ in., . .

No. 0566–2 blades, with cork screw and champagne opener, stag handle, brass lined, crocus polished, 3½ in., ...

No. 0567–2 blades, with cork screw and champagne opener, pearl handle, brass lined, crocus polished, 3½ in, ...

No. 0699–2 blades, with fleams, cork screw, hoof pick, harness reamer and tweezers, stag handle, iron lined, crocus polished, 3⅝ in., ...

HALF DOZEN IN A BOX.

Gold Filled Pocket Knives — Latest Shapes

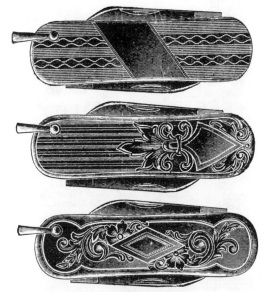

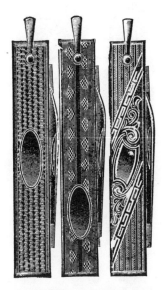

G.N. 6222. Gold-filled assortment. Bright polish English finish; two Sheffield blades; designs are latest in floral and bar effect; engine turned and engraved; bail attached for vest chain. Per doz..

G.N. 6220. Assortment latest oval shape with two Sheffield steel blades, engraved engine turned and raised model effects; floral, scroll, and bar designs; each knife has bail attached for vest chain. Per doz..................

G.N. 6221. Square-shaped thin model double blade **Knives.** Fancy engine turned and engraved designs with signet centers; very choice patterns in this gold-filled assortment. Per doz....

ALL ABOVE ASSORTMENTS ARE EXACT SIZE AS ILLUSTRATED

G.N. 6217. A quick-selling assortment of 1 dozen gold-filled **Knives,** put up on easel back card; Sheffield blades; assorted shapes and sizes; all bright and engraved finish. Per card of one dozen..

G.N. 6218. Same as above, but **platinoid finish.** Rapid sellers for jewelers, novelty dealers, cigar stores, etc. Per card of one dozen.........

G.N. 6219. An art figure assortment; ivory finish figures and design inlaid on gold-filled handles; Sheffield steel blades. This assortment has been a feature number for premium and salesboard work. Specially priced at, per doz..

POCKET KNIVES

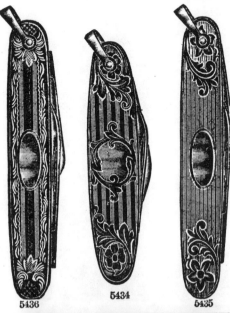

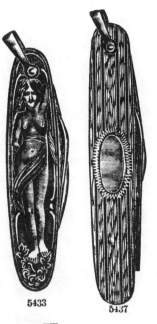

AMERICAN MANUFACTURE STANDARD QUALITY

GN. 5433, 5434, 5435, 5436, 5437. Five assorted patterns of Embossed, Engraved and Chased Pocket Knives, suitable for watch chains. Knives are electro-plated gold finished, with two blades of fine quality steel. Per dozen.........

5436   5434   5435   5433   5437

GN. 5429. Gold Filled Knife Assortment, warranted ten years. Each has two blades of high-grade steel. All are neatly engraved, with space left for initial. One dozen to display easel, marked 98c. each. Per dozen....................

GN. 5430. Gold Filled Pocket Knife, set with diamond chip, fitted with two good quality steel blades, with chain ring. Roman finish, handsome appearance.
Per dozen ....

GN. 5431. Gold Filled Pocket Knife, with three diamond chips set in bright cut stars; two steel blades; fine finish, with chain ring. Exceptional value.
Per dozen ....

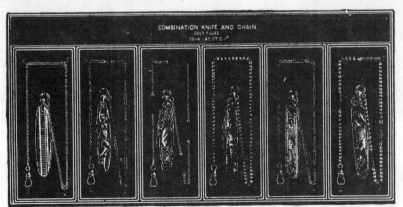

G.B. 3015. Rolled Plated Waldemar Chain, with fancy design gold plated pocket knife, put up half dozen on lined easel pad. Per dozen....................................

ASSORTED JACK AND HUNTING KNIVES

No. 4318 — Abalone Shell Handle Knife. Two highly polished steel blades. Assorted shapes. Polished brass bolsters. 3½ in. long. One dozen assorted on 6-color rainbow display card.

Dozen . . . .

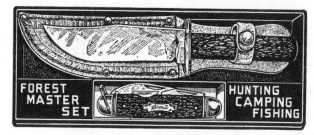

No. 4301—Boy Scout Outing Set. Consists of a three bladed scout knife and hunting knife in sheath, put up in a neat gift box. Knife has a spear blade, can opener and a combination screw driver and cap lifter. Both pieces have stag handles. Hunting knife 7½ inches overall.

Each . . . . .   **Dozen** . . . . .

No. 4319—G-Man Pocket Knife. Two highly polished steel blades nickel polished bolsters. Imitation pearl handles with characters printed on both sides. One dozen on card, 3 inches long.

Dozen . . . .

No. 4310X—Two Blade Pop-eye Pocket Knife. Polished blades and bolsters. Imitation handles with 3-color imprints. 5½ inches when open.

Dozen . . . .

No. 4338—Sportsman's Delight. A combination hunting knife and utility axe knife. Unbreakable celluloid handles. Highly polished nickel silver bolsters and cap. Size of knife closed 5½ inches. Each in box.

Each . . . .   **Dozen** . . . .

No. 4306—2 Blade Jack Knife. Assorted conventional and curved handles made of stag and mottled composition; with shield fine quality clip and pen steel blades. Nickel-silver bolsters. One dozen to display box.

Dozen . . . .

No. 4333—Novelty Leg Shaped Two Blade Pocket Knife. Nickel bolster cap lifter on end. Tinted art model pictures under transparent non-breakable handles.

Dozen . . . .

No. 4375 — Sportsman's Heavy Duty Hunting and Fishing Knife. Two steel blades, one long 4 inch blade and one serrated edge for scaling with a hook remover. Unbreakable handles in assorted colors, size 5¼ inches closed. Six in display carton.

Dozen . . . .

No. 4372—Waldemar Knife, finished in yellow or white finish. Conventional shapes with neat engine-turned designs. Polished steel blade and nail file. Bale for chain.

Dozen . . . .

No. 4308—Midget Knife Assortment. An ideal pocket or chain knife for all. Each consists of a pen and spear blade. Composition handles in mottled colors. Length 2½ inches with bale. Put up as illustrated.

Dozen . . . .

No. 4346—Boy Scout Knife Ensemble. Consists of a three blade stag handle scout knife and a magnifying glass with accurate compass imbedded in body. Each set put up in an attractive lithographed gift box.

Each . . . . .   **Doz.**

No. 4356—Hunting Knife. With leather sheath. 6¼ inches long. Abalonite composition handles. Full length solid tang. Durable sheath protected with 3 rivets.

Dozen . . . .

NOVELTY POCKET AND ART CHARM KNIVES

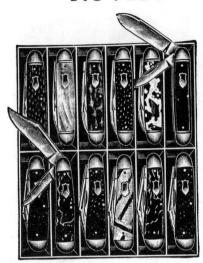

No. 4369—Jumbo Jack Knife. Two polished steel blades. Brass lined, polished bolsters and shield. Mottled composition and stag handles. Put up 1 dozen to display box.

Dozen . . . .

No. 4323—Art Pocket Knife. Two polished steel blades. Brass lined. Hand tinted art model pictures under non-breakable transparent handles. 2¾ inches when closed.

Dozen . .

No. 4332—Art Pocket Knife. 2 polished steel blades with tintet art model pictures on both sides. 3½ in. long. Brass lined. Non-breakable transparent handles.

Dozen . .

No. 4312—Lucky Pocket Knife. 2 polished steel blades. Pearl effect handles with embossed good luck symbols. 3⅛ inches when closed, 5⅝ inches when open. One dozen on counter display card.

Dozen . . . .

No. 4376 — Hunting Knife. Simulated stag. handle 4¼ inch high grade steel blade, with serrated back. 8¾ in. long overall. Each complete with leather sheath and snap button fastener.

Each . . . .

No. 4315—Novelty Polished Silver Finish Two Blade Charm Knife. Engine turned effects. Assorted shapes. Bulk packed. Steel shackle. Length 2¼ inches.

Dozen . . . . . .

Gross . . . . . .

No. 4309—Sportsman's Knife. 4 inch full polished steel blades. Nickel silver bolster. Steel lining. Imitation pearl handles in assorted bright colors. 9 inches when open.

Dozen . . . .

No. 4310—Sportsman's Knife. Full polished 4 inch blade. Steel bolster and lining. Assorted colored mottle handles. 9 inch long when open. One dozen assorted in compartment box.

Dozen . . . .

No. 4300—Fisherman's Knife. Highly polished 4 inch clip blade with serrated back for scaling fish. Simulated stag handle. Polished bolster with hook remover on one end. Size of knife when closed, 5 inches. One dozen in display box.

Dozen . . . .

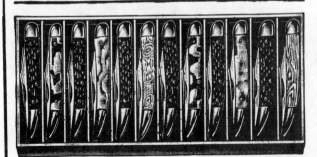

No. 4305—Spring Blade Knife. Full polished 4 inch blade. Nickel silver bolsters and lining. Assorted stag and colored mottled handles. One dozen in compartment box.

Dozen . . . .

No. 4336 — Fisherman's Knife. Simulated stag handle. Four inch clip blade with serrated back for scaling fish, high carbon steel blade, mirror finish. Nickel bolsters with hook remover. Compass imbedded in handle.

Dozen . . . . . .

No. 4355 — Mickey Mouse Pocket Knife. Two polished blades. Imitation pearl handles with 3-color prints. 5½ inches when open. One dozen in display box.

Dozen . . . . . .

Miniature Knives for Charms, Hunting Knives, Etc.

Toilet Knives

S8668 — Toilet Knife. Consists of earspoon, toothpick and spear point metal blade, celluloid handles, asstd. colors, iron lined, small metal shield. 1 gross in box. Gro.......

S8670—Same as above, Japanese make. 1 gro. in box. Gro. ......

S8669—Toilet Knife. Colored celluloid handle with five attachments, earspoon, toothpick, nail file, button hook and polished blade. 1 gross in box. Gro.................................

Midget Jack Knife Assts.

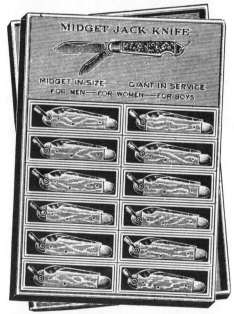

C7109—Midget Jack Knife Asst. (Mfrs. 22). Assorted brilliant color celluloid handles, 2 blades, master blade crocus polished, brass linings, full nickel silver trim including shackle. Each in box, 1 doz. in carton. Doz. ....

C7019—Midget Jack Knife Asst. (Mfrs. 54). Two blades solid Novo pearl handles, brass lined, nickel silver cap and bolster, fitted with shackle for attaching to chain, each in box, 1 doz. in display carton. Doz......................

C7020—Midget Jack Knife Asst. (Mfrs. 22½). Black and white Novo pearl handles, 2 blades, brass lined, nickel silver bolsters, fitted with shackle for attaching to chain, each in box, 1 doz. in carton. Doz......................

Photo Handle Pocket Knives

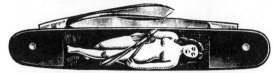

C6489—Art Photo Pen Knife. Length, 2¼ in., one large spear and one small pen blade, transparent celluloid handles with photo reproductions of famous art subjects, brass lined. Doz..................................

C6488—Art Photo Pen Knife. Length, 3¼ in., two blades, one large spear and small pen blade, transparent celluloid handles, nickel silver bolsters, photo reproductions of famous art subjects, brass lined. Doz..............................

Hunting and Outing Knives

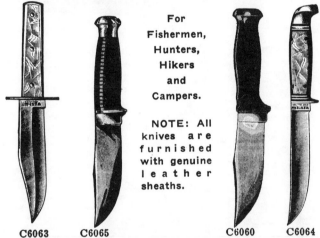

For Fishermen, Hunters, Hikers and Campers.

NOTE: All knives are furnished with genuine leather sheaths.

C6063   C6065   C6060   C6064

All blades are forged from the finest grade, special formula, crucible chrome steel, hand hammered, full mirror finished and hand honed.

C6063—Camper's Knife. (Mfrs. X235). 5⅞ in. overall 3¼ in. blade, pearl celluloid handle. Doz......................

C6061—Camper's Knife. (Mfrs. X245). Same as C6063, length overall 8⅝ in., length of blade 5 in., pearl celluloid non-breakable handles. Doz...................................

C6062—Camper's Knife. (Mfrs. 645 Jr.) Same as C6061, length overall 8 in., length of blade 4½ in., bone stag handle. Doz.................................

C6065—Hunter's Knife. (Mfrs. NX243). Length overall 8½ in., blade 4¾ in. long, full brown leather washer handle. A sturdy, well balanced, popular priced knife. Doz. ....

C6060—Hunter's Knife. (Mfrs. BX43). Moulded bakelite handle, length overall 9 in., asstd. mottled colors, blade 4¾ in. long, metal front guard. Doz......................

C6064—Hunter's Knife. (Mfrs. X248). Length overall 7¾ in., Finnish pattern, long and slender, keen edged blade, length 4½ in., pearl celluloid handle with black under-lay, metal and fibre washers at each end of handle, curved metal end knob. Doz...........................

Popular Priced Knives for Profitable Selling

C7294 — Boys' Chain Knife. Length, 2⅞ in. gun metal handle, one large spear blade, equipped with bail and chain. Knives mounted 1 doz. on display card, chains in separate pkg. Doz..................

Note chains may be ordered separately if desired.

Doz..................   Gro..................

Celluloid One-blade Knives.—Iron tips, iron lining. Glazed blade of special high quality cutlery steel. Length of knives 2¾ in. when closed.

C3851—One doz in bulk box, assorted colored handles. Doz. ....

One-blade Stag Chain Knives —Iron tips, iron lining, glazed blade, length of knives 2¾ in. when closed, high quality cutlery steel, chain attached.

C3852—One doz. in bulk box all with Stag handles.

Doz. ....

Assortment of large size single-blade Cattle Knives— Iron bolsters, iron lining, Length of knives, 3⅝ in. when closed. Blades made of special high quality cutlery steel.
C3853—One doz. in display box, all with assorted colored handles. Doz..................

Assortment of standard size Barlow Knives —Iron bolsters, iron lining, blades made of special high quality cutlery steel, length of knives, 3⅜ in. when closed.

C3854—1 doz. in display box all with Stag handles.

Doz. ....

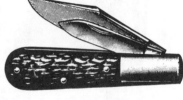

Large single-blade knives — Iron lining, polished blade of special high quality cutlery steel, length of knives, 5 in. when closed.
C3855—1 doz. in display box with half Stag and half Colored Celluloid handles. Doz..................

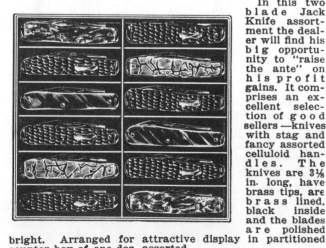

In this two blade Jack Knife assortment the dealer will find his big opportunity to "raise the ante" on his profit gains. It comprises an excellent selection of good sellers —knives with stag and fancy assorted celluloid handles. The knives are 3⅛ in. long, have brass tips, are brass lined, black inside and the blades are polished bright. Arranged for attractive display in partitioned counter box of one doz. assorted.
CB1825t—Two Blade Jack Knife Assortment.
Doz. ....

Favorite Style Pocket Knives for Quick Sale

Boy Scout Pocket Knives

C6491—American Made Scout Knife. (Mfrs. 826S). Jack knife style, size 3 in., 2 blades, stag handle, brass lined, nickel silver shield. One blade is a combination cap lifter and screw driver. Metal chain with button fastener attached. 1 doz. in box. Doz. ....

C350—Scout Knife. Standard size, brass lined, full polished, stag handle with nickel silver shield and bail for chain attachment. Size 3⅝ in.

Doz. ......

C250—Scout Knife. Three blade, length closed 3⅝ in., assorted, unbreakable stag and compo-pearl handles, full polished spear blade, can opener, combination screwdriver and bottle opener, polished bolsters and shackle. 1 doz. in display box. Doz............................
C3857—Same as above with inset, Stag handle. Doz...

Fancy "Nigger Chaser" Knife Assortment

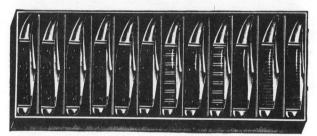

Fancy shaped one-blade "Nigger Chaser" type pocket knife, 5 in. long with assorted stag and fancy celluloid handles. These have beautiful nickel-silver trim, are brass lined and cleaned inside. Blades are polished. Asstd. 1 doz. in display box.
C6872—"Nigger Chaser" Pocket Knife Asst. Doz.........

Two Three-Bladed Pocket Knives

Assortment of Premium Stock Knives—Nickel silver bolsters, brass lining, nickel silver shield, full polished blades, polished springs. Clip, Spey and Punch blades made of special high quality cutlery steel. Length of knives 3½ in. when closed.
C3859—1 doz. in bulk box, all with Celluloid handles. Doz............

Cattle Knives—Nickel silver bolsters and shield, brass lining. Clip, Spey and punch blades, full polished, special high quality cutlery steel, polished springs. Length of knives 3⅝ in. when closed.
C3860—1 doz. in box all with Celluloid handles. Doz. ....

Cattle Knives—Nickel silver bolster and shield, brass lining, clip, spey and punch blades of special high quality cutlery steel. Full polished, polished springs. Length of knives 3⅝ in. when closed.
C3861—½ doz. in box all with Celluloid handles. Doz. ....
C3862—Same as above, all Stag handles. Doz.......

Premium Stock Knives — Brass lining, nickel silver shield and bolsters. Clip, Spey and Punch blades full polished, of special high quality cutlery steel. Polished springs. Length of knives 4 in. when closed.
C3863—½ doz. in box all with Celluloid handles. Doz. ....
C3864—Same as above, all with Stag handles. Doz...........

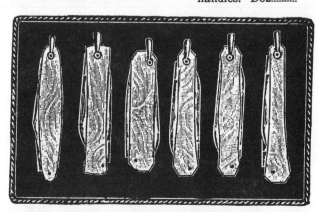

C7232—Genuine Mother of Pearl Mounted Knife Asst.—Two keen cutting polished steel blades, carefully selected pearl handles. Put up 6 assorted styles on velvet easel pad. Doz...

Assortment of 2-blade Jacks and Pens— Brass tips, brass lining, nickel silver shield, blades made of special high quality cutlery steel. Length of knives 3¼ in. when closed.

C3856—1 doz. in display box all with Imitation Pearl handles. Doz.....

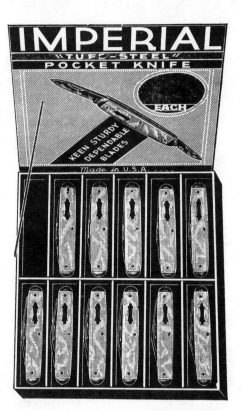

Hunting Knives

Guard Knife—One large clip blade, crocus polished on one side, brass lined, nickel silver guard and cap, asst. colored and black celluloid handles, length closed 3⅞ in. ½ doz. in box.
C7057—Asst. colors. Doz...

Sportsman's Fish Knife

Fish Knife—One-blade knife, iron bolsters, iron lining, lower bolster arranged to remove fish hook and is stamped "Hook Remover." Blade made of special high quality cutlery steel, has serrated back for fish scaling. Length of knife 5 in. when closed.
C3865—One doz. in display box all with Stag handles. Doz. ....

This Jack Knife assortment contains knives 3⅛ in. long, consisting of a fine variety in stag and assorted handled knives with brass tips and brass lined. They are black inside and the blades are polished. Asstd. 1 doz. in partitioned box designed for effective counter display.
C1450—Jack Knife Assortment.
Doz. ....

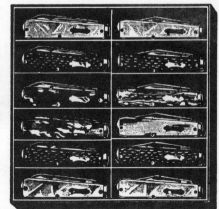

Assortment of Hunting Knives—Single iron bolster, iron lining, nickel silver shield, blade made of special high quality cutlery steel. Length of knives 5 in. when closed.
C3857—½ doz. to the display box all with celluloid handles. Box...................$2.05 Doz..........................
C3858—Same as above, all stag handles. Box, Doz. ....

,RMY AND NAVY COMBINATION KNIFE.

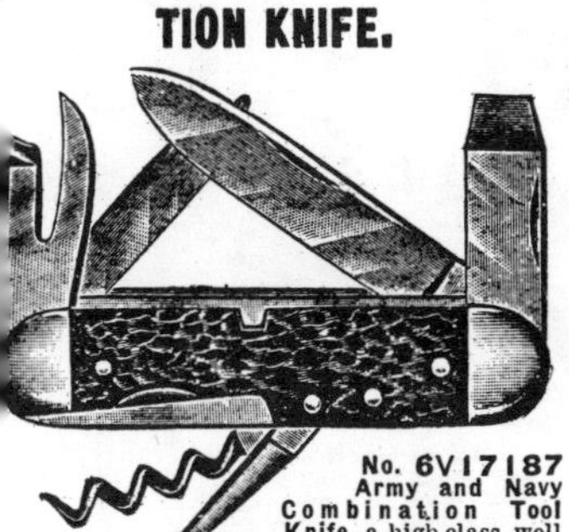

No. 6V17187 Army and Navy Combination Tool Knife, a high class, well made knife, brass lined, fine stag handle, double bolsters, fitted with corkscrew, swaging awl, can opener, screw-
:iver, one large spear blade and one medium
ze pen blade. Six tools in all, and all of
em forged of the very best material and
iaranteed to give satisfaction. Our price for
is knife, with stag handle and double bol-
ers, is lower than that asked by others for a
iife with plain handle and without bolsters.
ength of knife when closed, 3½ inches.
Price ....
If mail shipment, postage extra, 6 cents.

NINE TOOLS IN ONE,

No. 6V17186 This knife will cut wire, wood or leather and embodies a pocket knife, leather punch, swage awl, wire cutter, wire pliers, alligator wrench, hoof hook, screwdriver and screw bit. This knife is no clumsier than the ordinary pocket knife. The pliers and wire cutter are made from drop forged tool steel, the blade is made from the best cutlers' steel, full gauge, tempered and will stand hard usage. All tools are practical and serviceable; one tool does not interfere with the free use of the other. This knife has stag handle, German silver bolsters, and is steel lined. Length of handle, 4⅛ inches.
Price........................
If mail shipment, postage extra, 6 cents.

Congress Four-Blade Knife.

No. 6V17158 Wilbert Large Congress Knife, has two large blades and two pen blades, stag handle, German silver bolsters and shield, brass lined, nicely finished throughout. Length of handle, 3¾ inches; length with large blade open, 6⅛ inches.
Price....(Postage extra, 5 cents)....

Four-Blade Stockman's Knife, 88 Cents.

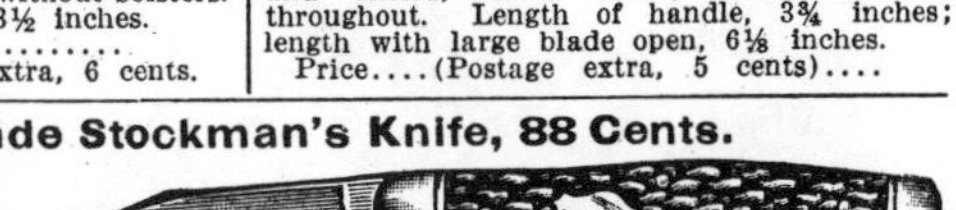

**No. 6V17157 Wil-
ert Four-Blade Stockman's
nife.** Stag handle, four heavy
ades, clip, pen, sheep's foot
id spaying blade, nicely pol-
hed, finely tempered and ground. German silver bol-
ers and shield. A good, strong, serviceable knife. The
ur blades permit of a great variety of work. Length of handle,
⅞ inches; length with large blade open, 6½ inches. This is a
iife that would ordinarily retail for $1.25. Price..........
If mail shipment, postage extra, 5 cents.

Push Button Knives.

**These knives are fitted with a push button in the bolster. By pressing this button you
:lease a flat spring which opens the blade and locks it so that it cannot be closed accident-
lly. The material used in these knives is the best. The push button arrangement is very
mple and the knife cannot get out of order.**

4¾-
nch

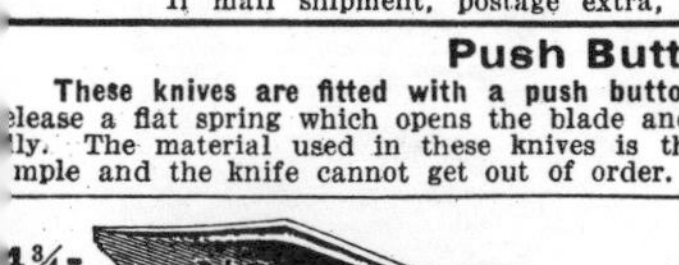

No. 6V17181 Push Button Knife.
ne blade, clip point, stag handle, single
olster, iron lined. Length of handle, 4¾
iches; length, with blade open, 8¾ inches.
Price ....
If mail shipment, postage extra, 6 cents.

3⅞-
inch

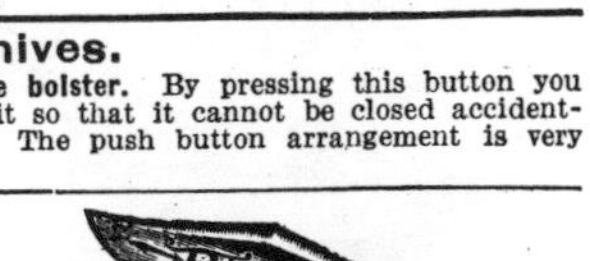

No. 6V17182 Push Button Knife. One blade, clip point, stag handle, single bolster, iron lined. Length of handle, 3⅞ inches; length with blade open, 6⅞ inches.
Price ....
If mail shipment, postage extra, 5 cents.

JOSEPH ALLEN & SONS'
'AMOUS NON-XLL KNIVES
Imported From Sheffield, England.

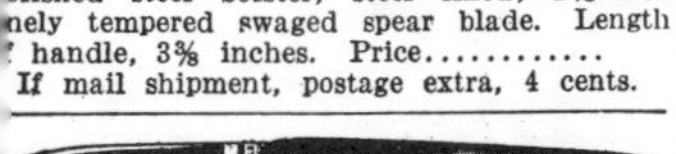

**No. 6V17224 Non-XLL One-Blade Bar-
w Pattern Jackknife.** Genuine horn handle,
olished steel bolster, steel lined; 2⅝-inch
nely tempered swaged spear blade. Length
handle, 3⅝ inches. Price...........
If mail shipment, postage extra, 4 cents.

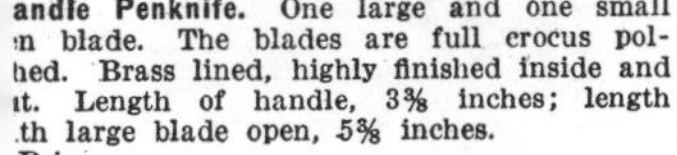

**No. 6V17226 Non-XLL Two-Blade Horn
andle Penknife.** One large and one small
n blade. The blades are full crocus pol-
hed. Brass lined, highly finished inside and
it. Length of handle, 3⅜ inches; length
th large blade open, 5⅝ inches.
Price ....
If mail shipment, postage extra, 4 cents.

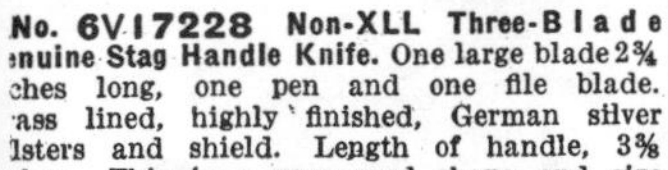

**No. 6V17228 Non-XLL Three-Blade
enuine Stag Handle Knife.** One large blade 2¾
ches long, one pen and one file blade.
ass lined, highly finished, German silver
lsters and shield. Length of handle, 3⅜
ches. This is a very good shape and size
ife; every knife guaranteed. Price....
If mail shipment, postage extra, 4 cents.

IMPORTED ENGLISH KNIVES.
Geo. Wostenholm & Sons' IXL Pocket Knives.

We show some of the most desirable patterns of George Wostenholm & Sons' Celebrated IXL Pocket Knives, which are favorably known all over the world.

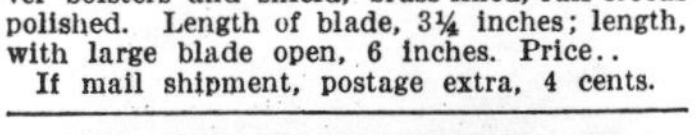

No. 6V17243 George Wostenholm & Sons' IXL Two-Blade Jack Knife. German silver bolsters and shield, brass lined, full crocus polished. Length of blade, 3¼ inches; length, with large blade open, 6 inches. Price..
If mail shipment, postage extra, 4 cents.

No. 6V17244 George Wostenholm & Sons' IXL Pocket Knife, stag handle, German silver bolsters and shield, brass lined. Length of handle, 3¾ inches. Price..........
If mail shipment, postage extra, 4 cents.

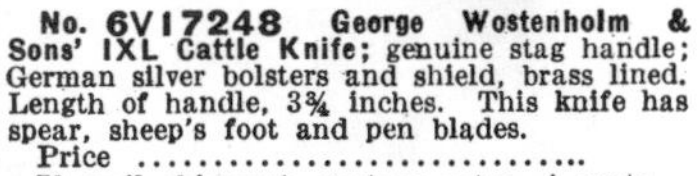

No. 6V17248 George Wostenholm & Sons' IXL Cattle Knife; genuine stag handle; German silver bolsters and shield, brass lined. Length of handle, 3¾ inches. This knife has spear, sheep's foot and pen blades.
Price ....
If mail shipment, postage extra, 4 cents.

IMPORTED GERMAN KNIVES

The following pocket knives are imported from Europe and are not guaranteed. In order that our customers may not be misled, we have described them as good, fair and cheap. The cheap grade is good for the price, but the price is not enough for a good knife. **Fair, will** usually give satisfaction. The good grades are commonly sold as warranted, but we do not warrant them. Any of these goods will be better value than you can secure elsewhere for the same money.

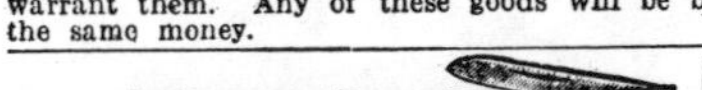

No. 6V17282 Rifle Pattern Knife. Has one blade, one pen and one lead pencil. The blade is of the best steel, finely ground and finished. German silver handle, brass lined. The pen and pencil slide in and out of the barrel. A very useful and practical article.
Price ....
If mail shipment, postage extra, 4 cents.

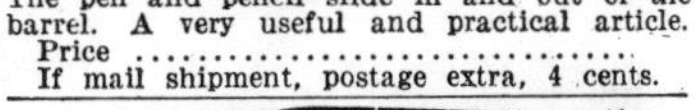

No. 6V17284 Two-Blade Knife with dark red composition handle. Length of handle, 3¼ inches; length of large blade, 2¼ inches. This knife is surprisingly good. Regular 20-cent value. Price..............
If mail shipment, postage extra, 2 cents.

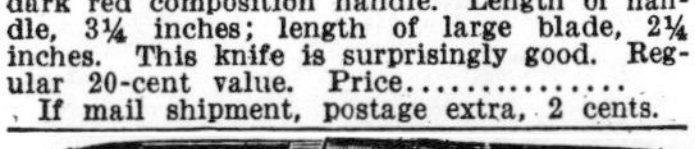

No. 6V17288 Boys' White Bone Handle Knife, with bolster and shield. Two blades, iron lined, 3½ inches. Cheap grade.
Price ....
If mail shipment, postage extra, 4 cents.

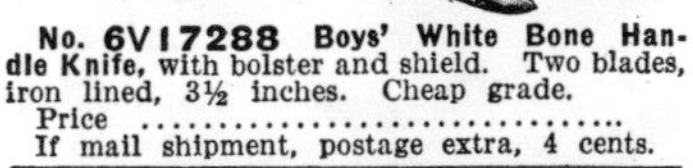

No. 6V17302 Stag Clip. A fair grade German Knife. Stag handle, clip blade. Entire length open, 6¼ inches; length of handle, 3½ inches. Price..............
If mail shipment, postage extra, 6 cents.

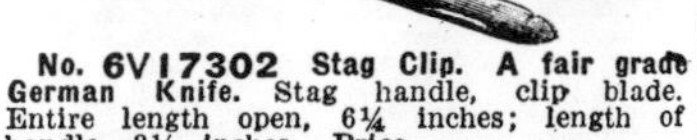

No. 6V17305 This knife has the easy opening feature, which saves the finger nails, and an 18-inch security chain, which prevents loss. Has two blades, stag handle and is iron lined. Length of handle, 3¾ inches; length with large blade open, 6 inches. A fair grade German knife. Price..................
If mail shipment, postage extra, 6 cents.

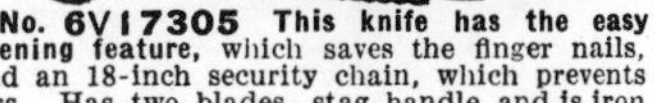

No. 6V17307 Good Quality, Equal End Three-Blade Cattle Knife, stag handle, brass lined, one large spear blade, one sheep's foot and one pen blade. Polished bolsters and shield. Length, 3½ inches; length with large blade open, 6¼ inches. Price....
If mail shipment, postage extra, 8 cents.

No. 6V17309 Combination Tool Knife. Stag handle, brass lined, German silver bolster. One large finely tempered and ground blade, 3⅝ inches long; one saw blade, 3½ inches long, will saw the hardest kind of wood; one awl blade for punching holes in leather or wood. Price................
If mail shipment, postage extra, 6 cents.

No. 6V17314 Stockman's Knife, three blades, stag handle, brass lined. Length of handle, 4 inches; length with large blade open, 7 inches. This is a good grade German knife. Price..........................
If mail shipment, postage extra, 7 cents.

No. 6V17318 Good Quality, Pearl Handle Premium Stock Knife. Three blades, one 3-inch clip blade, one sheep's foot and one spaying blade. Brass lined, polished brass bolsters and shield; a well finished, neatly made knife. Full size, 4 inches long. Price....
If mail shipment, postage extra, 7 cents.

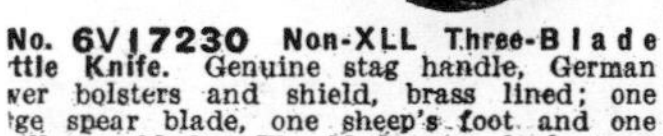

**No. 6V17230 Non-XLL Three-Blade
ttle Knife.** Genuine stag handle, German
ver bolsters and shield, brass lined; one
ge spear blade, one sheep's foot and one
all pen blade. The blades are finely tem-
ed and ground. Length of handle, 3¾
ches; length with large blade open, 6⅝
ches. Price ....
If mail shipment, postage extra, 6 cents.

No. 6V17338 Shoe Pattern Knife, composition handle, one blade. Makes a very pretty knife for the work basket.
Price, per dozen, **85c;** each..........
If mail shipment, postage extra, 2 cents.

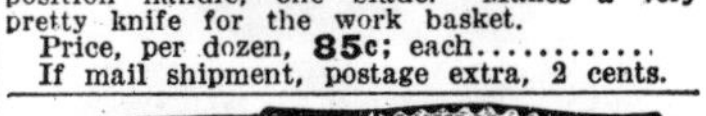

No. 6V17340 Ladies' Two-Blade Pearl Handle Penknife, brass lined. Length of handle, 2⅝ inches. A pretty knife. **Fair** grade. Price....(Postage extra, 2c)....

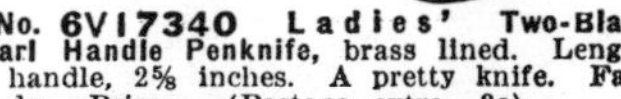

No. 6V17343 Ladies' Two-Blade Corrugated Pearl Handle Penknife, polished steel blades. Length, 2¾ inches. Cheap grade.
Price......(Postage extra, 2c)........

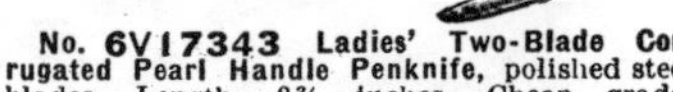

No. 6V17349 Ladies' Two-Blade Penknife. Pearl handle, brass lined, finely finished. Good grade. Length of handle, 2¾ inches. Price.........................
If mail shipment, postage extra, 2 cents.

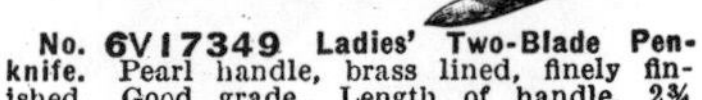

No. 6V17361 Two-Blade Pearl Handle Jackknife, 3 inches long; length with large blade open, 5¼ inches. Good grade. Serviceable, neat looking knife. Price..........
If mail shipment, postage extra, 5 cents.

Pearl View or Picture Knife.

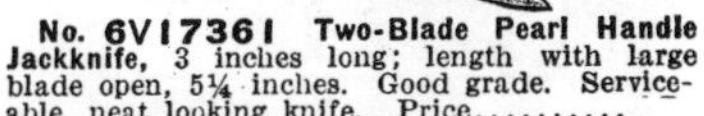

No. 6V17364 These knives have miniature pictures of actresses fitted between brass bolsters, which pictures are magnified by a small lens. This knife is 3 inches long, two blades, brass lined, nickel plated brass bolster and shield and neatly finished. Good quality. Price....(Postage extra, 2c)....

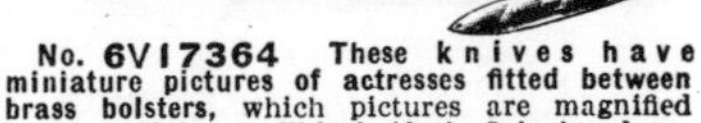

No. 6V17365 Four-Blade Pearl Handle Penknife. One large blade, two small pen blades and one nail file, brass lined, nickel plated brass bolsters and shield. Length of knife, 3 inches; length with large blade open, 5 inches. Good quality. Price.........
If mail shipment, postage extra, 3 cents.

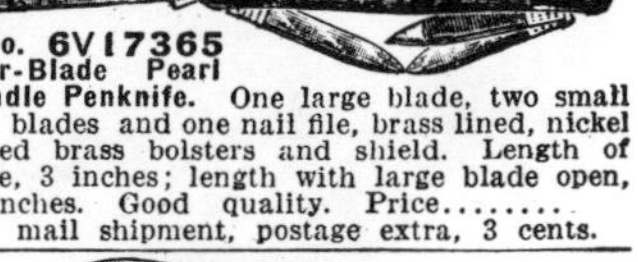

No. 6V17367 Imitation Tortoise Shell Handle Penknife. A great big value in a combination penknife and scissors. Has one 2¼-inch finely tempered full crocus polished steel blade on one side, and one 2-inch forged steel scissors on the other; brass lined, highly finished inside and out. This knife is well worth 75 cents. Price.................
If mail shipment, postage extra, 3 cents.

No. 6V17368 Black Crow Four-Blade Penknife. One large, two small and one file blade. Brass lined, finely finished inside and out. Length of handle, 3⅜ inches. Guaranteed and worth treble the price we ask.
Price.......(Postage extra, 3c.).......

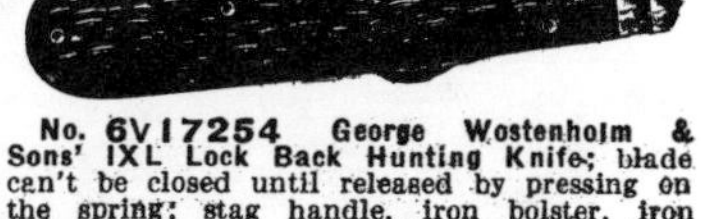

No. 6V17254 George Wostenholm & Sons' IXL Lock Back Hunting Knife; blade can't be closed until released by pressing on the spring; stag handle, iron bolster, iron lining, saber clip point blade. Length of handle, 4⅝ inches. Price..................
If mail shipment, postage extra, 5 cents.

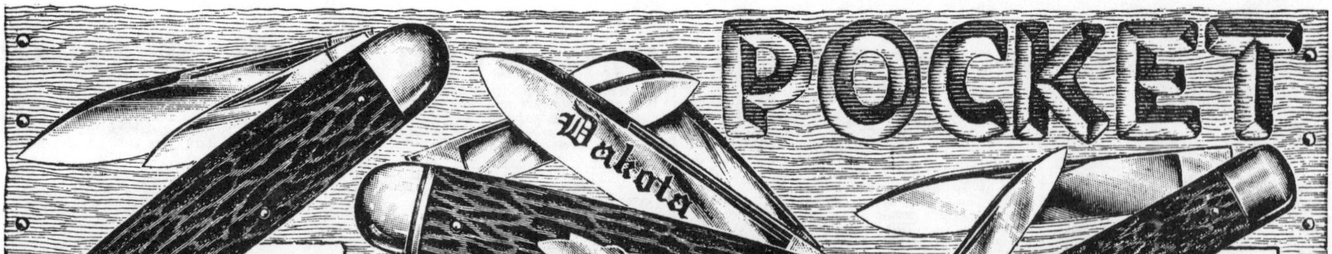

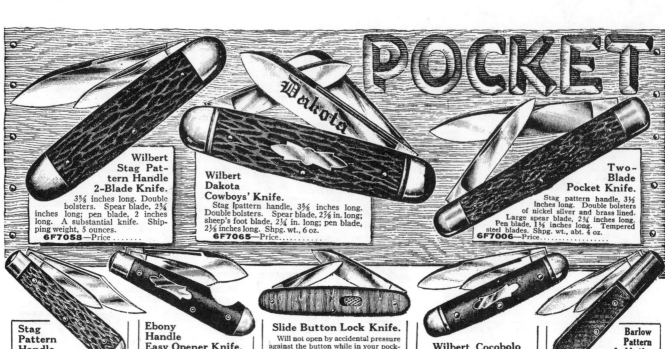

Wilbert Stag Pattern Handle 2-Blade Knife. 3⅝ inches long. Double bolsters. Spear blade, 2¾ inches long; pen blade, 2 inches long. A substantial knife. Shipping weight, 5 ounces.
6F7058—Price......

Wilbert Dakota Cowboys' Knife. Stag pattern handle, 3⅝ inches long. Double bolsters. Spear blade, 2⅞ in. long; sheep's foot blade, 2¼ in. long; pen blade, 2⅛ inches long. Shpg. wt., 6 oz.
6F7065—Price..........

Two-Blade Pocket Knife. Stag pattern handle, 3½ inches long. Double bolsters of nickel silver and brass lined. Large spear blade, 2¾ inches long. Pen blade, 1⅝ inches long. Tempered steel blades. Shpg. wt., abt. 4 oz.
6F7006—Price.................

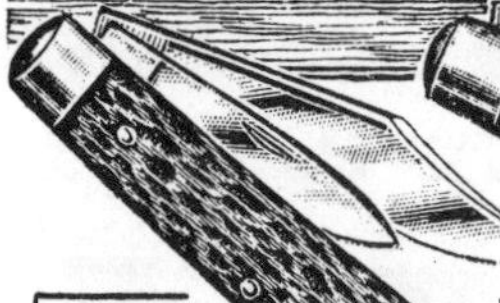

Stag Pattern Handle Jackknife. Length, 3¼ inches. Two blades. Double bolsters. Clip blade, 2⅝ inches long; pen blade, 2 inches long. A well made knife. Nicely polished and ground to insure a good edge. Shpg. wt., 5 oz.
6F7020—Price..

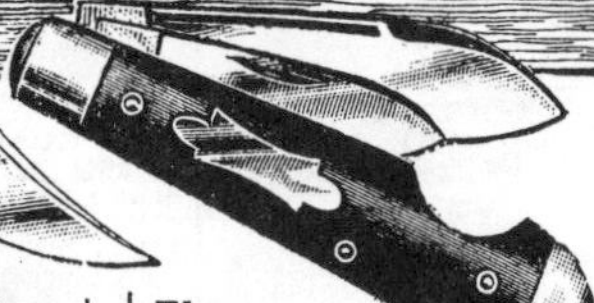

Ebony Handle Easy Opener Knife. Length, 3⅝ inches. Double bolsters and fancy nickel silver shield with easy opener feature. Large blade, 2⅞ inches long; pen blade, 2 inches long. Blades and handle are extra wide. A very strong knife. Shipping weight, 5 ounces.
6F7008–Price.....

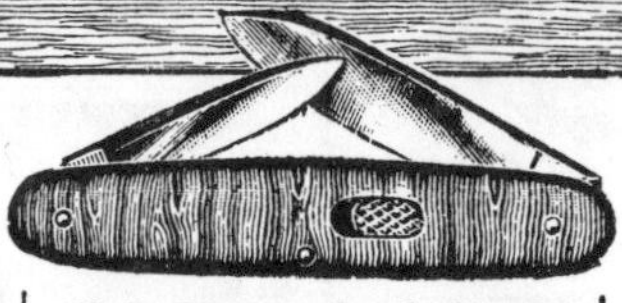

Slide Button Lock Knife. Will not open by accidental pressure against the button while in your pocket, but must be pushed sideways to be opened. Remains locked when opened or closed. Celluloid imitation rosewood handle, 3¾ in. long, brass lined. Large blade, 2¼ in. long; small blade, 2 in. long. Shpg. wt., 4 oz.
6F7082—Price.....
Same as above with jet black handle.
6F7083—Price........

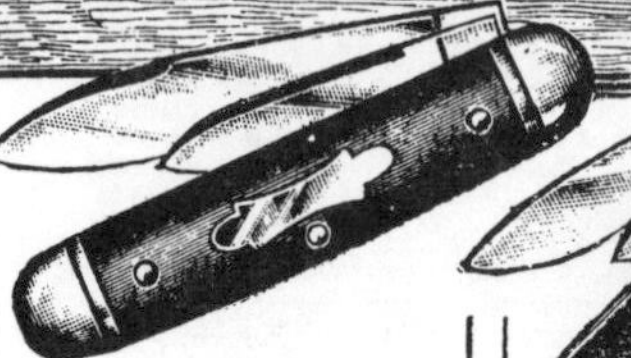

Wilbert Cocobolo Handle Jackknife. Polished cocobolo handle, 3¼ inches long. Double bolsters and nickel silver shield. Spear blade, 2½ in. long; pen blade, 1⅞ inches long. A well made knife. Shipping weight, 5 oz.
6F7002
Price................

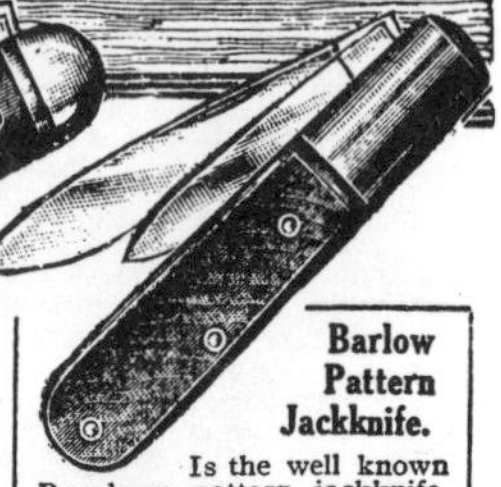

Barlow Pattern Jackknife. Is the well known Barlow pattern jackknife. Bone handle, 3⅝ inches long. Heavy single steel bolster, 1⅛ in. long, making the knife extra strong. Spear blade, 2¾ in. long; pen blade, 2 inches long. Shpg. wt., 5 oz.
6F7016—Price..

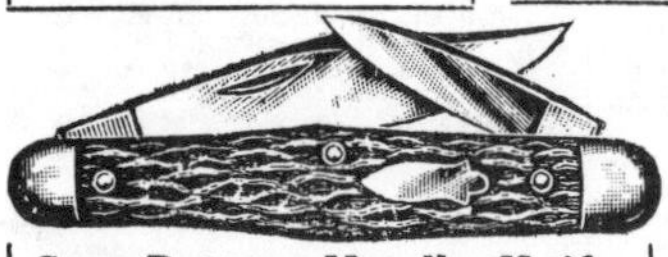

Stag Pattern Handle Knife. Three and a half inches long. Double bolsters and nickel silver shield. Clip blade, 2¾ inches long; pen blade, 1¾ inches long. Good quality steel, well tempered. Shpg. wt., 4 oz.
6F7018—Price............

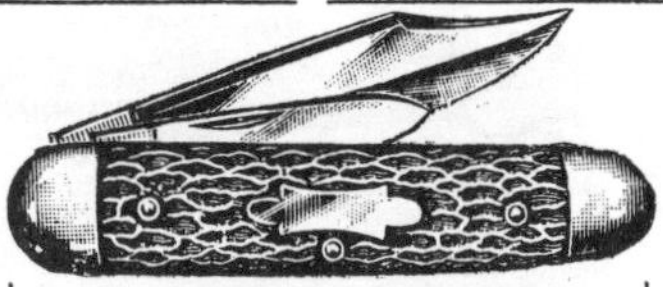

Wilbert Jackknife. Stag pattern handle, 3¼ inches long. Double bolsters and fancy nickel silver shield. Saber clip blade, 2½ inches long; pen blade, 1⅞ inches long. A strong medium size knife. Shipping weight, 5 ounces.
6F7023—Price............

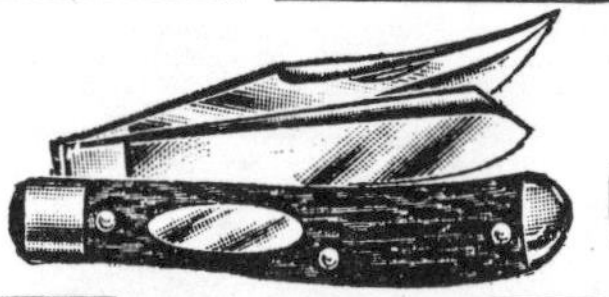

Wilbert Cattlemen's Knife. Stag pattern handle, 3⅞ inches long; with clip point blade open, 7 inches. Spaying blade is 3 inches long from bolster. Nickel silver bolsters. Shipping weight, 5 ounces.
6F7034—Price......

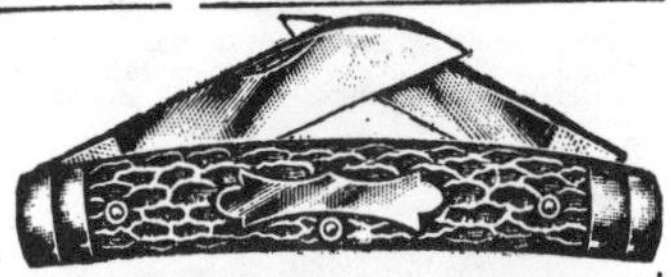

Wilbert Congress Jackknife. Stag pattern handle, 4⅛ inches long. Double bolsters and fancy nickel silver shield. Sheep's foot blade, 2⅝ inches long; pen blade, 2⅛ inches long. Heavy, high grade steel blades. Shipping wt., 5 ounces.
6F7026—Price...........

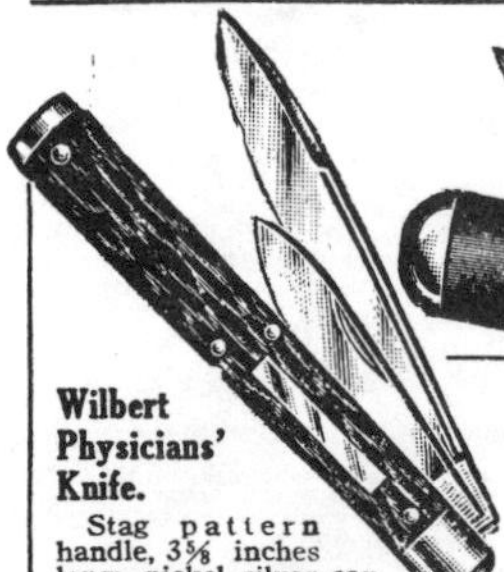

Wilbert Physicians' Knife. Stag pattern handle, 3⅝ inches long; nickel silver cap and bolster. Large blade, 3⅛ inches long; small blade 2¼ inches long. Shipping wt., 4 ounces.
6F7052—Price.

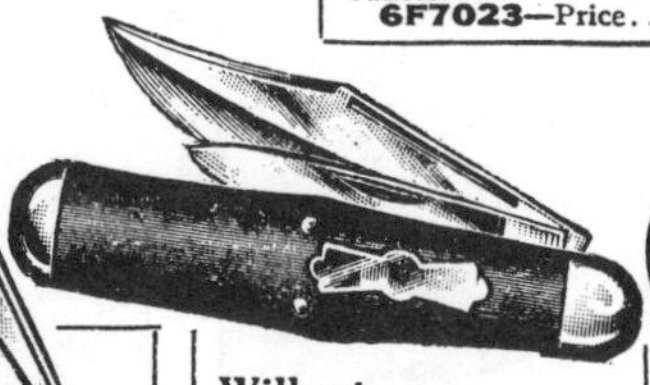

Wilbert Handle Jackknife. Genuine ebony handle, 3¾ inches long. Double bolsters and shield of nickel silver. A very strong knife. Clip blade, 3 inches long; pen blade, 2¼ inches long. Shpg. wt., 5 oz.
6F7013–Price.

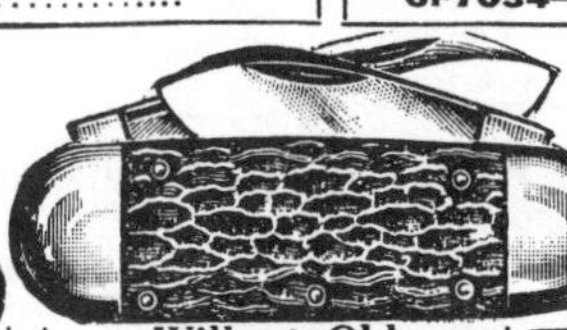

Wilbert Old Faithful. Stag pattern handle. Extraordinarily heavy, durable knife, 4¼ inches long, with two large spear blades, one 3 inches long and one 2¼ inches long. Back of blade ⅛ inch thick. Shipping weight, 9 ounces.
6F7043–Price.

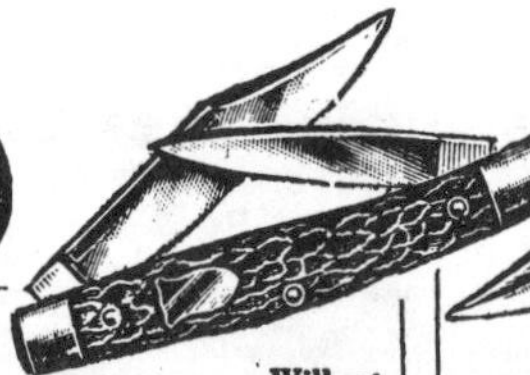

Wilbert Stag Pattern Handle Knife. Length, 3¼ in. Double bolsters. Clip blade, 2¼ in. long; pen blade, 1¾ in. long. Very good steel and well tempered. Shpg. wt., 4 oz.
6F7044–Price......

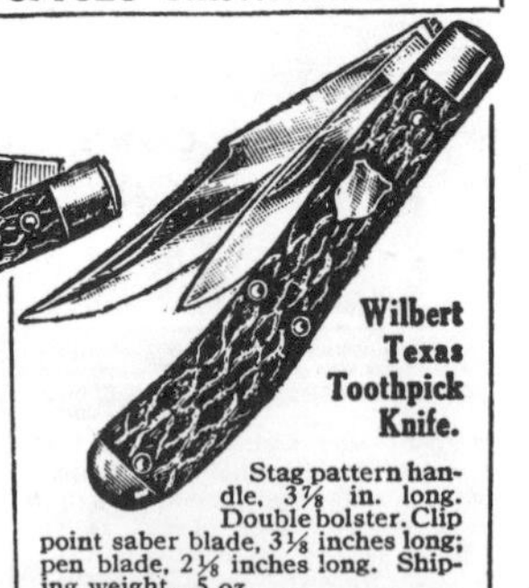

Wilbert Texas Toothpick Knife. Stag pattern handle, 3⅞ in. long. Double bolster. Clip point saber blade, 3⅛ inches long; pen blade, 2⅛ inches long. Shipping weight, 5 oz.
6F7032—Price..

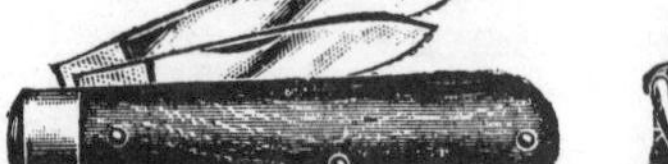

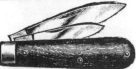

Vermilion Handle Knife. Polished genuine vermilion wood handle, 3 inches long. Single bolster. Blades are of good steel, nicely polished and well tempered. Spear blade, 2⅝ inches long; pen blade, 2⅛ inches long. Shipping weight, 4 ounces.
6F7001—Price.........

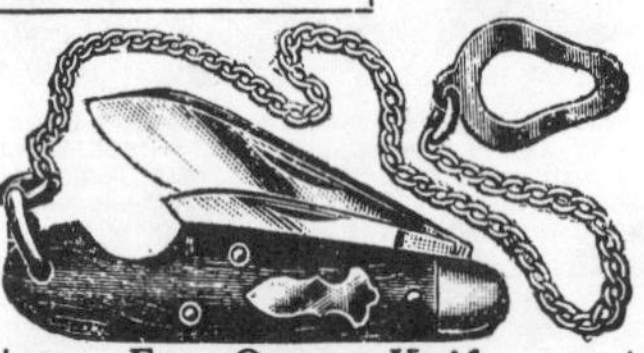

Easy Opener Knife. Polished dark wood handle, 3¼ in. long. Large spear blade, 2⅝ in.; small blade, 1⅝ in. long. Strong chain, securely fastened, with attachment to fasten to button of clothing. Shpg. wt., 6 oz.
6F7012—Price............

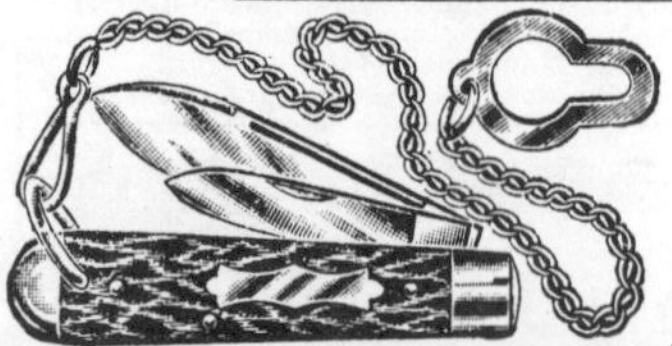

Stag Pattern Handle Knife. Two blades. Handle, 3½ inches long. Large blade, 2⅞ inches long. Small blade, 2 inches long. Double bolsters and shield of nickel silver. Strong chain, securely fastened, with attachment to fasten to button of clothing. Shpg. wt., 6 oz.
6F7010—Price...............

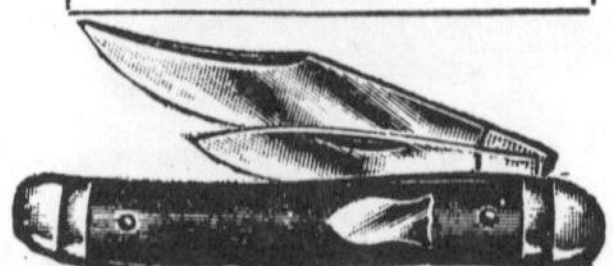

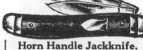

Horn Handle Jackknife. Handle of selected horn, 3½ inches long. Double fluted bolsters and shield of nickel silver. Clip blade, 2⅝ inches long; pen blade, 2 inches long. Shpg. wt., 5 oz.
6F7047—Price.....

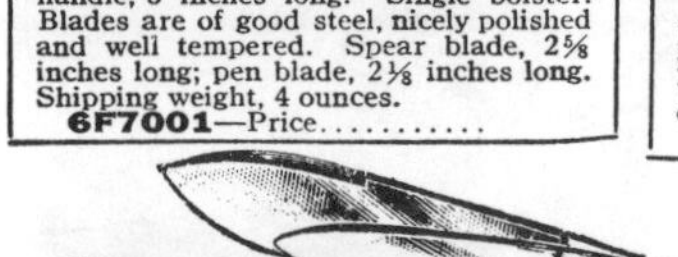

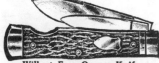

Wilbert Easy Opener Knife. Stag pattern handle, 3½ inches long. Double bolsters. Spear blade, 2⅞ inches long; pen blade, 2 inches long. A strong, all around, practical knife. Shpg. wt., 5 oz.
6F7030—Price...........

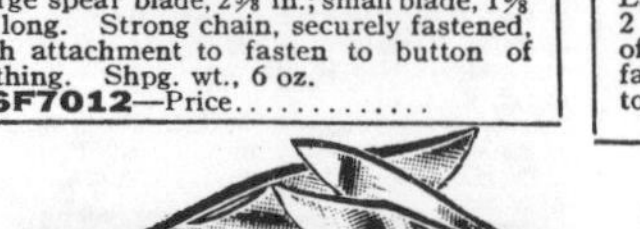

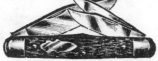

Wilbert Three-Blade Knife. Stag pattern handle, 3½ inches long. Large clip blade, 2¾ inches long; small clip blade, 1¾ inches long; pen blade, 1¾ inches long. Shipping weight, 5 ounces.
6F7062—Price...

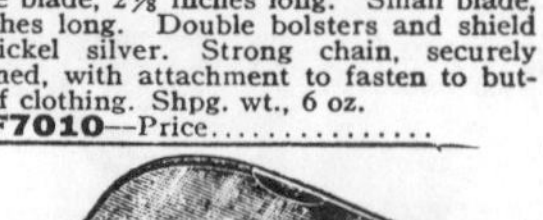

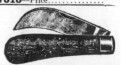

Wilbert Pruning Knife. Cocobolo handle, 3⅞ inches long. Single bolster. Heavy gauge steel pruning blade, 3 inches long. Shipping weight, 6 ounces.
6F7041—Price........

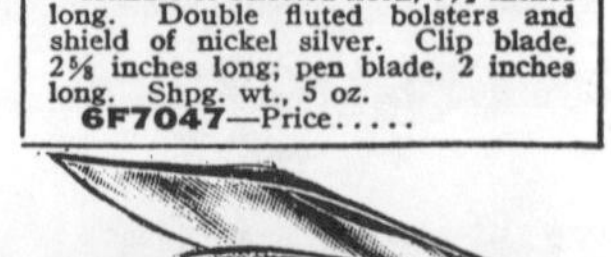

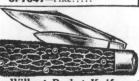

Wilbert Pocket Knife. Stag pattern handle, 3⅝ inches long. Clip blade, 2½ inches long. Small blade, 2 inches long. Single bolster. A very strong, practical knife for any boy. Shpg. wt., 5 oz.
6F7015—Price........

SEARS, ROEBUCK AND CO.

KNIVES

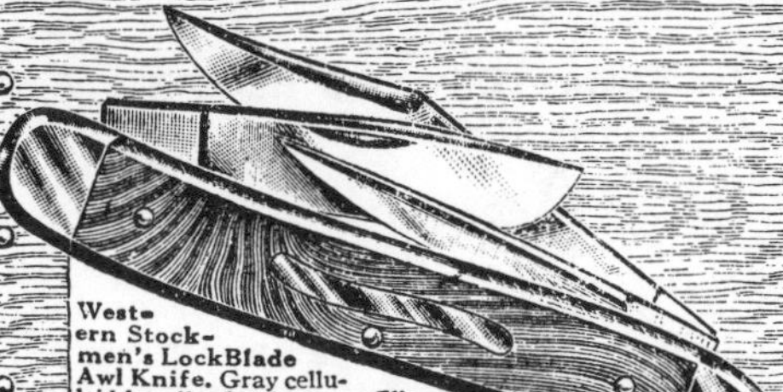

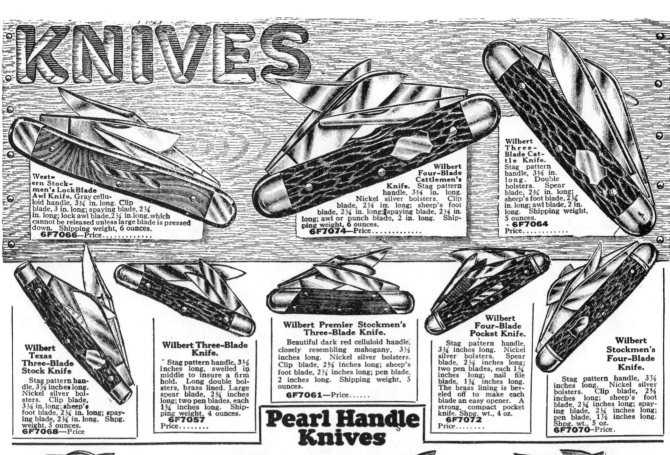

Western Stockmen's LockBlade Awl Knife. Gray celluloid handle, 3¾ in. long. Clip blade, 3 in. long; spaying blade, 2¼ in. long; lock awl blade, 2¼ in. long, which cannot be released unless large blade is pressed down. Shipping weight, 6 ounces.
6F7066—Price............

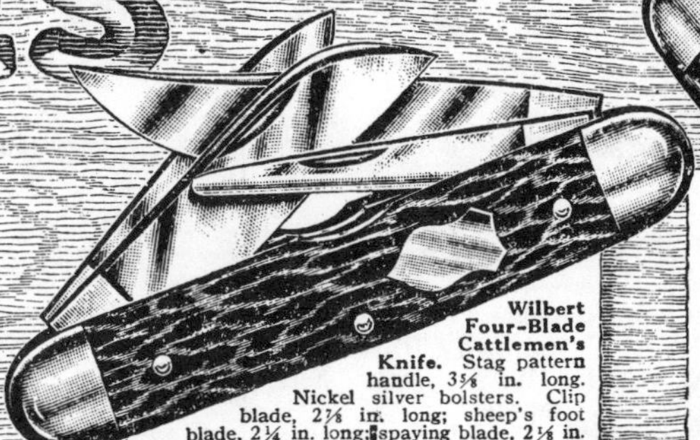

Wilbert Four-Blade Cattlemen's Knife. Stag pattern handle, 3⅝ in. long. Nickel silver bolsters. Clip blade, 2⅞ in. long; sheep's foot blade, 2¼ in. long; spaying blade, 2⅛ in. long; awl or punch blade, 2 in. long. Shipping weight, 6 ounces.
6F7074—Price............

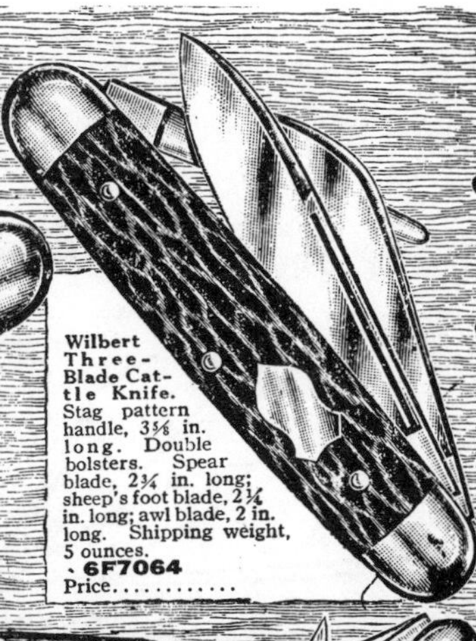

Wilbert Three-Blade Cattle Knife. Stag pattern handle, 3⅝ in. long. Double bolsters. Spear blade, 2¾ in. long; sheep's foot blade, 2¼ in. long; awl blade, 2 in. long. Shipping weight, 5 ounces.
6F7064
Price............

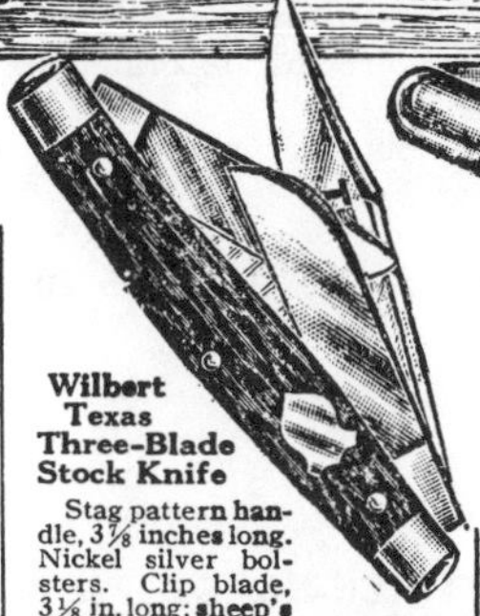

Wilbert Texas Three-Blade Stock Knife

Stag pattern handle, 3⅞ inches long. Nickel silver bolsters. Clip blade, 3⅛ in. long; sheep's foot blade, 2¼ in. long; spaying blade, 2¼ in. long. Shpg. weight, 5 ounces.
6F7068—Price

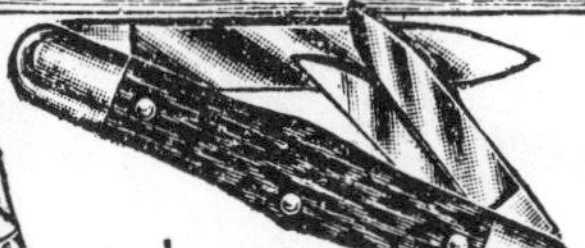

Wilbert Three-Blade Knife.

Stag pattern handle, 3½ inches long, swelled in middle to insure a firm hold. Long double bolsters, brass lined. Large spear blade, 2¾ inches long; two pen blades, each 1¾ inches long. Shipping weight, 4 ounces.
6F7057
Price........

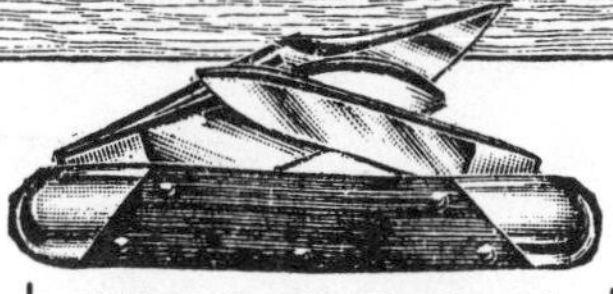

Wilbert Premier Stockmen's Three-Blade Knife.

Beautiful dark red celluloid handle, closely resembling mahogany, 3½ inches long. Nickel silver bolsters. Clip blade, 2⅝ inches long; sheep's foot blade, 2¼ inches long; pen blade, 2 inches long. Shipping weight, 5 ounces.
6F7061—Price......

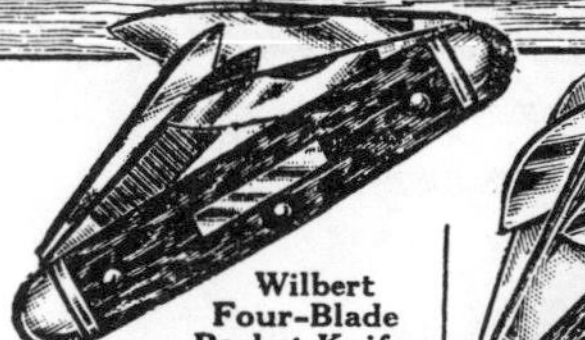

Wilbert Four-Blade Pocket Knife.

Stag pattern handle, 3¼ inches long. Nickel silver bolsters. Spear blade, 2⅛ inches long; two pen blades, each 1¾ inches long; nail file blade, 1¾ inches long. The brass lining is beveled off to make each blade an easy opener. A strong, compact pocket knife. Shpg. wt., 4 oz.
6F7072
Price........

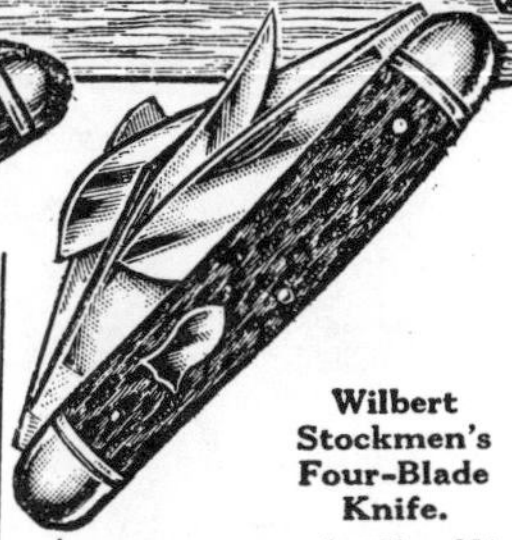

Wilbert Stockmen's Four-Blade Knife.

Stag pattern handle, 3⅞ inches long. Nickel silver bolsters. Clip blade, 2⅝ inches long; sheep's foot blade, 2¼ inches long; spaying blade, 2¼ inches long; pen blade, 1⅞ inches long. Shpg. wt., 5 oz.
6F7070–Price.

Pearl Handle Knives

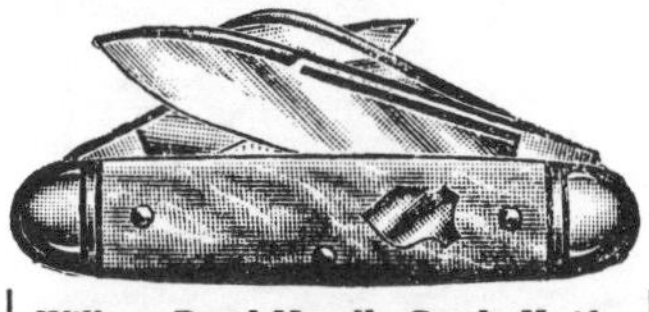

Wilbert Pearl Handle Cattle Knife.

Pearl handle, 3⅝ inches long. Nickel silver bolsters and shield, brass lined. Spear blade, 2¾ inches long; sheep's foot blade, 2⅛ inches long; pen blade, 2 inches long. Shipping weight, 5 oz.
6F7049—Price.........

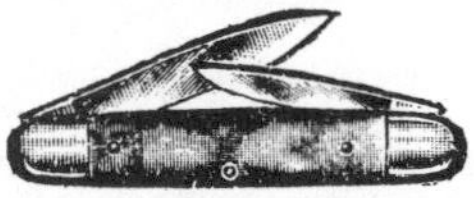

Pearl Handle Penknife.

Pearl handle, 2½ inches long. Double bolsters of nickel silver, and brass lined. Large blade, 1½ inches long; small blade, 1⅛ inches long. A very handsome, neat looking knife. Shipping weight, about 2 ounces.
6F7111—Price..

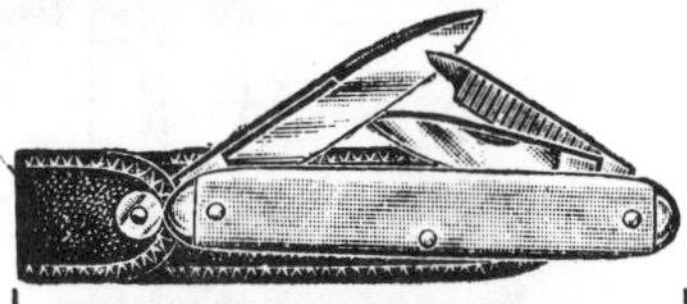

Wilbert Three-Blade Pearl Handle Penknife With Leather Purse.

3-inch handle. Nickel silver bolsters. Large blade, 1⅞ inches long; small blade, 1⅝ inches long; nail file, 1½ inches long. Shipping weight, 4 ounces.
6F7059—Price.........

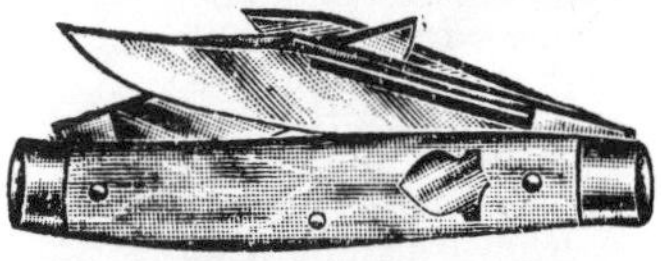

Wilbert Pearl Handle Three-Blade Stockmen's Knife.

3⅞ inches long. Nickel silver bolsters and shield. Clip blade, 3⅛ inches long; sheep's foot blade, 2⅛ inches long; spaying blade, 2⅛ inches long. This knife is strongly made. Shipping weight, 5 ounces.
6F7050—Price.........

Pen Knives

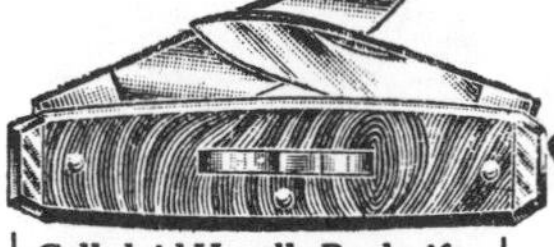

Celluloid Handle Penknife.

Handle of brown celluloid in artistic design resembling shell, very thin and flat, 2¾ inches long with nickel silver tips and shield. Large blade, 2⅛ inches; pen blade, 1½ inches long. Can be carried in vest pocket. Shpg. wt., 3 oz.
6F7103—Price.....

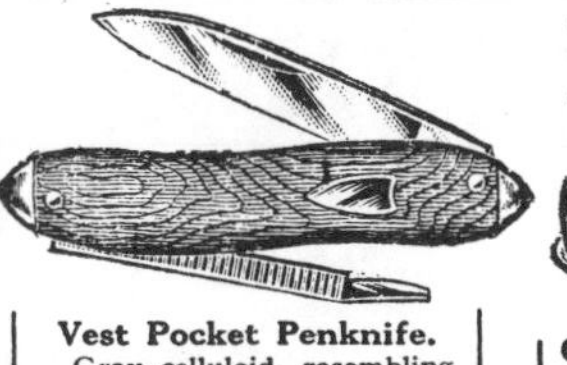

Vest Pocket Penknife.

Gray celluloid, resembling smoked pearl. The handle is very flat and thin, 3 inches long. Pen blade, 2¼ inches long; manicure file with sharp blade end, 2¼ inches long. Shpg. wt., 3 oz.
6F7054–Price.

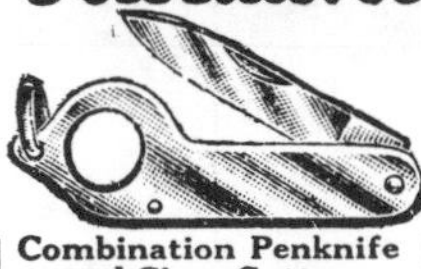

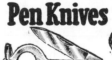

Combination Penknife and Cigar Cutter.

Nickel silver handle, 2¼ inches long. Pen blade, 1⅝ inches long. Press down pen blade to cut cigar end. Has linked end to fasten to watch chain or key ring. Flat shape. A good vest pocket size. Shipping weight, 2 ounces.
6F7108
Price..............

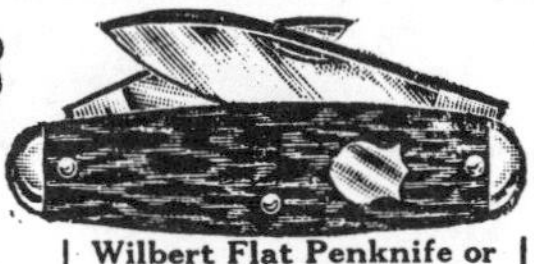

Wilbert Flat Penknife or Vest Pocket Knife.

Stag pattern handle, 3 in. long. Nickel silver tips and shield, brass lined. The wide flat shape makes this a convenient vest pocket knife. Very strongly made. Spear blade, 2¼ inches long; small blade, 1¾ inches long. Shipping weight, 4 oz.
6F7055–Price....

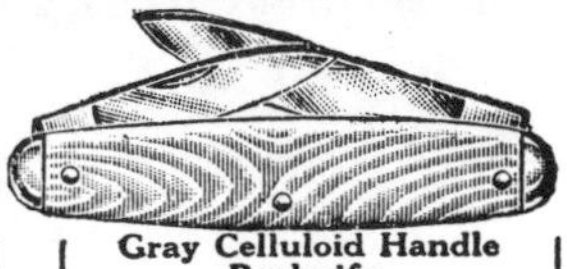

Gray Celluloid Handle Penknife.

Handle of gray celluloid resembling smoked pearl, 2¾ inches long with nickel silver tips. Large blade, 1¾ inches; pen blade, 1½ inches long. The small size makes it an attractive ladies' knife as well as a penknife. Shipping weight, 2 ounces.
6F7101—Price....

Tool Knives

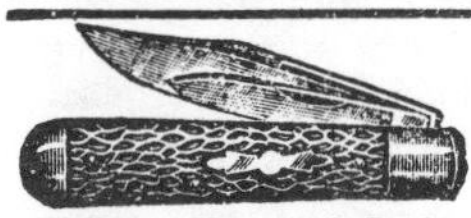

Wilbert Hunters' Pride Knife.

Stag pattern handle, 4½ inches long. Long heavy nickel silver bolsters and shield—brass lined. Clip blade, 3⅝ inches long; small blade, 2⅝ inches long. A strong, practical knife for hunters and campers. Shipping wt., 6 oz.
6F7035–Price.

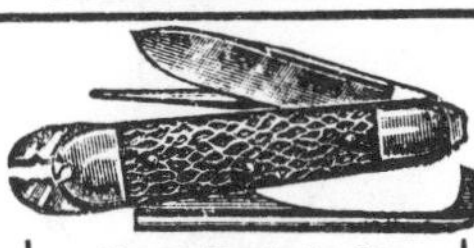

Seven Tools in One. Cuts wire, wood or leather and is a knife, leather punch, swage awl, wire cutter, pliers, hoof hook and screwdriver. Stag pattern handle, nickel silver bolsters and steel lined. Handle, 4⅛ in. Shipping weight, 6 oz.
6F7081
Price........

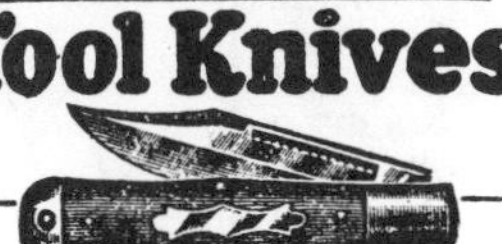

Wilbert Daniel Boone Hunting Knife.

Cocobolo handle, 5¼ inches long. Steel bolsters and cap, steel lined. Strong saber clip blade, 4¼ inches long. Shpg. wt., 7 oz.
6F7037—Price....

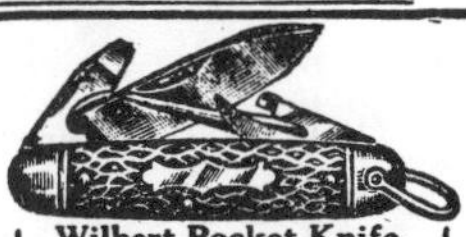

Wilbert Pocket Knife.

Suitable for Boy Scouts. Stag pattern handle, 3⅝ inches long. Nickel silver bolsters. Large spear blade, 2⅞ inches long; one swedging awl, one combination bottle opener and screwdriver and one can opener. Shipping weight, 6 ounces.
6F7080
Price........

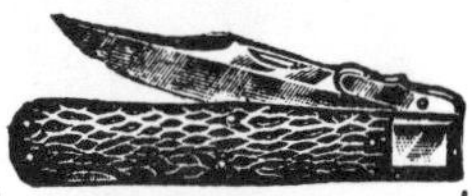

Hunting Knife With Guard.

Stag pattern handle. Clip point, saber blade, flush lock back. Nickel silver bolsters and guard. When blade is closed, guard lies flat with blade. Handle, 4¾ inches; with blade open, 8¾ in. long. Shpg. wt., 6 oz.
6F7038–Price.

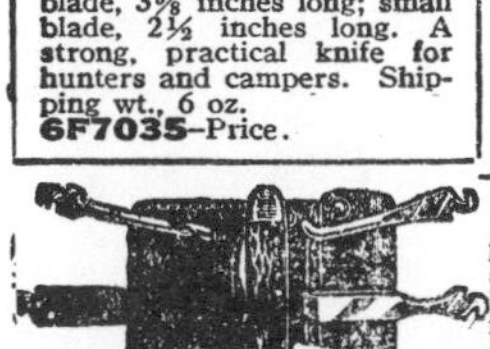

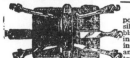

Pocket Tool Kit. Consists of a cocobolo handle pocket knife, 3¾ inches long; nickel silver bolsters, 2½-inch spear point blade; also six useful tools: 3½-inch file, 3⅝-inch screwdriver, 3-inch chisel, 3-inch awl, cork puller and drill. Either tool can be fastened in a moment's time to end of knife. The spring rigidly holds tool in place. In neat leather case. Shipping weight, 12 ounces.
6F7076—Price..............................

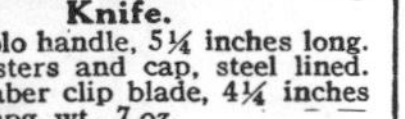

Leather Knife Purse.

For pocket knives having handles not longer than 4 inches. Give length of knife you intend to carry in purse. Keeps knife from rusting. Shipping weight, 1 ounce.
6F7124—Price.......................

Perfection Pocket Knife Desk Hone.

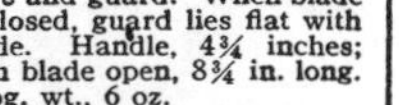

Will keep pocket knife or small cutting tool sharp. Every pocket knife owner should have one. 4 inches long by ⅞ inch wide. Shipping weight, 4 ounces.
6F7142—Price.......................

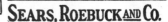

SEARS, ROEBUCK AND CO.

POCKET KNIVES

IMPERIAL—BARLOW

3 ⅜ inches. It is made up with full nickel type bolster stamped "Barlow" With buck horn handle.

The blading is master clip, spear, sheepfoot ass't.

(Illustration of Master Clip Blade.)

C3-CM281 _____Doz **$25 20**

One doz in box; wt doz 2 lbs.

IMPERIAL—JACK KNIFE
SERPENTINE PATTERN

3 ¼ inches in length. Made with full nickel type bolsters. The blades are made of high carbon stainless steel, heat treated, tempered and deep hollow ground blades.

Kameo handle with shield decoration.

Stainless.

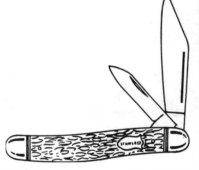

C3-CM685-SS _____Doz **$25 20**

One doz in box; wt doz 2 lbs.

IMPERIAL—JACK-MASTER—TWO BLADES
STRAIGHT PATTERN

Full non-corrosive bolsters. 3 ⅜ inches in length. The blading is master clip and pen, with Kameo Karved deer head handles.

C3-CM400 _____Doz **$25 20**

One doz in box; wt doz 1 lb.

IMPERIAL—JACK-MASTER—TWO BLADES
SERPENTINE PATTERN

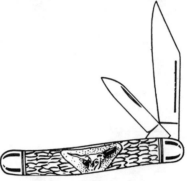

3 ¼ inches in length. Full non-corrosive bolsters. Clip and pen blades. Handles have the shields and cover pins.

Kameo handle with steerhead decoration.

C3-CM685 _____ Doz **$25 20**

One doz in box; wt doz 1 ½ lbs.

IMPERIAL—KAMP KING—THREE-BLADE
STRAIGHT PATTERN

Scout knives with full nickel type bolsters. 3 ⅜ inches in length.

Master spear, can opener, screw driver and cap lifter blades. The blades are made from special high carbon cutlery steel. The handles are made of buck horn, the handles having shields and cover pins.

C3-CM413 _____Doz **$25 20**

One in box; wt doz 2 lbs.

IMPERIAL—JACK-MASTER—THREE BLADES
SERPENTINE PATTERN

2 ¾ inches in length. Knives are made up with full non-corrosive bolsters and have shields and cover pins.

Master clip, spey and pen blades. The blades and springs are made of special high carbon cutlery steel.

Imitation pearl and maize handle with shield.

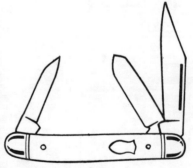

C3-CM787 _____Doz **$25 20**

One doz in box; wt doz 1 lb.

edge. Herter's Canadian Big game Skinning Knife will hold a sharp edge even if you use it to cut wire or to split backbones of big game animals.

The blade is six inches long and has a 2 inch upsweep. Overall length is 11 inches. The handle is triple riveted African tiger wood which will withstand all kinds of abuses that would damage or destroy other knife handles.

This knife does not have a hilt. You can be sure that a hilt on a knife is the first sign of an inferior knife. Instead, Herter's has designed a special hand fitting, five inch by 11/16 inch thick handle which will not slip.

Comes complete with Herter's World famous Professional Guide book.

No.		Each	Shpg. Wt.
AJ5F1	Knife, Sheath & Book	$3.10	1 lb.
AJ5F2	Skinning knife	2.47	8 oz.
AJ5F3	Sheath	.75	4 oz.
AJ5B4	Guide book	.45	3 oz.

HERTER'S MEAT HUNTER CLEAVER

This high quality cleaver has the finest tempered hammer forged blade of high carbon steel. The steel is a full quarter inch thick with a heavy guard and full length

tong. Handle is walnut with 3 brass rivets. Chopping blade is seven and one quarter inches long and two and one quarter inches wide.

Extremely handy for chopping meat, vegetables, bone or any other food products. Back of blade has a serrated tenderizer. An absolute necessity in cutting up deer, beef, pork, moose or other meat carcasses.

Order one out and see for yourself the fine quality in this cleaver. No kitchen or camp should be without one.

AJ5K12 Shpg. wt. 2 lbs. **$3.97**

HERTER'S ENGLISH-MADE SHEFFIELD STEEL STOCKMAN'S KNIFE

Made of the finest hand ground Sheffield steel known throughout the world for quality. This high quality knife has a 2½ inch clip blade and also a 2½ inch castrator blade. A very good knife for stockmen, hunters and outdoorsmen. Bone handle with stag scales is 3¾ inches long. Heavy bolster and proportionate length of blade to handle keeps blades extremely tight, which is very desirable in any knife of this type. Tempered heavy duty spring. One of the finest stockmen's knives made. This knife was used by the Herter's on the Western frontiers as early as 1853.

Order one out and see what a high quality knife this is.

AJ5K11 Shpg. wt. 8 oz. **$4.97**

HERTER'S "TOOTHPICK" KNIVES

In addition to the famous "chisholm" knife made in pocket knife style we developed a few other models from old standbys for serious trappers, fishermen, hunters and outdoorsmen for uses found in the field. These are not hardware store knives nor drugstore specials which are good-for-nothing in the field. You can sharpen our "toothpick" knives and they stay sharp. Some of the features in our knives are blades made from tool

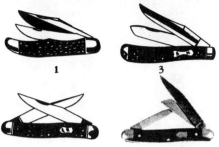

steel with grain running length of the blade; blades and springs electronically heat treated; blades expertly tapered vertically and horizontally for perfect sharpening; handles firmly riveted to the knife sides and fitted by hand; each part put into the knife: blades, springs, covers, rivets are carefully inspected and tested before assembly of the knife; each knife is hand polished, checked for blade alignment, blade "clicks" into position open and closed; knife edges are hand honed to razor sharpness and finally each knife is cleaned, hand oiled and final inspected. You will instantly see and feel the difference between our "toothpick" knives and others when you examine and compare them. We have a special leather sheath made to fit these knives. Snap fastener closed, heavy stitched with belt slits for those who prefer to carry the knives in a sheath while riding horses, or hunting where the knife could fall from a pocket and be lost. Model 5 special "Razor-Blade" stainless steel blades. Shpg. wt. ea. —3 ozs.

No.	Length	Model	Each
AJ5K2	5¼"	1	$4.47
AJ5K3	4 "	2	3.27
AJ5K4	3⅞"	3	3.27
AJ5K7	2⅛"	4	2.97
AJ5K8	3⅞"	5	4.95
AJ5K5	Sheath		each .45

HERTER'S RAZOR BLADE STAINLESS STEEL POCKET KNIVES

Thinline   Standard

THINLINE

This extremely thin and light pocket knife can be carried in any pocket without noticing any weight. The blades are made of razor blade stainless steel and are very sharp. Handles are of the finest materials and workmanship. Riveted simulated bone. Nickel plated bolsters and brass case. 2⅞ inches long. 1 blade 1⅝ inches and 12⅛ inches.

STANDARD

Razor blade stainless steel blades. Simulated bone handle. Nickel plated bolsters and brass case. A fine pocket knife. New grinding and honing process makes these sharper than ever. Length 3⅜ inches. One blade 1⅝ inches.

One blade 2½ inches.

AJ5K9	Thinline Shpg. wt. 3 ozs.	$1.87
AJ5K10	Standard Shpg. wt. 4 ozs.	1.97

HERTER'S ENGLISH SHEFFIELD STAINLESS STEEL STEAK KNIVES

Made in Sheffield, England of famous Sheffield stainless steel. The blade is forged in a scimitar pattern with serrations on

forward edge. These beautiful knives have a laminated wooden handle.

You owe it to yourself to try these knives and compare them to any available at twice this price.

AJ5K13 Set of 6 boxed Shpg. wt. 1½ lbs. **$6.97**

HERTER'S GOLDEN BEAR HAMMER FORGED STEAK KNIVES

These fine steak knives were used in some of the better watering and eating places of the Old West. However, few were used after 1880 because customers would usually walk off with them. Needless to say many of these customers were very difficult to take the knives back from. The knives were

made in Pennsylvania and were just as expensive then as they are now. Most places such as the Golden Bear in Abilene discontinued using them about 1880 because it was impossible to keep them in the place.

These knives were used by customers for cutting steaks, roasts and chops. This meat was even tougher than it is now. The knives were also used for minor surgery, population control, shaving and kitchen work by the regular customers.

The knife has a four-inch hammer forged carbon steel blade with forge marks showing and a full length tang. Rosewood handle with 3 brass rivets. The knife is not dainty but will prove to be the best steak knife you have ever used. The forged carbon steel blade is much easier to hone than stainless steel.

Be sure to get a set for your home and camp. Try at least one to see how good they really are. Watch your guests carefully after the meal. Shpg. Wt. 3 ozs.

	Each	Per 6	Per Doz.
AJ5K14	$1.45	$7.97	$14.97

HERTER'S POCKET SHARPENING STEEL

This handy sharpening steel is only 5½ inches long and can be carried in a pocket

or in a sheath. Made in England of Sheffield steel, this is the finest quality sharpening steel we have seen.

Put a fine edge on your hunting knife or other cutlery right when you need it by carrying one of these steels.

AJ5K15 Shpg. wt. 8 ozs. **$1.47**

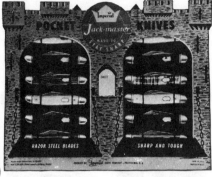

POCKET KNIVES

IMPERIAL

JACK-MASTER—THREE BLADES

Serpentine Pattern

HANDLES—Imitation pearl and colored celluloid. Shields and cover pins.
BLADES—Three: master clip, spey and pen. High carbon cutlery steel full polished.
BOLSTERS—Full nickel type.
LINING—Brass.
LENGTH—3¼ inches.

C3-N687_ Doz **$28 35**
One doz on display card; wt doz 2 lbs.

POCKET KNIVES
ASSORTMENT OF 30 KNIVES—IMPERIAL

An attractive assortment of 30 knives. Consists of six only 4-blade utility knives with simulated stag handles. Six only fish knives with serrated blades and safety locks to keep blades in position when scaling. Six only 2-blade serpentine jack knives with stainless blades. Twelve assorted 2-blade jack knives with attractive cameo carved handles. They are all put on attractive multi-colored display card. Each assortment furnished with vinyl carry-all bag.

C3-MS60
                    Ass't **$50 40**

One ass't in box;
wt ass't 5 lbs.

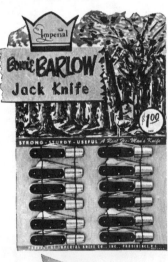

IMPERIAL
Barlow

Standard size Barlow knife. Full nickel type bolster stamped "Barlow".
Simulated bone type handle. Master clip and pen blade.
Length knife 3⅜ inches.

C3-278
Doz **$25 20**
One doz on display card; wt doz 2 lbs.

POCKET KNIVES
IMPERIAL
CHANGE MAKER ASSORTMENT

An assortment consisting of 2, 3-blade knives. Patterns are assorted Jack, Barlow, and 3-blade outdoor utility knives. All are made with attractive Nuloy bolsters. Blades are made of special cutlery steel fully heat treated and tempered. Forty of the knives have the new attractive Buck Horn handles. Eight are assorted simulated pearl and yellow maize—These are packed in a serviceable Wood Change Maker display case with glass cover to prevent loss. Case FREE.

(See page 2625 for open stock)
C3-CM48_ _ _ _ _ _ _ _ _ _ _ _ _ _ _ _ _Ass't **$100 80**
One ass't in shp ctn; wt ass't 10 lbs.   *$48 00*

If your competitors sell for less than you do, it shouldn't worry you. He knows the value of the stock he is offering at a lower price better than you.

POCKET KNIVES
IMPERIAL

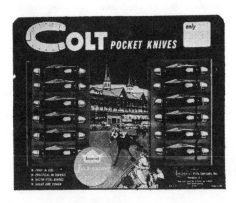

COLT—TWO BLADES
Serpentine Pattern
Handle—Simulated stag and color-ed pyralin. Shields and cover pins.
Blades—Two: clip and pen. High carbon cutlery steel full polished.
Bolsters—Full nickel type.
Lining—Brass.
Length—2¾ inches.

C3-N785 _____ Doz $18 90
One doz on display card; wt doz 1 lb.

IMPERIAL—PONY JACK

Medium size, dog-leg jack knives.
Full non-corrosive bolsters and shields. Master clip blade and pen.
Simulated stag handles.
Overall length 2¾ inches.

C3-N60 _____ Doz $18 90
One doz on display card; wt doz 1¼ lbs.

IMPERIAL

JACK-MASTER—TWO BLADES
Serpentine Pattern
Handles—⅛ dozen each on card: simu-lated stag, imitation pearl and colored celluloid. Shields and cover pins.
Blades—Two: clip and pen. High car-bon cutlery steel, full polished.
Bolsters—Full nickel type.
Lining—Brass.
Length—3¼ inches.

C3-N685 _____ Doz $20 85
One doz on display card; wt doz 1 lb.

POCKET KNIVES
ULSTER

Slim Premium Stock Knife, 3-1/4 inches long; Genuine BONE STAG Handles; 3blades (Clip, Spey & Pen); Brass Linings; Nickel Silver Bolsters; Master Blade Polished Mark Side Only and Etched; Other Blades Glazed on Both Sides. Packed six in a box.

No. 55G—

Small serpentine knife. Blades (3) Clip, Sheepfoot and Pen Handles; Simulated Pearl. Length Closed: 2-9/16'inches. Packed 1/2 dozen in a box. Weight per dozen approximately 3/4 lb.

No. 89-P—

Slim premium stock knife, 3¼ inches long; genuine STAG HEAD Handles; 3 Blades (Clip, Spey & Pen); Brass Linings; Nickel Silver Bolsters; Blades Full Mirror Polished. Packed 1/2 dozen in a box. Weight per dozen 1½ lbs.

No. 55-D—

POCKET KNIFE ASSORTMENT
ULSTER

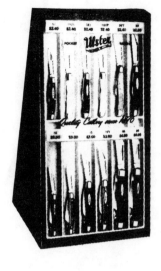

Profit packed assortment. The "Dealer Doubles Dollar" Deal. With purchase of only two (2) dozen "ULSTER" knives, every pattern a popular priced proven seller, Mr. Dealer gets the handsome display case illustrated above FREE!
Total Retail Value $68.80
Dealers Cost Only. 34.40

The case is compact — easy to handle— 8" wide, 6" deep, 13" high. Made of hard wood with limed oak finish, it has real beauty and will harmonize with most expensive fixtures. Display panel accessible only from rear of Case, protecting stock from pilferage. Front is of clear washable shadowproof acetate. Each knife is packed in a clear cellophane purse. Display and knives are packed in a strong cushioned carton for safe and easy re-shipment. Contains two of each of the following:

$2.40 — 50

$2.40 — 81

$2.40 — 183P

$2.40 — 183Y

$3.00 — 55Y

$3.00 — 55

$4.00 — 98

$2.40 — 50Y

$2.40 — 183

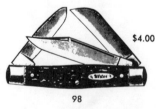
$4.00 — 98

$3.00 — 89Y

$3.00 — 89

Packed one deal in a carton. Weight 6 pounds.

No. UK-2D—

POCKET KNIFE ASSORTMENTS
IMPERIAL

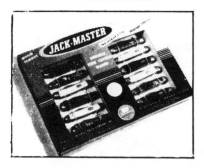

"JACK – MASTER"

Assortment of medium size pen knives. Knives measure 2-3/4 and 3-1/8" in length. Full nickel type bolsters. Straight pattern. Blades spear and pen. Blades high carbon cutlery steel. Handles assorted colors. Shields and cover pins. Packed one dozen to the attractive display card.

No. N83—

11.60 Asst. of 12 knives

"JACK – MASTER"

Assortment of medium size two blade jacks. Knives measure 2-3/4 and 3-1/8" in length. Full nickel type bolsters. Patterns assorted straight and serpentine. Blades clip and pen. Blades high carbon cutlery steel. Handles attractively assorted imitation pearl and colors. Handles have shields and cover pins. Packed one dozen to the card.

No. N84—

11.60 Asst. of 12 knives

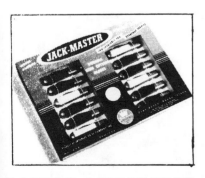

BARLOW ASSORTMENT

Medium size Barlow knives. Measures 3-1/8" in length. Full nickel type bolsters marked Barlow, blades are clip and pen. Packed one dozen to the display card. The weight per dozen is 2 pounds.

No. JM-435—

11.60 Asst. of 12 Knives

POCKET KNIFE ASSORTMENTS
IMPERIAL

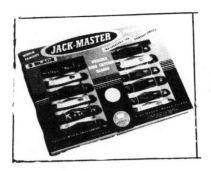

"JACK – MASTER"

Assortment of 3 blade jack knives. Full nickel type bolsters. Lengths closed 3-1/4". Blades—1 clip, 1 spey, and 1 pen. Blades of high carbon cutlery steel. Handles assorted colors, simulated stag. All have shields and cover pins. Packed one dozen in a display card.

No. N76—

16.00 Asst. of 12 knives

"KAMP – KING"

Assortment of 4 blade outdoor knives. Lengths closed 3-5/8". Full bolsters. Blades special high carbon cutlery steel. Blades — 1 spear, 1 can opener, 1 combination cap lifter and screw driver, 1 leather awl. Handles simulated stag and imitation pearl. Packed one dozen in a display unit.

No. 615—

16.00 Asst. of 12 knives

POCKET KNIFE ASSORTMENTS
IMPERIAL

BOWIE – BARLOW

Two blade standard barlow knife. 3-3/8" long. Full nickel type bolster stamped "Barlow". Simulated bone type handle attractive and serviceable. Blades are master CLIP and pen. Packed one dozen to the attractive display card. We will break cards.

No. 278—

14.40 card of 12 knives

HENCKEL KNIVES

C6904H Stag handles, double bolster; two cutting blades and file; length 3 in.; weight 2 oz.
Price ....$3.25 net

C6905H Same knife as above but with pearl handles.
Price ....$5.25 net

C6906H Stag handles; two bolsters; tipt pattern; three blades and flexible file; length 3 in.; weight 2 oz.
Price ....$3.50 net

C6907H Same knife as above but with pearl handles.
Price ....$5.75 net

C6908H Gun metal handles; one blade and file: length 3 in.; a convenient flat knife, easily carried in one's pocket; weight 1 oz.
Price ....$2.25 net

C6909H Same knife as above but with pearl handles.
Price ....$5.25 net

C6910H Gun metal handles; two blades and file; length 3 in.; weight 2 oz.
Price ....$3.50 net

C6911H Same knife as above but with pearl handles.
Price ....$6.00 net

C6912H Stag handles; two blades and file; double bolsters; length 3¼ in.; weight 2 oz.
Price ....$3.25 net

C6913H Stag handles; 2 blades and file; double bolsters; length 3½ in.; weight 2 oz.
Price ....$3.25 net

C6913HA Stag handle, two-blade; 3-in. double bolster; wt., 2 oz.
Price, each ....$1.50 net

C6913HB Black handle; otherwise same as C6913HA.
Price, each ....$1.50 net

HENCKEL KNIVES

C6914H Same knife as C6913H but with white handles.
Price ....$3.25 net

C6915H Same knife as C6913H, but with bone handles.
Price ....$3.25 net

C6916H Stag handles; 3 blades; double bolsters; length 3½ in.; weight 3 oz.
Price ....$3.00 net

C6917H Same knife as above but with bone handles.
Price ....$3.00 net

C6918H Nine tool, stag handle knife; has two cutting blades, saw, can opener, gimlet, punch, cork screw, screw driver, hoof cleaner; length 3¾ in.; weight 4 oz.
Price ....$11.75 net

GENUINE SHEFFIELD I. X. L. KNIVES

C6919 I.X.L. Stag handle, Wharncliffe, pen and file blades. Iron lined, double bolster, 3¼ in. closed; weight, 2 oz.
Price, each ....$4.25 net

C6920 I.X.L. Ivory handle, two cutting blades, full polished, double bolster, 3¼ in. long, closed; weight, 1½ oz.
Price, each ....$3.50 net

C6920A I.X.L. Same as C6920, except stag handle.
Price, each ....$3.50 net

AMERICAN MADE CAMP KNIFE
Lobster Pattern

C6925 Stag handle, two heavy cutting blades, full polished, double bolster, fully warranted, heavy service knife, 4 in. long closed, 1½ in. wide; weight, 6 oz.
Price, ea., **$2.50 net**

POCKET KNIVES

No. 0100—PRESS BUTTON

No. 0100—3¼-inch patent stag handle; brass lined.
 Has one large spear and one pen blade.

Per Dozen_____

No. 510—PRESS BUTTON

No. 510—4-inch patent stag handle; German silver
 press button and bolsters; brass lined. Has one
 large clip blade_____

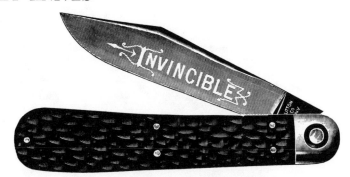

No. 1000—PRESS BUTTON

No. 1000—5-inch patent stag handle; German silver
 press button and bolsters; brass lined.

Per Dozen_____

KNIFE PURSES

Made from dressed kid, silk stitched, with clasp button.
 Assorted colors—black, gray and tan.

Lengths 2¾, 3, 3¼, 3½ and 4 inches_____

I. X. L. HORSE FLEAMS

No. 5167—3-inch brass handle, three assorted fleams_____

RUSSELL BARLOWS

Showing No. 60—One blade, Spear Point.

Showing No. 63—One blade, Sheep Foot Point.

Showing No. 66—Two blade, Large Blade, Clip Point.

No. 60—Russell Barlow, one blade, spear

No. 63—Russell Barlow, one blade, sheep foot

No. 65—Russell Barlow, one blade, clip

No. 62—Russell Barlow, two blade, spear

No. 64—Russell Barlow, two blade, sheep foot

No. 66—Russell Barlow, two blade, clip

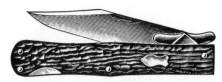

1347. Jos. Warren & Sons' Sportsman's Knife.
Extra Quality Swaged Cimeter Shaped Steel Blade, Full Polished. Spring Back and Folding Guard to Prevent Blade Closing on the Hand. Fully Warranted. Length, 4¾ inches.

1348. Genuine Deerfoot Hunting Knife.
Long Cimiter Shaped Blade, Made of Finest Tempered Steel. Fancy Engraved Bolster. Patent Spring to Release Blade When Open, and Folding Guard. Length, 5 inches.

3305. Jos. Warren & Sons' Hunting Knife.
Deerfoot Shaped. Lock Back. Large Blade When Open Stands Locked, to Release Press on Pen Blade. Patent Corkscrew. India Steel Blades, Fully Polished. Brass Lined. German Silver Bolster and Shield. Stag and Buffalo Horn Handle. Length, 4 inches.

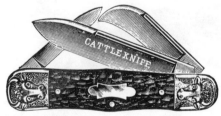

3401. Jos. Warren & Sons' Cattle Knife.
Stag and Buffalo Handle. One Large Spear Blade Etched "Cattle Knife." One Medium Pen and One Hoof Blade, Made from Best English Razor Tempered Steel. Heavy Embossed Bolsters. German Silver Shield. Brass Lined. Length, 3⅞ inches.

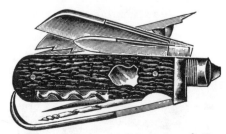

103. Jos. Warren & Sons' Sportsmans' Combination Knife.
Consisting of the Following Tools : One Large and One Small Blade, Corkscrew, Hoof Pick, Gimlet, Reamer, Nut Crack, Saw and Fleam Stag Handle. Fully Warranted. Length, 3⅞ inches.

2700. Ladies' Inlaid Shell Handle Knife.
Assorted Handles. Polished Metal Bolster. Nicely Finished Pen Blades. Length, 2½ inches.

2805. Ladies' Pearl Knife.
German Silver Bolster. Two Well Ground Blades. Metal Lined. An Excellent 15c. Value.

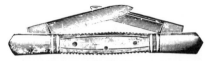

2118. Gem Ladies' Pearl Knife.
German Silver Bolster. Clear Polished Pearl Handle. Full Polished Blades. This Knife Never Retails Less Than 25 Cents Apiece.

2119. Special Pearl Handle Pocket Knife.
German Silver Bolster. Fancy Corrugated Pearl Handle. Two Polished Steel Blades. Brass Lined. Length, 3 inches.

2120. Favorite Pearl Pocket Knife.
Fancy Corrugated Plate. German Silver Fancy Bolster. Two Extra Well Finished Blades, Fully Polished. Length, 2⅞ inches.

2502. Novelty Two Blade Pocket Knife.
Imitation Stag Handle, Polished Tips. Strongly Riveted. Blades are Good and Durable. A Practical Gentleman's Knife. Length, 3⅜ inches.

2503. Fancy Gentleman's Pocket Knife.
Scored Imitation Stag Handle, with Fancy Nickel Horse-Shoe Tips and Whip Shield. Two Well Finished Polished Steel Blades. Length, 3⅜ inches.

VANCO POCKET KNIVES

FULLY WARRANTED

Illustrations Half Size

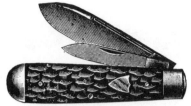

Two blades, stag handle; one large spear and one pen blade; glazed; brass lined; steel bolsters; nickel silver shield; length closed, 3½ inches.

No. V321—Pocket knives ....

Weight per dozen, 2 lbs.; half dozen in a box.

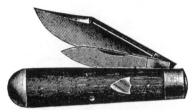

Two blades; rosewood handle; one large clip and pen blade, glazed; brass lined; steel bolsters; nickel silver shield; length closed, 3½ inches.

No. V221—Pocket knives ....

Weight per dozen, 2 lbs.; half dozen in a box.

Two blades; one large spear blade and one pen blade, glazed; brass lined; steel bolsters; nickel silver shield; length closed, 3½ in.; equipped with chain.

No. V221CH—Rosewood handle ....
No. V321CH—Stag handle ....

Weight per dozen, 2 lbs.; half dozen in a box.

Two blades, one spear and one pen blade, glazed; rosewood handle; brass lined; easy opener; steel bolsters; nickel silver shield; length closed, 3½ inches.

No. V222—Pocket knives ....

Weight per dozen 2 lbs.; half dozen in a box.

Two blades, stag handle; one spear and one pen blade, glazed; brass lined; easy opener; steel bolsters; nickel silver shield; length closed, 3½ inches.

No. V322—Pocket knives ....

Weight per dozen 2 lbs.; half dozen in a box.

Two blades, one large spear blade, crocused; one glazed pen blade; brass lined; steel bolsters; nickel silver shield; length 3¼ in.

No. V123—Ebony handle ....
No. V323—Stag handle ....

Weight per dozen 1½ lbs.; half dozen in a box.

Two blades; stag handle; one large spear blade, crocused; one pen blade glazed; brass lined; nickel silver tips and shield; length closed, 3 inches.

No. V326—Pocket knives ....

Weight per dozen 1 lb.; half dozen in a box.

Two blades; large spear blade, crocused; pen blade glazed; brass lined; nickel silver bolsters and shield; length closed, 3⅛ inches.

No. V327—Stag handle ....
No. V427W—White celluloid handle ......
No. V427SH—Shell handle ....

Weight per dozen 1 lb.; half dozen in a box.

Two blades; stag handle; one large spear blade, crocused, and one pen blade glazed; brass lined nickel silver tips and shield; length closed, 3¼ inches.

No. V324—Pocket knives ....

Weight per dozen 1¼ lbs.; half dozen in a box.

Two blades; stag handle; one large spear blade, crocused; one pen blade glazed; brass lined; nickel silver shield and bolsters; length closed, 3¼ inches.

No. V325—Pocket knives ....

Weight per dozen 1¼ lbs.; half dozen in a box.

Three blades; stag handle; one large clip blade, crocused; one spey and one sheep foot blade glazed; brass lined; nickel silver shield and bolsters; length, 3¼ inches.

No. V3311—Pocket knives ....

Weight per dozen 1½ lbs.; half dozen in a box.

POCKET KNIVES
MISCELLANEOUS

Chain Knives

Handle of metal to resemble stag; metal lining and bolster; o n e spear b l a d e; embossed "Easy Opener" on handle; equipped with chain; size closed, 2½ inches.

No. 01118 . . . .
Weight per doz. 1½ lbs.; one dozen in a box.

American Made

Two blades, one sheep foot and one pen blade, glazed; brass lined; steel bolsters; length, closed, 3⅛ inches.

No. 265—Stag handle . . . .
Weight per dozen, ¾ lb.; half dozen in a box.

RUSSELL BARLOW

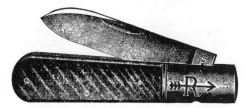

D a r k b o n e h a n d l e; one blade, g l a z e d; steel lined; steel bolster; length, closed, 3⅜ in.

No. 60—Spear blade . . . .
No. 65—Clip blade . . . .
Weight per dozen, 1¾ lbs.; one dozen in a box.

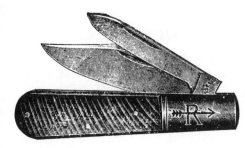

D a r k b o n e h a n d l e; t w o blades, large clip blade and small pen blade, glazed; steel lined; steel b o l s t e r; length, c l o s e d, 3⅜ inches.

No. 66—Clip blade . . . .
No. 62—Spear blade . . . .
Weight per dozen, 2 lbs.; one dozen in a box.

POCKET KNIVES
ADOLPH KASTOR & BROS.

Boy Scout
Stag handle; one large spear blade, one com b i n a t i o n cap lifter and screw driver, new improved can opener and sturdy leather punch b l a d e; all blades are full mirror polished on both sides; b r a s s lined; nickel silver bolsters and shield; length closed 3⅝ in.

No. 68590 . . . .
Weight per dozen, 2¾ lbs.; one half dozen in a box.

POCKET KNIFE ASSORTMENTS

VAN CAMP
Fancy Pen Knives

Six fancy patterns of pearl handle knives each in red gift box with gold embossing; s u e d e leather purse included with each knife; assortment packed in fancy red counter display box with attractive gilt lettering inside cover.

No. 6P . . . .
Weight per asst., 9 oz.; one asst. in a box.

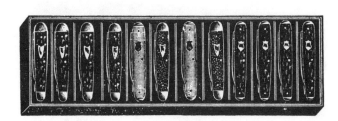

VAN CAMP

Twelve patterns of two, three and four bladed knives; assorted pearl, stag and celluloid handles.
No. 1931 . . . .
Weight per asst. 1¾ lbs.; one assortment in a partitioned cardboard box.

POCKET KNIFE ASSORTMENTS
VANCO

Two-Blade Punch Knives

Twelve stag handle knives; large spear and punch blades, spear blade polished; brass lined; nickel silver bolsters, cap and shield; length closed 3½ inches.

No. V3216..............................

Weight per assortment, 2⅜ lbs.; one assortment in a partitioned cardboard box.

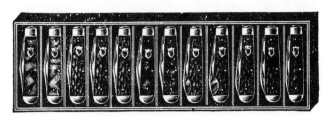

Two-Blade Jack Knives

Twelve patterns assorted stag and celluloid handles and clip and spear blades, two of them being easy openers; brass lined; steel bolsters; nickel silver shields; large blades polished; length, closed, 3⅜ inches.

No. 129..............................

Weight per assortment, 1⅞ lbs.; one assortment in a partitioned cardboard box.

VOOS

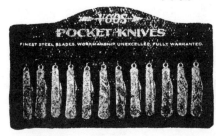

One-Blade Pen Knives

Twelve chatelaine knives with ring for attaching to watch chain; pearl handles; one blade; brass lined; nickel silver ring; blade polished; length 1¾ inches.

No. 4041 ....

Weight per card, 4 oz.; one assortment on a card.

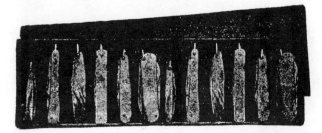

Two-Blade Pen Knives

Twelve fancy pearl handle knives with loop for attaching to watch chain; two pen blades; brass lined; nickel silver loop; length 2¾ inches.

No. 600P ....

Weight per assortment, 1 lb.; one assortment in a partitioned cardboard box.

POCKET KNIFE ASSORTMENTS

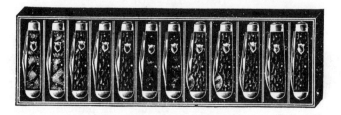

Two Blade Jack Knives

Twelve assorted colors pyralin handle knives; large spear and small pen blade; front side of large blade full polished, small blade glazed finish; brass lined; nickeled cap, bolster and shield; length closed 3⅛ inches.

No. 78AC ....

Weight each, 1½ lbs.; one assortment in a partitioned cardboard box.

CUB SCOUT

Assortment consists of twelve knives with Pyralin handles, in assorted colors; three blades; one large spear blade crocus polished; one combination bottle opener and screw driver blade; one can-opener blade, glazed finish; brass lined; nickel silver bolsters, shield and shackle; length closed 2¼ inches.

No. 236 ....

Weight per asst., 13 oz.; one asst. in a display box.

KNIFE PURSES

Gray mocha leather, unlined; silk stitched; snap fastener on flap with VanCamp trade mark.

No.	2¾	3	3¼	3½	4
Inches	2¾	3	3¼	3½	4
Oz. per dozen	2	2	2	2	2
Per dozen					

Three dozen in a box.

VANCO POCKET KNIVES

Illustrations Half Size

Two blade office knife; white handle; one large spear and one spey blade; brass lined; engraved and black inlaid wording as shown; length closed, 3½ inches.

No. V4210—Office knives . . . .

Weight per dozen 1½ lbs.; half dozen in a box.

Two blades, large sheep foot polished small pen blades glazed; brass lined; nickel silver bolsters and shield; length 3¾ in.

No. V3219—Stag handle . . . .

Weight per dozen 1½ lbs.; half dozen in a box.

Two blades, large sheep foot, small pen; large blade polished, small blade glazed; brass lined; nickel silver bolsters; length 3⅜ inches.

No. V3218—Stag handle . . . .

Weight per dozen 1½ lbs.; half dozen in a box.

Two blades, one pen blade, one sheepfoot blade; large blade crocused, small blade glazed; brass lined; steel bolsters; length 3 inches.

No. V3217—Stag handle . . . .

Weight per dozen 1 lb.; half dozen in a box.

Three blades, large clip, sheepfoot and spey; clip blade polished, others glazed finish; brass lined; nickel silver bolsters and shield; length closed, 3⅜ in.

No. V3316—Stag handle . . . .

Weight per dozen, 1 lb.; half dozen in a box.

Three blades, large spear, sheepfoot and spey; spear blade polished, others glazed finish; brass lined; nickel silver bolsters and shield; length closed, 3⅜ in.

No. V3317—Stag handle . . . .

Weight per dozen, 1 lb.; half dozen in a box.

Three blades, large clip, sheepfoot and spey; clip blade polished, others glazed finish; brass lined; nickel silver bolsters and shield; length closed, 3⅞ in.

No. V3318—Stag handle . . . .

Weight per dozen, 1¼ lbs.; half dozen in a box.

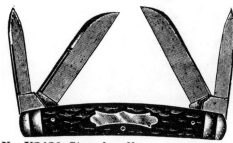

Four blades, two large sheep foot crocused; two small pen; glazed finish; brass lined; steel bolsters, nickel silver shield; length closed, 3¾ in.

No. V3420—Stag handle . . . .

Weight per dozen 2 lbs.; half dozen in a box.

Four blades, two large sheep foot, two small pen; large blades crocus finish, small blades glazed; brass lined; steel bolsters; nickel silver shield; length, closed, 4 inches.

No. V3421—Stag handle . . . .

Weight per dozen 2½ lbs.; half dozen in a box.

Quality Stamp

249

POCKET KNIFE ASSORTMENTS

POPEYE

Two Blades.

Jack knives with character of Popeye stamped on handle. Steel lining; polished blades.

Each box contains a window streamer size 6x24 inches.

No. 25 P1—Length knives 3⅛ ins _ _ _ _ _ _ _ _ _ _ _ _ _ _ _ _

(Sold only in full dozens.)

One doz in cardboard display box; wt doz 1½ lbs.

MICKEY MOUSE

Two Blades.

High quality cutlery steel blades, full polished.

All white handle with reproduction of Mickey Mouse in colors.

No. MM25—Length 3⅛ ins _

(Sold only in full dozens.)

One doz on counter display card; wt doz 1½ lbs.

POCKET KNIFE ASSORTMENTS

IMPERIAL "TOPSY"

One Blade.

Assortment includes 12 knives with nickel silver bolsters and brass lining. High quality cutlery steel clip blade, fully polished. Assorted colored pyralin handles.

No. 910—Length knives 2½ ins _

One doz on display card; wt doz 1½ lbs.

RABBIT FOOT AND KNIFE COMBINATION

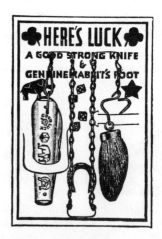

One Blade.

High quality cutlery steel blade, fully polished.

White handle printed on one side with good luck symbols.

Complete with 14 inch jack chain and genuine Rabbit's foot charm.

No. RFK—Length knife 3⅛ ins _ _ _ _ _ _ _ _ _ _ _ _ _ _ _ _ _ _

One on card wrapped in cellophane; one doz in cardboard box; wt doz 1⅜ lbs.

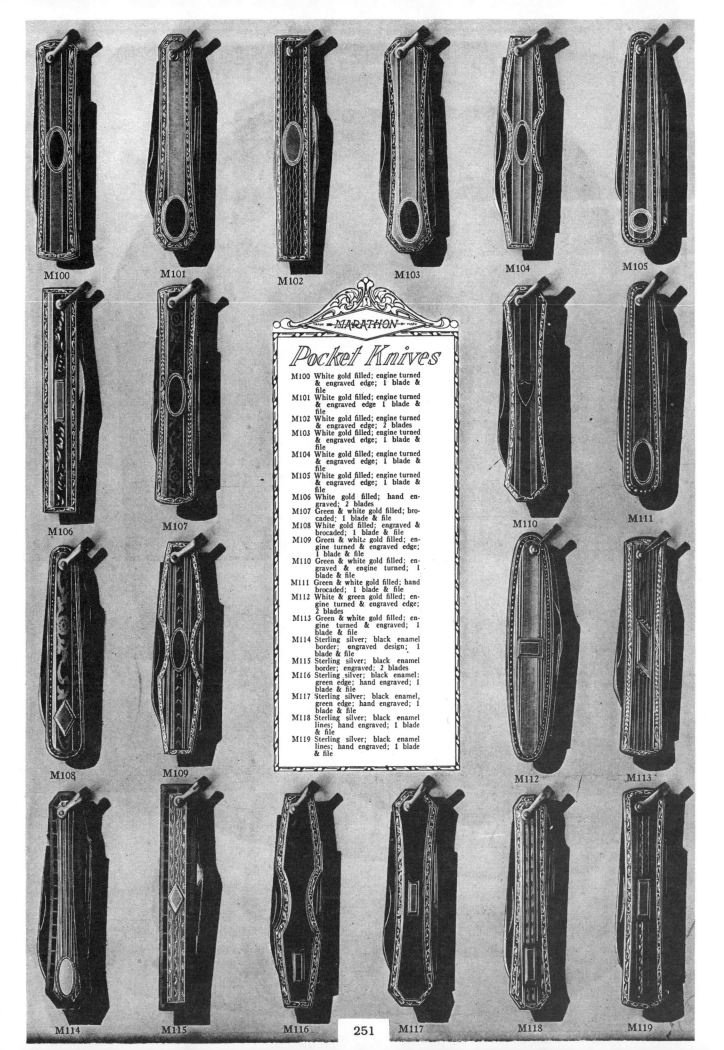

M100

M101

M102

M103

M104

M105

M106

M107

M110

M111

MARATHON

Pocket Knives

M100 White gold filled; engine turned & engraved edge; 1 blade & file

M101 White gold filled; engine turned & engraved edge 1 blade & file

M102 White gold filled; engine turned & engraved edge; 2 blades

M103 White gold filled; engine turned & engraved edge; 1 blade & file

M104 White gold filled; engine turned & engraved edge; 1 blade & file

M105 White gold filled; engine turned & engraved edge; 1 blade & file

M106 White gold filled; hand engraved; 2 blades

M107 Green & white gold filled; brocaded; 1 blade & file

M108 White gold filled; engraved & brocaded; 1 blade & file

M109 Green & white gold filled; engine turned & engraved edge; 1 blade & file

M110 Green & white gold filled; engraved & engine turned; 1 blade & file

M111 Green & white gold filled; hand brocaded; 1 blade & file

M112 White & green gold filled; engine turned & engraved edge; 2 blades

M113 Green & white gold filled; engine turned & engraved; 1 blade & file

M114 Sterling silver; black enamel border; engraved design; 1 blade & file

M115 Sterling silver; black enamel border; engraved; 2 blades

M116 Sterling silver; black enamel; green edge; hand engraved; 1 blade & file

M117 Sterling silver; black enamel, green edge; hand engraved; 1 blade & file

M118 Sterling silver; black enamel lines; hand engraved; 1 blade & file

M119 Sterling silver; black enamel lines; hand engraved; 1 blade & file

M108

M109

M112

M113

M114

M115

M116

M117

M118

M119

Solid Gold Waldemar Knives

PRICES EACH

No. W8890—14 k solid white gold very heavy. One side hand engraved with shield, other side engine turned. 1 stainless steel blade and 1 file........................ ....

No. W8821—14 k solid white gold very heavy. Engraved border with shield on one side. Straight line pattern. 2 stainless steel blades...'

No. W5000—10 k solid white gold very heavy. Straight line pattern both sides. Engraved border with shield on one side. 1 stainless steel blade and 1 file..

No. W4806x—10 k solid white gold very heavy. Engraved pattern, both sides alike. 2 stainless steel blades and scissors.

No. 2713—14 k solid white gold. Engine turned both sides. Engraved border on side with shield, 1 steel blade and 1 file...

No. 2705—14 k solid green gold. Engine turned both sides. Engraving around shield. 1 steel blade and 1 file......................

No. 2708—14 k solid white gold. Engine turned both sides. Engraved border on side with shield. 1 steel blade and 1 file....

No. 2704—14 k solid green gold. Engine turned both sides. Engraving around shield. 1 steel blade and 1 file....................

No. 2711—14 k solid white gold. Engine turned both sides. Engraving around shield. 1 steel blade and 1 file....................

No. W3 569/3—14 k solid white gold very heavy. Engine turned pattern, both sides alike. 3 stainless steel blades....

No. 2707—14 k solid white gold. Engine turned both sides. Shield on 1 side for initials. 1 steel blade and 1 file..................

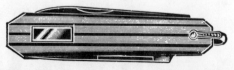

No. 2710—14 k solid white gold. Engine turned both sides. Shield for initials 1 side. 1 steel blade and 1 file......................

4205. Jos. Warren & Sons' "Special" Pocket Knife.
Genuine Stag Handle. German Silver Milled
Lining, Shield and Tips. Extra Refined Sheffield
Steel Blades. All Crocus Finish. Finished in
Best Possible Manner. Cannot Fail to Please.
Fully Warranted. Length, 3¼ inches.

**4203. Joseph Warren & Sons' Gentleman's Congress
Shape Pocket Knife.** Stag Handle. Has German
Silver Lining, Tips and Shield. Lining is Milled,
Making a Rich Finish. Blades are Full Crocus
Polished and Guaranteed. Length, 3⅜ inches.

4206. Jos. Warren & Sons' 4 Blade Pocket Knife.
Stag Handle. Blades are All Perfect, Hand
Forged English Steel, Extra Well Finished. Ger-
man Silver Bolster and Shield. Guaranteed
Quality. Length, 3⅜ inches.

**3602. Joseph Warren & Sons' Combination Genuine
Stag Handle Pocket Knife.** One Medium and One
Pen Blade and Scissors; All Made from Guaran-
teed English Steel, Full Crocus Polish. German
Silver Tips and Shield. Good, Sensible Pocket
Knife. Length, 3 inches.

3606. Joseph Warren & Sons' Combination Knife.
Genuine Stag Handle. German Silver Bolster and
Shield. One Medium Blade, One Wire Cutter
and Patent Corkscrew; Full Crocus Finish and
Made by Most Skilled Workmen. A Very Use-
ful Article. Length, 3¾ inches.

3605. Jos. Warren & Sons' Ideal Pearl Pocket Knife.
One Large. One Medium and One File Blade,
Made of Guaranteed English Steel, Full Crocus
Polished. German Silver Shield and Milled
Lining. Handles Selected from Best Grade
Pearl. Length, 3 inches.

**4604. Joseph Warren & Sons' Pearl Congress Pattern
Knife.** German Silver Hollow Bolster and Lin-
ing. Greatest Care is Exercised in Tempering and
Fitting. The Blades and the Cutting Qualities
are Fully Guaranteed. Fully Crocus Polish
Throughout. Length, 3¼ inches.

4603. Jos. Warren & Sons' Genteel Pearl Pocket Knife.
German Silver Lining, Tips and Shield. The
Edges of the Lining are Milled. The Blades
are All Crocus Polish, Making a Beautiful Finish.
Will Prove a Favorite Wherever Introduced.
Length, 3 inches.

4602. Jos. Warren & Sons' Pearl Handle Knife.
Popular Pattern of English Knives. German
Silver Bolster and Milled Lining. One Spear,
Two Pen and One Patent File Blade. We
Guarantee the Cutting Qualities Equal to Any
Knife. Length, 3⅛ inches.

4705. Joseph Warren & Sons' Highest Grade.
Full Crocus Polished Sheffield Steel Blades. One
Spear, Two Pen and One File Blade. Full
Mother of Pearl Handle. German Silver Lined.
Finished in Very Best Possible Manner. Length,
3 inches.

4304. Four-Blade Pearl Knife.
Triple Riveted Pearl Handle. One Large, 2 Pen and 1 File Blade of Highly Tempered Finely Polished Steel. Brass Lined. German Silver Bolsters and Shield. Length, 3½ inches.

3309. American Pattern Pearl Handle Pocket Knife.
Heavy German Silver Bolster and Fancy Shield, Brass Lined. One Large Spear, 1 Pen and 1 File Blade of High Quality Refined Steel. Length, 3⅜ inches.

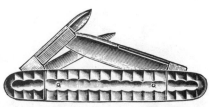

3308. Corrugated Pearl Handle Pocket Knife.
Brass Lined, Fancy German Silver Bolster. One Large, 1 Medium Pen and 1 File Blade, Full Crocus Polish and Well Tempered. A good, strong, durable article. Length, 3 inches.

4306. English Congress Pattern Pearl Handle Pocket Knife. Well Finished. German Silver Bolster, Brass Lined. One Large, 2 Pen and 1 Nail File Blade, Best Refined Steel, Crocus Polish throughout. Length, 3 inches.

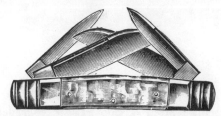

4303. Strong Pearl Handle Pocket Knife.
Fancy German Silver Bolster, First Quality Pearl Handle, Brass Lined. Two Large and 2 Pen Polished Steel Blades. A Durable Gentleman's Knife, 3¼ inches.

4305. Gentleman's Pearl Pocket Knife.
German Silver Bolsters and Shield, Brass Lined. Clear Mother-of-Pearl Handle. Has four blades made from High Grade Polished India Steel, well Tempered. Length, 3 inches.

JOSEPH WARREN & SONS' GUARANTEED POCKET KNIVES
Sold in Any Desired Quantity.

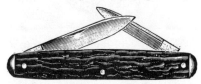

2207. Jos. Warren & Sons' Gentleman's Pocket Knife.
German Silver Tips and Lining. Blades are made of Best Sheffield Steel, Full Crocus Polished and fully Guaranteed. Length, 3⅛ inches.

3204. Jos. Warren & Son's Unrivalled Pocket Knife.
Stag and Buffalo Horn Handle. One Large Blade, 1 Pen and 1 File Blade, made of English Steel, Full Crocus Polish. Finished in best possible manner. Length, 3⅛ inches.

4208. Beautiful 4-Blade Knife. Genuine Stag and Buffalo Handle. German Silver Tips, Shield and Lining. Three Pen and 1 File Blade, all Crocus Polish, of Best English Steel. This knife cannot fail to please. Length, 2⅞ inches.

4207. Jos. Warren & Sons' 4-Blade Stag Handle Gentleman's Knife. Congress Pattern. German Silver Bolster and Shield. Four Strong English Steel Blades, Crocus Finish and a Keen Cutter. Length, 3¾ inches.

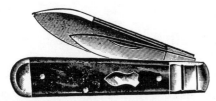

2302. Joseph Warren & Sons' Special Jack Knife.
Stag and Buffalo Horn Handle. Full Crocus Polish.
Best Sheffield Steel Blades, fully Tempered. Extra
German Silver Cap, Bolster and Shield. Nothing
better made and fully Warranted. Length, 3⅛
inches.

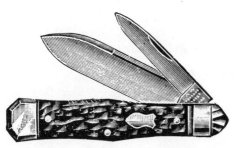

2303. Jos. Warren & Sons' Gentlemen Jack Knife.
Heavy German Silver Cap, Shield and Bolster. Refined Razor Steel Crocus Finish Blades. Stag and
Buffalo Horn Handle. Fully Warranted. Length,
3¾ inches.

Jos. Warren & Sons' Sportsmen and Hunting Knives.

3200. Celebrated Cattle Knife.
Stag Horn Handle. German Silver Bolsters and
Shield. Brass Lined. Fully Polished. One Large
Blade, Etched "Cattle Knife," one Curved and one
Pen Blade. Elegantly Polished. Length, 3½ inches.

2304. Swedish Pattern Lock Back Knife.
Heavy German Silver Bolster and Shield. Two
Select Swedish Steel Blades, Fully Polished. Large
Blade has Automatic Lock to close, press on small
Blade. Adapted for Heavy Cutting. Length, 4
inches.

**1000. Our Celebrated 1000 "Hunter's Own" Sportsmen
Knife.** Finely Tempered English Steel Blade, Hand
Forged, and Etched "Hunter's Own." Ebony and
Rosewood Handle. This Knife is Guaranteed for
Heavy Cutting. Length, 5¼ inches.

3304. Special Sportman's Knife.
Fancy Shape, Swell Center. One Large Clip and
one Pen Blade, made from best Swedish Steel, and
Patent Cork Screw. Stag and Buffalo Handle. Brass
Lined. Full Crocus Polish Throughout. Length,
3⅞ inches.

3307. Fancy Wharncliffe Sportsman's Knife.
Stag and Buffalo Horn Handle. German Silver
Shield. Brass Lined. One Large Clip, one Pen and
one Curved Blade, made from Genuine India Silver
Steel. A Popular and Practical Knife. Length, 4
inches.

3306. Gladiator Cattle Knife.
Stag and Buffalo Handle. German Silver Shield
Full Brass Lined, and Crocus Polished. Blades are
made from best Razor Tempered India Steel. Length,
4 inches.

POCKET KNIVES.

Each year the demand for our Cutlery has greatly increased until to-day it is one of our lines. For twenty-five years we have been working steady at this line, making special offers to g greatest values for the least money and it is hardly necessary for us to say that for well made and finished goods our various brands cannot be excelled. Our Joseph Warren & Sons Cutlery stands f most to-day, and shall always continue to hold its well earned reputation. We give an exact descriptio and cut of each knife and we are sure that a trial order will make you a steady customer.

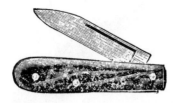

1203. Boys' Cocoa Handle Knife.

One Blade. Nicely Finished. A Good 5c. Value.

1204. Boys' Ebony Handle Knife.

One Blade. Scored Handle, Metal Lined, with Strong Blade.

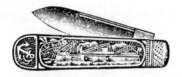

1200. Fancy Nickel Metal Handle Boys' Knife.

Embossed with **U. S. Cruiser "Maine"** on Both Sides. Well Made and Very Popular. Length, 2¾ inches.

1201. Boys' 5c. Knife, Fancy Metal Handle.

Embossed on Both Sides. Metal Lined. One Good Blade and Strong Spring. Length, 2¾ inches.

1202. Fancy Metal Boys' Knives.

Embossed with Picture of **"Our Boy"** on Both Sides. Metal Lined. Fancy Bolsters. Length, 2¾ inches.

2402. Same as Above, 2 Blades.

2401. Boys' 2-Blade Jack Knife.

Bright Metal Handle, Embossed with **U. S. Flag.** Two Good Blades. Plain Bolster and Frame. Length, 2¾ inches.

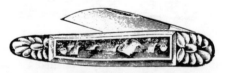

1300. Boys' Shell Handle Pocket Knife.

Fancy Embossed Bolsters. Imitation Shell Handle. Nicely Finished Steel Blade. Length, 3½ inches.

1400. Favorite Nickel Jack Knife.

Bright Fluted Handle. Polished Bolster and Heart Shield. One Strong, Nicely Finished Blade. Length, 3¼ inches.

Joseph Warren & Sons Celebrated Jack Knives.

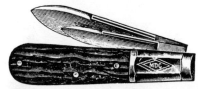

2205. Joseph Warren & Sons' M. D. C. Barlow.
Strong and Durable, with Blades of Best Tempered English Steel. Genuine Stag Handle. Full Crocus Polish. For cutting qualities this Knife cannot be excelled. Length, 3¼ inches.

2210. Joseph Warren & Sons' Practical Jack Knife.
Stag Handle. Two Fully Polished India Steel Blades, Brass Lined, German Silver Bolster and Shield, with Patent Seal Head. This Knife is especially adapted to Mechanics and Farmers use. Length, 3¾ inches.

2209. Joseph Warren & Sons' Extra Jack Knife.
Stag Handle, German Silver Shield and Cap. Octagon Shaped Bolster, Brass Lined, Full Crocus Finish. Two Best Ground Norwegian Polished Steel Blades, Fully Warranted. Length, 4 inches.

2206. Joseph Warren & Sons' Cattle Jack Knife.
Fancy German Silver Bolster and Shield. Finely Tempered India Steel Blades, Crocus Finish Throughout. Stag and Buffalo Horn Handles. Length, 3½ inches.

2202. Joseph Warren & Sons' Patent Easy Opener.
Stag, White Bone, Ebony and Dogwood Handles. Two English Steel Blades, Full Crocus Polish. Large Blade etched "Easy Opener." German Silver Cap, Bolster and Shield. Length, 3½ inches.

2208. Jos. Warren & Sons' Genuine Physician's Knife.
German Silver Bolster and Cap. Full Brass Lined. Stag and Buffalo Horn Handle. Two Refined Sheffield Steel Blades. One 3¾ inch Spear Blade and 1 Medium Pen. Fully Polished Throughout. Length, 3¾ inches

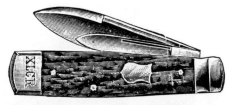

2203. Joseph Warren & Sons' XLCR Jack Knife.
Swell Center, Heavy German Silver Cap, Bolster and Crest Shield. Genuine Stag and Buffalo Horn Handle. Two Razor Tempered English Steel Blades, Fully Warranted. Length, 3½ inches.

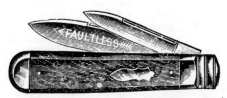

2201. Jos. Warren & Sons' English Pattern Jack Knife.
German Silver Shield and Cap, with Fancy Extension Bolster. Brass lined, Full Crocus Polish. Genuine English Steel Blades. Well Made and Warranted. Length, 4 inches.

2204. Jos. Warren & Sons' Celebrated "Faultless" Jack Knife. Genuine Stag and Buffalo Horn Handle. German Silver Cap, Bolster and Shield. Brass Lined, Full Silver Crocus Polish. Two Best English Tempered Steel Blades, etched. Length, 4 inches.

2211. Jos. Warren & Sons' Celebrated M D C Brand Jack Knife. German Silver Cap, Bolster and Shield, with Full Brass Lined Double Spring. Stag and White Bone Handles. Two Refined Sheffield Steel Blades. Guaranteed to give satisfaction. Length, 3⅝ inches.

PRICE GUIDE

Page 14
K343 – $100+
K32566 – 80+
K42566 – 75+
K429 – 100+
K4979 – 100+
K4679 – 100+
K4299 – 50+
K4297 – 75+
K3769 – 75+
K3113 – 75+
K4408 – 75+
K4849 – 75+
K3483 – 75+
K3808 – 50+

Page 15
K488 – $50+
K0488 – 50+
K3908 – 50+
K3489 – 50+
K3486 – 75+
K3488 – 75+
K4328 – 100+
K02339 – 75+
K02337 – 75+
K32339 – 75+
K32337 – 100+
K0382 – 50+
K03833 – 50+
K38333 – 50+
K48333 – 50+
K3389 – 50+

Page 16
K4429 – $100+
K4429E – 100+
K44288 – 125+
K4428 – 125+
K4426 – 125+
K4829 – 100+
K3008 – 100+
K44833 – 125+
K3219 – 75+
K3216 – 75+
K32188 – 75+
K3215A – 100+
K37288 – 100+

Page 17
K3433 – $125+
K34333 – 125+
K3434 – 125+
K32322 – 125+
K3828 – 125+
K3825 – 125+
K3829 – 125+
K3903 3/4 – 125+
K8433 – 125+
K3278 – 100+
K32788 – 100+
K3276 – 100+
K3277 – 100+
K3375 – 100+
K3378 – 100+
K72085 – 75+
K72086 – 75+
K72088 – 75+
K738 3/4 – 100+
K73878 – 100+

Page 18
K1201 – $75+
K1200 – 75+
K22033 – 75+
K1203 – 75+
K2621 – 75+
K2623 – 75+

K26233 – 75+
K2623 3/4 – 75+
K25233 – 75+
K21988 – 100+
K2613 – 75+
K2611 – 75+
K2048 3/4 – 75+
K2273 3/4 – 75+
K2063 – 75+
K20633 – 75+

Page 19
K2850 – $75+
K2851 – 75+
K2853 – 75+
K28533 – 75+
K2851 3/4 – 75+
K2853 3/4 – 75+
K2695 – 50+
K98 – 75+
K95 – 75+
K93 – 75+
K90 – 75+
K2719 – 75+
K50 – 75+
K51 – 75+
K2778 – 75+
K2778 3/4 – 75+
K2780 – 75+
K2781 – 75+
K2783 – 75+
K20333 – 75+
K2030/SC – 75+
K2780 3/4 – 75+
K2781 3/4 – 75+
K2783 3/4 – 75+
K26755 – 50+
K26756 – 50+
K23758 – 50+

Page 20
K601 – $100+
K600 – 100+
K2305 – 75+
K2305 3/4 – 75+
K2306 – 75+
K2306 3/4 – 75+
K2105 – 75+
K2105 3/4 – 75+
K2106 – 75+
K2160R – 75+
K510 – 75+
K511 – 75+
K512 – 75+
K513 – 75+
K514 – 75+
K500 – 75+
K1883 – 75+
K2583 – 75+
K2583 1/2 – 75+
K2580 – 75+
K2580 1/2 – 75+

Page 21
1005WG – $300+
115PB – 200+
116PB – 200+
117PB – 200+
1000PB – 250+
1100PB – 250+
1007PB – 250+
1200PB – 250+
500PB – 200+
501PB – 200+
507PB – 200+
517PB – 200+
105PB – 150+
100PB – 150+

102PB – 150+
103PB – 150+
107PB – 150+

Page 22
K830 – $200+
3H – 200+
3 – 25+
829 – 50+
828 – 50+
135R – 100+

Page 23
28V916 – $75+
28V920 – 75+
28V945 – 90+
28V946 – 90+
28V884 – 50+
28V925 – 50+
28V969 – 50+
28V980 – 75+
28V982 – 75+
28V890 – 50+
28V892 – 50+
28V911 – 50+
28V912 – 50+
28V881 – 50+
28V899 – 50+
28V901 – 50+
28V949 – 50+
28V904 – 50+
28V954 – 50+
28V928 – 50+
28V931 – 50+
28V906 – 50+
28V960 – 50+
28V963 – 50+

Page 24
28V830 – $50+
28V833 – 50+
28V836 – 50+
28V838 – 75+
28V840 – 50+
28V842 – 50+
28V847 – 50+
28V854 – 50+
28V849 – 50+
28V850 – 50+
28V875 – 50+
28V860 – 50+
28V861 – 50+
28V878 – 50+
28V864 – 50+
28V869 – 50+
28V856 – 50+
28V857 – 50+
28V866 – 50+
28V908 – 50+
28V845 – 50+
28V886 – 50+
28V1328 – 75+
28V895 – 50+
28V896 – 50+

Page 25
28V959 – $50+
28V932 – 50+
28V935 – 50+
28V953 – 50+
28V955 – 50+
28V956 – 50+
28V966 – 50+
28V936 – 50+
28V940 – 50+
28V941 – 50+
28V985 – 50+
28V989 – 50+

28V990 – 50+
28V1324 – 200+
28V1320 – 200+
28V1326 – 100+
28V1135 – 100+
28V1310 – 100+
28V1311 – 100+
28V1312 – 100+
28V1315 – 100+
28V1316 – 100+
28V1000 – 40+
28V1004 – 40+
28V1005 – 40+
28V1006 – 40+
28V1007 – 50+
28V1012 – 50+
28V1020 – 50+
28V1021 – 40+
28V1023 – 40+
28V1026 – 40+
28V1029 – 40+
28V1030 – 40+

Page 29
R4425E – $150+
R3413 – 175+
R6534 – 200+
R3415 – 150+
R4653 – 175+
R100A – 150+
R100B – 150+
R3183 – 250+
R3203 – 250+
R3553 – 225+

Page 30
R3415H – $150+
R100B – 150+
R3413 – 150+
R4683 – 150+
R3183 – 200+
R3963 – 150+
R3063 – 200+
R3065 – 150+
RS3333 – 225+

Page 31
RC8 – $100+
R2605M – 100+
R2605R – 100+
R2603 – 100+
RB43 – 200+
RB44 – 200+
RB44W – 200+
R2203 – 125+
R2213 – 125+
R2215M – 100+

Page 32
R2043 – $150+
R2053 – 150+
R2073 – 125+
R2045 – 150+
R2055 – 150+
R2075 – 150+
R1323 – 125+
R921 – 100+
R33 – 125+
RB43 – 200+
RB44 – 200+
RB44W – 200+
RB45 – 200+
RB46 – 225+
RB040 – 150+
RB041 – 150+

Page 33
R-100A – $150+

R-100B – 150+
R3123 – 250+
R3113 – 200+
R4593 – 200+
R953 – 225+
R955 – 225+
R4103 – 150+
R1225W – 200+
R7833 – 200+
R333 – 175+
R1343 – 250+
R1853 – 200+
R1863 – 150+
R555 – 150+

Page 34
R153 – $150+
R1065W – 100+
R1823 – 125+
R1873 – 150+
R1113 – 125+
R1073 – 225+
R1075 – 225+
R623 – 175+
R603 – 150+
R605 – 150+
R3533 – 175+
R2103 – 125+
R2105 – 150+
R2215 – 150+
R2213 – 150+
R2205 – 150+

Page 35
3358 – $40+
3553 – 40+
3568 – 40+
31635M – 40+
4508 – 65+
RC091 – 100+
RC953 – 200+
RC955L – 200+
R1303 – 1000+
RC6 – 100+

Page 36
R3555W – $175
R3563 – 225+
R3565W – 125+
R3873 – 200+
R4135R – 175+
R3963 – 225+
R3973 – 200+
R3993 – 200+
R1763 – 150+

Page 37
R6623 – $140+
R6473 – 200+
R6785W – 150+
R6175W – 150+
R3442 – 150+
R4593 – 150+
R7223 – 125+
R6194 – 250+
R3535S – 125+
R8023 – 150+
R4683 – 125+

Page 38
R605G – $150+
R555L – 175+
R573 – 175+
R1853 – 150+
R995N – 150+
R875D – 150+
R1973 – 175+
R1643 – 150+

R1653 – 175+
R1225W – 200+

Page 39
R983 – $175+
R985 – 175+
R6464 – 150+
R3253 – 200+
R6703 – 200+
R6032 – 325+
RB1240 – 250+
RS3333 – 250+
RS4233 – 250+

Page 40
R3553 – $200+
R3555W – 200+
R3563 – 250+
R3555G – 225+
R3565W – 200+
R3973 – 225+
R3975 – 225+
R3993 – 250+
R3965 – 150+
R3963 – 200+
R4405 – 150+
R3485 – 150+
R4133 – 250+
R4135 – 175+
R3493 – 250+
R4005 – 180+

Page 41
R6483 – $125+
R6843 – 175+
R6643 – 125+
R7425C – 150+
R6623 – 140+
R7773 – 150+
R7423 – 125+
R7233 – 100+
R6653 – 125+
R6723 – 250+
R6904 – 125+
R7633 – 200+
R7854 – 125+
R1623 – 150+
R1573 – 125+
R1622 – 125+
R1582 – 125+
R1882 – 150+

Page 42
RB44W – $350+
R1825W – 100+
R1075T – 125+
R1595P – 100+
R8015W – 100+
R6643 – 125+
R7854 – 125+
R6904 – 125+
R6645D – 120+

Page 43
102E – $50+
272CH – 50+
23R – 75+
0354E – 35+
7338CH – 75+
334CH – 50+
7342CH – 50+
4100 – 75+
229 1/2 – 80+

Page 44
R953 – $275+
R693 – 100+
R1673 – 100+

258

RB43 – 200+
RB44 – 225+
R33 – 100+
R23 – 125+
R1072 – 125+
R1073 – 100+
R1063 – 125+

Page 45
RB1240 – $250+
RS4783 – 200+
RS3333 – 250+
R6043 – 250+
R6073 – 275+
R6693 – 175+
R6163 – 150+
R6093 – 150+
R6143 – 150+
R6103 – 150+
R3535 – 125+
R6785 – 125+
R6175 – 150+
R7853 – 125+
R6499 – 150+
R6463 – 125+
R8003 – 125+

Page 46
R1065W – $125+
R1753 – 150+
R1783 – 150+
R1283 – 175+
R153 – 150+
R1323 – 150+
R1903 – 125+
R1593 – 125+
R1905E – 150+
R1833 – 150+
R603 – 150+

Page 47
R4593 – $200+
R3535S – 150+
R6645C – 100+
R6643 – 125+
R3533 – 175+
R7423 – 125+
R6623 – 100+
R7425MW – 100+
R7543 – 125+
R7233 – 100+
R6499 – 75+
R6914 – 75+

Page 48
R2223 – $150+
R2205B – 150+
R2103 – 100+
R2105MW – 100+
R1855M – 100+
R155 – 125+
R153 – 150+
R1323 – 150+
R603 – 150+
R605G – 140+

Page 49
R8065H – $175+
R8063 – 200+
R7854 – 125+
R6244 – 100+
R4845M – 125+
R4825R – 100+
R4843 – 100+
R3485H – 150+
R4635G – 100+
R105AMW – 125+

Page 50
R1853 – $125+

R1823 – 125+
R1653 – 125+
R1225W – 225+
R2111 – 100+
R1153 – 300+
RC7853 – 150+
R6463 – 150+
R6785IW – 125+
R6465MW – 125+
R6905MW – 75+

Page 51
RS195 – 125+
RS190 – 125+
JM3 – 400+
JM4 – 1200+
RJ9 – 1250+
DC60 – 5000+

Page 52
R4633 – $125+
R100A – 150+
R4135B – 175+
R3055 – 250+
R3053 – 275+
R3993 – 250+
R7593 – 200+
R6534 – 200+
R4835M – 200+
R4833 – 175+

Page 53
RS4783 – 225+
R4723 – 200+
RB1240 – 250+
65 – 400+
66 – 250+
62 – 250+
1850C – 80+
KK – 125+

Page 54
4991 – $350
2877 – 325
2879 – 600
3963 – 250
1613 – 110
2205 – 120
2681 – 125
1610 – 100
1614 – 100

Page 55
3009 – $350
4950 – 200
2852 – 250
3341 – 350
3942 – 290
3962 – 250
3959 – 250
4963 – 390
3916 – 200

Page 56
2079 – $125
3933 – 250
3932 – 250
3043 – 250
3044 – 250
2842 – 140
2945 – 150
3904 – 250
2302 – 75
2967 – 300
3915 – 275

Page 57
4931 – $300
2996 – 200
2933 – 185

3927 – 200
2978 – 275
2974 – 250
2962 – 125
2086 – 125
2107 – 125
1924 – 200
1051 – 200
1936 – 225
1050 – 225

Page 58
1938 – $165
1922 – 165
1921 – 165
2983 – 170
1701 – 175
1785 – 175
1704 – 425
1703 – 425
2630 – 175
2098 – 175
2940 – 175
1920 – 1000
2851 – 225

Page 59
5958 – $45
5294 – 325
5206 – 250
6228 – 250
8468 – 325
8277 – 125
6230 – 150
5230 – 200
5653 – 45
5202 – 200

Page 60
157 – $75+
519 – 75+
411 – 75+
444 – 75+
412 – 75+
448 – 75+
153 – 75+
159 – 75+
154 – 75+
160 – 75+
155 – 75+
161 – 75+
445 – 75+
413 – 75+
449 – 75+
446 – 75+
414 – 75+
450 – 75+

Page 61
458 – $60+
459 – 60+
460 – 60+
451 – 60+
452 – 60+
501 – 75+
502 – 75+
503 – 75+
515 – 75+
456 – 75+
457 – 75+
453 – 75+
454 – 75+
455 – 75+

Page 62
480 – 75+
481 – 75+
482 – 75+
483 – 75+
491 – 75+

492 – 75+
493 1/2 – 75+
484 – 75+
521 – 75+
500 – 75+

Page 63
447 – 75+
511 – 75+
514 – 75+
506 – 75+
489 – 75+
490 – 75+
418 – 75+
419 – 75+
477 – 75+
478 – 75+
256 – 75+

Page 64
165 – 75+
534 – 75+
509 – 75+
512 – 75+
443 – 75+
510 – 75+
513 – 75+
517 – 100+
158 – 100+
479 – 100+

Page 65
582P – 125+
204P – 125+
203P – 125+
205P – 100+
479P – 100+
120P – 125+
219P – 125+

Page 66
211P – 125+
244P – 125+
212P – 150+
321P – 125+
322P – 125+
323P – 125+
571P – 125+
572P – 125+
573P – 125+

Page 67
245P – 125+
268P – 125+
269P – 125+
270P – 125+
216P – 125+
431P – 125+
425P – 125+
426P – 125+
427P – 125+
428P – 125+
259P – 125+
260P – 125+
430P – 125+
378P – 125+
223P – 150+
272P – 175+

Page 68
275P – 125+
281P – 125+
282P – 125+
271P – 125+
227P – 125+
213P – 125+
214P – 125+
215P – 125+
206P – 125+
348 1/2 – 125+

349 – 125+
374 – 125+

Page 69
291P – $150+
291 1/2P – 150+
292P – 150+
273P – 150+
579P – 150+
581P – 150+

Page 70
277P – $125+
278P – 125+
298P – 125+
285P – 125+
286P – 125+
225P – 125+
371P – 125+
372P – 125+
373P – 125+
308P – 125+
331P – 150+
369P – 200+
370P – 200+

Page 71
0604 – $75+
0603 – 75+
0605 – 75+
0607 – 75+
0606 – 75+
0608 – 75+
0610 – 75+
0609 – 75+
0611 – 75+
0371 – 75+
0372 – 75+
0433 – 75+
0406 – 75+
0407 – 75+

Page 72
3202N – 150+
3206N – 150+
3208N – 150+
3718N – 150+
3215N – 200+
4215N – 150+

Page 73
821P – $75+
817P – 75+
816P – 75+
818P – 75+
819P – 75+
820P – 75+
812P – 75+
813P – 75+

Page 74
799P – $75+
623P – 75+
676P – 75+
677P – 75+
678P – 75+
682P – 100+

Page 75
329P – $75+
330P – 75+
570P – 75+
295P – 75+
296P – 75+
293P – 75+
294P – 75+
317P – 75+
318P – 75+
319P – 75+
320P – 75+

Page 76
620P – $90+
811P – 100+
628P – 90+
629P – 90+
619P – 90+

Page 77
300P – $90+
299P – 90+
343P – 90+
344P – 90+
345P – 90+
316P – 80+
309P – 90+
310P – 90+
311P – 90+
313P – 80+
312P – 80+
315P – 75+
314P – 75+

Page 78
608P – $75+
609P – 75+
610P – 75+
617P – 75+
616P – 75+
618P – 75+
611P – 75+
612P – 75+
613P – 75+
621P – 75+
622P – 75+

Page 79
109 – $75+
110 – 75+
111 – 75+
231 – 75+
207 – 75+
208 – 75+
232 – 75+
233 – 75+
239 – 75+
112 – 75+
209 – 75+
210 – 75+
210 1/2 – 75+
122 – 75+
142 – 75+

Page 80
741 – $80+
742 – 80+
727 – 80+
728 – 80+
663 – 90+
664 – 90+
814 – 100+
815 – 100+
755 – 90+
756 – 90+

Page 81
119 – $75+
222 – 75+
263 – 75+
266 – 75+
377 – 75+
377 1/2 – 75+
366 – 75+
367 – 75+
148 – 75+
204 – 75+
267 – 75+
431 – 75+
203 – 75+
243 – 75+
147 – 75+

425 – 75+
426 – 75+
149 – 75+
205 – 75+
429 – 75+
229 – 75+
230 – 75+

Page 82
461 1/2 – $75+
461 – 75+
462 – 75+
463 – 75+
439 – 75+
440 – 75+
441 – 75+
442 – 75+
540 – 75+
541 – 75+
542 – 75+
546 – 90+
547 1/2 – 90+
162 – 90+

Page 83
240 – $75+
241 – 75+
227 – 75+
213 – 75+
214 – 75+
215 – 75+
298 – 75+
246 – 75+
247 – 75+
248 – 75+
225 – 75+
371 – 75+
372 – 75+
373 – 75+
352 – 75+
350 – 75+
306 – 75+
307 – 75+
304 – 75+
308 – 75+

Page 84
216 – $75+
237 – 75+
238 – 75+
123 – 100+
340 – 100+
339 – 100+
430 – 100+
226 – 100+
341 – 100+
242 – 100+
223 – 100+
251 – 100+
563 – 100+

Page 85
211 – $75+
244 – 75+
212 – 75+
252 – 75+
253 – 75+
379 – 90+
844 – 90+
845 – 100+
562 – 100+
846 – 100+
847 – 100+

Page 86
261 – $75+
264 – 75+
262 – 75+
265 – 75+
257 – 75+

258 – 75+
259 – 75+
260 – 75+
427 – 75+
428 – 75+
274 – 75+
276 – 75+
120 – 75+
219 – 75+

Page 87
605 – $100+
666 – 100+
601 – 100+
604 – 100+
606 – 100+
683 – 100+
684 – 100+
686 – 100+
687 – 100+

Page 88
228 – $125+
128 – 100+
129 – 100+
164 – 100+

Page 89
101 – $100+
201 – 100+
691 – 200+
561 – 250+
370 – 200+

Page 90
249 – $100+
250 – 100+
348 1/2 – 75+
349 – 75+
374 – 75+
676 – 75+
677 – 75+
678 – 75+
667 – 75+
682 – 75+

Page 91
574P – $75+
237P – 75+
238P – 75+
251P – 75+
280P – 75+
575P – 75+
576P – 75+
578P – 75+
577P – 75+
580P – 75+

Page 92
683P – 100+
684P – 100+
685P – 200+
691P – 200+

Page 93
252P – $75+
254P – 75+
253P – 75+
327P – 75+
328P – 75+
614P – 75+
615P – 75+
627P – 75+
626P – 75+
625P – 100+

Page 94
604P – $100+
666P – 100+
667P – 100+

624P – 100+
631P – 100+

Page 95
782 – $100+
783 – 100+
784 – 100+
785 – 100+
743 – 100+
838 – 100+
843 – 125+
828 – 150+

Page 96
724 – $125+
723 – 150+
156 – 200+

Page 97
707 – $75+
393 – 75+
394 – 75+
406 – 75+
407 – 75+
700 – 100+
701 – 100+
702 – 100+
703 – 100+
794 – 100+
718 – 100+

Page 98
432 – $75+
433 – 75+
434 – 75+
434 1/2 – 75+
435 – 75+
422 – 75+
423 – 75+
424 – 75+
387 – 75+
388 – 75+
389 – 75+
396 – 75+
397 – 75+
398 – 75+
408 – 60+

Page 99
102 – $75+
202 – 75+
104 – 75+
111 1/2 – 75+
234 – 75+
117 – 75+
220S – 75+
118 – 75+
221 – 75+
236 – 75+
235 – 75+
116 – 75+
217 – 75+
218 – 75+

Page 100
469 – $75+
496 – 75+
497 – 75+
499 – 75+
498 – 75+
392 – 75+
402 – 75+
390 – 75+
391 – 75+
400 – 75+
401 – 75+
704 – 75+
705 – 75+
706 – 75+

Page 101
325 – $80+
409 – 60+
410 – 60+
583 – 60+
584 – 60+
585 – 60+
504 – 60+
505 – 60+
495 – 60+
744 – 75+
776 – 75+

Page 102
740 – $60+
745 – 75+
761 – 75+
380 – 75+
528 – 75+
530 – 75+
363 – 75+
360 – 75+
362 – 75+

Page 103
798 – $80+
757 – 80+
527 – 75+
127 – 75+
143 – 75+

Page 104
793 – $75+
753 – 75+
754 – 75+
709 – 75+
822 – 75+
531 – 75+
532 – 75+
533 – 75+
837 – 75+
520 – 75+
839 – 75+

Page 105
544 – $75+
545 – 75+
848 – 75+
535 – 75+
536 – 75+
780 – 75+
781 – 75+
777 – 75+
778 – 75+
779 – 75+
473 – 75+
474 – 75+
475 – 75+
476 – 75+
842 – 100+

Page 106
759 – $75+
760 – 75+
769 – 75+
762 – 75+
791 – 75+
792 – 75+
729 – 75+
730 – 75+
731 – 75+
735 – 75+

Page 107
736 – $75+
739 – 75+
567 – 75+
568 – 75+
569 – 75+
537 – 75+

538 – 75+
539 – 75+
849 – 75+
850 – 75+
851 – 75+
790 – 75+
763 – 75+
775 – 75+
908 – 100+

Page 108
827 – $100+
833 – 100+
712 – 75+
713 – 75+
714 – 75+
787 – 75+
788 – 75+
789 – 75+
715 – 75+
716 – 75+
717 – 75+
830 – 75+
831 – 75+
832 – 75+
719 – 75+
720 – 75+
746 – 75+
747 – 75+

Page 109
796 – $100+
797 – 100+
552 – 100+
553 – 100+
554 – 100+
558 – 100+
559 – 100+
560 – 100+
555 – 100+
556 – 100+
557 – 100+
786 – 75+

Page 110
550 – $75+
551 – 75+
381 – 75+
399 – 75+
823 – 80+
825 – 80+
824 – 80+
131 – 80+
133 – 80+
152 – 75+

Page 111
695 – $75+
696 – 75+
696 1/2 – 75+
695 1/2 – 75+
770 – 75+
771 – 75+
772 – 75+
764 – 75+
765 – 75+
766 – 75+
768 – 75+
773 – 75+
774 – 75+

Page 112
464 – $90+
464 1/2 – 90+
465 – 90+
466 – 90+
522 – 90+
523 – 90+
467 – 90+
375 – 90+

468 – 90+
436 – 90+
437 – 90+

Page 113
852 – $90+
854 – 90+
841 – 90+
834 – 90+
835 – 90+
829 – 90+

Page 114
749 – $100+
840 – 125+
751 – 100+
630 – 100+

Page 115
485 – $75+
486 – 75+
487 1/2 – 75+
488 – 75+
301 – 75+
524 – 75+
525 – 75+
526 – 75+
470 – 75+
471 – 75+
472 – 75+
420 – 75+
421 – 75+
416 – 75+
417 – 75+

Page 116
289P – $150+
290P – 150+
337P – 150+
338P – 150+
287P – 150+
288P – 150+
283P – 150+
284P – 150+
306PP – 150+
307P – 150+
304P – 150+
352P – 150+
350P – 150+

Page 117
5745MP – $40+
5745PP – 40+
5754SSC – 40+
5755C – 40+
5232S – 50+
5264S – 50+
5478JP – 40+
5600I – 40+
5751SP – 40+
5344P – 40+
5030P – 40+
5332P – 40+
5231S – 50+
4806S – 50+
JPEK – 50+
5106R – 50+

Page 118
C1-5279S – $60+
C1-5763P – 50+
C1-5763S – 50+
C1-902S – 60+
C1-5344S – 60+
C1-5323S – 60+
C1-901NP – 50+
C1-4987S – 75+
C1-4942S – 100+

Page 119
5224S – $50+
5222S – 50+
5222P – 50+
5433S – 100+
5409S – 75+
5278S – 60+
5279S – 60+
5280S – 60+
5755S – 50+
5736S – 50+
5736PP – 50+
5130S – 40+
5330S – 40+
5408S – 40+
5410S – 50+
5652S – 40+
5344S – 40+
5230S – 40+
5230P – 40+
3000SP – 40+
3000SS – 40+
5444S – 40+

Page 120
5286S – $50+
5285MP – 50+
5269S – 50+
5270S – 60+
5373S – 60+
4988S – 50+
5389S – 75+
5283S – 75+
4989S – 50+
4987S – 50+
4983JP – 50+
5751PP – 50+
4994S – 40+
4994SP – 50+
4815S – 50+
4815R – 50+
5727W – 60+
5204GS – 60+
5180S – 75+

Page 121
5190S – $75+
4860S – 50+
4861S – 50+
4955S – 50+
4961JP – 50+
5035S – 75+
5037S – 75+
4942S – 75+
4941S – 60+
5140S – 60+
5132S – 60+
5134S – 60+
4984S – 60+
5072S – 50+
5073S – 50+
5123S – 50+
5124S – 50+
5125S – 50+
4845S – 60+
05670S – 50+
5175S – 50+

Page 122
57390P – $50+
4844S – 50+
4855S – 50+
5147S – 50+
4938GP – 50+
4938S – 50+
4937S – 50+
4992S – 50+
4993S – 50+
5746GP – 40+
5726S – 40+

4950JP – 40+
4950S – 40+
5753S – 40+
4920S – 50+
4927GS – 50+
4927S – 50+
4927P – 50+
4923S – 50+
4923PP – 50+
4933MP – 50+
5715S – 40+
5749S – 50+

Page 123
1751 – $60+
3450 – 75+
370-1 – 75+
53W – 50+
22S – 60+
24S – 75+
27S – 75+
850 – 40+

Page 124
5748S – 50+
5750S – 50+
5758S – 50+
5759S – 50+
5010S – 50+
5012S – 50+
5008S – 50+
4952S – 50+
4813R – 40+
5516S – 75+
5394GS – 75+
5512S – 75+
5324GS – 75+
5369GS – 75+
5509S – 75+
5432S – 50+
5228S – 50+
5437S – 50+
5223S – 50+
5458S – 50+

Page 125
5371JP – $50+
05371JP – 50+
5378JP – 50+
3001SJP – 50+
5370JP – 60+
5386S – 60+
5380SP – 60+
5385S – 75+
5385NH – 75+
5374S – 75+
5381S – 75+
5383S – 75+

Page 126
C1-708S – $75+
C1-708NP – 75+
C1-5390S – 75+
C1-5390NP – 75+
C1-5617S – 100+
C1-5514S – 100+
C1-5511S – 100+
C1-5512S – 100+
C1-711S – 100+
C1-732S – 100+

Page 127
C1-5727S – $125+
C1-913S – 100+
C1-5133S – 100+
C1-4861S – 100+
C1-4860S – 100+
C1-4984S – 75+
C1-701S – 75+
C1-910S – 100+
C1-4952S – 100+

Page 128
C1-732NP – $100+
C1-3335S – 150+
C1-5228S – 75+
C1-5222S – 75+
C1-900S – 75+
C1-5224S – 75+
C1-4983S – 100+
C1-4983JP – 125+
C1-4995S – 75+

Page 129
C1-4953S – $60+
C1-4992S – 75+
C1-702S – 75+
C1-5733NP – 50+
C1-5733S – 50+
C1-728S – 50+
C1-728NP – 50+
C1-5100S – 50+
C1-908S – 50+
C1-4927S – 50+
C1-4927NP – 40+
C1-4923S – 50+
C1-4923NP – 40+

Page 130
C1-5371JP – $50+
C1-5371Y – 50+
C1-5371S – 50+
C1-5385S – 70+

Page 131
C4-1957-1 – $1000+

Page 132
C2-1975 – $100+

Page 133
C4-1950N-N – $2000
  with knives

Page 134
C4-87WN-N – $4000
  with knives

Page 135
C1-707S – $50+
C1-707NP – 50+
C1-20S – 100+
C1-923S – 75+
C1-7007S – 150+
C1-7007NP – 150+

Page 136
C1-5373S – $50+
C1-914S – 75+
C1-915S – 75+
C1-932Y – 50+
C1-731NP – 50+
C1-731S – 75+
C1-786S – 75+
C1-703S – 75+
C1-703Y – 75+
C1-921S – 50+

Page 137
C1-713Y – $75+
C1-5019S – 100+
C1-700S – 50+
C1-5922 – 75+
C1-5921 – 75+
C1-5924 – 75+

Page 138
C1-5372S – $75+
C1-917S – 75+
C1-933Y – 50+
C1-916S – 75+
C1-916Y – 75+

C1-5386S – 75+
C1-5380S – 75+
C1-5264S – 75+
C1-769S – 75+
C1-5370S – 50+

Page 139
C1-5722 – $150+
C1-5721 – 150+
C1-5724 – 150+

Page 140
C4-1960-N – $4500+
  including knives

Page 142
125N – $100+
226N – 100+
209N – 100+
2430N – 100+
2450N – 100+
2451N – 100+
2460N – 100+
2461N – 100+
138N – 100+

Page 143
241N – $100+
2449N – 100+
2444N – 100+
2222N – 100+
2223N – 100+
2225N – 100+
2224N – 100+
2672N – 100+
2625N – 100+
2628N – 100+
228N – 100+
2420N – 100+
2525N – 100+
2526N – 100+
2528N – 100+

Page 144
2348N – $100+
2755N – 100+
2965N – 100+
2742N – 100+
2743N – 100+
2762N – 100+
2339N – 100+
2294N – 100+
2872N – 150+
275N – 150+

Page 145
2425N – $100+
2731N – 100+
2403N – 100+
2738N – 100+
2434N – 100+
2811N – 100+
2813N – 100+

Page 146
242N – 100+
2288N – 100+
2299N – 100+
2301N – 100+
2303N – 100+
2521N – 100+
2522N – 100+
2540N – 100+
2542N – 100+
2543N – 100+

Page 147
2358N – $100+
2333N – 100+
2335N – 100+

2705N – 100+
2205N – 100+
2208N – 100+
2601N – 100+
2602N – 100+
2636N – 100+
2431N – 100+
2535N – 100+

Page 148
4054N – $100+
4037N – 100+
4057N – 100+
4999N – 100+
4164N – 100+
4167N – 100+
4415N – 100+
4417N – 100+
4772N – 100+

Page 149
291N – $100+
2045N – 100+
2621N – 100+
2022N – 100+
2369N – 100+
2370N – 100+
2355N – 100+
2164N – 100+
2382N – 100+
2167N – 100+

Page 150
304N – $100+
3154N – 100+
3157N – 100+
3051N – 100+
3053N – 100+
3378N – 100+
3381N – 100+
3081N – 100+

Page 151
2010N – $100+
2395N – 100+
2771N – 125+
253N – 100+
2991N – 100+
2307N – 100+
260N – 100+
261N – 100+
263N – 100+

Page 152
1S – $100+
1C – 100+
1SF – 100+
1R – 100+
2S – 125+
2C – 125+
2SF – 125+
50SF – 100+
8094 – 125+
7681 – 125+
11169 – 125+
7001 – 125+

Page 153
2294 – $75+
2060 – 75+
2148 – 75+
2289 – 75+
2408 – 75+
2152 – 75+
2154 – 75+
2156 – 75+
2061 – 75+
2065 – 75+
16157 – 100+
15523 – 100+

Page 154
6917 – $100+
6920 – 100+
6926 – 100+
6974 – 100+
6988 – 100+
17009 – 125+
17003 – 125+
17005 – 125+
17015 – 125+
14151 – 75+
7696 – 75+
8049 – 100+

Page 155
2191 – $100+
2192 – 100+
2193 – 100+
2160 – 100+
2163 – 100+
2402S – 75+
2044 – 75+
2045 – 75+
2018 – 75+
2401 – 75+
2402P – 100+

Page 156
305W – $100+
306W – 100+
8018 – 100+
8019 – 100+
7967 – 100+
11169 – 100+
2000 – 100+
2001 – 100+
2036 – 100+
2164 – 100+
2165 – 100+
2167 – 100+
2168 – 100+
2169 – 100+
2171 – 100+
2172 – 100+
2173 – 100+
2175 – 100+

Page 157
2153 – $100+
2154 – 100+
2156 – 175+
2136 – 100+
14360 – 100+
14364 – 100+
2197 – 100+
14387 – 100+
2141 – 100+
2195 – 100+
2143 – 100+
2145 – 100+
2144 – 100+
17021 – 100+

Page 158
17023 – $100+
13401 – 100+
2017 – 100+
2018 – 100+
2060 – 100+
2044 – 100+
2020 – 100+
2015 – 100+
2061 – 100+
2045 – 100+
2064 – 100+
2067 – 100+
2065 – 100+
2069 – 100+
2070 – 100+
14284 – 125+
15712 – 200+
15713 – 200+

Page 159
2053 – $125+
2054 – 125+
16551 – 125+
16226 – 125+
16227 – 125+
16228 – 125+
16229 – 125+
2225 – 125+
16692 – 125+
7940 – 125+
12825 – 125+
16584 – 100+

Page 160
2122 – $100+
2160 – 100+
2161 – 100+
2162 – 100+
16711 – 100+
16580 – 100+
14392 – 100+
2199 – 100+
2210 – 100+
2216 – 100+
16573 – 100+
2055 – 100+

Page 161
5166 – $100+
5167 – 100+
1335 – 200+
13950 – 250+
2998 – 300+
7577 – 350+

Page 162
7691 – $100+
14151 – 125+
11270 – 125+
11950 – 100+

Page 163
12056 – $100+
2004 – 100+
2038 – 100+
9890 – 100+
8926 – 100+
9881 – 100+
17009 – 100+
14958 – 100+
16145 – 175+
16148 – 175+
16144 – 175+
16485 – 175+

Page 164
13575 – $100+
17095 – 100+
2013 – 100+
2040 – 100+
2033 – 100+
2043 – 100+
14126 – 100+
12044 – 100+
17011 – 100+

Page 165
6202P – $100+
7234 – 75+
11615 – 75+
11618 – 75+
6157 – 75+

Page 166
5839 – $100+
7236 – 100+
6228 – 100+
6204 – 100+
6911 – 100+
6189 – 150+

Page 167
6554 – $100+
5950 – 100+
5595 – 100+
6007 – 100+
6006 – 150+
6243 – 150+
5753 – 150+
5973 – 150+

Page 168
5605 – $100+
5615 – 100+
6005 – 100+
6153 – 100+
5613 – 100+
5614 – 100+
5639 – 100+
5960 – 100+
6597 – 100+

Page 169
7069 – $100+
6598 – 100+
6512 – 75+
5738 – 75+
6453 – 125+
6835 – 150+
6111 – 125+

Page 170
9817SF – $75+
9817SP – 75+
9722 – 75+
9335 – 75+
6720 – 90+

Page 171
201 – $100+
202 – 100+
9732SF – 100+
9732SP – 100+
9830SF – 100+
9830SP – 100+
9830C – 100+

Page 172
7238 – $75+
7251 – 75+
7237 – 75+
11617 – 75+
6292 – 75+
4998 – 75+
7381 – 100+

Page 173
C3-6089 – $50+
C3-7585 – 75+
C3-7367 – 75+
C3-285 – 75+
C3-6085 – 75+
C3-7474 – 75+
C3-5452 – 90+
C3-5464 – 90+
C3-5474 – 90+

Page 174
C3-7593 – $35+
C3-435 – 150+
C3-N1499 – 150+

Page 175
C3-225 – $75+
C3-7614 – 50+
C3-280 – 75+
C3-2020 – 100+
C3-8388 – 75+
C3-7588 – 75+
C3-6066 – 100+
C3-7616 – 40+

Page 176
C3-8288 – $60+
C3-5252 – 75+
C3-240 – 75+
C3-93 – 75+
C3-93NP – 75+
C3-7288 – 100+
C3-230 – 75+
C3-220 – 75+
C3-210 – 75+
C3-7612 – 50+
C3-215 – 75+
C3-235 – 75+

Page 177
02063 – $75+
02064 – 75+
02065 – 75+
02066 – 75+
02067 – 100+
02068 – 100+

Page 178
02053 – $100+
02054 – 100+
02055 – 100+
02056 – 100+
02058 – 100+
02057 – 100+
02059 – 100+
02060 – 100+
02061 – 100+
02062 – 100+

Page 179
02026 – $125+
02027 – 125+
02028 – 100+
02029 – 100+
0326 – 150+
0146 – 150+
0467 – 100+
02031 – 100+
02032 – 100+
02033 – 100+
02034 – 100+
02035 – 100+
02036 – 100+
02037 – 100+
02038 – 100+

Page 180
02039 – $100+
02040 – 100+
02041 – 100+
02042 – 100+
02043 – 100+
02044 – 100+
02045 – 100+
02046 – 100+
02047 – 100+
02048 – 100+
02049 – 150+
02050 – 150+
02051 – 150+
02051 – 150+

Page 181
02019 – $150+
02020 – 175+
02021 – 150+
02022 – 150+
02023 – 150+
02024 – 200+
02025 – 200+

Page 182
02000 – $125+
02001 – 125+
02002 – 125+
02003 – 125+
02004 – 125+
02005 – 125+
02006 – 125+
02007 – 125+
02008 – 150+
02009 – 150+
02010 – 150+

Page 183
02011 – $125+
02012 – 125+
02013 – 125+
02014 – 125+
02015 – 125+
02016 – 125+
02017 – 125+
02018 – 125+

Page 184
C3-774 – $50+
C3-708 – 40+
C3-234K – 40+
C3-236 – 50+
C3-272 – 50+
C3-233 – 50+
C3-242 – 50+
C3-766 – 100+
C3-787 – 75+
C3-293 – 75+
C3-208 – 75+

Page 185
60 – $400+
65 – 400+
62 - 500+
66 – 500+
601 – 500+
600 – 500+
6000 – 500+
1553 3/4 – 100+
1543 3/4 – 100+
7444-K – 75+
7503T – 75+
7404-0 – 75+
7404-H – 75+
7404-GP – 75+
7403 – 75+
7404-ST – 75+
17003G – 100+
2154 – 100+
2191 – 100+
2193 - 250+
16584 – 75+

Page 186
272 – $30+
234K – 30+
204 – 35+
10G – 35+
11G – 35+
45G – 30+
40G – 30+
114S – 40+
50G – 30+
RJ-619 – 10+
50-D – 30+
81-P – 25+
81-Y – 30+

Page 187
C3-225SW – $75+
C3-835Y – 30+
C3-834 – 50+
C3-808 – 50+
C3-808Y – 50+
C3-882Y – 40+
C3-890 – 40+
C3-881 – 50+
C3-881Y – 50+
C3-896K – 40+
C3-899 – 40+

Page 188
766 – $40+
896K – 40+
895 – 50+
808 – 40+
856 – 50+
804 – 50+
708 – 40+
793 – 25+
294 – 40+
236 – 40+
242 – 40+

Page 189
C3-861 – $50+
C3-974 – 50+
C3-80T – 65+
C3-TL29 – 40+
C3-13C – 50+
C3-186 – 50+
C3-174 – 50+

Page 190
0272CS – $40+
0259S – 40+
0392P – 40+
0389P – 40+
0363P – 40+
0396P – 40+
04100P – 50+
0397P – 40+
0393P – 40+
0499P – 50+
0498P – 50+
04101P – 50+

Page 191
228 1/2 – $50+
130 1/2 – 50+
0365CB – 40+
0364S – 40+
0355S – 40+
0355CH – 40+
0476S – 50+
0479GS – 50+
0480S – 50+
0481S – 50+
0482S – 50+

Page 192
26618V – $30+
25613 – 30+
2683S – 35+
2688 – 35+
2055BP – 30+
2058 – 30+
25663 – 40+
29763 – 35+
2888 – 35+
2680RM – 35+
22243 – 35+
2243 – 40+

Page 193
24478 – $30+
21475M – 30+
21348 – 25+
21318 – 25+
23878 – 30+
21710W – 25+
21645H – 25+
34578 – 40+
33788 – 40+
33885 – 40+
34473 – 40+
34478 – 40+

Page 194
2263 – $40+
22433 – 40+
22348 – 40+
29345M – 40+
288 – 40+
24330M – 40+
22110M – 50+
21333 – 25+
21315M – 25+
21538 – 40+
21638 – 40+

Page 195
201 – $75+
535 – 75+
595 – 90+
587 – 90+
241 – 75+
224 – 90+
584 – 75+
565 – 75+
251 – 90+
250 – 90+
240 – 75+
213 – 75+
524 – 90+
212 – 90+
575 – 90+
221 – 90+

Page 196
605 – $90+
585 – 90+
245 – 90+
265 – 90+
410 – 50+
400 – 50+
415 – 50+
405 – 75+
505 – 90+
345 – 90+

Page 197
315 – $90+
305 – 90+
300 – 90+
208 – 75+
207 – 90+
254 – 100+
252 – 100+
226 – 100+
227 – 100+

Page 198
210 – $75+
234 – 75+
244 – 90+
306 – 75+
230 – 50+
220 – 50+
235 – 75+
275 – 75+

Page 199
202 – $75+
219 – 75+
215 – 75+
218 – 75+
211 – 90+
206 – 90+
301 – 75+
302 – 90+
303 – 75+
304 – 75+

Page 200
130 – $75+
135 – 75+
120 – 90+

124 – 90+
125 – 90+
205 – 90+
200 – 90+
204 – 90+
525 – 90+
285 – 90+
105 – 75+
545 – 90+
209 – 90+
100 – 90+
515 – 90+

Page 201
0454 – $75+
0455 – 75+
0496 – 75+
0497 – 75+
0574 – 75+
0573 – 75+
0589 – 75+
0590 – 75+
1622 – 75+
1632 – 75+
1662 – 75+

Page 202
0570 – $75+
0571 – 75+
0572 – 75+
0657 – 75+
0656 – 75+
0661 – 100+
0662 – 100+
0660 – 100+
0492 – 75+
0493 – 75+
0491 – 75+
0331 – 75+
0332 – 75+
0333 – 75+
0598 – 100+

Page 203
2801 – $40+
2703 – 60+
2804 – 40+
2104 – 40+
2101 – 40+
2102 – 50+
2107 – 40+
2111 – 50+

Page 204
3101 – $50+
2113 – 50+
2112 – 50+
2109 – 75+
2116 – 40+
2117 – 40+
2114 – 50+
2212 – 50+

Page 205
1500 – $50+
2403 – 150+
1602 – 100+
2900 – 150+
7250 – 100+
2610 – 50+
2704 – 75+
2800 – 100+

Page 206
2803 – $100+
2702 – 75+
2115 – 50+
100 – 40+
2103 – 40+
2110 – 50+

Page 207
0613 – $50+
0614 – 50+
0533 – 50+
0308 – 50+
0186 – 50+
0409 – 50+
0306 – 50+
0309 – 50+
0307 – 50+
0413 – 50+

Page 208
0410 – $50+
0411 – 50+
0412 – 50+
0253 – 50+
2422 – 50+
0348 – 50+
0543 – 50+
0542 – 50+
0478 – 50+
0479 – 50+

Page 209
1392 – $50+
0674 – 50+
0675 – 50+
092 – 50+
091 – 50+
0673 – 50+
0693 – 50+
1502 – 50+
0557 – 50+
0708 – 50+

Page 210
52 – $2500+
57 – 1200+
55 – 1000+
8920 – 200+
8921 – 200+
6721 – 250+
6722 – 250+
7721 – 250+
7722 – 250+
BG5717 – 250+
BG5718 – 250+
BG5721 – 250+
BG5722 – 250+
BG5723 – 250+
BG5724 – 250+
BG5725 – 250+
10CH – 100+

Page 211
0643 – $50+
0524 – 50+
0448 – 50+
0513 – 50+
0509 – 50+
0525 – 50+
0526 – 50+
0500 – 50+
0501 – 50+
0690 – 50+
0691 – 50+

Page 212
0489 – $75+
0490 – 75+
0486 – 75+
0487 – 75+
0488 – 75+
0659 – 75+
0658 – 75+
0582 – 75+
0581 – 75+
0334 – 75+
0335 – 75+
0482 – 75+
0483 – 75+

Page 213
0387 – $75+
0388 – 75+
0385 – 75+
0386 – 75+
0696 – 75+
0695 – 75+
0650 – 75+
0684 – 75+
0683 – 75+
0682 – 75+
0681 – 75+
0617 – 75+
0618 – 75+
0592 – 200+
0591 – 200+

Page 214
0529 – $75+
0528 – 75+
0469 – 100+
0285 – 75+
0577 – 100+

Page 215
1 – $150+
2 – 150+
0160 – 150+
0161 – 150+
10 – 300+
603R – 300+
60 – 250+
62 – 250+
52 – 250+
062R – 250+
42 – 250+

Page 216
0354 – $200+
0355 – 200+
0359 – 125+
0360 – 125+
0312 – 125+
0313 – 125+
0665 – 125+
0315 – 125+

Page 217
0593 – $300+
0594 – 300+
0600 – 300+
0601 – 300+
943 – 300+
944 – 300+
0278 – 125+
7619 – 125+
7633 – 125+

Page 218
0602 – $100+
0800 – 100+

Page 219
03 – $100+
02 – 100+
01 – 100+
144 – 100+
145 – 100+
146 – 100+
156 – 100+
0156 – 250+
4839 – 250+

Page 220
3025 – $150+
3028 – 150+
6217 – 150+
7203 – 150+
6741 – 150+
6891 – 150+

3836 – 150+
22068 – 150+
1984 – 150+
1784 – 175+

Page 221
3001 – $75+
0713 – 150+
0714 – 150+
0217 – 175+
0218 – 175+
0402 – 175+
0403 – 175+
16 – 175+

Page 222
010 – $100+
011 – 100+
0356 – 50+
0357 – 50+
0105 – 50+
0210 – 50+
0634 – 50+
0687 – 50+
0686 – 50+
0639 – 50+
0640 – 50+
0296 – 50+

Page 223
0671 – $100+
0670 – 100+
0672 – 100+
0667 – 100+
0668 – 100+
0669 – 100+
0361 – 100+
0362 – 100+
0337 – 75+
0338 – 75+
0576 – 75+
0575 – 75+
0663 – 75+
0664 – 75+

Page 224
0505 – $150+
1655 – 125+
0566 – 150+
0567 – 150+
0699 – 175+

Page 225
6222 – $100+
6220 – 100+
6221 – 100+
6217 – 400+
6218 – 400+
6219 – 200+

Page 226
5436 – $300+
5434 – 300+
5435 – 300+
5433 – 300+
5437 – 300+
5430 – 150+
5431 – 150+
5429 – 400+
3015 – 500+

Page 227
4318 – $100+
4301 – 50+
4319 – 500+
4310X – 50+
4306 – 150+
4333 – 100+
4375 – 20+
4372 – 20+

4308 – 100+
4346 – 100+

Page 228
4369 – $150+
4323 – 100+
4332 – 100+
4312 – 150+
4309 – 35+
4310 – 35+
4300 – 25+
4315 – 20+
4305 – 200+
4336 – 25+
4355 – 75+

Page 229
S8670 – $10+
S8669 – 10+
C6489 – 50+
C6488 – 50+
C7109 – 100+
C7019 – 100+
C7019 – 100+
C7020 – 100+

Page 230
C7294 – $20+
C3851 – 10+
C3852 – 20+
CB1825t – 100+
C3853 – 100+
C3854 – 15+
C3855 – 10+

Page 231
C6491 – $50+
C250 – 50+
C6872 – 150+
C3859 – 15+
C3860 – 15+
C3861 – 15+
C3862 – 15+
C3863 – 15+
C3864 – 15+
C7232 – 150+

Page 232
C3856 – $150+
C7057 – 20+
C3865 – 20+
C1450 – 100+
C3857 – 20+
C3858 – 20+

Page 233
6V17187 – $100+
6V17186 – 40+
6V17158 – 40+
6V17157 – 30+
6V17181 – 200+
6V17182 – 200+
6V17224 – 75+
6V17243 – 75+
6V17226 – 50+
6V17244 – 75+
6V17228 –50+
6V17248 – 75+
6V17282 – 100+
6V17284 – 40+
6V17288 – 50+
6V17302 – 50+
6V17305 – 75+
6V17307 – 40+
6V17309 – 75+
6V17314 – 40+
6V17318 – 40+
6V17230 – 50+
6V17338 –100+
6V17340 – 40+

6V17343 – 40+
6V17349 – 40+
6V17361 – 40+
6V17364 – 100+
6V17365 – 40+
6V17367 – 75+
6V17368 – 40+
6V17254 – 100+

Page 234
6F7058 – $50+
6F7065 – 75+
6F7006 – 40+
6F7020 – 30+
6F7008 – 30+
6F7082 – 30+
6F7083 – 30+
6F7002 – 30+
6F7016 – 20+
6F7018 – 30+
6F7023 – 30+
6F7034 – 30+
6F7026 – 30+
6F7052 – 40+
6F7013 – 30+
6F7043 – 60+
6F7044 – 30+
6F7032 – 40+
6F7001 – 30+
6F7012 – 40+
6F7010 – 40+
6F7047 – 30+
6F7030 – 30+
6F7062 – 30+
6F7041 – 30+
6F7015 – 30+

Page 235
6F7066 – $30+
6F7074 – 30+
6F7064 – 30+
6F7068 – 30+
6F7057 – 30+
6F7061 – 30+
6F7072 – 30+
6F7070 – 30+
6F7049 – 20+
6F7111 – 20+
6F7059 – 20+
6F7050 – 20+
6F7103 – 20+
6F7054 – 20+
6F7108 – 20+
6F7055 – 20+
6F7101 – 20+
6F7035 – 20+
6F7081 – 30+
6F7037 – 30+
6F7080 – 30+
6F7038 – 30+
6F7076 – 30+
6F7124 – 30+
6F7142 – 30+

Page 236
C3-CM281 – $20+
C3-CM685-SS – 20+
C3-CM400 – 25+
C3-CM685 – 25+
C3-CM413 – 30+
C3-CM787 – 20+

Page 237
AJ5K11 – $25+
AJ5K2 – 40+
AJ5K3 – 20+
AJ5K4 – 20+
AJ5K7 – 20+
AJ5K8 – 20+
AJ5K9 – 15+
AJ5K10 – 15+

Page 238
C3-N687 – $175+
C3-MS60 – 200+
C3-278 – 150+
C3-CM48 – 300+

Page 239
C3-N785 – $150+
C3-N60 – 150+
C3-N685 – 175+

Page 240
55G – $30+
89P – 30+
55D – 30+
50 – 20+
81 – 20+
183P – 20+
55Y – 20+
55 – 20+
98 – 20+
89Y – 30+
89 – 20+

Page 241
N83 – $125+
N76 – 125+
278 – 150+
N84 – 100+
615 – 150+
JM-435 – 125+

Page 242
C6904H – $30+
C6905H – 20+
C6906H – 30+
C6907H – 20+
C6908H – 20+

C6909H – 20+
C6910H – 20+
C6911H – 20+
C6912H – 20+
C6913H – 30+
C6913HA – 30+
C6913HB – 30+
C6914H – 30+
C6915H – 30+
C6916H – 40+
C6917H – 40+
C6918H – 40+
C6919 – 40+
C6920 – 40+
C6920A – 40+
C6925 – 50+

Page 243
0100 – $100+
510 – 100+
1000 – 150+
5167 – 100+

Page 244
60 – $400+
63 – 400+
66 – 400+
65 – 400+
62 – 400+
64 – 400+
66 – 400+

Page 245
1347 – $100+
1348 – 125+
3305 – 100+
3401 – 100+
103 – 150+

2700 – 50+
2805 – 50+
2118 – 50+
2119 – 50+
2120 – 50+
2502 – 75+
2503 – 75+

Page 246
V321 – $50+
V221 – 50+
V221CH – 75+
V321CH – 75+
V222 – 75+
V322 – 75+
V123 – 50+
V323 – 50+
V326 – 50+
V327 – 40+
V427W – 40+
V427SH – 40+
V324 – 40+
V325 – 40+
V3311 – 50+

Page 247
01118 – $20+
265 – 20+
60 – 400+
65 – 400+
66 – 400+
62 – 400+
68590 – 50+
6P – 200+
1931 – 300+

Page 248
V3216 – 600+

129 – 600+
4041 – 400+
600P – 400+
78ACV – 600+
236 – 1000+

Page 249
V4210 – $40+
V3219 – 50+
V3218 – 50+
V3217 – 50+
V3316 – 40+
V3317 – 40+
V3318 – 40+
V3420 – 50+
V3421 – 50+

Page 250
25P1 – $300+
MM25 – 500+
910 – 150+
RFK – 75+

Page 251
M100 – $75+
M101 – 75+
M102 – 75+
M103 – 75+
M104 – 75+
M105 – 75+
M106 – 75+
M107 – 75+
M108 – 75+
M109 – 75+
M110 – 75+
M111 – 75+
M112 – 75+
M113 – 75+

M114 – 75+
M115 – 75+
M116 – 75+
M117 – 75+
M118 – 75+
M119 – 75+

Page 252
W8890 – $200+
W8821 – 200+
W5000 – 200+
W4806X – 200+
W2713 – 200+
2705 – 200+
2708 – 200+
2704 – 200+
2711 – 200+
W3569/3 – 200+
2707 – 200+
2710 – 200+

Page 253
4205 – $50+
4203 – 50+
4206 – 50+
3602 – 60+
3606 – 60+
3605 – 40+
4604 – 40+
4603 – 40+
4602 – 40+
4705 – 40+

Page 254
4304 – $40+
3309 – 40+
3308 – 40+
4306 – 40+

4303 – 50+
4305 – 50+
2207 – 50+
3204 – 50+
4208 – 50+
4207 – 60+

Page 255
2302 – $50+
2303 – 50+
3200 – 60+
2304 – 60+
1000 – 50+
3304 – 60+
3307 – 75+
3306 – 75+

Page 256
1203 – $50+
1204 – 50+
1200 – 150+
1201 – 100+
1202 – 150+
2402 – 175+
2401 – 150+
1300 – 100+
1400 – 75+

Page 257
2205 – $75+
2210 – 75+
2209 – 75+
2206 – 50+
2202 – 50+
2208 – 75+
2203 – 75+
2201 – 50+
2204 – 75+
2211 – 75+